P9-CJL-365

305.8
B812

RACE IN THE AMERICAN SOUTH
FROM SLAVERY TO CIVIL RIGHTS

David Brown and Clive Webb

WITHDRAWN

LIBRARY ST. MARY'S COLLEGE

University Press of Florida

Florida A&M University, Tallahassee
Florida Atlantic University, Boca Raton
Florida Gulf Coast University, Ft. Myers
Florida International University, Miami
Florida State University, Tallahassee
New College of Florida, Sarasota
University of Central Florida, Orlando
University of Florida, Gainesville
University of North Florida, Jacksonville
University of South Florida, Tampa
University of West Florida, Pensacola

Copyright 2007 by David Brown and Clive Webb

First published in the UK by Edinburgh University Press
Printed in Great Britain
All rights reserved

12 11 10 09 08 07 6 5 4 3 2 1

WITHDRAWN

12/3/08 $21.08 YBP

Library of Congress Cataloging-in-Publication Data

Brown, David, 1968 Apr. 25-
Race in the American South: from slavery to civil rights / David Brown and Clive Webb.
p. cm.
Includes bibliographical references and index.
ISBN 978-0-8130-3202-3 (cloth: alk. paper)—ISBN 978-0-8130-3203-0 (pbk.: alk. paper)
1. Southern States—Race relations. 2. Racism—Southern States—History. 3. African Americans—Southern States—Social conditions. 4. Slavery—Southern States—History. 5. African Americans—Civil rights—Southern States—History. 6. Civil rights movements—Southern States—History. 7. United States—Race relations. 8. Racism—United States—History. I. Webb, Clive, 1970– II. Title.
E185.92.B76 2007
305.800975—dc22
2007012091

The University Press of Florida is the scholarly publishing agency for the State University System of Florida, comprising Florida A&M University, Florida Atlantic University, Florida Gulf Coast University, Florida International University, Florida State University, New College of Florida, University of Central Florida, University of Florida, University of North Florida, University of South Florida, and University of West Florida.

University Press of Florida
15 Northwest 15th Street
Gainesville, FL 32611
www.upf.com

CONTENTS

ACKNOWLEDGEMENTS

A book of synthesis such as this is only as good as the literature it has to work with. We must, therefore, acknowledge our debt to many varied historians for the rich and stimulating literature on race in the American South written in the last two decades. Many of the interpretations contained in this book have been shaped in debates with students. David Brown would like to acknowledge all students who have taken his southern and civil war modules, but particularly those at Sheffield University on the special subject 'Slavery and the Old South' in 2004–05 and 2005–06. He would also like to note the support of the late Peter J. Parish, who many years ago provided a crucial fee waiver allowing him to register at the Institute of United States Studies in London. Peter's synthetic skill as a historian and beautiful prose style were qualities we could only hope to match. Clive Webb is similarly grateful to William Dusinberre, who not only inspired his initial enthusiasm for southern history, but has also remained a guiding influence.

The support of friends and colleagues has also been essential. Simon Middleton typically did not guard his evaluations of early chapters on the colonial and revolutionary periods (anyone who knows Simon will know what that means!). Trevor Burnard also read the early chapters, providing a timely evaluation and much needed encouragement. Tim Lockley read the whole of the first half of the book, improving the prose and picking up errors of fact and interpretation. Michael Tadman also read the first half of the book and, once again, his searching comments and unwavering support was gratefully received and immensely valuable. Martin Crawford, David Gleeson and Emily West looked at specific chapters. Brian Ward provided an outstanding critique at a late stage in this project, which helped to improve both the style and the conceptualisation of the manuscript. We cannot thank these friends enough for their help. Robert Cook picks up the MVP award for reading the whole manuscript and parts of it more than once. His incisive evaluation and refusal to accept sloppy or inaccurate prose improved all chapters immeasurably. He truly is the Martin O'Neill of British Americanists! We also thank Robert F. Pace for providing the maps, and the School of Arts, Histories and Cultures at the University of Manchester for providing financial support.

Family and friends were also essential. David Brown expresses his deep appreciation to all family members who looked after his children (they were relieved as much as he was that this book did not take as long as the last one). He would especially like to warmly thank Sarah, Joe and Sam. Joe and Sam showed great patience (most of the time) when Dad was writing and they never had any trouble negotiating the obstacle course that was 'the study' at times, unlike their Mum! This book would not have been completed without them. Clive Webb thanks his parents, Brian and Marjorie, and his brothers, Paul and Neil. Above all, he is indebted to Kathleen Kendall for her inestimable intellectual wisdom and emotional support, without which the book would not have been completed.

MAPS

THE MODERN SOUTH
Nebraska
Iowa
Illinois
Indiana
Ohio
Pennsylvania
Del.
Md.
Colorado
Kansas
Oklahoma
New Mexico
MEXICO
Missouri
Kentucky
West Virginia
Virginia
Tennessee
North Carolina
South Carolina
Arkansas
Mississippi
Alabama
Georgia
Texas
Louisiana
Florida
Kansas City
St. Louis
Springfield
Louisville
Lexington
Wheeling
Baltimore
Arlington
Alexandria
Washington D.C.
Richmond
Norfolk
Virginia Beach
Roanoke
Winston-Salem
Raleigh
Knoxville
Nashville
Charlotte
Wilmington
Memphis
Greenville
Myrtle Beach
Little Rock
Huntsville
Columbia
Atlanta
Augusta
Birmingham
Charleston
Montgomery
Selma
Savannah
Albany
Fort Worth
Dallas
Shreveport
Jackson
Natchez
Mobile
Jacksonville
Tallahassee
Biloxi
Baton Rouge
New Orleans
Austin
Houston
Galveston
San Antonio
Orlando
St. Petersburg
Miami
Atlantic Ocean
Gulf of Mexico
N
W
E
S
Miles 0 200 400
Kms 0 200 400
Robert F. Pace

INTRODUCTION

At the London Pan-African conference in 1900, the African American scholar and political activist W. E. B. Du Bois declared that 'The problem of the twentieth century is the problem of the color-line, – the relation of the darker to the lighter races of men in Asia and Africa, in America and the islands of the sea.' In his seminal book *The Souls of Black Folk*, published three years later, Du Bois explained the significance of the colour line. African Americans lived in the United States in their millions but were denied membership of its society. They were accorded second-class status in a system built on the pervasive ideology of innate white superiority and black inferiority that privileged whites above all other groups.

The problem of the colour line was not confined to the southern states, by any means, but it was more systematically enforced there than anywhere else in the United States. Dilemmas of race and racism have afflicted all modern nations, but in the twentieth century only the South African apartheid regime was built on the same fundamental rationale of racial inequality as the American South, arguably constituting 'the highest stage of white supremacy'.[1] Jim Crow laws strictly regulated race relations in the southern United States, effectively creating two worlds in which whites and blacks were kept apart from one another as far as possible. Although a northerner by birth, Du Bois was fully aware of the hardships that American apartheid imposed upon all but the most fortunate southern blacks who endured inferior housing, schools and public facilities. However, it was not the outward, physical manifestation of segregation visible in separate parks, hospitals, restaurants, hotels, drinking fountains and even cemeteries that worried him most. Du Bois was more concerned with the inner turmoil caused by notions of racial inferiority. He identified a destructive feeling of 'double-consciousness' sapping the collective spirit of American blacks. African Americans were regarded as, and to an extent considered themselves to be, 'a problem'; they lived in a society that recognised their presence but did not admit their claim as legitimate citizens. Du Bois felt himself to be striving for acceptance in a world that would never accept him: 'One ever feels his two-ness, – an American, a Negro; two souls, two thoughts, two unreconciled strivings; two warring ideals in one dark body, whose dogged strength alone keeps it from being torn asunder.'[2]

Racism has both an ideological and material power, as suggested by Du Bois. Race shapes and can even subsume individual identity and societies can structure their institutions to prioritise one so-called racial group above another. Notions of whiteness and blackness have been crucial in all areas of southern life and history, although they have never been static but subject to constant evolution. Yet not all southerners neatly fit into categories of white and black. Native Americans in particular complicate the binary colour line, but so have immigrant groups such as Jews, Sicilians and the Irish. Free blacks proved a very troublesome presence in the antebellum South, when to be white was to be free and to be black was supposedly to be slave.

We strive to include all groups in this history of race in the South, not just the most populous, in so far as they have influenced ever-changing constructions of southern racial ideology. Consequently, some groups feature more heavily than others at different historical moments. Native Americans, for example, were a powerful and extremely important presence in the first two centuries of European settlement, strongly shaping white ideas about race. However, after the expulsion of Indian tribes from the South in the 1830s, their influence waned. The racial status of immigrant minorities such as Jews and Sicilians was fiercely contested during the late nineteenth and early twentieth centuries, but by the Second World War they had become absorbed into the dominant white mainstream.

Southern racial ideology posited the superiority of whites over African Americans and Native Americans. Blacks and Indians had their own interpretations of race, it should be emphasised, and they did not passively accept dominant views but, nonetheless, white supremacy inexorably became embedded in southern political and legal structures over the course of the colonial period. In the seventeenth and eighteenth centuries, when the notion of separate races was inchoate, the rights of free Englishmen became increasingly sacrosanct. At the same time, however, race constitutes just one element in the complex construction of southern identity: gender and class have been equally significant, if often less obvious, components. The privileging of white males is a constant theme in southern history and historians have shown white women to be distinctly disadvantaged, although not necessarily in the same ways or to the same extent as African Americans. A history of race in the South must pay very careful attention to changing formulations of gender, especially in the way concepts of masculinity and femininity have reinforced, and sometimes challenged, the racial order. With the codification of slavery in the early 1700s, 'whiteness' – a powerful form of institutional power giving white men legal, social and psychological authority over blacks, Indians and women – became enshrined in southern law, granting immense power to white male southerners. White male authority was never absolute, however, and was always contested by supposedly inferior or weaker groups. Moreover, class cannot be ignored. Different kinds of inter-racial relationships developed, depending on the status of those involved. Racial superiority was most keenly felt and projected by elite white males, reflecting the great power that the southern ruling class wielded. It was not necessarily the same lower down the social scale. Some poor whites, for example, allied themselves with blacks when labouring on the colonial Chesapeake tobacco plantations, in the informal economy of antebellum slavery and in the populist movement of the late nineteenth century.

On balance, there is much to be said for Ulrich B. Phillips's famous declaration that the quest for white supremacy was no less than 'the central theme of southern history'.[3] Southern historiography has strongly reinforced the pervasive importance of race to the historical and cultural development of the South, to an extent unmatched in the history of other American regions or of most other countries. Phillips was an early historian of American slavery, regarded as one of the giants of the academy in his era, who believed absolutely in the racial inferiority of blacks. Phillips's racism was not a hindrance to his career; indeed, the majority of professional historians of his generation shared similar views, illustrating just how ingrained racism had become across the whole of the United States in the first half of the twentieth century.[4] The entrenchment of American, not just southern, racism represented the culmination of an ideological assault on black character. Racial discourse sought to justify slavery on the grounds of black inferiority and then argued that the alleged shortcomings of newly enfranchised African American citizens required the passage of segregation laws. The South was not unique in holding such views, it needs stressing, as blacks suffered in both the North and the West, but undeniably southerners took a leading role in the national construction of white supremacy.

This book explores the power of race in the American South, pinpointing shifting notions of whiteness and blackness and the ways in which both have shaped southern race relations. It outlines the institutionalisation of white supremacy and considers attempts to challenge the racial status quo. Given their immense significance to the history of the American South, race and racism have often appeared to be timeless. Like virtually all contemporary scholars, we reject the idea that race is a natural, fixed category – race is a construction, persistently fluctuating and transforming in differing circumstances. Racial ideology is historicised: it is tied to specific historical moments and contexts which give it shape and substance, without which race becomes meaningless. As Ira Berlin stresses, race is 'a historical construction' that 'cannot exist outside of time and place'.[5] Nonetheless, this does not alter the fact that race has been an immense force influencing southern historical development and that racial difference did appear to be timeless, natural and all-encompassing to southerners.

In the 1950s, segregationist politicians engaged in 'massive resistance' made frequent reference to a southern way of life that had not changed for generations. White solidarity in keeping blacks down is often presented as crucial to understanding the South, overriding class differences within southern society. This is an oversimplification and one of the key aims here is to de-mythologise and contextualise race, complicating claims that white southerners have always acted in unison. The South has had more than its fair quota of poor; something that remains the case to the present day, as the impact of Hurricane Katrina in 2005 forcibly reminded us. Poverty has never followed the colour line exclusively in the history of the South, as a small elite kept control of the bulk of the wealth and large numbers of blacks and whites lived in squalid conditions.

White supremacy has been a powerful slogan and rallying call but white southern unity was not continually maintained in practice, not least because of vast disparities in wealth and status. Class differences within the white community have deeply influenced the course of southern history, from colonial times to the present. Race relations may appear to be rigid in certain relationships, such as those between master and slave or factory owner and mill hand, but relations between lower-class whites and blacks were far more fluid and flexible, markedly so before the American Civil War. Indeed, separation of the races has almost always been impossible to achieve in practice. Historian John W. Blassingame describes the 'Americanization of the slave and the Africanization of the South' and white and black interaction in the South has been unstoppable. Charles Joyner explicitly counters Phillips's view in arguing that 'The central theme of Southern history is racial integration'. Joyner encapsulates what many scholars have been showing in detail recently: white, black and indigenous southerners interacted with one another in a myriad of diverse ways from first contact. They ate, drank, worked, socialised and slept with each other, much to the consternation of the southern elite. Southern culture is a fusion of African, European and

Native American influences and any suggestion that these distinctive elements were not intertwined cannot hold true. At the same time, the institutional and ideological development of the South has in practice been strongly influenced by the quest to maintain, and to resist, white supremacy.[6]

We ask a series of questions in this book. Was race planted in the southern colonies by the first settlers bringing prejudiced Old World values with them? (To reformulate Du Bois, the colour line was the problem of the twentieth century, but was that also the case in the seventeenth, eighteenth and nineteenth centuries?) Was racism generated from the top down as a means to establish order and maintain control or was it more a bottom-up process, giving ordinary white men opportunities and a sense of superiority? Did racism emerge primarily as a justification for the system of slavery that became the backbone of the southern economy or was it reflective of deeper social attitudes? How did race buttress ruling interests and intersect with class and gender? Why did racial concerns become so central to the society, culture and politics of the South? In what ways did the structural changes that occurred in southern society during the twentieth century undermine white racial unity and stimulate the rise of a black protest movement that overthrew segregation? Was Jim Crow eventually overthrown by a civil rights movement rooted in institutions and social networks that segregation had actually helped to create? Should black agency or federal government intervention be regarded as the decisive factor precipitating the downfall of southern apartheid? We also distinguish clearly between ideas about race, mostly written and disseminated by intellectuals and politicians, and their reception by the mass of ordinary southerners, white and black. How did racial ideology affect daily interactions between different groups of southerners, across time and space?

Although our primary focus is on the fraught and complicated relationship between black and white southerners, race alone cannot account for the dynamics of the southern past. While the binary division between black and white has been fundamental in shaping the course of southern history, race should not be emphasised to the exclusion of other factors such as class and gender, which have been critical features of the southern past and present, despite their downplaying by historians over the years. It is a false distinction to claim that we can understand the South only in terms of either race or class or gender. On the contrary, it is the interaction between these forces that has determined the course of southern history. Thus, we attempt to delineate the simultaneous interplay of race, class and gender – the ways in which these forces have ebbed and flowed – during the course of southern history.

The South has often been seen as a region set apart from the mainstream of American life. Following the Second World War in particular, repressive racial practices were perceived by northern liberals as being antithetical to their idealised image of the United States as the most democratic nation on earth. There was a substantial element of self-deception to the criticisms made of the South by northerners. The northern ghetto riots of the 1960s ruthlessly exposed the fallacy that racism was a regional problem confined to the southern states. This book recognises that racial discrimination was – and remains – a phenomenon that afflicted the entire United States. It provides points of comparison that allow the reader to assess southern race relations within a broader national framework. The South is part of the Atlantic world and connections to the Caribbean slave colonies were particularly significant in the seventeenth, eighteenth and nineteenth centuries. Transatlantic discourses (such as the Enlightenment) and movements (such as anti-slavery) paid no respect to national borders, impacting upon the South as they did elsewhere. The racist intellectual climate of the late nineteenth and twentieth century was heavily shaped by European colonialism in Africa and Asia. And the liberal critique of race, which contributed greatly to the South's isolation in the decades after the Second World War, was more or less a global phenomenon. That said, the authors rationalise their focus on the American South by emphasising that there were many exceptional aspects to racial practices in the region. Only in the South was white supremacy enforced so relentlessly through the power of law as well as custom (with the exception of southern Africa). No other region witnessed racial violence of the same epidemic proportions that it reached below the Mason–Dixon Line.

This last reference to a line on the map of the United States separating North from South leads to a further point. There is no consensus among scholars as to what precisely constitutes 'the South'. It is in some respects a state of mind as much as a geographical reality. There are many good reasons to divide the South into upper and lower sections – states below North Carolina were historically far more committed to slavery and segregation. Race relations in the urban South often differ from those in rural areas. Even the attempt to determine which states constitute the South relies to some extent on arbitrary decisions. Kentucky, for instance, had more slaves during the antebellum era than Texas and Florida combined, yet it did not join other slaveholding states in seceding from the Union. The status of other border states such as Delaware, Maryland and Oklahoma is also indeterminate. Maryland was an important slave state in the colonial era but from the 1800s onwards slavery became less important and the state became more like its mid-Atlantic neighbours such as Pennsylvania. Even so, Maryland had most of the apparatus of Jim Crow in the twentieth century. Thus, this book will broadly delineate the dynamics of race within the various sub-regions of the American South over the course of the last four hundred years.

We try to keep jargon and theory to a minimum in the chapters that follow. The dense sociological, anthropological and cultural literature about race is not only vast but also highly contentious. There is no single, authoritative interpretation of the origins, effects and variable meanings of race and racism. Nonetheless, some key theoretical positions inform our analysis. First, it is important to distinguish between race and racism. Race usually refers to the constellation of (empirically false) ideas about the supposedly essentialist and determinative physical and mental attributes of distinct human types, most powerfully realised when placed within a hierarchy of superior and inferior races. Racism is the organised system of oppression of one so-called inferior racial group to the benefit of a superior group built into the institutional structure of society. Race is false but racism is very real and has dreadful consequences for its victims. Historian Barbara J. Fields vociferously criticises her peers for their continued neglect of this point.[7]

Second, although masquerading as natural and commonplace, race is never fixed but is continually refined and re-ordered. Racial identity is not primordial but historically contingent, manifesting itself in subtly discrete forms in different times and different places, and constantly evolving (one might say mutating). Racialisation, or 'racial formation', to borrow a term employed by the American sociologists Michael Omi and Howard Winant, is a continual process. The state plays a leading role in this process through the instruments of government (local, state and federal in the American context) and law, adjusting and enforcing racial labels as 'a variety of previously racially undefined groups have required categorization to situate them within the prevailing racial order'.[8]

Third, racism is much more than cultural prejudice or xenophobia towards another group. Racism reflects power relations within any given society's social structure and is buttressed by a powerful and widely diffused ideology determining not just the opportunities available to allegedly superior and inferior groups, but fundamentally shaping individual identity itself. George M. Fredrickson uses the important idea of a 'racial order' to distinguish levels of prejudice between different societies. Racism 'is more than theorizing about human differences or thinking badly of a group over which one had no control. It either directly sustains or proposes to establish *a racial order,* a permanent group hierarchy that is believed to reflect the laws of nature or the decrees of God' (or both, of course). Racial ideology is at its most powerful when human beings internally accept its logic, gauging their own abilities and the abilities of those around them though the lens of the body and idea of racial stock.[9]

Fourth, a word about this book's relationship to the relatively recent field of 'whiteness studies'. The 1990s witnessed a new and exciting departure in the study of American race. Usually associated with Alexander Saxton, David R. Roediger and Matthew Frye Jacobson (even though each takes very different approaches), whiteness scholars argue that the problem of race was not just the story of African Americans and their struggles within the United States, which was, they assert, what most historians really meant when writing about race relations.[10] The problem of race was equally, perhaps even predominately, the problem of *whiteness*: the complex and contested meanings and prerogatives of being white. The curious thing about whiteness studies, however, is its relative lack of attention to the South – especially as the South had been a central focus of the voluminous literature on American race relations that had been written in the post-Second World War period. With a few notable exceptions, this has not changed, and we seek to apply the insights of whiteness scholarship to this study of the South. We are equally mindful of recent critiques, however – especially those by Peter Kolchin and Eric Arnesen – that question the explanatory power of whiteness as a concept and note its propensity to minimise the importance of class and gender.[11]

Finally, a word about our use of 'white' and 'black' as synonyms for European American and African American. To borrow from Kirsten Fischer's excellent discussion of the difficulties of using these terms, '*black* and *white* are problematic because they reinscribe the very categories [we] examine in this book'. Despite these problems, we share Fischer's contention that they are 'convenient' descriptors and they will be used throughout the text. Likewise, we will not place *race* in quotation marks, which can become confusing, but share current scholarly concern about a word devoid of legitimacy.[12] In sum, we contend that while southern history was never only about race, race and racism were critical to the historical development of the South. In order to understand that history, we need to grapple with the convoluted history of race.

Notes

1. John W. Cell, *The Highest Stage of White Supremacy: The Origins of Segregation in South Africa and the American South* (Cambridge: Cambridge University Press, 1982).
2. W. E. B. Du Bois, *The Souls of Black Folk* (Chicago: A. C. McClurg and Co., 1903), pp. 13, 2, 3.
3. U. B. Phillips, 'The Central Theme of Southern History', *American Historical Review*, 34 (October 1928), pp. 30–43.
4. Peter Novick, *That Noble Dream: The 'Objectivity Question' and the American*

Historical Profession (Cambridge: Cambridge University Press, 1988), pp. 74–80, 225–9.

5. Ira Berlin, *Many Thousands Gone: The First Two Centuries of Slavery in North America* (Cambridge, MA: Harvard University Press, 1998), p. 1.
6. John W. Blassingame, *The Slave Community: Plantation Life in the Antebellum South*, revised and enlarged edition (New York: Oxford University Press, 1979), pp. 49–104; Charles Joyner, 'A Single Southern Culture: Cultural Interaction in the Old South', in Ted Ownby (ed.), *Black and White: Cultural Interaction in the Antebellum South* (Jackson: University Press of Mississippi, 1993), p. 3.
7. Barbara J. Fields, 'Of Rogues and Geldings', *American Historical Review*, 108 (December 2003), pp. 1397–405. British sociologist John Rex made much the same point as long ago as 1970: John Rex, 'The Concept of Race in Sociological Theory', in Sami Zubaida (ed.), *Race and Racialism* (London: Tavistock, 1970), pp. 35–55.
8. Michael Omi and Howard Winant, *Racial Formation in the United States: From the 1960s to the 1990s* (New York: Routledge, 1994), p. 81. There is currently an important conceptual debate among sociologists over the meaning and significance of 'racialisation'. See Karim Murji and John Solomos (eds.), *Racialization: Studies in Theory and Practice* (Oxford: Oxford University Press, 2005).
9. George M. Fredrickson, *Racism: A Short History* (Princeton, NJ: Princeton University Press, 2002), p. 6. Not all scholars, it should be stressed, agree with this definition, and some argue that race and racism have been pervasive throughout world history. See, for example, Robert Bartlett, *The Making of Europe: Conquest, Colonization, and Cultural Change, 950–1350* (Princeton, NJ: Princeton University Press, 1993).
10. Alexander Saxton, *The Rise and Fall of the White Republic: Class Politics and Mass Culture in Nineteenth-Century America* (New York: Verso, 1990); David R. Roediger, *The Wages of Whiteness: Race and the Making of the American Working Class* (London: Verso, 1991); Matthew Frye Jacobson, *Whiteness of a Different Color: European Immigrants and the Alchemy of Race* (Cambridge, MA: Harvard University Press, 1998).
11. Peter Kolchin, 'Whiteness Studies: The New History of Race in America', *Journal of American History*, 89 (June 2002), pp. 154–73; Eric Arnesen, 'Whiteness and the Historians' Imagination', *International Labor and Working-Class History*, 60 (Fall 2001), pp. 3–32. See also the other articles in this special issue of *International Labor and Working-Class History*, as well as Eric Arnesen, '"Like Banquo's Ghost, It Will Not Down": The Race Question and the American Railroad Brotherhoods, 1880–1920', *American Historical Review*, 99 (December 1994), pp. 1601–33.
12. Kirsten Fischer, *Suspect Relations: Sex, Race, and Resistance in Colonial North Carolina* (Ithaca, NY: Cornell University Press, 2002), p. 3.

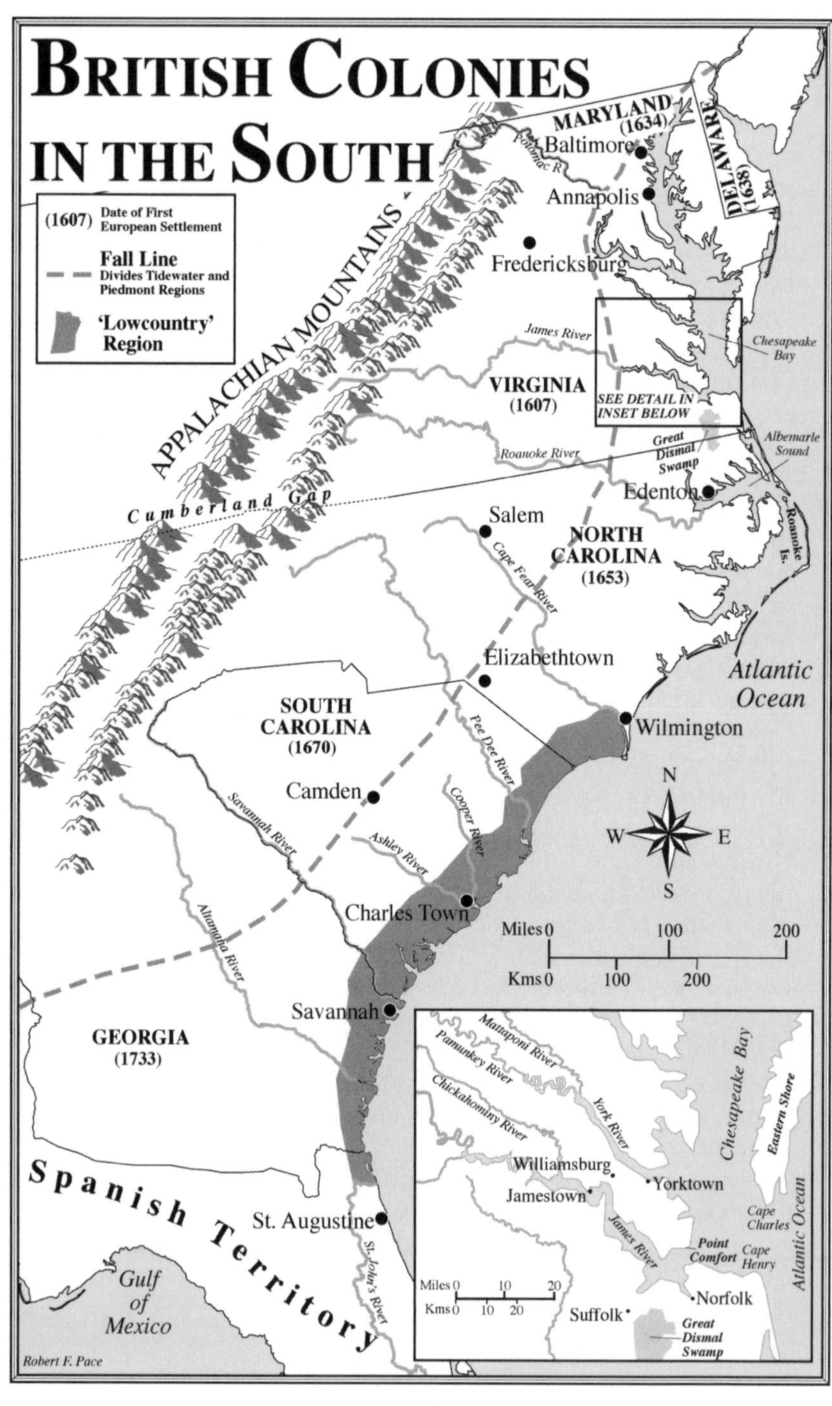
British Colonies in the South
(1607) Date of First European Settlement
Fall Line
Divides Tidewater and Piedmont Regions
'Lowcountry' Region
Appalachian Mountains
Cumberland Gap
Maryland (1634)
Delaware (1638)
Potomac R.
Baltimore
Annapolis
Fredericksburg
James River
Virginia (1607)
See detail in inset below
Chesapeake Bay
Great Dismal Swamp
Albemarle Sound
Roanoke River
Edenton
Salem
North Carolina (1653)
Roanoke Is.
Cape Fear River
Elizabethtown
Atlantic Ocean
Wilmington
South Carolina (1670)
Pee Dee River
Camden
Savannah River
Cooper River
Ashley River
N
W
E
S
Charles Town
Miles 0 100 200
Kms 0 100 200
Altamaha River
Savannah
Georgia (1733)
Spanish Territory
St. Augustine
St. John's River
Gulf of Mexico
Mattaponi River
Pamunkey River
York River
Chickahominy River
Chesapeake Bay
Eastern Shore
Williamsburg
Yorktown
Jamestown
James River
Cape Charles
Atlantic Ocean
Point Comfort
Cape Henry
Miles 0 10 20
Kms 0 10 20
Norfolk
Suffolk
Great Dismal Swamp
Robert F. Pace

Chapter 1

RED, WHITE AND BLACK? NATIVE AMERICANS, EUROPEANS AND AFRICANS MEET IN THE CHESAPEAKE

On 21 March 1861, Confederate vice-president Alexander H. Stephens declared that the 'corner-stone' of the new nation formed by southern states leaving the Union 'rests upon the great truth, that the negro is not equal to the white man; that slavery – subordination to the superior race – is his natural and normal condition'.[1] Like Stephens, the modern mind tends to consider slavery and freedom as binary opposites and usually takes the existence of separate races for granted. The scientific concept of race may have been exposed as fallacious by twentieth-century scholars, but racial ideology continues to exert a powerful influence in everyday life, as it has done since the nineteenth century. It was not always this way. A sharp dividing line between slave and free took decades to emerge in both thought and daily practice in colonial America and the idea of separate and unequal races took even longer to mature. Truths that seemed certain to Stephens in 1861 were actually only very recent insights and his statement would most likely have puzzled colonists founding Virginia in 1607.

Slavery made an indelible mark on North American society and slaves made a critical contribution to the success of the British colonies, although there were significant regional variations in their use and importance. American slavery took considerable time to develop into a fully-fledged institution in an uneven rather than a uniform process. The experiences of the enslaved were variable. In the subsistence agriculture of the northern colonies that rapidly developed into a market economy, the use of slaves was sporadic. New York had the largest slave population outside of the South, mainly because the Dutch were heavily involved in the slave trade in the seventeenth century, but it never amounted to more than 15 per cent of the colony's total population. Things were dramatically different in the South. Virginia became a 'slave society' during the course of the seventeenth century, when 'slavery stood at the center of economic production, and the master–slave relationship provided the model for all social relations'. South Carolina was conceived as a slave society, but took time to find a staple crop.[2]

And yet all this seemed very far off when considered from the perspective of the first English arrivals at Jamestown, Virginia, who were heavily outnumbered by Native Americans. Their priority was survival and co-existence with their Indian neighbours, although that changed as the colony grew in size and population. Africans were present in Virginia from at least as early as 1619 and historians have disagreed about the status they were accorded. Uppermost in the minds of the colonists, however, was the need to get along with Indians and then, when their position was strong enough, to obtain land vital to the developing tobacco economy. This was a period in which identity was predominately shaped by class and gender, not by race. Plantation owners needed workers for their land and used various groups, including Indians and white indentured servants, before bondspeople became the principal labour force. Europeans and Africans mingled with the indigenous population as three continents met in the Chesapeake and later in the Carolinas. Each group carefully evaluated the other, noting cultural and physical differences, but a sense of racial identity, defined as the permanent and inherent separation of human beings into separate types based on physical and hereditary characteristics, took much longer to develop.

ESTABLISHING A FOOTHOLD IN NORTH AMERICA

At the beginning of the seventeenth century, when the English were looking to establish colonies in North America, Great Britain played only a minor part in the international slave trade. It would become more heavily involved in the late 1600s, which partly explains why slave imports to the mainland increased towards the end of the century, although changing economic circumstances were also significant. A far more pressing concern was their relationship with the powerful Native Americans. The first permanent English settlement in North America was Jamestown, established in 1607. Situated along the James River, the Virginia colony (named after Elizabeth I, the virgin queen) grew in size and importance during the seventeenth century, as settlers moved into the Tidewater region of the Chesapeake Bay. Slavery would eventually take root on the banks of the Chesapeake and its meandering river systems, spreading out from the Bay area in the seventeenth century to the Tidewater. Maryland was founded to the north of Virginia in 1634. The first generation of settlers was fully aware that slaves were used by the Spanish and the Portuguese in their New World colonies but they had no intention of following a similar model. The

Jamestown community had its hands full trying to survive in unfamiliar circumstances.

The Virginia Company of London included a diverse mixture of merchants, aristocrats and philanthropists who had recruited an equally diverse group of colonists, including artisans, labourers and soldiers, as well as several gentlemen and an Anglican minister. The plan of this private company was simple: to make as much profit as possible by trading furs, fish, timber, and searching for gold, but for a decade the settlement struggled on the brink of disaster. Initially, 104 men and boys arrived in the Chesapeake on 26 April 1607, establishing a foothold on the banks of the James River shortly afterwards. A handful of others followed in their wake, motivated by the seemingly endless supplies of gold brought back by Spanish galleons to Europe, and a common desire to find their own immediate riches. This mentality, combined with a disdain for manual labour and a severe lack of agricultural expertise, was not conducive to survival in a harsh, inhospitable environment. Jamestown was situated adjacent to a mosquito-infested swamp which spread malaria and other diseases to the settlers, who were already coping with a severe shortage of food. That Virginia survived at all was largely due to the autocratic leadership of John Smith, Thomas Gates and Thomas Dale.

The Virginia colonists were also indebted to the Native Americans they encountered. At the time of arrival there were approximately 15,000 Algonquian-speaking Native Americans in the Chesapeake Bay region, loosely organised into a confederacy led by Chief Powhatan. Most likely, Indians initially considered the newcomers a source of mild amusement rather than a threat. Over two decades earlier, attempts to establish an English colony at Roanoke Island, on the outer banks of North Carolina, had ended in disaster with the disappearance of settlers, probably killed by local Indians. No members of this 'lost' colony were found when a relief ship returned in 1590. These memories, combined with the faltering efforts of the Virginian colonists to establish themselves on the North American mainland, served to minimise any threat posed by their new neighbours.

If some Indians were complacent, no doubt many others were a little more anxious. Waves of devastating epidemics had decimated the native population of North and South America since Christopher Columbus first established a Spanish presence in the Caribbean during his voyage of 1492–93. This was a crucial feature of the colonisation process in the South, as it was elsewhere – thousands of natives died before Europeans established permanent settlements. Indigenous peoples seemingly lacked immunity to European diseases, although this was not the only significant factor causing depopulation and tribes were affected in different ways.[3] Measles, influenza, diphtheria, tuberculosis, smallpox, scarlet fever, cholera and typhus had a calamitous impact. Disease was the major factor aiding European conquest, claiming infinitely more lives than warfare. However, it should not be forgotten that Europeans also struggled to survive in the different ecosystem of the Chesapeake. Typhoid, malaria and dysentery were major killers in Virginia and the colonists suffered from salt poisoning, as they failed to understand the tidal system that contaminated their wells with saltwater. For at least the first half-century of contact, disease drastically hampered both Indians and Europeans in the Chesapeake.

The first Virginian colonists relied on Indian corn to survive and were well aware that without it they were doomed. The relationship between the colonists and the Native Americans was complex. Although Chief Powhatan of the Pamunkey nation had effectively subdued neighbouring tribes who were obliged to pay him an annual tribute, he could hardly be said to have led an organised group. Longstanding rivalries existed and the decentralised nature of tribal leadership, based upon consent rather than autocracy, was something that Europeans found difficult to understand but advantageous to exploit. Historian Edmund S. Morgan aptly describes 'an uneasy truce' that was 'punctuated by guerrilla raids on both sides' in the colony's first decade. Individual colonists and Indians were prone to act contrary to public agreements, making it very difficult to realise the Virginia Company's goal of establishing cordial relations. Although the political situation was delicate, there was a great deal of cultural interaction and exchange. John Rolfe's marriage to Pocohontas was the most famous example of intermarriage. John Smith also displayed a keen interest in the Indian way of life, recording a great deal of information about Native Americans in his published works.[4]

At the same time, however, the English arrived in Virginia with tangible, but inchoate, notions of superiority in comparison to their hosts. This was a feeling partly based on the technological superiority of English culture. Despite struggling themselves to tame the environment, colonists viewed with condescension the primitive housing of the natives and their small-scale, agricultural and semi-nomadic economy. Indians seemed to lead an extremely parochial way of life, with a simple form of government, in contrast to the much larger and more complex nature of English society. Centuries of warfare in Europe had fostered a sense of national identity, encouraging the English to rank themselves in comparison to other countries. National rivalry was intensified in the first half of the seventeenth century, as English explorers sailed across the globe claiming new lands for their sovereign. Most significantly, the English were Protestants and the Indians were heathens and for many this translated into a crucial difference between civilised and savage. In an age when religion was probably the most important marker of identity and status, Christianity was used in a number of ways to justify the expulsion of Indians from their land. The European political tradition of civic humanism also served to exclude the indigenous people from colonial government. In making these judgements, Virginian colonists followed a well-worn script justifying English colonisation in Ireland that would be repeated around the globe as Great Britain forcibly acquired colonies in Africa and Asia.

Nonetheless, the English did not hold an explicit sense of racial superiority in relations with Native Americans at this time. There were clearly a number of important contrasts between the two groups – religious, economic, political and cultural – but those differences did not signify an innate and permanent separation of the races, much less an overarching explanation for the supposed superiority of the English. Race in the modern sense of the word did not exist at this time. Indeed, most early commentators noted the physical *compatibility* of Indians and Europeans. It was not differences but the essential similarities of the two groups that struck the first settlers. The development of racial ideology, rooted in the idea of physiologically distinct European, African and Native American bodies, was a long and complex process. Historian Alden T. Vaughan points out that 'not until the middle of the eighteenth century did most Anglo-Americans view Indians as significantly different in color from themselves, and not until the nineteenth century did red become the universally accepted color label for American Indians'. Nancy Shoemaker argues that not only were Europeans and Indians considered essentially similar in a physical sense, but that they also perceived the world around them in much the same way, identifying 'a bedrock of shared ideas' between the two. Most significantly, masculinity provided a bridge between the different cultures, as males generally held power, conducted political diplomacy and warfare, were heads of families and shared conceptions of 'manly' behaviour in protecting and providing for their dependents.[5]

Shoemaker's ingenious argument goes further than most historians in minimising the alien nature of the Indian in the eyes of the colonists, but reflects the positive view that many seventeenth-century commentators held toward the indigenous population. Indeed, there was a tension apparent in imagining and describing the Native American. On the one hand, the Indian was seen as barbarous and savage, standing outside the boundaries of civilised society. On the other was the myth of the Indian as Noble Savage. This latter image had romantic overtones, depicting Indians as naturally free and in tune with nature. In some accounts the Indian lifestyle was portrayed as almost idyllic. While ethnocentric in conception (because Indians were judged by European standards), the Noble Savage was at least deemed capable of assimilating into colonial society. Europeans considered it their duty to convert Indians to Christianity, believing all equal in the eyes of God. Some settlers, mostly runaway servants, found the native lifestyle highly appealing in the early years, seeking release from their servitude by joining tribes and marrying Indian women. As we will see, the harsh existence of indentured servants encouraged their flight. Any notions these runaways held about Indians as alien and inferior were seemingly put aside.

Positive views of the Indians conflicted with economic and political realities in Virginia, however. Land was at a premium as the settlers were cornered into the Jamestown peninsula. More territory was imperative if Virginia was to grow and prosper but land was in the possession of Indian tribes. Once Virginia had stabilised its position somewhat after the 'starving time' in the winter of 1609–10, and reached a stage where it might expect larger numbers of immigrants, the pressure to expand became irresistible. That point came when John Rolfe, after experimenting with several different strains, perfected a variety of West Indian tobacco ideal for the Virginian conditions. Rolfe's first export of four hogsheads of tobacco left in 1614. The potential profits to be made from tobacco cultivation, which required large acres of fresh land, concentrated the efforts and minds of the settlers for the rest of the decade and into the 1620s.

Relations with Indians became increasingly fractious as a result and Virginia's leaders took every opportunity to push their neighbours back. John Rolfe's marriage to Pocohontas in 1614 promised a period of relative calm, but in truth was merely a truce rather than an end to the conflict. The notion of the Indian savage was increasingly promulgated once Virginia became less reliant on Indian corn, encouraging colonists to take aggressive actions. The strategic outlook turned from a defensive to an expansionist policy. On 22 March 1622, Powhatan's successor Opechancanough took drastic steps to defend the native way of life by orchestrating an attack on the colonists. Estimates of those killed range between 330 and 350, including men, women and children. John Smith's response to the so-called Virginia massacre, which in reality was a desperate attempt to drive the English from Indian land, reflected the deteriorating relationship between the colonists and the natives. Some Virginians, Smith wrote, interpreted the massacre as 'good for the Plantation, because now we have just cause to destroy them by all meanes possible'.[6] The Virginia Company subsequently devoted substantial men and materials to a bloody war of attrition against the Native Americans that intensified after Virginia became a royal colony in 1624. Despite a last ditch attempt to repel the colonists in 1644, the hegemony of the Pamunkeys was effectively ended, leaving individual tribes to deal with the English on their own. Land was taken by negotiation, fraud and by force after 1622. The colonists exhibited an insatiable desire for more territory, which would be a major factor in causing Bacon's Rebellion in 1676. Indeed, there were frequent skirmishes between Indians and settlers on the Virginian and Maryland frontier throughout the seventeenth century.

THE INTERNATIONAL SLAVE TRADE AND THE ARRIVAL OF AFRICANS IN BRITISH NORTH AMERICA

In the summer of 1619, English corsairs attacked a slave ship captained by Manuel Mendes de Cunha off the coast of Campeche in the Gulf of Mexico. The *Sáo Joáo Bautista* was transporting 350 slaves from Luanda, the capital of Portuguese Angola, to the port of Vera Cruz in Mexico. More than half the slaves were taken by the English ship the *Treasurer*, working in consortship (a temporary agreement to combine forces in preying on Spanish vessels) with a Dutch man-of-war, the *Trier*. Slaves taken onboard the *Trier* headed east, where they would probably have been sold to one of the growing Caribbean colonies. However, the Dutch ship, perhaps running into trouble, eventually found its way to the Virginia colony several hundred miles to the north. When the *Trier* arrived in August 1619, Virginia had been in existence just twelve years and was not a destination that held much interest for slave traders. As we have seen, this British outpost had only barely managed to survive a precarious beginning. However, things had stabilised somewhat by 1619, and it was at the outlying settlement of Point Comfort, several miles downstream from Jamestown where the James River flows into the Chesapeake, that the first documented arrival of Africans to England's North American colonies took place.[7]

Like most slaves who arrived on the eastern seaboard during the nearly 200 years in which slave importing was legal (the international slave trade to the United States was banned in 1808, although illegal cargoes were sold in the American South up to the Civil War), these slaves came directly from Africa. This made them unusual in the context of early Virginia and South Carolina, however, as the small number of Africans arriving in the early decades were typically 'seasoned', originating from Caribbean plantations that had gone some way to acculturating Africans to European ways. Historians agree that these first arrivals, or charter generations, enjoyed more autonomy and flexibility than those coming afterwards, but with very different degrees of emphasis. For the first ninety years or so of Virginia's development, and for a much shorter period in South Carolina, Africans had the verbal and cultural skills enabling them to press their owners for better conditions, and freedom in some cases, as each colony took time to conceptualise and codify what slavery meant to both owners and slaves.[8]

Ira Berlin identifies four main waves of African slave arrivals in his influential history of American slavery: charter generations in the seventeenth century; plantation generations in the eighteenth century; the revolutionary generation in the final third of the 1700s; and migration generations in the nineteenth century (as well as the freedom generation in the 1860s, when slavery was finally ended). Broadly speaking, there were significant differences between these groups, but some characteristics were common to all. Every slave in the Americas originated from, or traced their ancestry to, diverse tribes and societies in the African continent. The first arrivals from the *Trier* were most likely from the Kingdom of Ndongo, across the Kwanza River to the south-west of Angola, enslaved victims of a Portuguese military campaign that transported approximately 50,000 Kimbundu-speaking Africans between 1618 and 1621. The shock of capture would have been made worse by a march of several hundred miles to Luanda, where the captives would have been held in pens before being transferred to slave ships bound for the New World. Europeans and their African partners built a system of slave fortresses along the west coast of Africa to regulate this process as the slave trade became increasingly systematised in the seventeenth and eighteenth centuries.[9]

The most vivid description of the experience of capture, transportation and eventual sale in the slave markets of the New World is provided by Olaudah Equiano. No single account can adequately stand for the many different experiences of the millions of individuals who were victims of the slave trade. Nonetheless, Equiano's autobiography, published in 1789, has unusual power and captures emotions shared by captives across time and space. Africans came from a myriad of diverse circumstances. Men and women, both young and old, were part of the estimated 12 million sold during the international slave trade. Equiano was from the upper ranks of his society, his father being an elder of some description. It was the young and the fit, particularly males, who were most likely to fetch the best price and were at greatest risk of capture. Slave societies in the Americas generated immense wealth, bringing planters power and prestige, and the inexorable need for slave labour was always pressing.

Captives like Equiano came from the African interior. They faced a long and uncertain journey to the African west coast from whence all slaves bound for the New World departed. After being kidnapped with his sister from their Igbo homeland (part of the kingdom of Benin somewhere in present-day

Nigeria), Equiano was sold several times and took at least six months to find his way to the Atlantic Ocean where he had to board a slave ship. This was a terrifying prospect. Equiano had never seen the sea before and was invasively 'handled and tossed up to see if I was sound' as the crew inspected their human cargo. He not only found the European sailors strange and unfamiliar, he was also bewildered by the 'multitude of black people, of every description, chained together, every one of their countenances expressing dejection and sorrow'. Equiano emphasises how Africans of many different ethnicities found themselves chained together. It would be easy, but a great mistake, to assume slaves came from the same cultural background and held similar values. Those interned on the decks of slave ships could not even be sure of speaking the same language.

From this point, captured Africans faced the ordeal of the journey to the New World. The four- to six-thousand mile voyage (depending upon point of origin and arrival) known as the 'Middle Passage' was hazardous in the extreme and ships lost between 15 and 20 per cent of their crew and human cargo because of disease and violent revolts. Equiano described 'the loathsomeness of the stench' as he was put 'under the decks' that made him 'so sick and low that I was not able to eat, nor had I the least desire to taste any thing'. Those who survived the journey taking from six to nine weeks were greeted by their prospective buyers as planters and traders came aboard the ship to make a preliminary inspection. Equiano and his shipmates anchored in Barbados but had to be coaxed ashore, as 'there was much trembling and dread among' them. Barbadian slaves were sent to calm Equiano and his companions, telling them that 'we were not to be eaten, but to work, and were soon to go on land, where we should see many of our country people'. Even before disembarking, then, slaves were forging relations with each other and helping one another to cope with the shock of bondage.

The final indignity was the slave auction. At root, slavery was the ownership of one human being by another human being, with the slaves' chattel status (chattel means 'movable possession') akin to that of any other item of property, such as a horse or a piece of furniture. Equiano recalled being lined up at his auction 'like so many sheep in a fold, without regard to sex or age'. The bidders 'rush at once into the yard where the slaves are confined, and make choice of that parcel they like best'. The excitement etched into the faces of the buyers disturbed Equiano, as did the 'noise and clamour' of the auction. This paled in comparison with the awful conclusion of events, however, as freshly acquired slaves left with their new owners for an uncertain future in which they could be put to work in a diverse variety of roles and tasks. 'In this manner, without scruple, are relations and friends separated, most of them never to see each other again', Equiano concluded. Approximately four out of five North American slaves came directly from Africa, enduring an experience perhaps similar to Equiano's.[10]

Slavery had been a prominent feature of human society since ancient times, but the Atlantic slave trade between the fifteenth and nineteenth centuries was by far the largest, most sustained and highly organised movement of people into bondage. Trafficking in slaves had been a feature of most African societies, but under the direction of the Portuguese and the Spanish, and later the Dutch and the English, it became more incessant and business-orientated. Moreover, what developed in the Americas was a much more tightly controlled and restrictive system of bondage that denied slaves a place in society, what historian Philip D. Curtin describes as 'the plantation complex'.[11] Previous forms of servitude had allowed some measure of flexibility, however slight.

Above all, the justification of New World slavery came to rest upon a pervasive ideology of black inferiority and white superiority. The exchange of European merchandise, such as weapons, alcohol and manufactured goods, for slaves enabled the mass production in New World colonies of staple plantation crops like sugar, tobacco and later cotton, which were sold on European markets. The 'triangular trade', as it was known, transformed the demography of the globe. Arguably, the Atlantic slave trade's most harmful legacy in the long run was the creation of a powerful racial ideology dividing human beings into distinct races. Historians disagree about the precise impact of this mass forced migration, but there is no question that the political, economic and cultural consequences were profound. North America actually received far fewer slave imports than colonies in the Caribbean and South America. Approximately 660,000 slaves disembarked on the shores of the American mainland, amounting to less than 7 per cent of the total international slave trade. Nonetheless, slavery would become as central to the American South as it was to Barbados or Brazil.

THE STATUS OF AFRICANS IN EARLY VIRGINIA

One of the fiercest debates between American historians concerns the status of blacks in early Virginia and the question of whether slavery or racism came first to the colony. Reflecting the turbulent state of contemporary race relations in the United States in the 1950s and 1960s, the so-called origins debate was pioneered by Oscar and Mary Handlin and Carl Degler. The Handlins argued that blacks in Virginia were treated in a similar fashion to white indentured servants up to the 1660s. The terms 'servant' and 'slave' were virtually interchangeable in practice, they found. This situation changed around mid-century, when planters realised that blacks could not only be tied to longer terms of service but were not necessarily bound by rules that applied to white servants. After that slavery was gradually written into the statute book. Africans became widely associated with the debased position of slave and white attitudes hardened. Racism was the product of slavery in this view.[12]

Carl Degler disagreed. He countered that it was far more likely 'that the Negro was actually *never* treated as an equal of the white man, servant or free', in a reversal of the Handlins' logic. A much more deep-rooted view of Africans as inferior existed in the English mind, according to Degler, and while it was undoubtedly the need for labour that brought Africans to Virginia, and racism probably got worse as a result, a negative view of Africans existed long before the 1660s. It was the lesser status of Africans that facilitated the establishment of bondage in Virginia and therefore prejudice existed before slavery.[13]

A decade after Degler's challenge, to which the Handlins replied robustly, historian Winthrop Jordan entered, and promised to resolve, this debate. Jordan's monumental *White Over Black* is a study of racial ideology in colonial North America that has been hugely influential and remains required reading. At first glance, Jordan seemed to provide the evidence proving Degler's thesis. Jordan probed the Elizabethan English view of Africans that had been emerging in plays, books and travel accounts since William Hawkins of Plymouth made the first recorded British visit to West Africa in 1530. Most significantly, Jordan argued that the colour black had negative connotations in the English mind, being associated with evil and filth. Africans were also heathens and were regarded as totally uncivilised, savage and ultimately irredeemable. In a way that did not apply to Native Americans, the popular view saw Africans ranked at the bottom of the scale, with little or no chance of assimilation into English society. They were regarded as permanent outsiders. Jordan also argued that Africans were considered libidinous by Britons, who believed that they instinctively had little or no control over their sexual urges.[14]

Jordan's sweep through early modern England was, as he admitted, not necessarily proof that Englishmen in Virginia were inherently prejudiced toward Africans. The logic of Jordan's argument pointed towards changing and flexible views of 'others' because he heavily emphasised the unique conditions of early Virginia. It was not only Africans but Native Americans who 'came to serve as two fixed points from which English settlers could triangulate their own position in America'. Thus, the precise historical context was critical and attitudes were changeable in different circumstances. Despite

Jordan's caution, Alden T. Vaughan argued shortly afterwards that two Virginia censuses taken in 1624 and 1625 confirmed the inferior status of blacks from a very early point. In both censuses, the small number of Africans were not given surnames and half were not named at all but denoted by 'negar'. Moreover, dates of arrival for Africans were not always recorded, dates that were crucial to indentured servants because they denoted their length of service. Were Africans, then, serving permanently? Evidence is far from conclusive and the same list refers to Frenchmen, Irishmen, Dutchmen and an Italian, which could be interpreted as English suspicion of anyone not originating from the mother country, rather than racial prejudice towards Africans.[15]

In order to evaluate these positions, it is necessary to consider the context of Virginia's development after the difficult first decade. Despite the high mortality rates, which would not come down until mid-century, the economy and society gained a measure of stability in the tobacco boom of the 1620s. The sweet-scented variety of Trinidadian tobacco cultivated by Rolfe was much prized in European circles and secured the economic future of the colony, shaping its development and character. Virginians rapidly shifted their focus to tobacco production. For this they relied on a specific type of unfree labour – white indentured servants. Usually contracted for a period of seven years to masters, indentured servants were disproportionately male and tended to come from a variety of moderate backgrounds, although some were skilled artisans. In 1618, the Virginia Company established the 'head-right' system granting fifty acres of land to all self-financed new arrivals and to those who paid for the passage of others across the Atlantic. Much greater interest in the colony followed as wealthy Englishmen rapidly accumulated vast tracts of land in return for assisting the passage of indentured servants, who would then be bound to work for them, thus solving the labour problem.

Cultivating tobacco was a painstaking and intricate process, and servants worked extremely hard. Circumstances varied according to owner, but corporal punishment was a constant threat (a 1641 Maryland statute made running away an offence punishable by death) and living conditions were primitive. Servants could be sold to different masters while under contract. Terms of service improved gradually during the seventeenth century, not least to make the colony more appealing, and shorter contracts of four or five years were signed according to age and circumstances of arrival. At the same time, 'freedom dues' customarily given on completion, consisting of provisions and sometimes land, became progressively less substantial over the decades.

As profits soared and more Europeans arrived, the relationship between the Virginia Company and the King became a concern. By 1624, the cost of campaigning against the Indians had put the company in financial difficulty and profits for shareholders were thin. Frequent accusations of fraud against leading officials led James I to revoke the company charter and reorganise Virginia as a royal colony. A royal governor was appointed to oversee affairs, but apart from that the colony was left largely to govern itself. This made the Virginia House of Burgesses, established in 1619, even more important. As a relatively democratic governing body, based upon the principle of elected representatives, the House of Burgesses made Virginia a far more attractive option to Englishmen who had no voice in politics at home.

Within this context, Africans arrived in Virginia in small numbers during the 1620s and 1630s. While American schoolchildren are taught that the first Africans arrived in Virginia on the Dutch ship *Trier* in August 1619, recent evidence indicates that they were present before this date. A census taken in the spring of 1619 shows 32 Africans in Jamestown, although we know nothing about their circumstances or when they arrived. We know for certain that numbers of Africans were low and would remain so until the latter half of the century, a critical demographic feature in considering the origins debate. In 1625 there were just 23 blacks and 1,227 whites; by 1649, 300 blacks and 15,000 whites; by 1660, about 950 blacks and 26,000 whites; and by 1670, 2,000 blacks and 38,000 whites. Up to around mid-century, Africans accounted for just 2 per cent of the total population and while that proportion had risen slightly by 1670, it still amounted to only 5 per cent. As long as numbers were low, Africans were relatively invisible, particularly in comparison with the much more imposing presence of Native Americans. For even though the Algonquians were pushed back, they remained a significant presence as the frontier slowly pushed outwards. Moreover, Anglo-Indian interest groups emerged in the 1630s, the most famous being an alliance between the Susquehannocks and a group exporting beaver pelts led by William Claiborne. The critical point of reference for the colonists, then, was the Native American.

There are other problems with trying to establish the existence of ingrained prejudice at this very early point. Can the absence of surnames for Africans be taken as a reliable guide to wider attitudes among the colonists as a whole, or merely of the leaders who ordered the census to be taken? In a society where the vast majority of people were unfree labourers of one sort or another, the clearest distinction was that between the free – the small number of landowners contracting a workforce – and those labouring in the fields. We must surely distinguish between the attitudes of planters and indentured servants. Even if some Africans were contracted for longer periods than others, there is no suggestion that they were slaves at this point; at least not slaves in the sense of the term as it would later evolve. Just how much status did a white skin guarantee when the reality was that servants worked side-by-side with Africans in the fields? The words of James Revel, a convict who became a servant in Virginia, are revealing:

> We and the Negroes both alike did fare,
> Of work and food we had an equal share;
> But in a piece of ground we called our own,
> The food we eat first by ourselves were sown.
>
> Much hardships then in deed I did endure,
> No dog was ever nursed so I'm sure,
> More pity the poor Negroe slaves bestowed,
> Than my inhuman brutal master showed.
>
> Forc'd from your friends and country for to go,
> Among the Negroes to work at the hoe;
> In distant countries void of all relief,
> Sold for a slave because you prov'd a thief.[16]

Slavery was not written into the statute books until Maryland passed a law in 1664 requiring Negroes to serve *durante vita* (for life). Even then, further laws were needed defining what it meant to be a slave. Legal bondage gradually evolved after 1660 and major slave codes were passed in Virginia in 1680 and 1705, and in South Carolina in 1690, 1696, 1712 and 1740. These codes were written in response to changing circumstances.

The clearest evidence in support of the Handlins' position that full-blown racial prejudice developed after slavery is provided by the existence of a number of free blacks living in the Chesapeake in the mid-seventeenth century. Not only were these individuals free, they were also accorded full status in society, using the court system, voting and taking advantage of headrights to import white and black servants and claim more land. The most celebrated free black was Anthony Johnson. Known as 'Anthony the Negro' in 1621 when he was sold in Jamestown, Johnson was commended for his actions during the 1622 attack by Native Americans. In addition to routine duties, his owners allowed him to work for himself, to marry and to baptise his children. The precise circumstances of his freedom are unknown but, like all free blacks in the Chesapeake, Johnson somehow extracted himself from a servile condition. Perhaps he agreed a term of service with his master on arrival. More likely, Johnson was rewarded for meritorious service – many slaves were released in wills – or he worked his way towards purchasing his own freedom.

Most servants, white or black, were allowed to own property and labour for themselves on garden plots. In time they might accumulate enough to buy their terms of service and those of their loved ones, even though this process could take decades. For example, Francis Payne signed an agreement with his owner on 13 May 1643 to deliver three servants in exchange for his freedom. On top of carrying out routine duties that required producing 1,500 pounds of tobacco and six bushels of corn by the end of the harvest, Payne also worked for himself. Just under six years later, he had secured two servants and sometime in the early 1650s he was granted his freedom. It then took Payne until November 1656 to secure the freedom of his wife and children.

Clearly Payne was a remarkable figure and it would be wrong to assume that all blacks within the colony prospered as he did. Moreover, he had to work extremely hard to succeed, far more so than ordinary white indentured servants. Still, in the 1660s and 1670s, ten out of fifty-three black men in Northampton county on Virginia's eastern shore owned their own home and some had done extremely well. Half of those men had English wives. By 1651, Anthony (who had taken the surname Johnson to emphasise his free status) had a substantial plantation of his own and obtained a patent of 250 acres that underscored his success. Johnson was a prominent figure in his local community who used the court system to his advantage. After a fire in 1653, Johnson received relief from the county court. Moreover, he bought an African slave called John Casor, who was bound to serve for life. When Casor ran away to a neighbouring white planter's estate, Johnson successfully sued for his return in court. Owning a black slave confirmed Johnson's standing and raises interesting implications for the notion that owners were always Europeans while Africans were only slaves. These examples led historians Timothy H. Breen and Stephen Innes to conclude that 'Englishmen and Africans could interact with one another on terms of relative equality for two generations' in the Chesapeake.[17]

More recently, in a thesis with significant implications for interpreting the experiences of the first blacks, Ira Berlin has stressed the creole origins of the first Africans in North America. The charter generations of slaves were, to an extent, much better prepared for life in the colonies than their successors. Resident in coastal areas in West Africa, and emerging in Europe and the Americas as well, Atlantic creoles were familiar with Europeans and with the triangular trade. They used their skills as merchants, sailors and interpreters to exploit opportunities created by the slave trade. Some, then, worked in conjunction with Europeans. As bondage became the primary labour system in the New World, however, the less fortunate among them became enslaved.

The charter generation of slaves from creole backgrounds had a much better ability to survive and make the best of slavery than did the plantation generations. They could communicate with their owners, a skill crucial in trying to gain concessions. Indeed, most Africans arriving in the South in the seventeenth century came from the Caribbean (from British, Spanish and Portuguese colonies) and were 'seasoned' – used to plantation routines and to the conditions and loopholes of bondage. They realised the benefits of becoming Christians, for example. At a stroke, conversion undermined the charge of being savage and baptised Africans sued for their freedom in Virginia courts.[18]

There is not enough evidence to establish decisively the status of blacks in the colony, but some observations can be made. We must be precise about the terms of the origins debate. It is vital to distinguish between racism, prejudice and slavery. Racism is an organised system oppressing and debasing on the basis of supposed biological differences. It rests on the ideology of racial supremacy separating allegedly superior and inferior groups and the implementation of institutional barriers between those groups. This did not exist in the Chesapeake in the seventeenth century, although it was slowly developing. Prejudice can take many forms, being sustained and widespread or more limited and ephemeral. There is little doubt that the English believed themselves superior to Native Americans and Africans in a variety of ways. However, this did not prevent free blacks in the colony making their mark and becoming significant members of their local communities. Moreover, because the majority of whites were unfree labourers, forced to endure similar conditions to the enslaved, the gap between whites and blacks that would develop in the eighteenth century was considerably reduced. Servants interacted with one another on a daily basis, forming mutual relationships borne out of shared hardships. They stole and ran away together, got drunk and mutually bemoaned their treatment at the hands of their owners. Men sought to assert their masculinity, seeking a measure of control over women in the colony, and interracial relationships flourished. Once this situation changed, and the majority of Africans became slaves with little hope of altering their condition, then the dynamics of the black–white relationship altered decisively.

THE SWITCH TO SLAVERY

Discriminatory laws restricting the rights of blacks were drawn up in the 1640s and 1650s and the transition to slavery was under way in earnest by the 1660s. These measures reveal that, by mid-century, a number of Africans were serving for life and that terms for other black servants were being extended to life as a punishment for misdemeanours. This did not automatically make Africans slaves, as they retained entitlements and opportunities, but the law gradually chipped away at their rights.

A Virginia tax of 1643 made black women tithable at the same rate as male servants, but did not apply to white female servants. It seems that English, yet not African, women were being removed from some kinds of field work. This constituted an attack on the status of black women and by extension their male partners, whether white or black. The same law made black wives of white husbands taxable and was the first of a number of measures seeking to penalise and ultimately prevent interracial relations. As historian Kathleen M. Brown shows, the Virginian elite wanted to control reproduction and marriage among servants, anxious not to lose the labour of their female servants to pregnancy. They were also aware that the severe gender imbalance in the Chesapeake lessened the availability of women, thereby heightening tension over relationships between black men and white females. As the century progressed, gender was manipulated to promote white unity and undermine black status as 'lawmakers began to define the social meaning of racial difference by reserving the privileges of womanhood for the masters and husbands of English women'. Kirsten Fischer outlines a similar course of action taken in colonial North Carolina. Jennifer L. Morgan also highlights the importance of gender. Morgan emphasises the significance of controlling the reproductive capacity of African women for the owner's benefit as intrinsic to the enslavement process in New World societies.[19]

After 1660, slavery's grip tightened as both Virginia and Maryland sought to close loopholes allowing blacks to seek freedom for themselves or their children. The Virginia General Assembly followed up a 1662 law defining a child's status by that of his mother with a further act in 1667 stipulating that the 'conferring of baptisme doth not alter the condition of the person as to his bondage or ffreedome'. Africans were thus denied the chance to sue for freedom by virtue of their Christianity. The children of black mothers became slaves regardless of the condition of their father. Any inconvenience caused to an owner by pregnancy was now outweighed by the beneficial addition to his labour force. Bondage became hereditary, passing from mother to child, reversing the paternal emphasis of English law. In so doing, notions of the permanent inferiority of blacks became much more plausible as slavery literally began to run through bloodlines. Over time, blackness became associated with a servile condition, whiteness with freedom. Paul Finkelman describes these laws as the '"cost of color" – a sort of civil penalty for being black'. However, they are perhaps better interpreted as the privileges of whiteness, as gender and race were used to the advantage of Englishmen no matter what their economic standing.[20]

Underlying, if not driving, these reforms was the shift from a system of servitude to a system of slavery. This was a slow and inconsistent process, not complete until around 1700, but gradually more Africans slaves were imported into the Chesapeake. A number of factors have been identified to explain this switch. Considerations of supply and demand were crucial. Slaves were an expensive option, costing more than indentured servants because they served for the duration of their lives rather than for a fixed term. The price of an indentured servant stood somewhere between one third and one half of what it cost to purchase a slave. Only the wealthiest tobacco planters could afford this expense and only after mortality rates fell in the colony did it make economic sense to invest in slaves.

It did not matter how much Virginians had to spend, however, until the international slave traders were willing to sell their cargo on the mainland. Travelling to North America from Africa added several hundred miles to the slave traders' journey and slavery was booming in the Caribbean. The Caribbean islands exhibited an insatiable appetite for slaves and virtually monopolised slave imports in the seventeenth century. Sugar production in colonies like Barbados soared by mid-century and proved to be even more lucrative than tobacco. Indeed, after the boom of the 1620s, average tobacco prices in the Chesapeake fell dramatically and did not reach a level comparable to that of sugar until much later in the century. Prices were subject to annual fluctuations depending on the size and quality of the tobacco harvest. The disparity between these staple crops was intensified because sugar was subject to a lower British import tax than tobacco, but this was somewhat offset by the lower price of land in the Chesapeake and the lower capital outlay required for growing tobacco (sugar planters required more slaves and had to build mills and boiling houses). Even if tobacco planters in the Chesapeake were as wealthy as their counterparts who sold sugar, however, they could only purchase slaves if they were available and it appears that this was not the case until about the 1690s.

In the middle decades of the seventeenth century it was the Dutch who controlled the slave trade. This changed in 1672 with the formation of the Royal African Company, which was given a monopoly to supply slaves to British colonies. In practice, however, supply remained haphazard until the Royal African Company lost its monopoly in 1698, for it failed to provide slaves in sufficient numbers, being unable to organise a regular supply from African sources and being reluctant to travel to Virginia. The vast majority of slaves arriving in the Chesapeake in the seventeenth century actually came on Dutch ships plying their trade between the Caribbean and the mainland. These ships carried a few slaves in addition to their regular merchandise, for there was considerable trade in both goods and foodstuffs between the islands and the Chesapeake, rather than being the kind of dedicated slave ships that would come regularly in the eighteenth century.

Another factor encouraging the growth of slavery was the decreasing supply of indentured servants, which pushed up the price that had to be paid for their labour. Numbers of servants coming to the Chesapeake declined from around the 1660s, although precise figures are difficult to gauge. Once the British economy recovered from a period of uncertainty in the mid-seventeenth century caused by the English Civil War, it was no longer considered economically prudent to send workers abroad. A falling birth rate in England, combined with the severe loss of life caused by the plague, eased problems caused by overpopulation. In any case, the hard work and progressively limited opportunities awaiting indentured servants in the Chesapeake was hardly attractive, as freedom dues dwindled. The latest study on this subject, by Anthony Parent Jr, suggests that it was in the 1680s that longer life expectancy and the reduced cost differential between buying servants or slaves made 'the slave trade economically viable' in Virginia.[21] Nonetheless, white servants continued to arrive in the southern colonies and a sharp transition from servitude to slavery did not take place. It is difficult, therefore, to cite fewer numbers of indentured servants as the primary cause of the switch to slavery, although this would eventually ensure that tobacco planters predominantly used slaves instead of servants.

Indeed, all of the factors cited thus far present structural reasons as to *how* slaves became more available; they do not explain *why* they became more appealing. As historian Betty Wood contends, 'economic and demographic factors' broadly engendered changes in the colonial Virginian labour force, but 'they do not provide a convincing explanation of why the legal status of "slave" became devised and reserved for people of West African ancestry'. Answers to this question hinge on the inferior status of blacks and the cultural, religious, and physical 'otherness' of Africans within Chesapeake society. Planters in Virginia, it is asserted, were more comfortable with English servants who spoke their language, shared their customs and were familiar with English agricultural practices. Africans had already been enslaved in the Spanish colonies and in the English Caribbean. In Winthrop Jordan's influential view, bondage emerged due to a combination of changing circumstances: more slaves became available at the same time that the supply of servants fell and white prejudice increased. No single overarching factor was decisive, Jordan argues; rather, a complex mixture of demographic, economic, political, cultural, social and religious forces, which cannot be unravelled from one another, added up to an 'unthinking decision' in Virginia. The shift from indentured servitude to bondage entailed 'a mutually interactive growth of slavery and unfavorable assessment [of Africans], with no cause for either which did not cause the other as well'.[22]

Recent scholarship challenges this interpretation and emphasises the elite planters' role above all other factors, structural or cultural. Robert McColley points towards a March 1660 Virginian law soliciting Dutch traders to bring greater supplies of slaves as a sign of the changing tide. John C. Coombs shows that the wealthiest Virginians had a strong preference for African slaves and had begun to acquire them wherever possible from mid-century onwards. Anthony Parent, building upon the pioneering materialist interpretation of Edmund S. Morgan, squarely blames the Virginian elite for the switch to slavery. Far from being unthinking, this was a deliberate and conscious decision, taken in no small part because of the considerable amounts of land accumulated by the great planters and their fear of a growing mass of discontented ex-servants who had served their time of indenture. Parent describes a 'landgrab' between 1650 and 1664, when almost a million acres of land were secured via the headright system. A further million acres were taken in the decade after 1664. 'Hoarded' land was rented out to tenants as the great planters extended the range of their activities beyond their own plantations, developing business ties both within their local communities (with small planters), and across the Atlantic (with British merchants). They needed a permanent dependent labour force and indentured servants were not adequate by the second half of the century. Slaves fitted the bill much better.[23]

Any anxiety that the planters may have felt about moving to a slave labour system was dispelled by events of 1676. In the face of continuing hostility on the western frontier, settlers were disappointed that Governor William Berkeley failed to authorise a raid against the Susquehannocks. Nathaniel Bacon, an ambitious young planter, ignored Berkeley's ruling and gathered a group of frontiersmen who carried out an attack anyway. This dispute escalated into a power struggle between the older, established, Tidewater elite and the younger planters who were both socially and geographically placed at the margins of the colony. On 23 June, Bacon led a force of 400 men (including the slaves of his opponents) to the General Assembly to demand a pardon for defying Berkeley and to seek permission to lead an expedition against the Indians. Berkeley agreed under duress but later declared Bacon a traitor. For the next few months, Bacon's mob threatened the property of

Berkeley and his allies, as well as attacking Indians indiscriminately. The affair only came to an end when Bacon died in October 1676 (probably after contracting dysentery).

Bacon's Rebellion scared the Virginian elite. This class conflict threatened their power and continued security. In the aftermath, the great planters consciously sought to raise the status of all white men while at the same time continuing to tighten the restrictions on blacks. Thus began a concerted attempt to provide whiteness with substance and tangible rewards. Most indentured servants welcomed these developments, as they promised more favourable working conditions and better future prospects. Many remained friends with their black neighbours and collusion continued between servants. Inexorably, though, the elevated status of whites created racial barriers and encouraged identification with the colonial elite, no matter how great the economic gulf. Whiteness gradually became a privilege and an important component of individual identity with social, political and economic benefits. Male servants in particular saw their desires to become patriarchal heads of households being enhanced by the new order. Virginian Reverend Godwyn Morgan's observation in 1680 was telling: '*Negroe*' and '*Slave*' had 'by custom grown Homogenous and Convertible; even as *Negro* and *Christian, Englishman* and *Heathen,* are by the like corrupt Custom and Partiality made Opposites'.[24]

The colonial authorities, prompted by the needs of elites in Virginia and Maryland, began to systematically undermine the status of Africans in the second half of the seventeenth century, as legal statutes defined the rights of whites and blacks. Unlike white indentured servants, blacks could be made to serve for life and could be controlled in a more ruthless fashion. From the planters' perspective, they were heathens and outsiders, which made them easier to enslave, especially after misgivings about enslaving blacks on religious grounds were put aside. Popular conceptions of whiteness and blackness would be influenced decisively by this process. Once Virginia and Maryland turned to slavery, other southern colonies facing the same labour problems would find it very easy to follow their lead. The Upper South (Virginia and Maryland) might conceivably have remained a society based on indentured servitude and thus developed very differently from other New World colonies that rapidly became slave societies in the seventeenth century. Having headed down this path, however, it was more likely a question of when, rather than if, the Lower South (Carolina and Georgia) would do likewise. As it turned out, South Carolina needed little encouragement from Virginia, as it followed a Caribbean model from the beginning, led by an influx of settlers from Barbados.

Notes

1. Alexander H. Stephens, 'The Cornerstone Speech', cited in Paul Finkelman (ed.), *Defending Slavery: Proslavery Thought in the Old South* (Boston, MA: Bedford/St. Martin's, 2003), p. 91.
2. Ira Berlin, *Many Thousands Gone: The First Two Centuries of Slavery in North America* (Cambridge, MA: Harvard University Press, 1998), p. 8. For more on the distinctions between 'slave societies' and 'societies with slaves', see David Turley, *Slavery* (Oxford: Blackwell, 2000), pp. 62–100.
3. David S. Jones cautions against monocausal explanations in 'Virgin Soils Revisited', *William and Mary Quarterly*, 60 (October 2003), pp. 703–42.
4. Edmund S. Morgan, *American Slavery, American Freedom: The Ordeal of Colonial Virginia* (New York: W. W. Norton, 1975), p. 72; John Smith, *A Map of Virginia; with a Description of the Countrey, the Commodities, People, Government and Religion* (Oxford: Joseph Barnes, 1612).
5. Alden T. Vaughan, 'From White Man to Redskin: Changing Anglo-American Perceptions of the American Indian', *American Historical Review*, 87 (October 1982), p. 918; Nancy Shoemaker, *A Strange Likeness: Becoming Red and White in Eighteenth-Century North America* (New York: Oxford University Press, 2004), p. 3.
6. John Smith (1624), cited in Gary B. Nash, *Red, White, and Black: The Peoples of Early America* (Englewood Cliffs, NJ: Prentice Hall, 1974), p. 61.
7. Engel Sluiter, 'New Light on the "20. and Odd Negroes" Arriving in Virginia, August 1619', *William and Mary Quarterly*, 54 (April 1997), pp. 395–8.
8. Berlin, *Many Thousands Gone*; Ira Berlin, *Generations of Captivity: A History of African-American Slaves* (Cambridge, MA: Harvard University Press, 2003).
9. John Thornton, 'The African Experience of the "20. and Odd Negroes" Arriving in Virginia in 1619', *William and Mary Quarterly*, 55 (July 1998), pp. 421–34.
10. *The Interesting Narrative of the Life of Olaudah Equiano, or Gustavas Vassa, the African*, in Henry Louis Gates, Jr (ed.), *The Classic Slave Narratives* (New York: Penguin, 1987), pp. 33, 37, 38. It should be noted that doubt has recently been cast as to Equiano's origins. He may have been born in South Carolina, not Africa. See Vincent Carretta, *Equiano the African: Biography of a Self-Made Man* (Athens: University of Georgia Press, 2005).
11. Philip D. Curtin, *The Rise and Fall of the Plantation Complex: Essays in Atlantic History* (Cambridge: Cambridge University Press, 1990).
12. Oscar and Mary Handlin, 'Origins of the Southern Labor System', *William and Mary Quarterly*, 7 (April 1950), pp. 199–222.
13. Carl Degler, 'Slavery and the Genesis of American Race Prejudice', *Comparative Studies in History and Society*, 2 (October 1959), pp. 49–66.
14. Winthrop D. Jordan, *White Over Black: American Attitudes Toward the Negro, 1550–1812* (Chapel Hill: University of North Carolina Press, 1968).

15. Ibid. p. 90; Alden T. Vaughan, 'Blacks in Virginia: A Note on the First Decade', *William and Mary Quarterly,* 29 (July 1972), pp. 469–78.
16. James Revel, 'The Poor Unhappy Transported Felon's Sorrowful Account of His Fourteen Years Transportation at Virginia in America', c.1680, in Warren M. Billings (ed.), *The Old Dominion in the Seventeenth Century: A Documentary History of Virginia, 1606–1689* (Chapel Hill: University of North Carolina Press, 1968), pp. 140–2.
17. Timothy H. Breen and Stephen Innes, *'Myne Owne Ground': Race and Freedom on Virginia's Eastern Shore, 1640–1676* (New York: Oxford University Press, 1980), p. 5.
18. Berlin, *Many Thousands Gone*; Berlin, *Generations of Captivity*.
19. Kathleen M. Brown, *Good Wives, Nasty Wenches and Anxious Patriarchs: Gender, Race and Power in Colonial Virginia* (Chapel Hill: University of North Carolina Press, 1996), p. 128; Kirsten Fischer, *Suspect Relations: Sex, Race, and Resistance in Colonial North Carolina* (Ithaca, NY: Cornell University Press, 2002); Jennifer L. Morgan, *Laboring Women: Reproduction and Gender in New World Slavery* (Philadelphia: University of Pennsylvania Press, 2004).
20. Willie Lee Rose (ed.), *A Documentary History of Slavery in North America* (New York: Oxford University Press, 1976), p. 19; Paul Finkelman, 'Crimes of Love, Misdemeanors of Passion: The Regulation of Race and Sex in the Colonial South', in Catherine Clinton and Michele Gillespie (eds), *The Devil's Lane: Sex and Race in the Early South* (New York: Oxford University Press, 1997), p. 127.
21. Anthony S. Parent, Jr, *Foul Means: The Formation of a Slave Society in Virginia, 1660–1740* (Chapel Hill: University of North Carolina Press, 2003), p. 55.
22. Betty Wood, 'The Origins of Slavery', in John B. Boles (ed.), *A Companion to the American South* (Malden, MA: Blackwell, 2002), p. 58; Jordan, *White Over Black*, p. 80.
23. Robert McColley, 'Slavery in Virginia, 1619–1660: A Re-Examination', in Robert H. Abzug and Stephen E. Maizlish (eds), *New Perspectives on Race and Slavery in America: Essays in Honor of Kenneth Stampp* (Lexington: The University Press of Kentucky), p. 20; John C. Coombs, 'Building the "Machine": The Development of Slavery and Slave Society in Early Colonial Virginia' (Ph. D Dissertation, College of William and Mary, 2003), pp. 69–99; Parent, *Foul Means,* pp. 9–79. See also Theodore W. Allen, *The Invention of the White Race, Volume One: Racial Oppression and Social Control* (London: Verso, 1994) and *The Invention of the White Race, Volume Two: The Origin of Oppression in Anglo-America* (London: Verso, 1997).
24. Reverend Godwyn Morgan (1680), cited in Jordan, *White Over Black*, p. 97.

COLONIAL SETTLEMENTS 1720
Fort St. Louis 1682
Maryland
Delaware
Virginia
Powhatan Confederation
Jamestown 1607
Williamsburg 1699
Tuscaroras
Roanoke Is. 1585
North Carolina
New Bern 1710
Cherokees
Catawbas
South Carolina
Charles Town 1680
Yamasees
Guales
Timucuas
St. Augustine 1565
FLORIDA
Apalachees
Fort Condé 1710
Fort Toulouse 1717
Creeks
Choctaws
Chickasaws
Natchez
Ohio
Tennessee
Mississippi
Arkansas
Red
Rio Grande
Cahokia 1698
Santa Fe 1609
Nuestra Señora de Guadalupe (El Paso) 1659
Comanches
Apaches
Caddos
Karankawas
Natchitoches 1714
Fort Rosalie (Natchez) 1716
Guadalupe Mission (Nacogdoches) 1716
San Antonio de Valero 1718
New Orleans 1718
Fort Maurepas 1699
Pensacola 1695
Gulf of Mexico
NEW SPAIN
Saltillo 1586
Guadalajara 1531
Mexico 1521
Vera Cruz 1519
Coast of Campeche
Mérida 1542
British Honduras
Guatemala 1542
Miskito (Mosquito) Coast
Pacific Ocean
Havana 1515
Cuba
Jamaica
Port Royal 1655
Saint Domingue
Santo Domingo
Hispaniola
Santo Domingo 1496
Puerto Rico
Virgin (Br.)
Leeward Is. (Br.)
Barbuda (Br.)
Antigua (Br.)
Guadalupe (Fr.)
The Saints (Fr.)
Dominica (Fr.)
Fort Royal 1638
Martinique (Fr.)
St. Lucia (Fr.)
St. Vincent
Barbados (Br.)
Grenada
Tobago
Trinidad
Caribbean Sea
Bahamas (Br.)
Atlantic Ocean
Bermuda
N
W
E
S
Miles 0 200 400
Kms 0 200 400
Areas of Settlement:
British
Spanish
French
Indian Tribes Encountered in the South in Bold Italics
Robert F. Pace

Chapter 2

SYSTEMATISING SLAVERY: THE MAKING OF THE PLANTATION SYSTEM IN THE EIGHTEENTH CENTURY

The eighteenth century proved a critical period in the evolution of slavery and race in the American South. The trajectory of the southern colonies was far from certain at its beginning, but became much clearer after the split from Great Britain in 1776 and the subsequent formation of the United States. Slavery grew in size and importance in the South throughout the 1700s, creating two mature slave societies based on different crops: tobacco in the Upper South and rice in the Lower South. During this period, the need for white unity increased as African slaves formed a much greater proportion of the population. Blackness became ever more firmly associated with a servile status, while whiteness, at least for men, granted some form of political inclusion – white males could vote, but most political offices were limited to those with substantial property. Class tensions did not go away, however, and a tight-knit Virginia planter elite emerged in the first half of the century, living sometimes uneasily alongside their less affluent neighbours. As slaves arrived in ever greater numbers, and numbers of indentured servants decreased, the demographic dynamics of the Chesapeake changed decisively. This was a society in flux, despite the stability of the staple crop tobacco.

The rapid growth of a second major English colony at the turn of the century did much to protect British interests in North America from colonial rivals Spain and France and ensure slavery's entrenchment in the South. Carolina was divided into northern and southern sections and Charles Town held the key to its future success, although in 1700 this settlement was threatened by Native Americans to the west and the Spanish to the south. Georgia was founded in the 1730s primarily to provide a buffer against Spanish incursions from Florida, and not until mid-century were slaves permitted. After that, slavery quickly became the principal labour system as Georgia essentially became an extension of South Carolinian society. Plantation slavery, organised on a much larger scale than in the Chesapeake, was concentrated in the Lowcountry, a slim strip of land about fifty miles wide stretching down the Atlantic coast from the Cape Fear River in North Carolina to the Saint Johns River in Florida. The South Carolina and Georgia Lowcountry, home of the biggest plantations, wealthiest planters – who were also vocal and influential political leaders as well – and the urban centres of Savannah and Charles Town, would play a leading role in the development of the American South.

The character of slavery changed dramatically after 1700. Ninety per cent of slave arrivals to the South came directly from Africa rather than the West Indies. No longer were these seasoned Africans familiar with European ways but saltwater slaves, or 'New Negroes', as contemporaries called them. The evolution of the plantation system in the eighteenth century attempted to control these strange newcomers, abruptly cutting short most if not all of the opportunities available to the charter generations. The plantation generations did not look or sound like their predecessors. Larger numbers of slaves, perhaps inevitably, led the colonists to tighten security, especially in South Carolina, which had a black majority from at least 1708 and probably before that date. The rhythm of the agricultural seasons and the intricacies of producing tobacco, rice and indigo shaped the lives of southern bondspeople and, to a lesser degree, those of their owners. There were some exceptions, as diversity always characterised American slavery, but the plantation system imposed a ruthless discipline on the enslaved while making planters some of the richest men in the Atlantic world. Indeed, colonial historian Peter H. Wood prefers the term 'slave labor camp' to plantation, because of the latter's romantic overtones in the present day which hide 'a world of perpetual exploitation and incessant degradation built on racist ideology and overwhelming physical force'.[1]

COMPETING COLONIAL POWERS

Spain and France had a significant presence in the South. Both nations were fierce rivals of England throughout the colonial period, as each hoped to establish hegemony over the North American continent. Sporadic and violent conflict marked relations between the powers. The Spanish hoped to extend northward their great empire acquired by conquering the Aztecs and Incas, and they took African slaves to North America long before the English. Lucas Vásquez de Ayllón was the first European to bring large numbers of slaves to the mainland. In 1526, he unsuccessfully endeavoured to build a Spanish colony (San Miguel de Gualdape) somewhere on the coast between present-day Savannah and St Helena Sound in South Carolina. He failed in no small part because the estimated one hundred slaves in his expedition revolted and escaped with the aid of Native Americans. In 1565, Spain built the first permanent European settlement in North America at St Augustine, Florida, with the primary aim of spreading Catholicism to the Indians. Missionaries and explorers travelled across the southern rim of the present-day United States (which they called the Borderlands), the most important areas of Spanish occupation being Florida, Texas, New Mexico and California. However, the northern edge of New Spain was never as important to the mother country's interests as control of Central America. Native American resistance and the failure to find gold undermined attempts at consolidation in the American South. Thus, Spanish settlements in Florida were primarily maintained for strategic and religious purposes. Fearful of the encroachment of the French and the English on the Atlantic Coast, Spain supported a number of thinly populated forts and missions across the Borderlands in the hope of keeping out rivals. The Spanish were right to fear the intentions of Great Britain, which claimed an interest in land stretching down the east coast from Virginia to Florida.

French interests were mostly concentrated far to the north, in present-day Canada. Following the exploration of Jacques Cartier in the 1530s, Samuel de Champlain founded Quebec in 1608. When Montreal was established in 1642, French control of the St Lawrence valley was confirmed. This had important implications for the development of the South because even though New France was located hundreds of miles to the north, from this position the French ventured into the heart of the North American continent. In 1682, Robert Cavalier, Sieur de la Salle, was the first European to navigate the Mississippi River down to the Gulf of Mexico. La Salle claimed the whole of the vast interior region in the name of Louis XIV, and over the next fifty years a line of trading posts and forts was established. New Orleans was founded in 1718 to secure French control of the area and quickly attracted a cosmopolitan mixture of French, Canadians, Germans, Swiss and African slaves. New Orleans was an extremely important port city linking trade from the Mississippi valley to European markets.

Race relations and slavery in French and Spanish areas developed somewhat differently from that in the British colonies. Both nations professed a more open policy granting Africans and Native Americans certain religious and legal rights, although this was not always the case in practice. Spanish settlements did not have such a diverse ethnic mix as the city of New Orleans, but did contain an important African presence. Indeed, slaves, free blacks and Indians were critical to the building and the defence of Spanish Florida. The majority of blacks in Florida were escapees from the British colonies. In 1738, the governor of Florida reaffirmed his commitment to a 1693 edict granting freedom to British slaves reaching Spanish lines, much to the annoyance of South Carolina and later Georgia.

Between 1719 and 1732, approximately 6,000 saltwater slaves were sent to Louisiana as the French hoped to stimulate hitherto unsuccessful attempts to grow tobacco and indigo. Their efforts to replicate the French Caribbean colonies of Saint Domingue and Martinique using African slaves were checked decisively by the Natchez Indians. In 1729, Indians, in conjunction with escaped slaves, killed more than 200 colonists encroaching on their land. These events served as a powerful reminder to all Europeans that a delicate balance of power existed in North America. By 1760, Louisiana's total population stood at just 10,000, as the government sent paupers and criminals to the colony. The failure of the Spanish and the French to attract large numbers of settlers to their southern possessions left them isolated, vulnerable and dependent on the goodwill of local tribes. Nonetheless, the legacy of French and Spanish influences on southern culture would be enduring.

It was Carolina's rapid growth in the opening decades of the eighteenth century that secured the British position and ensured a predominately Anglo-African presence in the South. Interest in the land lying between Virginia and Spanish Florida had been growing throughout the seventeenth century, despite the fears of potential colonists about living in close proximity to Britain's traditional enemy. A group of eight proprietors led by Sir John Colleton secured a patent from King Charles II on 24 March 1663 to explore the possibilities of building new settlements in the area. Three colonies would eventually be established: North Carolina, South Carolina and Georgia. South Carolina, the first and most important of the three, was situated at the beginning of the southern semi-tropical zone. In many ways, it was an economic, political and social offshoot of Barbados. South Carolina might have developed very differently had Barbados been geographically larger. Barbadian planters and their sons, as well as hundreds of indentured servants, simply had nowhere left to go on the overcrowded island and saw an ideal opportunity in taking the short trip to the American mainland.

Sir John Colleton was a prominent Barbadian planter and friend of Virginia governor William Berkeley. Not put off by earlier, unsuccessful forays, he organised a party leaving England in August 1669, picking up recruits from Barbados before setting down a few miles up the Ashley River in April 1670. After several false starts, the colony established itself on a firmer basis in 1680, when the settlement of Charles Town was moved downstream to the peninsula flanked on either side by the Ashley and Cooper rivers. This was an excellent location with deep harbours and a cool sea breeze flowing in from the Atlantic Ocean providing some relief from the blistering heat and humidity, a lethal combination. A number of tough Barbadian planters and their families and slaves settled in the nearby vicinity of Goose Creek, a tributary of the Cooper River. They constituted a significant presence and would challenge the autocratic rule of the proprietors. From an estimated population of just 300 in 1680, Charles Town – which became Charleston in 1783 – would become the most significant city in the South and a pivotal economic and cultural hub of the Atlantic world.

The southern portion of the Carolinas grew steadily from this point. Unlike Virginia, it was not tied to one staple crop, but relied on two specific economic markets before the advent of the transatlantic trade in rice. Most prominent was trade with the Caribbean and, in particular, Barbados. With all resources and manpower focused upon cultivating sugar, the tiny island of Barbados imported most of its essential foodstuffs. Carolina settlers practised mixed farming (corn, peas) and livestock grazing (cattle, hogs) that met this demand, as well as felling and exporting the abundant timber in Carolina (a resource that had been exhausted in Barbados). More lucrative was a second trade in deer skins. In conjunction with Native American allies who hunted and prepared the pelts for sale, Carolinians were exporting 50,000 deerskin hides a year, mostly to Europe, by the turn of the seventeenth century.

Pioneers also ventured into the northern section of the Carolinas. Most came from Virginia and migrated south across the Albemarle Sound into what is today north-eastern North Carolina. This location was poorly served by its shallow coastline and outer banks preventing easy access by sea and was of little concern to the proprietors who focused their efforts on Charles Town. Settlers here were essentially subsistence farmers who were connected to the Virginian economy, by virtue of their tobacco production, rather than to England or the Caribbean. Naval stores (tar, turpentine, pitch) were also cultivated, and in the eighteenth century this trade became especially lucrative in North Carolina. The two sections formally split into North and South Carolina in 1712. In 1729, both became royal colonies under the control of the English Crown, with a governor appointed by the monarch, putting them on an equal political footing with the Chesapeake colonies.

Georgia also reverted to the Crown in 1754, after a twenty-one-year period of governance by a group of trustees, among whom General James Oglethorpe and Sir John Percival were leading lights. King George II and Carolinian governor Robert Johnson were delighted at the founding of Savannah in February 1733, since it provided a buffer zone against the Spanish. Oglethorpe had philanthropic, idealistic intentions for the colony, seeing Georgia as a haven for the dispossessed, and the colony successfully attracted a diverse mixture of settlers from Britain, Austria, Germany, Italy and Switzerland. Slavery was believed to be incompatible with the Georgia 'plan' of providing the poor with a second chance. However, the economy failed to prosper and there was pressure from some quarters to reverse the ban on slavery. Once that prohibition was lifted in 1751, Georgia quickly followed the South Carolinian model. Large plantations came to characterise the Lowcountry, with smaller plantations and yeomen farms in the interior. Numbers of slaves in Georgia rose from 1,000 in 1750 to 16,000 in 1776, as rice production increased ten fold.[2]

SAWBUCK EQUALITY IN SOUTH CAROLINA

The 1661 Barbadian Master and Servant Act had explicitly sought to distinguish between slavery and indentured servitude, and settlers from Barbados brought with them the belief that blacks were servants for life and whites were entitled to the rights of freemen. The insecurity caused by a ratio of approximately one white to every four blacks on the island (which actually constituted a sizeable number of whites in comparison with other Caribbean slave societies) encouraged this legislation.[3] Planters importing slaves or indentured servants to South Carolina received 100 acres of land for each female and 150 acres for each male (later reduced to 50 acres regardless of sex). In practice, the rigid divide between black and white emerging in Barbados was impossible to recreate in South Carolina in the first few decades. Owner, slave and servant typically worked together in the harsh Lowcountry environment, defying notions of a natural disparity in status. As was the case in Virginia, the colour line only had tangible meaning and substance when clear divisions existed between the races. 'Sawbuck equality', as Ira Berlin puts it, reflected 'the primitive, labor-scarce' conditions of the South Carolina frontier which 'frequently placed master and slave face-to-face on opposite sides of a sawbuck, where shared labor reduced – if it did not dissolve – the differences of status and color'. Moreover, all available men, no matter their origin, were required to defend the colony from the Spanish and from various Native American tribes.[4] In 1706, a combined force of Europeans, Indians and Africans repelled a Franco-Spanish attack on Charles Town designed to sever trading links with Indians in the interior and drive the British northward.

Relations with Native American tribes were crucial to the early development of the colony, as they had been in Jamestown. South Carolina depended upon Indian allies , initially the Westos and then the Yamasee to pursue the fur trade. Indeed, the Yamasee were close allies of the colony for many years, and in 1702 they joined an unsuccessful expedition attacking the Spanish in St Augustine. The balance shifted a decade later in two bloody wars between the colonists and their former partners, the Tuscarora and the Yamasee. Both tribes were concerned at encroachment on their land and, like the Powhatans earlier, sought to remove the cause of that problem. Just as in Virginia, the colonial authorities relied on the policy of divide and conquer as they enlisted the aid of other Indian tribes. In 1711, it took a combined force of Yamasee, Cherokee, Creek and Catawba to defeat the Tuscarora (hailing from present-day western North Carolina). Conflict erupted again four years later and 400 colonists were killed as the Yamasee reached Charleston's outer limits. After a year of hostility the Yamasee were eventually subdued with the help of the Cherokee, who subsequently became the principal allies of the colonists.

Indian slavery was more extensive in South Carolina than it was in the Chesapeake. Colonists established relations with Indian allies who preyed on other tribes, providing a steady supply of slaves. Just as Carolina was becoming heavily involved in the international slave trade as a net importer, the colony simultaneously organised the internal trade of Indian slaves from the interior. Thousands of Indian captives were shipped through Charles Town to Britain's colonies, mostly in the Caribbean but also to the northern colonies on the American mainland. Historian Alan Gallay estimates that somewhere between 30,000 and 50,000 Indians from the South were sold by the British before 1715. 'The Carolinians, in comparison to Indians, were obsessed with the desire to own human labor,' he argues. Native Americans were familiar with the concept of slavery but usually took captives as prisoners of war and integrated them into tribal life, in contrast to their use in British colonies. Tribes sought economic gains and the opportunity to weaken their traditional enemies by participating in the slave trade, but slavery would gradually have a greater internal impact on Native Americans over the course of the eighteenth and the nineteenth centuries, as will be discussed in Chapter 4.[5] Indian tribes adjusted to the permanent and ever-growing numbers of Europeans as best they could. Southern tribes were not as powerful as the Iroquois in the North, but they became skilled in using the strategic needs of the colonial powers to their advantage. England, Spain and France each sought to ally themselves with Indian tribes to strengthen their position against one another.

In South Carolina itself there were approximately 1,400 Indian slaves out of a total population of 12,580 in 1708. Colonists needed as many hands as they could get to carve out their plantations in hostile terrain. However, it is likely that Africans were always preferred to Indians. Indian slaves had a much better chance of escape, having allies they might call upon, and in some cases a good knowledge of the local terrain. Indian males were not used to agricultural work, normally undertaken by women, and resisted tasks they considered beneath them. The colonists' relations with individual tribes were probably not quite so precarious as those in Virginia a century earlier, but there was no point unnecessarily antagonising Indians when African slaves could be purchased.

Once supply of African slaves matched demand, Indian slavery declined rapidly. From its peak of one in four in 1708, numbers of Native Americans within the ranks of the enslaved fell to approximately one in ten a decade afterwards; however, it is difficult to measure numbers accurately. Indian and African slaves intermingled and amalgamated with one another, just as servants and slaves had done in Virginia. Children of African and Native American partners were considered black by Europeans. Despite being physically different, Native American slaves became African slaves for all practical purposes, showing just how malleable notions of race and identity can be. Slaveholders in South Carolina had very little concern for 'matters of origins, nationality, or race in their haste to satisfy their need for labor'.[6] Native Americans had a long-lasting influence on the emerging culture of the Carolinas, although one that is very difficult to pin down precisely.

Rice was essential to the development of slavery in South Carolina. First imported into the colony in the 1690s, it was not until later that planters realised the remarkable potential of the crop. The Lowcountry was a coastal plain crisscrossed by rivers, creeks, inlets, marshes and swamps that provided an ideal environment for growing rice. Initially cultivated in the swampy interior, rice would eventually find its natural home in coastal plantations. An ingenious system of ditches, dams and canals, incorporating floodgates to keep out sea water but allow fresh water in, was built over the decades. In the latter half of the eighteenth century, planters shifted to tidal irrigation (flooding fields with fresh water from rivers), an even more efficient method of production.[7] Contemporaries in South Carolina and later historians have noted just how dramatically this changed the face of the environment. To take one example, something like six million cubic feet of earth was displaced by building dams and digging ditches at the Middleburg plantation on the Cooper River.[8] This system was built by the backbreaking labour of the enslaved; once in place it entailed less hoeing of the rice fields, but a considerable degree of skill in operating the sluice gates and managing the tides. During the eighteenth century, rice constituted somewhere between a half and two-thirds of the annual value of all exports leaving South Carolina. Rice defined and became synonymous with Lowcountry society as much as the Chesapeake was associated with tobacco.

Africans were critical to the success of rice production in South Carolina.

Planters considered African slaves ideally suited to work in the hot, humid rice swamps, and many did possess natural defences against the deadly malaria spread by mosquitoes. Malaria was common in Africa and hence locals developed immunity over the generations from its worst excesses; some black arrivals were therefore genetically less likely to suffer from certain types of the disease. Historian Judith A. Carney has recently and most decisively illustrated what many historians have long pointed towards: it is impossible to disentangle the shift to large-scale rice production from the importation of slave labour to South Carolina. Carney goes further than others, though, in suggesting that slaves from the West African rice coast 'tutored planters in growing the crop', stressing that it was the specific knowledge and skills of African men and women that counted. Planters had the acumen to purchase slaves used to working with rice and were extremely knowledgeable about the ethnic background of African slaves, but credit for the spectacular growth of what became known as 'Carolinian gold' lies elsewhere. Rice planters developed a powerful myth of their own ingenuity in the nineteenth century but Carney argues that their input was limited in comparison to that of their slaves. 'Rice cultivation in the Americas depended upon the diffusion of an entire cultural system, from production to consumption', states Carney, making an indelible mark on Lowcountry society. From the beginning, blacks formed approximately one quarter to one third of the colony's population. They became the most numerous group soon after 1700, with significant implications for the development of South Carolinian society.[9]

It was Africans best described as part of the charter generation who came in the first three decades of the colony's existence. The majority came with their masters from Barbados or were purchased from Britain's slave colonies in the Caribbean as part of the extensive trade between the regions. Master–slave relations in South Carolina went through a period of uncertainty as both sides adapted to their new environment. This process was much shorter than it had been in Virginia, though. Not only were numbers of slaves rising in the Chesapeake, assuaging any hesitations over the legality of slavery on Carolinian soil, but Barbadian planters were also used to exerting strict control over their property. Nonetheless, slaves used any small advantages to ease their load and pursue their interests as best they could in the small window of opportunity that opened in the final decades of the seventeenth century. They realised that white society was not firmly established and that control of the slave population not as tight as in Barbados. The hard labour required of the first slave arrivals in clearing the land was very different from the regimented work routines of Barbados. Some slaves earned enough money to buy their freedom by cattle ranching. Others gained freedom as a reward for defending the colony from attack. Regardless of time and space, the enslaved consistently exploited any opportunity to push for a better deal.

Once slavery in South Carolina became more stable, daily supervision by the owner was no longer essential and those planters who could do so withdrew to the less oppressive environment of Charleston, especially in summer. The large rice plantations were left under the supervision of white overseers hired by the owner. Indentured servants never really had a significant presence in South Carolina, which did not offer the same opportunities as the Chesapeake or indeed Pennsylvania or New York. Potential servants were also put off by the colony's well-deserved reputation for disease, especially malaria and yellow fever. In general, the proportion of those coming to the South as indentured servants declined in the eighteenth century. More free migrants, attracted by the availability of land, made the journey. Approximately 307,400 whites came to the British North American colonies as a whole between 1680 and 1775: roughly a third were servants, a half were free, and the rest were transported convicts. Specific numbers coming to the southern colonies are more difficult to calculate, but they pale in comparison with the massive importation of Africans.[10]

BUILDING THE PLANTATION: SLAVERY IN THE UPPER AND LOWER SOUTH

Slavery initially grew slowly in Virginia and South Carolina, followed by a rapid increase in the importation of saltwater slaves directly from Africa after 1700. The slave trade to the American mainland continued at a pace throughout the 1700s, but the volume of imports to the Chesapeake differed from that of the Lowcountry after mid-century. Numbers of slaves arriving roughly doubled in the 1720s in both colonies, up from 6,750 in the 1710s to 12,700 in Virginia, and from 6,000 to 11,600 in South Carolina. The peak decade was the 1730s, when 15,700 slaves were brought to Virginia and 21,150 to South Carolina. Such large numbers were not sustainable and they fell in the 1740s. South Carolinia authorities put a prohibitive duty on slave imports after the 1739 Stono Rebellion, but even if they had not, Lowcountry planters had as many slaves as they needed and imports would have fallen anyway. From mid-century, far fewer slaves came to Virginia: falling from about 9,500 in the 1750s and 1760s to just below 4,000 in the 1770s. By contrast, slave imports to South Carolina remained high: 16,500 in the 1750s; 21,850 in the 1760s; and 18,850 in the 1770s. Thus, the proportion of slaves arriving directly from Africa was much higher in the Lower South, with profound consequences.

The American slave population also increased through natural reproduction, a critical feature making the South unique among New World colonies. Slave society on the American mainland was far more stable as a result. This process took time, it should be emphasised, as mortality rates rose sharply with the importation of the plantation generations after 1700. Natural increase was happening in Virginia by the second decade of the eighteenth century, and by mid-century the colony 'grew *primarily* from natural increase, and at a rapid rate', something which would not happen in the Lowcountry until much later. Having said that, the slave community in South Carolina was also growing naturally by the 1750s, and by the 1770s the rate of increase had, according to Philip D. Morgan, 'reached a respectable 1.5 percent'. Even so, the reason for disparity in the numbers of slave imports to the South after mid-century is clear: natural increase was basically sufficient to meet economic needs in the Chesapeake but not in the Lowcountry.[11]

The key to natural growth, and hence to the possibility of slave families and ultimately of durable slave communities, was a favourable balance of men and women. Men outnumbered women transported along the Middle Passage, although historian David Eltis has recently shown that the gender imbalance of the international slave trade was far less pronounced than historians usually assume.[12] Numbers of African men and women reached something approaching parity in the South surprisingly quickly, notwithstanding that approximately one in four 'New Negroes' died within a year of arriving. Women lived longer than men, and those born in the colonies were generally healthier, more resistant to disease and able to bear children more regularly from an early age. These factors reduced the gender imbalance. Slowly but surely, as the century progressed, most bondspeople joined some type of family unit, with significant consequences. The family was the foundation of slave community and culture. Once the enslaved expected to get married and have children, this inevitably altered their perspectives and gave their lives a different emphasis in comparison to slaves in the Caribbean, whose brutal reality was an extremely low life-expectancy. Cross-plantation ties also developed over the decades, of great importance for the small-sized holdings of the Chesapeake.

The lives of the enslaved, whether African or native-born, were dominated by the demands of agricultural production. Work was central and all other considerations had to fit around its requirements. Slave life in the Chesapeake was tied to tobacco production as much as rice and indigo dictated the working lives of bondsmen and women in the Lowcountry. Indeed, Lorena S. Walsh demonstrates how surges in the importation of slaves to the

Chesapeake were linked to booms in the tobacco economy, as slavery expanded from the Tidewater to the interior (known as the Piedmont). Tobacco growers followed a system of rotation designed to preserve the soil, only utilising part of their land from year to year. African men, women and children toiled side-by-side as they carefully tended to precious tobacco plants, as well as growing maize and other food crops in the Chesapeake. Wheat grew in importance during the eighteenth century, both for home consumption and for sale. By the 1770s, somewhere in the region of 2.3 million bushels of wheat was being exported (mostly to Europe). Lowcountry plantations were usually much larger in terms of slave numbers and acreage. Rice was the major crop in the Lowcountry, although cultivation of the dye indigo was also widespread, peaking in the 1740s, and wheat was also grown. Slaves in the Lower South worked in dreadful conditions: 'no work can be imagined more pernicious to health than for men to stand in water mid-leg high, and often above it, planting and weeding rice', wrote Alexander Hewatt in 1779.[13]

The plantation generations worked flexibly in a variety of jobs. The most significant practical difference in work routines was use of the task system in the Lowcountry and the gang system in the Chesapeake. Slaves organised into gangs worked in small groups under the direction of the owner (or a driver on larger plantations), usually from sunup to sundown, with small rest breaks during the day. Slaves organised by the task system were not so regimented, as they had specific duties to complete on a daily basis. It is easy to underestimate the extent of the task, which always tested the limit of the slaves' capabilities. The standard size of the task was invariably set at a quarter of an acre – for weeding, planting, reaping and many other duties. Undeniably, though, Lowcountry slaves had more leeway to work at their own pace and some sought to complete their work as early as possible, giving them a few hours to themselves. If the complaints of Chesapeake masters are anything to go by, it was the gang system that was less productive, as they routinely commented on the poor work of their slaves.

Most importantly, tasking allowed slaves in the Lower South to develop their own plots, which could grow to the size of several acres. One of the few privileges retained by the plantation generations was the right to gardens provided by owners. This allowed slaves to supplement their provisions, which lessened dependence on the master but was also an effective way of encouraging slaves to identify with their plantation. Whether a means of resistance or compliance, slaves exploited their garden plots to the full as the domestic or informal economy grew in size and importance, especially in the Lowcountry, during the eighteenth century. Slaves would trade produce among themselves, with their owners and sometimes at the market. Contemporaries describe bondspeople having their own fields, not just gardens, and making large cash profits. For example, Lowcountry slaves were observed planting 'rice, corn, potatoes, tobacco' in their '5 or 6 acres of ground . . . of which the industrious among them make a great deal', and some also raised 'hogs and poultry'. This activity was not for mere 'subsistence, but for amusement, pleasure, and profit'.[14] Slaves in the Chesapeake usually did not have the time or the space to grow anything more than basic provisions for themselves.

Women were expected to labour as hard as men and faced the lash if they did not meet their owners' expectations. This contrasted greatly with white society, especially elite white society, in which the different gender roles of men and women became more sharply defined during the eighteenth century. Masters extracted as much work as they could by the incessant use of the whip, regardless of sex. Harsh expectations of bondswomen were somewhat tempered over the years and larger plantations began to count females as three-quarter hands in the latter half of the eighteenth century (with healthy males constituting 'full' hands), organising separate male and female gangs. Nonetheless, the average work routine was usually six days a week, and work might extend to Sundays and into the night, although this depended on the weather and the particular time of year. The pace of work varied. 'Rice was a roller coaster, tobacco a slow-moving train', notes historian Philip D. Morgan. In general, tobacco required constant vigilance, while rice demanded bursts of intense activity. For all slaves in the eighteenth century, though, the level of coercion was raised, the hours of work extended and the punishments made more severe. The charter generations had some measure of negotiation but the plantation generations were part of a total system intended to beat them down into submission in the aim of maximising profits.[15]

In terms of skilled work, slaves in the Lower South had far more opportunities than their Chesapeake counterparts. Carpentry was probably the most important trade carried out by bondsmen who also worked with leather and became bricklayers, brick-makers, coopers and blacksmiths. More skilled slaves were found in urban areas. Slaves were regularly employed by shipwrights, especially in Charleston. Basket-making and pottery were skilled trades in the Lowcountry, while slave iron workers were found in the Chesapeake. Most of the skilled work in the Chesapeake, however, was carried out by white artisans who rarely complained about competition from slaves. This was not the case further south. A plea from Charleston in 1734 complained that 'many Negroes are now train'd up to be Handicraft

Tradesmen, to the great discouragement of Your Majestys white Subjects'.[16] The growing size of plantations during the eighteenth century took more slaves, mainly males, from the fields into other more skilled activities. No longer were all bondspeople required in the fields, as planters diversified their activities.

Larger plantations presented new opportunities for the enslaved. Greater numbers demanded a more complex organisation of work and many slaves found themselves split into small groups of approximately ten members, led by drivers who were typically trusted, older bondsmen. In the Lowcountry, drivers had managerial functions, sometimes in conjunction with white overseers or stewards. They could be granted a surprising measure of responsibility and in some cases were handed sole control of plantation operations, indicating a remarkable level of trust on the part of the master. On the smaller plantations of the Chesapeake, drivers were used for the more basic function of leading the pace of work. Slaves were also put to work in plantation houses as cooks, butlers, maids and gardeners. The emergence of domestic slaves, working in the rice planters' summer retreats in Charleston and Savannah and in the great plantation houses of the Chesapeake, symbolised the growing wealth and power of the southern colonial elite.

Overseers hired to take over day-to-day running of operations had a growing input as the century progressed. They faced a difficult situation, being nominally in charge but in actuality responsible to the owner. Allan Kulikoff estimates that the proportion of slaves on Chesapeake plantations with overseers ranged from approximately 30 to 50 per cent by the 1770s. Undoubtedly there were many more overseers in the Lowcountry, which had a much longer tradition of absentee owners. Kulikoff notes how the enslaved 'became particularly adept at playing masters against overseers on large plantations'.[17] Little wonder that there was rapid turnover of overseers, who were usually appointed on yearly contracts.

The material conditions of slave life improved slowly over the decades. Traveller Johann Schoepf observed in 1786 that the lives of South Carolina slaves were 'in general harder and more troublous than that of their northern brethren'.[18] Bondspeople in the Chesapeake enjoyed more plentiful rations, better clothing and had more sturdy accommodation. This applied in particular to slaves on larger plantations because space was more cramped and supplies were not so abundant on smaller farms. Absentee owners in the Lowcountry had less incentive to upgrade the slave quarters or increase rations, whereas Chesapeake owners tended to have closer relations with their slaves. For some Virginian planters this heralded a desire to improve the conditions of their bondspeople. Slaves supplemented their diets by hunting and fishing the abundant game available in the countryside, especially in the Lower South, and growing their own vegetables and fruits on garden plots.

CULTURE, RESISTANCE AND REBELLION

The working lives of the enslaved in the eighteenth-century South have been extensively uncovered. We know far less about the cultural side, not least because few primary sources exist, in contrast to more plentiful documentation available for the antebellum period. In both the Upper and Lower South, however, it is clear that the impact of the plantation generations had significant consequences for the development of slave culture. A flood of 'New Negroes' hailing from the African interior arrived in the opening decades of the eighteenth century. They spoke strange languages, carried tribal markings and seemed utterly alien from the charter generations hailing from the Caribbean. These contemporaries of Olaudah Equiano no doubt faced as equally difficult a time as he did in adjusting to the shock of capture, transportation, sale and enslavement.

One of the key historical debates concerns the number of Africans born on American soil (creoles) versus natives coming from Africa (measured as those arriving in the previous decade) in the slave population. From a similar starting point in 1700, when Africans composed about half the total slave population in Virginia and South Carolina, the percentage diverged dramatically. In 1720, 45 per cent of Virginia's slaves were Africans; 58 per cent of South Carolina's. Twenty years later, the figures were 34 per cent and 66 per cent respectively. By 1760, just 14 per cent of slaves in Virginia were African-born, compared with 39 per cent in South Carolina, as the rate of natural increase among the slave population became critical. Twenty years after that, the African contingent in Virginia was almost insignificant at 5 per cent, but still constituted a third in South Carolina. Wherever there were greater numbers of Africans, acculturation to European ways took much longer and African customs proved more resonant.

The assimilationist culture of the charter generations was challenged, and in some cases transformed, by saltwater Africans in the first three decades of the eighteenth century. This process had its fullest effect in the Lowcountry, and was not quite as powerful in the Chesapeake. The combination of more native Africans, larger plantations and absentee owners allowed the development of a rich African culture on the rice plantations. Inevitably, slaves became somewhat creolised over the course of the century. The very different environment of North America forced considerable readjustment, as did the fact that Africans from many different ethnic and social backgrounds had to learn to get along with one another. However, black life in the Lowcountry was more heavily influenced by African cultural practices, in all their varied guises, due to the simple fact that the majority of slave communities were populated by native Africans and regularly infused by waves of fresh imports down to the abolition of the international slave trade in 1808. In the Chesapeake, slaves were creolised at a much earlier stage, and African influences were further attenuated by the small size of plantations and greater contact between owner and slave. Far fewer African names were retained in the Chesapeake, for example, in comparison with the Lowcountry.

These are complicated issues. Recent studies by Michael A. Gomez and Gwendolyn Midlo Hall remind us that we have a long way to go in understanding the development and function of slave culture in the eighteenth century. Both argue that far more attention needs to be paid to African ethnicity on the North American mainland. The enslaved in the American South came from distinct societies bringing unique cultural forms. The majority of slaves in the Upper South came from the Niger Delta (especially the Bight of Biafra and Angola). The largest groups in the Lower South were from the Guinea Coast (Angola, Gambia and Sierra Leone). Gomez emphasises that new arrivals were faced 'with two realms of acculturation'. First, and most difficult, was the negotiation between different African nationalities and the African American community. Second, was the process of adaptation to the white world. These two processes occurred simultaneously and each informed the other. Most intriguingly, slaves progressively readjusted their outlook and conception of self from an ethnic base – resting on the particular traditions, cultural practices and languages that they had left behind – to a proto-racial conception engendered by the slave experience in North America. Igbos and Gambians gradually became Africans as the 'creation of the African American collective involved a movement in emphasis from ethnicity toward race as the primary criterion of inclusion'. How far bondspeople came to accept *scientific* racial doctrines is questionable, though, as will be discussed further in Chapter 5. The enslaved in North America developed a sense of belonging and kinship based on culture and the shared experience of oppression, rather than supposedly common biological characteristics, transforming the localised view of the world with which the vast majority, if not all, arrived. This overarching group identity was overwhelmingly based on culture and community, not racial ties. As historian James Sidbury puts it, 'the relatively concrete lines of kinship and friendship dominated more abstract and imagined ties of race'.[19]

Whatever the extent of ethnic and cultural differences – one of the longest-running debates concerning American slavery centres on the issue of African survivals in the South – there is no doubt that the development of a distinctive African American culture was extremely important. It brought slaves together as a group, allowed them to express themselves in their own ways and provided a means, however inadequate, to counter the power of their masters. A rare glimpse of a slave gathering in Charles County, Maryland, in 1774 provides some insight. Nicholas Cresswell wrote that on Sundays slaves 'generally meet together and amuse themselves' by playing the banjo (an African instrument), singing and dancing. Cresswell found the spectacle odd – 'Their poetry is like the music: Rude and uncultivated' – as he did the energetic dancing of the slaves. It was because he witnessed something so different from the European styles with which he was familiar that it made such an impression. Most intriguingly, Cresswell remarked that the slave songs 'generally relate the usage they have received from their Masters or Mistresses in a very satirical stile [sic] and manner'. Thus slaves not only appropriated songs for themselves but also used them to pass comment on their owners and their conditions. Cresswell's conclusion that the participants 'appear to be exceedingly happy at these merry-makings and seem as if they had forgot or were not sensible of their miserable condition' was way off the mark but did suggest that cultural expressions could provide relief from the oppression of bondage, however temporary.[20]

Such moments were important because callous disregard for the lives of their slaves marked the slaveholders' outlook at the beginning of the eighteenth century. Barbaric punishments were administered as a matter of routine, indicating little respect for human life and certainly none for the rights of Africans. The demographic imbalance between black and white probably ensured that punishments were carried out more severely and with more frequency in the Lower South. Reverend Francis Le Jau, a minister for the Society for the Propagation of the Gospel in Foreign Parts based in Goose Creek, South Carolina, recorded some particularly horrific incidents. In 1712, he wrote of rising levels of cruelty following a rumoured slave rebellion as masters 'hamstring mai[m] & unlimb these poor Creatures for small faults'. One slave was punished for losing a bag of rice by being chained up by day and placed 'into a hellish machine' resembling a coffin at night.[21] South Carolinian slaves might have their ankle-cords cut, be burnt to death and face castration (a punishment also found on the Virginia statutes until 1769 for rape cases). However, it was frequent use of the whip and routine punishment that regulated master–slave relations, not the law. As Ira Berlin powerfully argues, 'violence was not only common' but was purposely 'systematic and relentless' because 'the planters' hegemony required that slaves stand in awe of their owners'. Historian Donald R. Wright suggests that 'the equivalent of medieval torture' was used 'to keep the slave population docile'.[22]

Slaves reacted in a variety of ways to this brutality but resistance typified the plantation generations. Their unfamiliarity with Europeans and with plantation slavery encouraged hostility and non-compliance. Most bondspeople coming in the 1700s were anything but docile. The runaway was a troublesome problem for the eighteenth-century slaveholder, particularly at harvest time when work demands peaked. Newspapers carried thousands of adverts about runaway slaves who remained at large for anything from a few days to years. New arrivals were particularly likely to leave together, especially if from the same ethnic background. Historian Michael Mullin stresses the important connection between ethnicity and resistance – where ethnicity was sustained, slaves were far 'more likely to resist by organizing with others', whereas acculturated slaves were more cautious.[23] Runaways escaped to the towns and to the geographical margins in the Upper and the Lower South. Both regions grew rapidly during the eighteenth century and a lawless frontier zone marked the edges of colonial settlement where slaves might seek the assistance of Native Americans or congregate in maroon colonies (formed by runaways in areas of inaccessible terrain such as mountains and swamps). Those in the Lowcountry headed for Spanish settlements in Florida. The Spanish encouraged these efforts by establishing a town of escaped slaves, Gracia Real de Santa Teresa de Mose, just outside St Augustine, in 1738.[24]

Slave rebellions were dreaded by southern whites. There were a number of attempted rebellions in the eighteenth century and many more conspiracies. They were generally more spontaneous than nineteenth-century revolts, which were intricately planned. Large concentrations of native Africans and the dire circumstances confronting the plantation generations appear to be the main causal factors. The most famous uprising of the colonial era took place just twenty miles from Charleston at the Stono River, beginning on 9 September 1739. Approximately twenty blacks, led by a recently arrived Angolan called Jemmy, stole guns and roamed the countryside, growing in number to about sixty, burning and looting houses and killing thirty whites, although notably sparing the life of an innkeeper who was kind to slaves. The South Carolinian authorities took a savage revenge on the insurgents, placing their heads on poles as a warning. In 1740, a number of statutes were passed in the aftermath of the rebellion, including a prohibitive duty on slave imports, intended to tighten control of slaves. It is likely that more uprisings took place across the British colonies, but because colonial authorities repressed details that might frighten whites and encourage blacks, there is limited documentation. Anthony S. Parent Jr has uncovered evidence of a series of insurrections in Virginia in the late seventeenth and early eighteenth centuries as Africans engaged in what he terms 'mass resistance'. This included the flight of as many as 300 slaves to the Dismal Swamp in southern Virginia in October 1730.[25]

The vast majority of bondspeople, if not all, resisted in one way or another – breaking tools, working poorly, being careless, feigning illness, stealing – regardless of time or space. Women pretended to be pregnant to stay out of the fields. That slaveholders were fearful of being poisoned by their slaves indicates just how volatile the master–slave relationship became as the black population expanded. Revolts were far more frequent in other New World slave colonies than they were in the South. This reflected the different structural circumstances of the enslaved in the Caribbean and in South America: much bigger plantations, large numbers of African males and the presence of far fewer whites. Slavery was universally harsh and cruel, but the low life-expectancy of Caribbean slaves and the killing pace of sugar production caused desperation that encouraged drastic and dangerous actions. Resistance took a different form in the American South. The unique natural increase of American slaves, allowing the development of families and communities, somewhat ameliorated the worst aspects of bondage. Overt resistance generally became channelled along individual, not collective, lines, although there were rebellions in the nineteenth century. Historians John Hope Franklin and Loren Schweninger estimate that a minimum of 50,000 slaves absconded annually by the antebellum period and argue that their actions disrupted the system more profoundly than is generally accepted by historians. Peter Kolchin is more cautious, suggesting that slaveholders regarded runaways as a 'routine annoyance' – certainly most returned to their plantations after a short while, although some escaped to the North. In this way, running away acted as a kind of safety valve, releasing pressure when the daily grind of bondage became too much, preventing discontent from escalating into anything more serious.[26]

A void separating Africans and Europeans emerged as the black population grew rapidly in the eighteenth century. A state of war existed most immediately between owner and slave, partly explaining why notions of permanent racial difference were so plausible. In these circumstances, the barbaric behaviour of planters remains abhorrent but their actions become more comprehensible. Like so many other slaves in world history, Africans in the South were outsiders denied basic human rights, with no claim to be part of civil society. Not only were the rights of citizenship or inclusion denied, but basic human rights such as marriage and family life depended on the consent of the master; 'natal alienation' as sociologist Orlando Patterson terms it.[27] Such was the fate of the plantation generations. Any ties that bound master and slave in a common sense of humanity were severed around the turn of the eighteenth century. Masters held no illusions that their slaves were content. They were fully aware of the hardships slaves endured, that the only way to make them comply was by force and that all bondspeople wanted to be free.

PLANTERS, PATRIARCHY AND WHITE SOCIETY

As the harsh plantation system was codified in the eighteenth century, a new and potentially mediating ideology was developing in the mind of the planter class: patriarchy. Drawing on a patriarchal tradition with strong roots in early modern Britain, wealthy planters – like their counterparts across the Atlantic world – increasingly liked to think of themselves as kings of their own domain. Their little world was a microcosm of wider society in which individuals were assigned to specific ranks on a hierarchical basis. Wives, sons and daughters were included within the planter's purview, as well as slaves. Much like a monarch demanding the loyalty of his or her subjects, planters demanded obedience from slaves and from family members alike. All dependants were subject to the justice and mercy of the patriarch. Reciprocal obligations increasingly characterised the patriarchal relationship. Owners provided food and shelter while slaves had to work and obey in return.

The patriarchal impulse reflected broad developments in the religious and intellectual landscape of the eighteenth century that will be discussed further in Chapter 3. It was also brought on by a crisis of confidence in the 1720s, as planters in the colonies were reminded that ultimate power lay with the Crown in England. Possibly the constant war between owner and slave took a psychological toll on planters; certainly masters wanted to find an understanding of their position more noble than that of solely enforcing discipline and control. Whatever the combination of factors, planters gradually began to perceive their slaves in different ways and treat them with less overt hostility and cruelness. Punishment was still administered, it needs stressing, but rather than being arbitrary it required some kind of justification, however self-serving. Above all, patriarchalism sought to explain and enhance the planter's position. It was an ideology subject to reformulation in changing circumstances and probably reached its fullest expression in the Chesapeake, where owners lived permanently on their plantations, although was prominent in the Lowcountry as well.[28]

The great planters emerged as a cohesive class in the first half of the eighteenth century. Carefully arranged marriages ensured that elite sons and daughters intermarried within the planter class. Wives found their movements increasingly restricted as gender conventions confined them to the household. In 1726, William Byrd memorably captured the patriarchal creed: 'I have a large family of my own, and my Doors are open to Every Body. . . . Like one of the Patriarchs, I have my Flocks and my Herds, my Bond-men and Bond-women. . . . I must take care to keep all my people to their Duty, to set all the Springs in motion and to make every one draw his equal Share to carry the machine forward.' Byrd regularly referred to 'my' slaves in his diary – 'my people were still ill', 'visited my sick people again', 'my sick people were better thank God' – suggesting that there was more to master–slave relations than the business of extracting work. Several decades later Landon Carter depicted himself as the great patron of his community, slave and free, not just their leader but, as historian Mechal Sobel put it, 'their mentor, their teacher, and even their saviour'. Planters also expected the respect of whites outside the household, in a deferential culture. The imposing plantation house stood at the apex of a web of power and control that extended across white and black worlds – the masculine domain of the great planter.[29]

Non-slaveholding whites are among the least studied social groups in the eighteenth century and much remains to be discovered about them. Often divided by contemporaries into 'middling' and 'lower' sorts, we especially need more studies of the latter. Historian Edmund S. Morgan's argument that slavery and freedom became so intertwined in colonial Virginia as to ensure social consensus remains extremely influential. Morgan interprets race trumping class, as economic and status differences between white Virginians were bridged by a unifying whiteness filtered through the political ideology of republicanism: 'the forces which dictated that Virginians see Negroes, mulattoes, and Indians as one also dictated that they see large and small planters as one. Racism became an essential, if unacknowledged, ingredient of the republican ideology that enabled Virginians to lead the nation'.[30]

A majority of whites were not only free, but property holders in the Chesapeake by mid-century, somewhat lessening the divide that existed between indentured servants and planters in the seventeenth century and magnifying and sharpening differences between whites and blacks. The privileges of whiteness continued to grow in colonial society. It has been estimated that as many as 85 per cent of adult white males could vote for members of their local county court, granting them a political voice and lending credence to the idea that Virginia was a republican, not an aristocratic, society. Moreover, eighteenth-century historians seeking to explain the existence of a broad franchise and white social consensus have suggested that ordinary Virginians deferred to the gentry as natural social leaders without 'too much resentment', as J. G. A. Pocock put it. Gender was equally significant: if togetherness was encouraged by having a white skin, it was also bolstered by shared masculinity. White men considered themselves economically, culturally and politically superior to non-whites and women.[31]

Morgan's thesis is compelling, but the development of racism as an ideology was only at a formative stage in the eighteenth century, as will be discussed in the next chapter. Whiteness granted colonial males group identity in a cultural, political and religious sense, but whether this was a racial unity, grounded in the physical distinctiveness of white bodies, is open to question. Moreover, whiteness did not erase huge differences in wealth, status and political power. The colonial elite conspicuously displayed their affluence by mid-century in the homes that they built, the furniture they bought and the clothes that they wore. Although more white men held the franchise than in the seventeenth century, they voted for local positions, and members of the richest families not only held the highest offices but considered it their right to do so.

Gentry claims about the harmonious nature of Virginian society work best in justifying their own power and position, rather than in explaining actual social relations. The reality was that the House of Burgesses continued to be the exclusive preserve of the elite who claimed to guard the best interests of the colony. The views of ordinary whites towards planters and slaves need far greater investigation, especially as the theory of deference has been heavily criticised by historian Michael Zuckerman for ignoring considerable discontent and resentment. As Michael A. McDonnell states, eighteenth-century Virginia was 'a deeply divided and carefully defined hierarchical society', despite claims to the contrary, and a more complex interpretation of white class relations is emerging in current scholarship.[32]

Greater class cohesion among whites is apparent over time (though it was never absolute), but this is because of shared interests and growing economic opportunities as much as some kind of proto-racial solidarity. There were no overt clashes like Bacon's Rebellion between white southerners in the 1700s, even though differences in wealth and power remained acute. Poorer whites had the option of moving westwards to acquire land, relieving some of the tensions causing conflict, as Native Americans continued to fall victim to disease and chose to move themselves in response to settler encroachment. Moreover, tobacco cultivation was so widespread in the Chesapeake, at all levels of white society, that perhaps a shared set of values bridging gaps between great planters and ordinary farmers emerged. Historian T. H. Breen describes a 'tobacco mentality' created by 'a vocabulary of work imprinted so deeply upon the minds of people who grew it that they were barely conscious of how many assumptions and ideas they actually shared'.[33] Large planters were bound to their neighbours in the processing, transportation and sale of the tobacco crop, and by a system of debt that was pervasive in the Chesapeake. Moreover, the locally-based society of the Chesapeake ensured that planters, farmers and the poor interacted at church, in the county court and as part of the militia. Planter patronage was not confined to the household.

Unity was probably even stronger in the Lowcountry which had a much smaller white population. Slaveholding was more widespread there than in the Upper South. Growing rice and indigo was physically gruelling work carried out only by slaves precisely because it was so demanding, clearly demarcating the colour line. Lower-class whites did not carry out what was commonly held to be slave work. The law also privileged whiteness in South Carolina and sought to divide blacks and whites. As early as 1683 measures were taken to outlaw 'Trading between Servants and Slaves', and numerous subsequent measures punished whites trading and interacting with slaves. The demographic ratio of blacks to whites in South Carolina was not nearly as extreme as in Jamaica (the ratio went as high as 15 to 1 in places), where class antagonisms were mitigated 'out of fear', according to historian Trevor Burnard – whites simply had to unify in order to meet the threat posed by slaves.[34] Even so, a similar need for white solidarity existed in the Lower South. The large black majority in South Carolina – and by 1790 eleven rural parishes were 80 per cent black – was a powerful aid to white consensus.

At the margins, both geographically and economically, unity was less assured. In rural districts away from the plantation belt, blacks and whites interacted more freely. Ebenezer Hazard noted how South Carolina's 'common countrey people . . . talk very much like Negros'.[35] Sporadic incidents of bi-racial criminal activity continued throughout the eighteenth century. Historian Rachel N. Klein describes the menace posed by gangs of bandits roaming the South Carolina upcountry in the 1760s. These gangs included whites, Indians, free blacks and slaves. Although details are hazy, it is clear that their actions threatened the stability of slave society. In 1779, the *South Carolina Gazette* reported the existence of 'a large body of the most infamous banditti and horsethieves', including 'a corps of Indians, with negro and white savages disguised like them, and about 1,500 of the most savage disaffected poor people, seduced from the back settlements of this State and North Carolina'. More respectable whites in the frontier regions of the Carolinas, calling themselves 'Regulators', responded by trying to enforce law and order. They also protested, sometimes violently, against elite control of political offices, displaying their discontent at the older, more established coastal sections of the state, which they believed ruled autocratically.[36]

Where blacks and whites remained side-by-side in the Chesapeake there was much greater likelihood of collusion. Slaves and servants who worked together in the fields continued to run away together. This did not happen as frequently as earlier in the seventeenth century but still took place. We need to know much more about collusion at the lower levels before the American Revolution, between Europeans, Africans and Native Americans. Within the urban environment, blacks and whites mingled more freely than anywhere else during the eighteenth century. Indeed, it is possible to distinguish two different racial environments emerging in the South as a whole. In the bustling towns of Richmond, Charleston and Savannah, in the grog shops, gambling houses and brothels, there was little notion of a hard racial demarcation. Slaves sold their goods at regularly held markets. Sexual relations between poor white women and black men continued in urban areas. To be sure, it was lower-class whites and blacks, both free and slave, mingling together, while rich planters resided in the better parts of town. Nonetheless, the hard colour line that was being drawn on the plantation was effectively absent from the towns.

As relations between the colonies and Great Britain became increasingly fractious in the 1770s, relations between whites, blacks and Indians, and between men and women, in the South had become more ordered and rigidly structured. Despite Mechal Sobel's argument that Africans and Europeans were moving closer together in the Chesapeake, it seems more likely that the opposite was true; certainly, that was the case in the Lower South. The planter elite stood firmly on top of colonial society. Their position was based on the subjugation of blacks and Indians, as well as patriarchal rule over women. All white men considered themselves superior to these groups, but ordinary farmers and artisans were excluded from high society and knew that power lay with the gentry. The outlook of the great planters was domineering. Historian Kathleen M. Brown argues forcefully that 'Domestic tranquillity became the ideal of planters who dreamed of hegemonic authority over compliant wives, children, and slaves, and of unquestioned political leadership over less privileged men.'[37] Southern elites considered themselves to be as powerful and as important as any ruling group in the British Empire and regarded Charleston as fine a city as any other in the Atlantic world.

The southern colonies grew considerably in size and in economic power because tobacco and rice reaped lucrative rewards on European markets. From chaotic beginnings, in which the priority was to survive amidst dreadful mortality rates, society became 'settled, cohesive, and coherent' in Jack

P. Greene's influential formulation.[38] Economic, political and social gaps between different social groups had become wider and deeper by the eve of the American Revolution. Most prominent was the gap between blacks and whites, which reached seismic proportions with the arrival of the plantation generations and the inexorable growth of a ruthlessly enforced system of bondage. Even so, it would not be until after the American Revolution that race emerged as an important scientific and intellectual concept and, eventually, as a powerful ideological force intimately shaping individual identity. The foundations of the southern racial order were laid in the eighteenth century, however, as the social structure and legal system took firm shape. Slaveholders speculated whether there were inherent and permanent differences between blacks and whites, not just between slaves and freemen, and the vast majority probably came to believe that there were. Revolutionary ideology would also emphasise the idea of universal white male equality, something that challenged deferential elite culture in the post-war period. Both of these developments would have profound consequences.

Notes

1. Peter H. Wood, 'Slave Labor Camps in Early America: Overcoming Denial and Discovering the Gulag', in Carla Gardina Pestana and Sharon V. Salinger (eds), *Inequality in Early America* (Hanover, NH: University Press of New England, 1999), p. 234. A useful survey of recent historical writing on the Atlantic world is David Armitage and Michael J. Braddick (eds), *The British Atlantic World, 1500–1800* (Basingstoke: Palgrave Macmillan, 2002).
2. Julia Floyd Smith, *Slavery and Rice Culture in Low Country Georgia, 1750–1860* (Knoxville: University of Tennessee Press, 1985), p. 22; Betty Wood, *Slavery in Colonial Georgia, 1730–1775* (Athens: University of Georgia Press, 1984).
3. Robin Blackburn, *The Making of New World Slavery: From the Baroque to the Modern, 1492–1800* (London: Verso, 1997), p. 254.
4. Ira Berlin, *Many Thousands Gone: The First Two Centuries of Slavery in North America* (Cambridge, MA: Harvard University Press, 1998), p. 66.
5. Alan Gallay, *The Indian Slave Trade: The Rise of the English Empire in the American South, 1670–1717* (New Haven: Yale University Press, 2003), pp. 299, 357.
6. Ira Berlin, *Generations of Captivity: A History of African-American Slaves* (Cambridge, MA: Harvard University Press, 2003), p. 69.
7. Joyce E. Chaplin, 'Tidal Rice Cultivation and the Problem of Slavery in South Carolina and Georgia, 1760–1815', *William and Mary Quarterly*, 49 (January 1992), pp. 29–61.

8. Leland Ferguson, *Uncommon Ground: Archaeology and Early African America, 1650–1800* (Washington, DC: Smithsonian Institution Press, 1992).
9. Judith A. Carney, *Black Rice: The African Origins of Rice Cultivation in the Americas* (Cambridge, MA: Harvard University Press, 2001), pp. 81, 165. Not all historians agree with Carney's thesis: see Philip D. Morgan, *Slave Counterpoint: Black Culture in the Eighteenth-Century Chesapeake and Lowcountry* (Chapel Hill: University of North Carolina Press, 1998), pp. 182–83.
10. Kenneth Morgan, *Slavery and Servitude in North America, 1607–1800* (Edinburgh: Edinburgh University Press, 2000), p. 44.
11. Morgan, *Slave Counterpoint*, pp. 81–5.
12. David Eltis, *The Rise of African Slavery in the Americas* (Cambridge: Cambridge University Press, 2000), p. 96.
13. Lorena S. Walsh, 'Slave Life, Slave Society, and Tobacco Production in the Tidewater Chesapeake, 1620–1820', in Ira Berlin and Phillip D. Morgan (eds), *Cultivation and Culture: Labor and the Shaping of Slave Life in the Americas* (Charlottesville: University of Virginia Press, 1993), pp. 170–99; Alexander Hewatt (1779), cited in Morgan, *Slavery and Servitude*, p. 74.
14. 'A Curious New Description', *Universal Museum*, I (September 1762), p. 477, cited in Morgan, *Slave Counterpoint*, p. 187.
15. Morgan, *Slave Counterpoint*, p. 203.
16. 'The humble Remonstrance of Your Majesty's Governor, Council and Assembly of Your Majesty's Province of South Carolina', 9 April 1734, in Elizabeth Donnan (ed.), *Documents Illustrative of the History of the Slave Trade to America, Vol IV* (Washington, DC: Carnegie, 1935), p. 288.
17. Allan Kulikoff, *Tobacco and Slaves: The Development of Southern Cultures in the Chesapeake 1680–1800* (Chapel Hill: University of North Carolina Press, 1986), p. 409.
18. Johann David Schoepf, *Travels in the Confederation [1783–1784]*, translated and edited by Alfred J. Morrison, 2 vols (Philadelphia: William J. Campbell, 1911), II, p. 220.
19. Michael A. Gomez, *Exchanging Our Country Marks: The Transformation of African Identities in the Colonial and the Antebellum South* (Chapel Hill: University of North Carolina Press, 1998), pp. 8, 11; Gwendolyn Midlo Hall, *Slavery and African Ethnicities in the Americas: Restoring the Links* (Chapel Hill: University of North Carolina Press, 2005).
20. Nicholas Cresswell, *The Journal of Nicholas Cresswell, 1774–1777* (New York: The Dial Press, 1924), pp. 18–19.
21. Francis Le Jau, *The Carolina Chronicle of Dr. Francis Le Jau*, edited by Frank J. Klinberg (Berkeley: University of California Press, 1956), p. 129.
22. Berlin, *Many Thousands Gone*, p. 98; Donald R. Wright, *African Americans in the Colonial Era: From African Origins through the American Revolution* 2nd edition, (Wheeling: Harlan Davidson, 2000), p. 149.
23. Michael Mullin, *Africa in America: Slave Acculturation and Resistance in the*

American South and the British Caribbean, 1736–1830 (Urbana: University of Illinois Press, 1992), p. 15.

24. Jane Landers, 'Gracia Real de Santa Teresa de Mose: A Free Black Town in Spanish Colonial Florida', *American Historical Review*, 95 (February 1990), pp. 9–30.
25. Anthony S. Parent, Jr, *Foul Means: The Formation of a Slave Society in Virginia, 1660–1740* (Chapel Hill: University of North Carolina Press, 2003), pp. 148, 160–2.
26. John Hope Franklin and Loren Schweninger, *Runaway Slaves: Rebels on the Plantation* (New York: Oxford University Press, 1999), p. 282; Peter Kolchin, *American Slavery* (London: Penguin Books, 1993), p. 159.
27. Orlando Patterson, *Slavery and Social Death: A Comparative Study* (Cambridge, MA: Harvard University Press, 1982), p. 5.
28. On patriarchy in Virginia, see Kathleen M. Brown, *Good Wives, Nasty Wenches and Anxious Patriarchs: Gender, Race and Power in Colonial Virginia* (Chapel Hill: University of North Carolina Press, 1996), pp. 319–66; for the Lowcountry, see Robert Olwell, *Masters, Slaves, and Subjects: The Culture of Power in the South Carolina Low Country, 1740–1790* (Ithaca, NY: Cornell University Press, 1998), pp. 181–219.
29. William Byrd II to Charles, Earl of Orrery, 5 July 1726, cited in Rhys Issac, *The Transformation of Virginia, 1740–1790* (Chapel Hill: University of North Carolina Press, 1982), pp. 39–40; Maurice H. Woodfin (ed.), *Another Secret Diary of William Byrd of Westover, 1739–1741* (Richmond VA: The Dietz Press, 1942), pp. 7, 8, 130; Mechal Sobel, *The World They Made Together: Black and White Values in Eighteenth-Century Virginia* (Princeton, NJ: Princeton University Press), p. 167.
30. Edmund S. Morgan, *American Slavery, American Freedom: The Ordeal of Colonial Virginia* (New York: W. W. Norton, 1975), p. 386.
31. Robert E. Brown and B. Katherine Brown, *Virginia, 1705–1786: Democracy or Aristocracy?* (East Lansing: Michigan State University Press, 1964), p. 142; J. G. A. Pocock, 'The Classical Theory of Deference', *American Historical Review*, 81 (June 1976), p. 516; Brown, *Good Wives, Nasty Wenches and Anxious Patriarchs*.
32. Michael Zuckerman, 'Tocqueville, Turner, and Turds: Four Stories of Manners in Early America', *Journal of American History*, 85 (June 1998), pp. 13–42; Michael A. McDonnell, 'Class War? Class Struggles During the American Revolution', *William and Mary Quarterly*, 63 (April 2006), p. 309. This special issue of the *William and Mary Quarterly* goes a long way towards refocusing the debate over class in the colonial period. See also the essays in Billy G. Smith and Simon Middleton (eds), 'Deference in Early America: The Life and/or Death of an Historiographical Concept', special issue of *Early American Studies: An Interdisciplinary Journal*, 3 (Fall 2005).

33. T. H. Breen, *Tobacco Culture: The Mentality of the Great Tidewater Planters on the Eve of Revolution* (Princeton, NJ: Princeton University Press, 1985), p. 46.
34. Trevor Burnard, *Mastery, Tyranny, and Desire: Thomas Thistlewood and His Slaves in the Anglo-Jamaican World* (Chapel Hill: University of North Carolina Press, 2004), p. 74.
35. Ebenezer Hazard (1778), cited in Morgan, *Slave Counterpoint*, p. 302.
36. *South Carolina Gazette*, 7 July 1779, cited in Rachel N. Klein, *Unification of a Slave State: The Rise of the Planter Class in the South Carolina Backcountry, 1760–1808* (Chapel Hill: University of North Carolina Press, 1990), p. 99.
37. Brown, *Good Wives, Nasty Wenches and Anxious Patriarchs*, p. 321.
38. Jack P. Greene, *Pursuits of Happiness: The Social Development of Early Modern British Colonies and the Formation of American Culture* (Chapel Hill: University of North Carolina Press, 1988), p. 81.

Chapter 3

SLAVERY, RACE AND THE AMERICAN REVOLUTION

When Samuel Johnson asked 'How is it that we hear the loudest *yelps* for liberty among the drivers of negroes?', he not only provided one of the most frequently quoted lines in American history, he also put the problem of the American Revolution squarely in focus. For Edmund S. Morgan, 'the central paradox of American history' was the simultaneous rise of slavery and freedom.[1] As the ink dried on Thomas Jefferson's Declaration of Independence in July 1776, pronouncing the split from Great Britain, approximately half a million slaves worked in the thirteen colonies, the majority in six southern colonies: Maryland, Delaware, Virginia, North Carolina, South Carolina and Georgia. Given the vocal rallying cry of the revolutionaries attacking British tyranny for treating the colonists like slaves, this might seem a curious anomaly. No less a figure than George Washington, like Jefferson a Virginian slaveholder, wrote of 'a struggle which was begun and has been continued for the purpose of rescuing America from impending Slavery'. And yet, viewed in the context of republican ideas of virtue and citizenship, the contradiction between slavery and freedom was not as great as it might first appear. In order to be worthy of freedom, men had to act honourably and courageously and, above all, resist enslavement. Republican ideology blamed the weak for allowing themselves to exist in bondage, encouraging the view that some were naturally stronger than others.[2]

The revolutionary era proved a major watershed. Slavery came under the national spotlight for the first time as the British colonies eventually became the United States. An anti-slavery strain of thinking emerged, hastening slavery's extinction in the North and briefly threatening its place in the South as well. The southern states hoped to return to normal when the war ended in 1783, but master–slave relations had changed in significant ways, as had the attitudes of many whites toward slavery. The revolutionary generation of slaves utilised wartime chaos to reclaim rights taken away from them by the plantation system and, contrary to the republican critique of black character, showed themselves to be anything but content in servitude. Upper South planters, influenced by Enlightenment ideals and the revolutionary experience, displayed considerable unease as the intellectual tide turned against slavery in the late eighteenth century. This contributed to the most dramatic development of the post-war period – the rapid growth of the free black population.

Although challenged, southern slavery was never really likely to follow northern emancipation for a variety of reasons. Indeed, the peculiar institution expanded rapidly in the revolutionary and early national period (c.1776–1820). In 1790, there were 700,000 slaves in the United States. By 1820, there were more than 1.5 million slaves, all but a tiny number living in the South. Kentucky, Tennessee, Louisiana, Mississippi, Alabama and Missouri were new states by 1821. The growth of cotton and sugar production breathed new life into the institution as the tobacco economy of the Chesapeake slowed down. 'The years of slavery's supposed decline,' historian Robert McColley shrewdly observes, 'were in fact the years of its greatest expansion.'[3] The American Revolution had contradictory effects and consequences. It produced the world's most important republican democracy and popularised the seminal notion of 'natural and unalienable rights' due to all members of society. This idea quickly spread throughout the western world and became an inspiration for many different causes in the nineteenth century. However, African Americans and Native Americans, as well as women, were not part of this vision. Their exclusion required justification, and the development of racial science offered a suitable rationale.

THE AMERICAN REVOLUTION IN THE SOUTH

Opinion is divided over the war's effect on slavery in the South. Sylvia R. Frey and Gary B. Nash stress its radical impact, but Philip D. Morgan is more cautious. These conflicting views partly reflect the divergent focus of each historian, as the war played out differently in the Upper and the Lower South.[4] Common to all those in bondage, no matter where they lived, were heightened expectations of better treatment and for many the unexpected opportunity to escape. Virginian Royal Governor Lord Dunmore issued an amnesty proclamation on 7 November 1775, offering freedom to slaves aiding the British. This news spread across the plantations like wildfire and as many as a thousand bondspeople took up Dunmore's offer. General Henry Clinton renewed this promise on 30 June 1779, during fighting in the Lower South.

In truth, the British made a strategic offer designed to disrupt rebel plans more than to liberate blacks. They did take in American slaves willing to enlist in the fight, but on the whole treated them appallingly and only a fortunate few actually gained their permanent freedom. Dunmore formed an Ethiopian regiment of black soldiers, but the majority of escapees reaching British lines found themselves in familiar work: labouring in the hot sun as they fetched and carried and built fortifications. In 1782, it was reported that just 700 blacks were fighting for the British. Disease was common in British camps and onboard ships with food in short supply. Lord Cornwallis quietly allowed loyalist Americans to retrieve escaped slaves. Many more blacks found themselves sold into slavery in the Caribbean or recaptured by the Americans. Both sides offered slaves as bounties to volunteers. Simon Schama's recent observation that British policy was 'dictated more by the cold-blooded needs of military self-preservation than by the warmth of humanity' tends to understate the dreadful treatment of the enslaved between 1776 and 1783.[5]

Nonetheless, Dunmore's announcement rattled American slaveholders. Just two weeks after the proclamation, the *Williamsburg Virginia Gazette* countered with a veiled threat: slaves 'have been flattered with their freedom. . . . To none . . . is their freedom promised but to such as are able to do Lord *Dunmore* service. The aged, the infirm, the women and children, are still to remain the property of their masters, masters who will be provoked to severity, should part of their slaves desert them.'[6] The wartime situation exacerbated fears of slave rebellion. The overwhelming riposte of the planters, especially in the Lower South, was to enforce discipline and tighten up the plantation system, with limited success. There were other courses of action available to the colonists, however, not least because manpower was needed for the war effort and it proved difficult to police the plantations, particularly those located close to the fighting. Some Americans argued that blacks could be very useful to the much smaller Patriot forces. This opinion was more common in the North but was not unheard of in the South. Slaves could be loaned or hired for support duties. They might also fight, either to earn their freedom or as substitutes for their masters. Although initially opposing the arming of free blacks, commander-in-chief of the American forces George Washington changed his mind in December 1775, after being persuaded of their strategic importance. Most states followed his lead and about 5,000 African Americans fought for the Patriots; only South Carolina and Georgia prohibited their participation.

The total number of runaways is extremely difficult to establish with any accuracy. Slaves were killed in the fighting, some died of natural causes and others were reclaimed by their owners or sold back into bondage. The standard figures cited by historians estimate that there were 25,000 fewer slaves in South Carolina in 1783 compared to 1775, a loss amounting to a quarter of the total pre-war population. In the same comparison, Georgia lost 5,000 slaves (approximately two-thirds of the pre-war population, the largest proportion of any colony). Five thousand slaves left the Upper South for the North, Canada and the West Indies, in a variety of circumstances, and it is possible that the same number remained at large within the Upper South. Maroon colonies of escaped slaves, congregating near swamps and on the frontier, grew in size during the 1770s and early 1780s, and some escapees blended in with the free black population. These figures, however, have recently been heavily criticised by historian Cassandra Pybus as being far too high. She estimates that only about 6,000 slaves from the Upper South and 6,000 from the Lower South made it to British lines and a much smaller number gained permanent freedom. Pybus also refutes the claim that the British went back on their promise of freedom by selling blacks back into slavery in the West Indies.[7]

The work regime was severely disrupted during the war. Out of necessity, plantations became self-sufficient and food production became more or less the sole responsibility of the slaves. The pace of work slowed, the average working week was reduced and collectively bondspeople were able to devote considerably more time to their interests and families. Slaveholders, and ordinary farmers, switched from tobacco to wheat production in the Upper South as tobacco markets collapsed because of the war, a trend which continued in the last quarter of the century. Attempts to return to the status quo after 1783 were hampered by the effects of the French Revolution, which pulled down the price of tobacco in the 1790s. Moreover, vast tracts of land in the Chesapeake were becoming infertile, as overproduction took its toll. Mixed farming (wheat, corn, dairy products, vegetables, fruits and herding) increasingly replaced tobacco. Growing wheat, which became the main cash crop, did not require the same exertion and year-round attention that tobacco did, and slaves were put to many new tasks. A significant number left the fields to work in tanneries, cooperages, iron works, flour mills, boat yards and a myriad of other pursuits, as slaveholders found that they had a surplus of labour. Bondswomen spent a lot more of their time spinning and weaving.

Slave management and discipline was dramatically disrupted in the Lower South, the region most heavily affected by fighting in the latter stages of the war. The majority of colonists remaining loyal to the Crown were found in the Lower South, and both the British and the Patriots confiscated slaves and other property, causing considerable upheaval. Planters were forced to move their bondspeople from the path of marauding armies, adding to the general sense of confusion as traditional structures of authority broke down. Loyalists sent their slaves as far as Natchez, on the Mississippi River, in British-controlled West Florida. This territory, stretching much further along the Gulf Coast to New Orleans than present-day Florida, was relinquished by the Spanish in 1763 but had mostly been reclaimed for Spain by 1783, as the British had other, more pressing, priorities.

Drivers continued to assume positions of greater authority on plantations in the Lowcountry as masters and overseers left to fight. Wartime disruption enabled slaves to negotiate better conditions, with some refusing to follow their orders. With the market for rice and indigo abruptly curtailed anyway, there was little point in sticking to the same routine. As in the Upper South, plantations were no longer running at full capacity and the break-neck speed required before the war slackened and was slow to return. Bondsmen and bondswomen demanded more time to work their gardens. Indeed, some refused the requests of their owners to evacuate plantations in the path of the British because they would not leave their gardens. In short, the wartime experiences of slaves were uncertain and varied. While the opportunity for escape and freedom presented itself – to the British, to the Spanish and to the frontier regions – reviving the rebellious spirit sapped by the plantation regime, this was an opportunity fraught with considerable risks.

SLAVERY'S PLACE IN THE NEW NATION

Eleven years after the Declaration of Independence and just four years after the Treaty of Paris formally ended British control of the American colonies, fifty-five men met in Philadelphia with the intention of drafting a new system of government to replace the outdated Articles of Confederation. The place of slavery in the new nation was likely to be a matter of controversy. Representatives from the thirteen states held differing viewpoints on slavery, and many other issues, during the long, hot summer of 1787. Out of these discussions emerged a blueprint for the political structure of the United States.

This was a point at which the interests of the South were potentially compromised by the priorities of the nation as a whole. Hitherto, slavery had been a matter for individual colonies to decide on, but with the formation of the new country it now became a national concern. The precise functions of federal government were vigorously contested at Philadelphia and the political system created in 1787 incorporated a series of checks and balances, the result of compromises between competing interests. As with most compromises, unresolved tensions remained, not least in the relationship between the states and the national (federal) government that was eventually located in Washington, DC. Southerners strongly asserted state power over that of the federal government – the doctrine of states' rights – a thorny problem of fundamental significance to the political development of the South.

Even at this early juncture, the United States appeared divided into northern and southern sections, as slavery was becoming isolated not only geographically, but in a moral and intellectual sense as well. Slavery had been an accepted part of virtually all past societies and a central feature of the Greek and Roman civilisations many southerners greatly admired. Growing unease over slavery was apparent in the North, as it was in Europe and particularly in Great Britain, as the institution came under sustained attack for the first time. Political, religious and moral objections were uppermost. Influenced by the rhetoric of the Revolution, and by the vocal protests of abolitionist groups such as the Quakers, the northern states prohibited slavery outright or made it moribund by gradual emancipation acts in the late eighteenth and early nineteenth centuries. The growth of the British anti-slavery movement in the 1770s was especially significant. Abolitionists on both sides of the Atlantic joined forces to exert increasing pressure on the South and they jointly conducted an impressively organised and highly effective campaign against slavery in the antebellum period. It should not be inferred, however, that abolitionists automatically promoted black equality and challenged racial doctrine. Some did, but abolitionists took up the cause for many different reasons; sometimes because they were hostile to blacks and wanted their removal and sometimes for the implicitly racist paternal motive of protecting their weaker brothers. Moreover, the abolitionists were a small minority. As John Wood Sweet shows, racial ideas of white superiority and African and Native American inferiority emerged just as pervasively in the American North as they did in the South, albeit in very different contexts.[8]

Another criticism, which would eventually become a contributory factor in the coming of the American Civil War, was the view that slavery was an inferior economic system, particularly in comparison with the rapidly developing capitalist system. Adam Smith's *The Wealth of Nations*, published in 1776, stated that the 'experience of all ages and nations demonstrates that the work done by slaves . . . is in the end the dearest of any'. This was because a 'person who can acquire no property, can have no other interest but to eat as much, and to labour as little as possible. Whatever work he does beyond what is sufficient to purchase his own maintenance can be squeezed out of him by violence only, and not by any interest of his own.' Free labour was considered to be vastly superior to slave labour. This critique quickly became the orthodox position among political economists in the late eighteenth century.[9]

Vocal objections were raised against slavery from some quarters in the North but, more significantly, slavery was never as economically important above the Mason–Dixon Line as it was in the South. This allowed northern states considerable room for manoeuvre, as southerners were not slow to point out. Banning slavery affected a relatively small percentage of the white population in the North. Moreover, when slavery was ended by gradual means, northern slaveholders were at liberty to sell slaves before the date at which they became free, somewhat lessening claims to moral superiority. Freedom did not come to blacks overnight by any means. Emancipation in the northern states was a messy process that took decades in some cases. Some northern slaveholders put up a strong fight, especially in the Mid-Atlantic states of New York and New Jersey. Slaves were also prominent in the North's great metropolitan areas, including Boston, Philadelphia and New York, and continued to feature in these cities for many years to come.

Southerners were also placed on the defensive by divisions within their own ranks. The Lower South vehemently opposed any changes to slavery but support in the Upper South was not so uncompromising. Important Virginians, including Thomas Jefferson, John Randolph and Robert Carter, were uneasy about slavery's moral and political implications in the new republic. It is not without some justification that historians such as Gary B. Nash see a great opportunity lost during the Constitutional Convention. Despite the fact that Rhode Island declined to send delegates to the Constitutional Convention, and those from New York left early, free states effectively outnumbered slave states by six to five at Philadelphia, if one counts Delaware as free. Delaware was part of Pennsylvania until 1701, and even though a few tobacco slaves worked on the eastern shore, it had more interests in common with the free states at the convention.

The prospect of employing radical measures to curtail slavery was never really likely, however. There was pressure for unity at the Constitutional Convention and concerns about slavery were far outweighed by the desire to protect private property. In general, the Founding Fathers did their best to avoid divisive issues, recognising that slavery was fundamental to southern interests. That said, heated debates at Philadelphia took place over the way in which slaves were to be incorporated and represented in the federal system, and especially over the continuation of the international slave trade. The Constitution is a remarkable document, not least in the way it avoids use of the term 'slave' within its various sections – a telling indication of changing views in the late eighteenth century. 'Other persons' were to count as three-fifths for the purposes of taxation and political representation: three slaves were equivalent to five free people. The fugitive slave clause made obligatory the return of runaway slaves crossing state borders, providing strong evidence that the protection of property was uppermost in the minds of the Founding Fathers. Most controversially, the international slave trade was guaranteed for twenty years, with an expectation of its end in 1808 but not necessarily an automatic curtailment. A distinction was made by most contemporaries between domestic slavery and the international slave trade; the latter was regarded as abhorrent by northerners and by many southerners as well. Failure to ban the international slave trade dashed the expectations of anti-slavery supporters.

Despite the influential argument of William W. Freehling, echoed more recently by Earl M. Malz, it is difficult to dispute Peter Kolchin's verdict that the Founding Fathers threw the weight of the federal political system behind the protection of slavery in 1787. Historian Paul Finkelman vehemently criticises the view that the Founding Fathers, and the documents that they wrote, were anti-slavery in intent, agreeing with abolitionist William Lloyd Garrison's verdict that the Constitution was a 'covenant with death' and 'an agreement with Hell'. The motive behind these conservative actions is less clear, however. Some planter delegates were undoubtedly protecting their own interests, but James Oakes contends that many genuinely believed that slavery would naturally wither away: 'The widespread assumption among the Founders that slavery would ultimately fail in the global competition between free and unfree labor helps explain the great paradox of the Revolutionary legacy; the reluctance of otherwise bold men, men who went on record opposing slavery, to do much to bring about its complete abolition.' The rights of Africans were of little or no consequence to the debates. This was emphasised when the first Congress passed the Naturalization Act in 1790, restricting citizenship to 'free white persons' resident for at least two years. The institutionalisation of whiteness at the federal level illustrated just how important and elevated white status was across the United States, not just within the South.[10]

CONCEPTUALISING RACE IN NORTH AMERICA

Underlying the conservative position taken by the Founding Fathers was the question of the supposed racial inferiority of Africans. Were African Americans capable of being included as citizens in the United States? How far were Africans similar to or different from white Americans? It was not for a lack of interest that there were no definitive answers to these questions. Thousands of speculative words had been written about the moral, religious, cultural and physical comparison between Europeans, Africans and Native Americans in the seventeenth and eighteenth centuries. A white identity gradually emerged in the South that, although somewhat amorphous, was nonetheless distinct from Africans and Indians. Whiteness conferred political status, legal protection and gave social standing and an overarching sense of superiority. For some historians, this was a cynical construction by a frightened elite; for others, it was more an unintentional consequence of European colonisation of North America that appropriated Indian lands and imported slaves to solve the labour problem.

The challenge for scholars is to understand how the wide variety of contrasts made between different groups in the colonial era became channelled into a narrow idea of a hierarchy of races by the nineteenth century. It is extremely difficult to distinguish race clearly from other measures of comparison. Joyce E. Chaplin's critique of current historical writing is instructive in this respect: 'Though much recent work on the English-speaking Atlantic world claims to discuss race, most of this scholarship in fact discusses questions of status, religious confession, superficial physical appearance, or cultural practice.' For Chaplin, the focus should be 'the definitive and insidious feature of racism: its grounding in the human body and in lineage, which thus defines it as inescapable, a non-negotiable attribute that predicts socio-political power or lack of power'.[11] Only when difference was primarily interpreted through the lexicon of biology and genetic inheritance did racism truly emerge. How and why, then, did this happen?

European society up to and including the early modern period usually adhered to a biblical interpretation of human origins, promoting the idea of monogenesis. Human beings descended from Adam and Eve. This view affirmed a common humanity and worked against ideas of different racial types. Mankind took its place near the top of the 'Great Chain of Being', a popular belief in the seventeenth and eighteenth centuries that all living creatures were ranked hierarchically from the simplest organism all the way up to God. If anything, the critical marker in the vast majority of societies up to the eighteenth century was gender, as men assumed control over women. The treatment of Jews and some groups of Africans indicated that more exclusionary ideas and practices were emerging in the Iberian peninsula, but on the whole nothing existed that really compared to modern racism.[12] To be sure, ethnocentric viewpoints, promoting the superiority of particular cultures or societies, were common. The key point is that such views were not based on racial criteria. Most glaringly absent was the understanding of genetic transmission between successive generations, a crucial concept underpinning the notion of distinct races.

The physical contrasts between peoples from different continents were placed in sharp relief as Europeans navigated the globe from the 1400s. Skin colour provided the most striking point of comparison, but hair, noses and skulls were also of great interest. A religious explanation for blackness was provided by the tale of Noah and his son Ham. For allegedly gazing on his naked father, the descendants of Ham were forever cursed and in some versions of the story that curse took the form of blackened skin. However, the most popular explanation of physical differences focused on the environment. In this widely held view, human beings were pretty much the same the world over but were transformed by the environments they inhabited. The blazing African sun created a darkened skin colour, whereas the more temperate European climate made for a lighter skin tone. According to Winthrop D. Jordan, 'the flowering of environmentalism was one of the major historical developments of the second half of the eighteenth century'.[13] While popular before that date, environmentalism perfectly complemented revolutionary notions of natural rights theory. Human beings were united both politically and biologically in this view.

Yet, concomitantly, scientists and philosophers speculated about alternative theories based on the allegedly unique physicality of Europeans, Africans and Indians. Circumstances in North America encouraged naturalists, who had hitherto concentrated their efforts on classifying plants and animals, to compare the bodies of the indigenous people and new arrivals in detail. Disease could kill indiscriminately and decimated Europeans, Africans and Native Americans alike. However, colonists noticed marked contrasts between themselves and others. Indians suffered hardest from the epidemics that swept the continent and became regarded as physically weak and susceptible to diseases of little consequence to Europeans. Drawing on experiences in the South and from explorations in Africa, it seemed as though whites suffered in hot environments to a much greater extent than Africans. African bodies seemed more hardy and durable as a consequence.[14]

Planters in South Carolina looked to an African labour force because they were regarded as ideal workers in Lowcountry conditions. One of the key arguments for opening Georgia to slavery was the alleged physical suitability of Africans to plantation slavery – without them, it was thought impossible to cultivate rice successfully. Patrick Tailfer, a leading 'malcontent' urging Georgia's trustees to end the slavery ban, asserted that Negroes were 'much stronger than white people, and the heat no way disagreeable nor hurtful to them; but in us it created inflammatory fevers of various kinds'. Charlestonian Samuel Eveleigh concurred, believing that 'without Negroes Georgia can never be a Colony of any great Consequence'. He was convinced that 'the Work is too laborious, the heat very intent [*sic*]' for the constitution of whites. Slave bodies were also disfigured by the whippings and other punishments inflicted upon them, encouraging notions of profound physical disparity. As historian Kirsten Fischer put it, 'The visible marks that corporal coercion imprinted on the bodies of slaves came to connote to whites an underlying physical difference in the victims – a nonwhiteness – that in turn served to justify the violence perpetrated against them.' Lower-class whites were protected by law from similar fates, making 'the marks of officially condoned brutality against blacks into an insignia of inferiority'.[15]

The social context was critical here. If race was to have meaning, it had to build on everyday circumstances, and it is no surprise to find that challenges to environmentalism came most vociferously from the slave colonies. Edward Long's *A History of Jamaica*, a vicious condemnation of the character of Africans published in 1774, contrasted the lineage of blacks and whites, pointing to distinct racial qualities. Long, a member of the Jamaican white elite, criticised racial mixing in Spanish America, contrasting it with the pure 'English breed', and he questioned whether blacks were a 'different species of the same GENUS'. Moreover, the first person to argue that skin colour was inherent and genetically transmitted from parent to child, rather than environmentally determined, was South Carolinian physician William Wells in 1813. Racial ideology was conceptualised throughout the Atlantic world in the late eighteenth century, but it emerged with considerable force and urgency in regions with slaves. Longstanding connections between the American South and the British Caribbean were rejuvenated by the shared endeavour of defending slavery and promoting racial doctrine. Historian Larry E. Tise asserts that British planters in the Caribbean, such as Edward Long, actually took the lead decades before their American counterparts in not only proclaiming 'slavery morally blameless and perfectly consistent with enlightened government' but insisting 'that it was a positive good – that it civilized and Christianized degraded Africans and that it ensured the best possible relationship between capital and labor'.[16]

The foundations of the theory of biologically determined races were laid in the mid-eighteenth century. Swedish botanist Carl von Linnaeus was the first to provide a taxonomy of the different forms of the species mankind ('Homo'), refined in the various editions of his *General System of Nature*. He pioneered use of the scientific binomial nomenclature of 'genus' (groups of living organisms sharing similar characteristics) and 'species' (distinct subgroups within the genus classification that had fundamentally remained similar since creation), used to this day in classifying plants and animals. Linnaeus put forward various types, the most recognisable being Europeans, Africans, Asians and Native Americans. He did not specifically rank each against the other but, by the tenth edition of his *General System*, published in 1758, qualities other than the physical, such as intelligence and honesty, differentiated each type. Others followed in a similar vein, forging links between the idea of global hereditary distinctions grounded in the body and differing mental, moral and cultural traits of the races, most notably the European philosophers Lord Kames and Voltaire. In 1759, Johann Friedrich Blumenbach used the term 'Caucasian' to distinguish the 'superior' qualities of those emanating from Europe. Linnaeus and Blumenbach were extremely cautious in their findings and both worked within the framework of monogenesis and environmentalism. They provided analytical tools used later in the nineteenth century but did not 'invent' scientific racism at this time.[17]

Moreover, these were the theories of scientists and intellectuals. In the eighteenth century, most, if not all, southern whites simply assumed their superiority to Africans and Indians and did not need a rationale of racism to explain their position. Whites were self-evidently superior to blacks because they were free. Black inferiority was not based on racial ideology. George M. Fredrickson argues that this position constituted 'implicit or societal racism that can be *inferred* from actual social relationships'. Without thinking too much about it in intellectual terms, whites in this instance acted as though they were superior and there may be some grounds for considering this to be racist, or proto-racist, behaviour. 'If one racial group acts as if another is inherently inferior,' Fredrickson suggests, this constitutes societal racism 'even if the group may not have developed or preserved a conscious and consistent rationale for its behavior.'[18] This case is not proven, however. If colonists believed that the greatest contrast between themselves and others existed in religious, political and material terms, rather than on biological grounds, then racial attitudes in the colonial South were significantly different to those of the late nineteenth century. Moreover, it is dangerous to assume that all whites considered blacks in the same way. Elite whites viewed and interacted with blacks very differently to poor whites. Class was extremely important in shaping different kinds of relationships between whites and blacks, and lower-class whites continued to associate with slaves and free blacks in a variety of ways during the eighteenth century.

Clearly the development of scientific racism was a key moment in the history of the South, as it was in the history of the western world. Science provided a seemingly objective and indisputable legitimacy to the concept of race that left no room for ambiguity but was explicit and fixed. There is no scholarly consensus as to a precise date heralding the arrival of scientific racism, much less agreement as to when its logic was widely accepted within society. The growth of racist thought and practice was a slow, messy and uneven process but, in general, historians see a significant change during the eighteenth century and especially during the revolutionary era. At this time, the orthodox view of human universalism and common origins was challenged by the notion of separate races (usually placed in relations of superiority and inferiority to each other). Early commentators were not sure whether the races were actually created separately (polygenesis), an idea that conflicted with religious doctrine, or whether they had become different over time. Nonetheless, the idea of a hierarchy of races was driven by an influential, secular, scientific discourse in the second half of the eighteenth century and was rapidly disseminated during the nineteenth century.

REFORM AND REACTION IN THE REVOLUTIONARY ERA

Debates about the relative status of blacks and whites were of great significance to understanding the actions of the Founding Fathers, especially those who owned slaves. Indeed, these debates meant a great deal to all southerners. There were certainly compelling reasons why white southerners might favour theories concerning the racial inferiority of blacks. Slaves were considered by definition to be of an inferior status. The idea of racial inferiority added legitimacy to that belief, justifying the enslavement of Africans in a changing moral climate. At the same time, environmentalism and the rhetoric of political equality stimulated the growth of anti-slavery thinking in the Upper South, as well as the North.

These intellectual cross-currents also need to be placed within the context of Enlightenment ideas that swept across the United States in the latter half of the 1700s. Enlightenment thinking, promulgated by elites across the Atlantic world, challenged established beliefs. It took a rational view of the world, seeking universal laws to explain human behaviour and historical development. For the first time, it was posited that man controlled his own destiny. Everything from politics to astronomy was included in the Enlightenment world view, as followers of Galileo and Newton began crafting a secular explanation of the natural and the social world. Perhaps most important was the emphasis on individual agency, stressing that all were capable of improvement. This opened the possibility of celebrating diversity, rather than automatically condemning different cultures or, for that matter, different races, on an ethnocentric basis. In many ways, the American Revolution and its aftermath was the natural culmination of such thinking. Enlightenment views of common humanity and universal political rights posed the greatest challenge to slavery's existence in the South since the institution came to North American shores.

Two figures – Thomas Jefferson from the Upper South and Henry Laurens from the Lower South – epitomise the changing views of elite southerners in the revolutionary era. Their examples illustrate how southern thinking on slavery changed considerably at this time, but never to the extent that immediate abolition was a serious prospect. Planters liked to think of themselves as progressive and the equal of their elite counterparts around the Atlantic world. None wrote more eloquently or was better versed in Enlightenment thought than Virginian Thomas Jefferson. Despite owning more than 200 slaves, Jefferson was also a historian, philosopher and scientist, with no admiration for slavery as an institution. His original draft of the Declaration of Independence had criticised King George III for forcing the international slave trade on the colonies. In 1784, his proposal outlawing slavery from the western territories that might become part of the United States in the future was defeated by just one vote. However, Jefferson's primary objection was based on slavery's harmful impact on whites, not on blacks. Moreover, Jefferson was one of the first prominent figures to declare openly that blacks were racially inferior to whites. He was cautious in this view, and knew very well that it contradicted the dominant position of environmentalism, but, by expressing such opinions, Jefferson provided a telling indication of the direction in which southern thinking on black–white relations was heading.

Jefferson wrote that blacks and whites could not continue to co-exist if emancipation was ever implemented: 'Deep-rooted prejudices entertained by the whites; ten thousand recollections, by the blacks, of the injuries they have sustained; new provocations; the real distinctions which nature has made; and many other circumstances, will divide us into parties, and produce convulsions, which will probably never end but in the extermination of the one or the other race.' He also held 'physical and moral' objections to African Americans. Jefferson's extended discussion of physiological differences emphasised the ugliness of blackness and the beauty of whiteness, speculating whether colour was 'not the foundation of a greater or less share of beauty in the two races?'. Whites had 'flowing hair' and 'more elegant symmetry of form', while blacks perspired more, having 'a very strong and disagreeable odour'. Blacks were supposedly inferior intellectually as well. They needed less sleep and enjoyed simple amusements, Jefferson alleged. While they were brave, this might be because of 'want of forethought' in fearing danger. Love was 'an eager desire', grief 'transient', and 'in reason [blacks were] much inferior'. In terms of the arts, only in music did blacks excel, and even then by mimicking tunes, not composing them. Any improvements that had been made seemed to reflect contact with whites, in Jefferson's opinion. He concluded 'as a suspicion only, that the blacks, whether originally a distinct race, or made distinct by time and circumstances, are inferior to the whites in the endowments both of body and mind'. Jefferson drew on emerging scientific discourse to support his claims: 'It is not against experience to suppose that different species of the same genus, or varieties of the same species, may possess different qualifications.'[19]

While abhorring slavery in the abstract, Jefferson simultaneously believed blacks to be innately inferior. They were incapable of becoming part of a republican society. Jefferson's position is made even more complex by his relationship with Sally Hemmings, a slave mulatto woman. This affair shows just how close masters and slaves could be, despite notions of an insurmountable racial divide. Jefferson also realised that the South could not exist without a fixed labour force – from personal experience as much as anything else. Jefferson was caught up in a cycle of debt that made it extremely difficult for him to emancipate his slaves. There is no evidence that this was what he wanted to do, however, for, like all planters, his status and privileged lifestyle relied on chattel slavery. During his lifetime, Jefferson freed just a handful of slaves. Idealistic motives were countered by material and racial priorities in Jefferson's way of thinking. He also expected the natural decline of slavery, although he was never specific about a timeframe. Moreover, the political legacy of the Revolution 'left a twinned ideology: a call to freedom linked with an obligation to resist'.[20] Slaves were not worthy of emancipation without claiming it for themselves, in this view, thus condoning their continued bondage. Jefferson became more conservative in his later career, seemingly abandoning any expectation of abolition. 'We have the wolf by the ears,' he famously wrote in 1820, 'and we can neither hold him, nor safely let him go. Justice is in one scale, and self-preservation in the other.'[21]

Henry Laurens of South Carolina also had misgivings about the institution of slavery, possibly because of religious convictions. As one half of the Charleston mercantile firm of Austin and Laurens, he became extremely wealthy in the mid-eighteenth century, much of that wealth generated by selling slaves. He bought considerable land with his profits and from 1762 devoted his time to planting rice. Laurens was the typical patriarchal master, expecting slaves to obey him and in return providing them with food and shelter. He described his slaves in 1765 as 'human creatures', an ambiguous phrase which perhaps suggests that he held a different racial view to Jefferson, but they were his property and if disobedient would be punished.[22] Laurens reached a critical moment in his life during the war, when the contradiction between fighting for liberty could not be reconciled with slaveholding. On 14 August 1776, he wrote to his son John advising him he was considering emancipating his slaves. Laurens was cautious: he was wary of impoverishing his heirs and emancipation could only happen at the right time, some time in the future. Even so, Laurens was willing to contemplate abolition – probably the only white man in the Lower South prepared to do so.

John Laurens responded enthusiastically to his father's letter and later proposed raising a regiment of slaves to fight against the British. In a classic example of environmentalism, John reasoned that blacks were sufficiently capable of fighting in spite of the debilitating conditions of slavery they endured. He saw a black regiment as the first step to their gradual freedom. His father, however, was horrified. He knew that such a regiment would never be approved in South Carolina and that slaves were unlikely to volunteer for service. John would not give up, though, and by 1779, with the war being fought in South Carolina, Henry was prepared to support him. The Continental Congress approved John's plan in 1779 and authorised the recruitment of 3,000 slave troops from South Carolina and Georgia, subject to the agreement of the respective state governments. Predictably, Laurens' plan met with resounding defeat. Both the South Carolina Privy Council and House of Representatives turned it down. The planters, who dominated proceedings, simply could not contemplate arming slaves for it would have turned their whole society upside down. The prospect of British invasion of South Carolina was preferable to Laurens' proposal. Georgia did not even debate this matter until 1782, when it also rejected the plan.

On 27 August 1782, John Laurens was killed in action. His kind of antislavery zeal was rare in the Lower South, although it was not uncommon in the Upper South. There were possibly a few others like Henry Laurens in the Lowcountry willing to envisage gradual emancipation but recognising the immense difficulty of freeing one's livelihood and the problematic position of freed blacks in the South. As historian Gregory D. Massey observes, Henry 'spoke much, but accomplished little'. Moreover, the majority of southern whites showed little concern for blacks or slavery. South Carolinians 'fought to protect their property and their freedom to dispose of it as they pleased; their vision of liberty and the American dream entailed the use of slave labor to accumulate more wealth'. Faced with the options of abandoning their property or maintaining slavery, Lower South planters overwhelming chose the latter and increasingly adopted racist views like those expounded by Jefferson as their justification. Upper South planters were less forthright, but nonetheless generally followed the lead of their Lowcountry peers, as the issues facing John and Henry Laurens and Thomas Jefferson were played out on a grand scale in the 1780s and 1790s.[23]

FROM PATRIARCHY TO PATERNALISM

'Austere patriarchalism slowly gave way to mellow paternalism' in the eighteenth century, argues historian Philip D. Morgan.[24] This deceptively simple statement belies an extremely complex process that proceeded at variable speeds in different places and was anything but uniform, as Morgan recognises. Pinpointing a date at which paternalism became the dominant frame of reference for southern planters is highly problematic. Elements of planter behaviour might indicate a change from very early in the eighteenth century; that change was undeniably under way by mid-century. However, the very idea of a wholesale shift from one position to the other is dubious, as historians Kathleen M. Brown and Jeffrey Robert Young point out.[25] Patriarchy and paternalism were idealised conceptions of the master–slave relationship projected by planters which, at first glance, were so similar that the differences were negligible. Paternalists could be cruel and saw punishment as an essential disciplinary tool. Patriarchs might be generous and consider that good leadership involved withholding the lash as much as applying it. Small changes characterised the transition. The cold, enforced discipline of the aloof patriarch gradually adjusted into a closer relationship requiring slaves to give more of themselves, not just their labour. This reflected longstanding relations developed over decades. Planters professed concern for their family, white and black, and were seemingly very conscions about how slaves viewed them. Diaries and instructions to overseers emphasised benevolent treatment of supposedly contented bondspeople, who were expected to reciprocate with gratitude and even affection. Quite what slaves made of this change is unclear, but paternalism would develop further in the antebellum period.

A growing sense of humanitarianism, a critical feature of Enlightenment thinking, was important to the emergence of paternalism. Cruelty became far less respectable and the strong were expected to take care of, rather than simply subjugate, the weak. Central to this intellectual shift in the colonies was the religious movement known as the Great Awakening. Originating in the North in the 1730s and spreading across North America in the 1740s, the Great Awakening questioned established religious orthodoxy. Evangelical denominations, such as the Baptists and the Methodists, strongly asserted that all individuals were equal before God, criticising the elitism of the established church, and seeking the conversion of souls no matter what their origins or how humble their backgrounds. Africans, Indians and the poor were included in this vision. Historian Rhys Isaac argues that this development constituted a serious attack on the hitherto unchallenged power of the Virginian gentry.[26]

The Baptists and the Methodists also called into question notions of racial difference. The leading light of the Great Awakening, George Whitefield, asked southern planters difficult questions about their relations with slaves in 1740. 'Think you,' he asked, 'are any way better by Nature than the poor

Negroes?' Whitefield answered in the negative: 'Blacks are just as much, and no more, conceived and born in Sin, as White Men are. Both . . . I am persuaded, are naturally capable of the same improvement'. The Methodist John Wesley repeated these sentiments in 1774, in a vehement denunciation of the institution of slavery which, although focusing on Caribbean slavery, was utilised by American abolitionists in their campaigns. What some scholars describe as the Second Great Awakening hit the South powerfully in the 1780s and evangelical religion would become ever more popular in the nineteenth century. Its basic principle of spiritual equality and the common origins of human beings sat uneasily alongside emerging intellectual conceptions of race.[27]

Humanitarian feeling made it even more difficult for slaveholders to re-establish the same level of control over the revolutionary generation of slaves as they held over the plantation generations. A more widespread sense of responsibility characterised their outlook, at least in terms of their rhetoric. Even if they could return to former levels of brutality, planters appeared reluctant to do so. A heightened concern for the slave family was evident – owners seemed averse to separating kin by sale. The Upper South reacted differently from the Lower South to the Revolution and the Enlightenment, but even Lowcountry planters on the whole failed to reassert their dominance in the same way as before the war. They spent more and more time in their urban residences, leaving plantations to overseers and drivers and allowing slaves a greater element of autonomy.

The slaveholders' embrace of paternalism was accelerated by the revolutionary rhetoric of rights and responsibilities. The spate of emancipations in the post-war era points to a decisive shift in thinking in the last decades of the eighteenth century. The will of Virginian George Corbin provides a good example:

> Know Ye that I George Corbin . . . Especially from motives of Humanity, Justice, and Policy, and as it is Repugnant to Christianity and even common Honesty to live in Ease and affluence by the Labour of those whom fraud and Violence have Reduced to Slavery; (altho' sanctioned by General consent, and supported by the law of the Land) Have, and by these presents do manumit and set free the following Persons [list of twenty-three names follows].[28]

Corbin's rationale for freeing his slaves included many elements of classical Enlightenment thinking. Manumission occurred more frequently and on a wider scale in the Upper South, but favoured slaves in the Lower South also benefited, as southern states made manumission easier. Maryland freed so many slaves that it set off down the road to becoming a society with slaves, not a slave society. Slaves were manumitted outright, or owners worked out agreements with their bondspeople to work towards their freedom, which might take decades. Most dramatic was the example of Robert Carter of Nomini Hall, who made plans to free 509 slaves over a period of 22 years. Cynics might suggest that the decline of the tobacco industry encouraged slaveholders in the Upper South to rid themselves of surplus slaves who no longer had an economic use, but that would misrepresent the convictions of many planters.

Rising rates of manumission, in combination with those slaves freed during the Revolution (by whatever means), boosted the free black population that had declined since the late 1600s. In the twenty years after the first federal census in 1790, the free black population increased from approximately 60,000 (7.9 per cent of the total African American population) to 186,000 (13.5 per cent). In Virginia, numbers of free blacks increased from 12,766 in 1790 (4.2 per cent of Virginian African Americans) to 30,570 in 1810 (7.2 per cent). Just under a quarter of blacks in Maryland were free by 1810 (nearly 34,000 in total, the highest number of any state). Delaware's relatively small slave population was rapidly set free after the Revolution; by 1810, three-quarters of blacks in the state were free. More than half the free black population of the United States was located in the Upper South by 1810, as one in ten African Americans in the region enjoyed freedom. Even in the Lower South, the free black population tripled between 1790 and 1810. Numbers involved there were minimal in comparison, however – just 6,000 free blacks by 1810, comprising only 2 per cent of the total black population. It should not be overlooked that manumission rates did go up, however. The free black population of Charleston and Savannah increased significantly as urban slaves were able to use their skills as artisans to press for their freedom.

These circumstances might point to the demise of slavery in the South, but the growth of conditional anti-slavery in the revolutionary era was halted by three main developments. First, white anxiety was stimulated by the prospect of emancipation as greater numbers of southerners adopted the Jeffersonian view of blacks. For some, but by no means all, this prospect led to the supposed horrors of interracial mixing. For others, the uncertainty and instability raised by the prospect of emancipation was too unsettling to proceed. For those in the Upper South who seriously contemplated slavery's end, the only solution was colonisation (removal of slaves from the United States). Virginian St George Tucker's 1796 *Dissertation on Slavery* called for a gradual end to slavery and the colonisation of African Americans. Significantly,

Tucker cited Jefferson as his authority: 'If it be true, as Mr Jefferson seems to suppose that the Africans are really an inferior race of mankind', then they must be deported. Many Virginians followed this line of thinking in the 1790s as the shining lights of revolutionary equality and natural rights faded. Not coincidentally, planter elites fought off the evangelical challenge to bring back a measure of hierarchy to the organisation of religion in the South. Colonisation, however, was simply not practical for logistical reasons, let alone because most blacks rejected the idea. Nonetheless, the American Colonization Society was founded in 1816 and removal of African Americans would remain a possible solution to the so-called race problem for many white southerners during the antebellum period.[29]

Second, the Upper and the Lower South grew increasingly fearful over their security. In 1791, slaves on the island of Saint Domingue began a violent and bloody struggle with their French captors which lasted throughout the 1790s. They participated in the largest slave rebellion in history and successfully established the republic of Haiti in 1804. This served as a powerful reminder to southern whites of the dangers of living in a slave society. The rebel leader, Toussaint L'Overture, was killed during the struggle but his name struck fear into the heart of the South as the ultimate symbol of the danger of failing to control African slaves. Refugees from the conflict, including planters, their slaves and free blacks, settled in the South in the 1790s, bringing the conflict much closer to home than southerners cared for. These fears were exacerbated in 1800 with the uncovering of an abortive slave uprising in Richmond.

Richmond was the largest town in Virginia, with around 6,000 residents in 1800, half of whom were black. One-fifth of the black population was free. Gabriel was a literate and charismatic blacksmith who enjoyed quasi-free status as a skilled artisan. He most probably worked for himself, giving his owner a share of his wages or an agreed yearly fee in return. Gabriel and his co-conspirators used their freedom of movement to spread word of the planned uprising over a wide geographical area in the spring and summer of 1800, probably reaching thousands of blacks, slave and free. On the night of 30 August 1800, 150 rebels gathered with the intention of meeting other groups, but torrential rain broke lines of communication. This gave the authorities, who had been tipped off by two slaves, time to prepare their defences and the uprising faltered. Suspects were arrested and the threat was averted, although Gabriel remained at large for some time afterwards. What frightened Virginians most was the scale of the attack, which aimed to take control of Richmond, as well as strong rumours about the involvement of two Frenchmen. Gabriel testified that he 'expected poor white people would also join him', giving an intriguing insight into black–white relations at the bottom of the social hierarchy.[30]

It emerged clearly at the trial that rebel leaders were motivated by revolutionary rhetoric, likening their actions to those of the Patriots. 'I have nothing more to offer than what General Washington would have to offer had he been taken by the British,' said one defendant. 'I have adventured my life in endeavouring to obtain the liberty of my countrymen, and am willing to sacrifice in their cause.' Virginian John Randolph wrote that the conspirators were unafraid of danger and had a proud 'sense of their rights'. St George Tucker had noticed such feeling growing stronger among slaves. Before the Revolution they had 'fought [for] freedom merely as a good, now they also claim it as a right'.[31] Freedom had been an abstraction for slaves before the war. Afterwards it became a tangible reality for many slaves who were emancipated, but its promise extended to all those held in bondage. The shift in consciousness was immense. In light of the Richmond plot, Virginia reversed its lenient stance on manumission, an action replicated by other southern states.

Third, and most decisively, slavery grew rapidly in the late eighteenth and early nineteenth centuries. This happened despite the voluntary closing of the international slave trade by southern states and its final federal termination on 1 January 1808. Greater numbers of imported slaves were sold in the South before the trade was closed – perhaps as many as 170,000 between 1783 and 1810. Southern states banned slave imports in the late 1700s on security grounds and because supply from the Upper South was enough to satisfy demand in the Lower South. Only South Carolina bucked this trend, reopening the international trade in 1803 after closing it in 1787. Just under 40,000 slaves were imported into South Carolina between 1803 and 1807.[32]

Most significantly, cotton slavery became commercially viable in the South Carolina and Georgia upcountry, and higher grades of cotton flourished in the sea islands off the coast. Cotton had been grown on many plantations in small amounts during the eighteenth century, but its appeal was lessened by the difficulty of separating sticky seeds from the cotton fibre. This problem was eased by the invention of the cotton gin, which is usually attributed to the northerner Eli Whitney in 1793, although others also claimed this distinction. In 1790, there were 29,000 slaves in the South Carolina upcountry; by 1810, 85,000. Slavery also moved westward and southward. Some 75,000 slaves moved from the Chesapeake to Kentucky and Tennessee between 1790 and 1810. Moreover, a huge territory opened up for slavery when the United States made the Louisiana Purchase in 1803. Between 1810 and 1820, a massive 137,000 slaves from the Chesapeake and North Carolina were sold west of the Appalachians as the internal slave trade developed at a pace.[33]

Slavery's place in the South was assured by this expansion and by the recovery of the rice industry in the Lowcountry. Demand for bondsmen and bondswomen was as high as ever at the turn of the century and, conveniently, an excess of slaves was found in the Chesapeake. Paradoxically, then, the slow death of the tobacco industry (it remained buoyant in the Piedmont region of the interior but was declining in the Tidewater) aided the growth of slavery as an institution. For those slaves remaining in the Upper South, the future was uncertain. The switch from tobacco to wheat and mixed farming left them without a plantation staple and slaves were hired out in ever greater numbers as a result, with important long-term implications as bondage became less significant in the Upper South.[34] This was not noticeable at the time, however, as small farmers and even tenants, who could never dream of buying a slave outright, eagerly took the opportunity to become slave hirers. The prospects of significant change for those held in bondage fizzled out by the turn of the nineteenth century. The revolutionary and the anti-slavery movements had been propelled 'by egalitarianism and by a belief in universal and natural rights', but in the long run only 'helped to produce a positive racism'. As historian David Brion Davis argues, race became 'the central excuse for slavery'.[35]

Notes

1. Samuel Johnson, cited in David Brion Davis, *The Problem of Slavery in the Age of Revolution 1770–1823* (Ithaca, NY: Cornell University Press, 1975), p. 275; Edmund S. Morgan, 'Slavery and Freedom: The American Paradox', *Journal of American History*, 59 (March 1972), p. 6.
2. George Washington (1781), cited in Adam Rothman, *Slave Country: American Expansion and the Origins of the Deep South* (Cambridge, MA: Harvard University Press, 2005), p. 8.
3. Robert McColley, *Slavery and Jeffersonian Virginia* (Urbana: Illinois University Press, 1964), p. 3.
4. Sylvia R. Frey, *Water From the Rock: Black Resistance in a Revolutionary Age* (Princeton, NJ: Princeton University Press, 1991); Gary B. Nash, *Race and Revolution* (Madison, WI: Madison House Publishers, Inc., 1990); Philip D. Morgan, 'Black Society in the Lowcountry', in Ira Berlin and Ronald Hoffman (eds), *Slavery and Freedom in the Age of the American Revolution* (Charlottesville: University of Virginia Press, 1983) and Morgan, *Slave Counterpoint: Black Culture in the Eighteenth-Century Chesapeake and Lowcountry* (Chapel Hill: University of North Carolina Press, 1998).
5. Simon Schama, *Rough Crossings: Britain, the Slaves and the American Revolution* (London: BBC Books, 2005), p. 108.

6. *Williamsburg Virginia Gazette*, 25 November 1775, cited in Gerald W. Mullin, *Flight and Rebellion: Slave Resistance in Eighteenth-Century Virginia* (New York: Oxford University Press, 1972), pp. 134–5.
7. Figures in Ira Berlin, *Many Thousands Gone: The First Two Centuries of Slavery in North America* (Cambridge, MA: Harvard University Press, 1998), pp. 263, 303–4; Cassandra Pybus, 'Jefferson's Faulty Math: The Question of Slave Defections in the American Revolution', *William and Mary Quarterly*, 62 (April 2005), pp. 243–64.
8. John Wood Sweet, *Bodies Politic: Negotiating Race in the American North, 1730–1830* (Baltimore: Johns Hopkins University Press, 2003).
9. Adam Smith, *An Inquiry Into the Nature and Causes of the Wealth of Nations. Books I–III* ([1776] London: Penguin, 1986), pp. 488–98.
10. William W. Freehling, 'The Founding Fathers and Slavery', *American Historical Review*, 77 (February 1972), pp. 81–93 (it should be noted that he later significantly qualified his position in Freehling, *The Reintegration of American History: Slavery and the Civil War* (New York: Oxford University Press, 1990), pp. 12–13); Earl M. Malz, 'The Idea of the Proslavery Constitution', *Journal of the Early Republic*, 17 (Spring 1997), pp. 37–59; Peter Kolchin, *American Slavery* (London: Penguin Books, 1993), p. 80; Paul Finkelman, *Slavery and the Founders: Race and Liberty in the Age of Jefferson*, 2nd edition (Armonk, NY: M. E. Sharpe, 2001), p. 3; James Oakes, 'The Peculiar Fate of the Bourgeois Critique of Slavery', in Winthrop D. Jordan (ed.), *Slavery and the American South* (Jackson: University Press of Mississippi, 2003), p. 35.
11. Joyce E. Chaplin, 'Race', in David Armitage and Michael J. Braddick (eds), *The British Atlantic World, 1500–1800* (Basingstoke: Palgrave Macmillan, 2002), p. 155.
12. James H. Sweet, 'The Iberian Roots of American Racist Thought', *William and Mary Quarterly*, 54 (January 1997), pp. 143–66.
13. Winthrop D. Jordan, *White Over Black: American Attitudes Toward the Negro, 1550–1812* (Chapel Hill: University of North Carolina Press, 1968), p. 287.
14. Joyce E. Chaplin, 'Natural Philosophy and an Early Racial Idiom in North America: Comparing English and Indian Bodies', *William and Mary Quarterly*, 54 (January 1997), pp. 229–52.
15. Patrick Tailfer, cited in Joyce E. Chaplin, *An Anxious Pursuit: Agricultural Innovation and Modernity in the Lower South, 1730–1815* (Chapel Hill: University of North Carolina Press, 1993), p. 119; Samuel Eveleigh, cited in Peter H. Wood, *Black Majority: Negroes in Colonial South Carolina from 1670 Through the Stono Rebellion* (New York: W. W. Norton, 1974), p. 84; Kirsten Fischer, *Suspect Relations: Sex, Race, and Resistance in Colonial North Carolina* (Ithaca, NY: Cornell University Press, 2002), pp. 160–1.
16. Edward Long, *A History of Jamaica*, 2 vols (London, 1774), cited in Jordan, *White Over Black*, p. 492; Chaplin, 'Race', p. 166; Larry E. Tise, *Proslavery: A*

History of the Defense of Slavery in America, 1701–1840 (Athens: University of Georgia Press, 1987), p. 78. See also David Lambert, *White Creole Culture, Politics and Identity During the Age of Abolition* (Cambridge: Cambridge University Press, 2005) and Mark J. Steele, 'A Philosophy of Fear: The World View of the Jamaican Plantocracy in a Comparative Perspective', *Journal of Caribbean History,* 27 (Spring 1993), pp. 1–20.

17. Alden T. Vaughan, 'From White Man to Redskin: Changing Anglo-American Perceptions of the American Indian', *American Historical Review,* 87 (October 1982), p. 945. A useful guide to these complex developments is Audrey Smedley, *Race in North America: Origin and Evolution of a Worldview* (Boulder, CO: Westview Press, 1993), while Emmanuel Eze (ed.), *Race and the Enlightenment: A Reader* (Oxford: Blackwell, 1997) provides a valuable collection of writings on the emergence of race in the colonial and revolutionary periods.
18. George M. Fredrickson, 'Social Origins of American Racism', in *The Arrogance of Race: Historical Perspectives on Slavery, Racism, and Social Inequality* (Middletown, CT: Wesleyan University Press, 1988), p. 189.
19. Thomas Jefferson, *Notes on the State of Virginia* ([1785] New York: Harper and Row, 1964), pp. 132–8.
20. François Furstenberg, 'Beyond Freedom and Slavery: Autonomy, Virtue, and Resistance in Early American Political Discourse', *Journal of American History,* 89 (March 2003), p. 1302.
21. John Chester Miller, *The Wolf by the Ears: Thomas Jefferson and Slavery* (New York: The Free Press, 1977), p. 241.
22. Gregory D. Massey, 'The Limits of Antislavery Thought in the Revolutionary Lower South: John and Henry Laurens', *Journal of Southern History,* 63 (August 1997), p. 498.
23. Ibid. pp. 529–30.
24. Morgan, *Slave Counterpoint,* p. 259. See also Philip D. Morgan, 'Three Planters and Their Slaves: Perspectives on Slavery in Virginia, South Carolina, and Jamaica, 1750–1790', in Winthrop D. Jordan and Sheila L. Skemp (eds), *Race and Family in the Colonial South* (Jackson: University Press of Mississippi, 1987), pp. 37–79.
25. Kathleen M. Brown, *Good Wives, Nasty Wenches and Anxious Patriarchs: Gender, Race and Power in Colonial Virginia* (Chapel Hill: University of North Carolina Press, 1996), pp. 322–4; Jeffrey Robert Young, *Domesticating Slavery: The Master Class in Georgia and South Carolina, 1670–1837* (Chapel Hill: University of North Carolina Press, 1999), p. 45.
26. Rhys Isaac, *The Transformation of Virginia, 1740–1790* (Chapel Hill: University of North Carolina Press, 1982).
27. George Whitefield, *Three Letters from the Reverend Mr. G. Whitefield . . . Letter III. To the Inhabitants of Maryland, Virginia, North and South-Carolina, Concerning Their Negroes* (Philadelphia, 1740), p. 15. For more on the

evangelical influence, see Alan Gallay, 'The Origins of Slaveholders' Paternalism: George Whitefield, the Bryan Family, and the Great Awakening in the South', *Journal of Southern History*, 53 (August 1987), pp. 369–94.

28. George Corbin's will (1787), in Rick Halpern and Enrico Dal Lago (eds), *Slavery and Emancipation* (Oxford: Blackwell, 2002), pp. 91–2.
29. St George Tucker, *A Dissertation on Slavery: With a Proposal for the Gradual Abolition of it in the State of Virginia* (1796), cited in Reginald Horsman, *The New Republic: The United States of America, 1789–1815* (Harlow: Longman, 2000), pp. 141–2; Eric Burin, *Slavery and the Peculiar Solution: A History of the American Colonization Society* (Gainesville: University Press of Florida, 2005).
30. Gabriel, cited in Douglas R. Egerton, 'Gabriel's Conspiracy and the Election of 1800', *Journal of Southern History*, 56 (May 1990), p. 204.
31. Ibid pp. 208–9. See also Robert A. Olwell, '"Domestic Enemies": Slavery and Political Independence in South Carolina, May 1775–March 1776', *Journal of Southern History*, 55 (February 1989), pp. 21–48.
32. James McMillin, 'The Final Victims: The Demography, Atlantic Origins, Merchants, and Nature of the Post-Revolutionary Foreign Slave Trade to North America, 1783–1810', (PhD Dissertation, Duke University, 1999). This estimate is higher than Patrick S. Brady, 'The Slave Trade and Sectionalism in South Carolina, 1787–1808', *Journal of Southern History*, 38 (November, 1972), pp. 614–15.
33. Allan Kulikoff, 'Uprooted Peoples: Black Migrants in the Age of the American Revolution, 1790–1820', in Berlin and Hoffman (eds), *Slavery and Freedom*, pp. 143 –71.
34. Sarah S. Hughes, 'Slaves for Hire: The Allocation of Black Labor in Elizabeth County, Virginia, 1782–1810', *William and Mary Quarterly*, 35 (April 1978), pp. 260–86; Lorena S. Walsh, 'Work and Resistance in the New Republic: The Case of the Chesapeake, 1770–1820', in Mary Turner (ed.), *From Chattel Slaves to Wage Slaves: The Dynamics of Labor Bargaining in the Americas* (London: James Currey Ltd, 1995), pp. 97–122.
35. Duncan J. MacLeod, *Slavery, Race and the American Revolution* (Cambridge: Cambridge University Press, 1974), p. 184; Davis, *Problem of Slavery*, p. 303.

Chapter 4

A WHITE MAN'S REPUBLIC IN THE ANTEBELLUM SOUTH

The United States doubled in size with the Louisiana Purchase of 1803, adding to the vast expanses gained in the trans-Appalachian West in the late eighteenth century, but this was hardly unoccupied land. The Mississippi Territory, organised in 1798, was home to the Choctaw and Chickasaw, while the Seminoles were a powerful presence in Florida. Moreover, large parts of Georgia remained occupied by the Cherokee and the Creek. In the first three decades of the nineteenth century, Native Americans faced a mounting challenge as settlers pushed both westward towards the Mississippi River and southward towards the Gulf Coast. This movement and the creation of new states along the Gulf Coast would ultimately result in the tragic forced expulsion of Native Americans. Settlers, including ordinary whites and slaveholders, as well as slaves migrating with their owners or sold via the internal slave trade, quickly moved into the prime cotton land of the Black Belt. The emergence of the cotton kingdom was extremely significant to the development of the South. This region became the heart of what scholars call the Old South but, with the exception of long-established French and Spanish settlements, was barely two generations old by 1860.

As Native Americans were pushed out and the contours of the present-day South took shape, the centrality of whiteness to southern society was not only confirmed but seemingly became enshrined. The process of westward expansion was intrinsically linked to debates about the racial and cultural superiority of American civilisation. New states opening in the Southwest wrote constitutions based on the democratic principles of universal white male suffrage and the election of political offices. Underpinning white political rights was a powerful pro-slavery argument, drawing on the latest scientific research, asserting that all white men were equal in their superiority over blacks. In these changing circumstances, status differences between whites, blacks and reds (as Native Americans were now known) became more rigidly defined and widely interpreted as natural and irrevocable racial differences.

Beneath the veneer of southern white social consensus, however, tensions persisted and the potential for conflict always existed in the Old South. The planter elite, only a tiny minority, continued to enjoy a power and influence way beyond their numbers. Unlike the colonial gentry, who expected deference from ordinary whites, antebellum planters had to concede some of their more aristocratic pretensions or else risk their social standing and potentially be voted out of office. Whether all white men were united *solely* on the grounds of race, as planters claimed, is open to question. The majority of southern yeomen saw their interests coinciding with those of the planters, or failing that, lived in largely independent upcountry communities away from the plantation districts. Male dominance over women and children was also crucial in bridging class divisions. Poor whites, owning no land or slaves, lived a precarious existence, and they mixed with blacks to a much greater extent than whites higher up the class structure. On balance, however, this was a relatively stable and unified society, which explains why a majority of southerners were prepared to follow the lead of slaveholders in leaving the Union in 1861.

SETTLING THE BORDERS: WESTWARD EXPANSION

Westward expansion proceeded at varying speeds in the nineteenth century. Sometimes it was fostered by government initiative, but more often than not it was the thousands of individual pioneers and their families who forced matters by pushing ever further into the American interior. The 1783 Treaty of Paris granted the United States a vast expanse of territory between the Appalachian Mountains and the Mississippi River, opening the way west from the original thirteen states hugging the Atlantic seaboard. Settlers were already moving beyond the Appalachians in the 1770s, particularly in the South (mostly through the Cumberland Gap in south-western Virginia). Kentucky and Tennessee became states in 1792 and 1796 respectively. The United States offered unparalleled opportunities for land ownership: between 1796 and 1820 the price of buying an acre of government land in the West fell from $2 to $1.25, and the minimum allowable purchase from 640 acres to just 80. The pace of westward movement was rapid, even though few Americans at that time conceived of a nation stretching from the Atlantic to the Pacific. The most important boundary in the antebellum period was the Mississippi River; beyond that, contemporaries believed, was the 'Great American Desert', a region supposedly unfit for human habitation.

The process by which the South came to incorporate Florida and Louisiana was lengthy and complex, as Britain, France and Spain all had an interest.

Indeed, the southern boundary of the United States was hotly contested in the late eighteenth century. The Old Southwest, as it was called, comprising land below Kentucky's southern border, was of vital importance for the development of southern interests. This region had a fluid culture and heritage reflecting the influence of the colonial powers. Just before withdrawing from North America in 1763, after defeat in the Seven Years War, France ceded Louisiana to Spain. At the same time, Britain took possession of Florida from Spain, creating two new colonies: East Florida, including most of the present-day state jutting southward toward the Caribbean; and West Florida, stretching from the Apalachicola River through Pensacola. East and West Florida briefly became the fourteenth and fifteenth colonies of British North America (remaining loyal to the crown between 1776 and 1783). New Orleans remained in Spanish hands, however.

Florida retained a strong Spanish influence, despite the change of government, with British forces far too stretched to exert firm control. The population remained comparatively sparse, but rice and indigo production was extended southward from Georgia to the Saint Johns River in East Florida under British rule. Authority was not nearly as assured in Florida as it was in the rest of the South. Free blacks had traditionally been employed by the Spanish in their military campaigns and the British were wary of antagonising them. Moreover, powerful maroon groups of armed escaped slaves, allied with Native American tribes in some cases, established permanent bases in the eighteenth century, taking advantage of the dense forests and impenetrable swamps of Florida and the Lower Mississippi Valley. Colonial conflicts between the European powers and the chaos of the revolutionary struggle allowed these groups a measure of autonomy, as both the British and the Spanish were afraid of forcing maroon groups into an alliance with the other. Maroons also established strong links with plantation slaves, raising the vexing prospect of mass rebellion if either group was pushed too hard. The delicate balance of power in the region gave Africans and Native Americans an unprecedented influence.

Despite being ousted from Florida, Spain maintained its presence in the South in Louisiana and Texas. Louisiana was not greatly changed by Spanish rule. Relations between whites, slaves, free blacks and Indians in the Lower Mississippi Valley remained remarkably flexible. Indeed, the Spanish offered the most generous terms of manumission found in North America under the law of *coartación,* which effectively compelled owners to grant freedom if slaves could match their market value and afford to purchase a freedom certificate.[1] The frontier lifestyle encouraged, even depended on, extensive interactions between different cultural groups. As Daniel H. Usner Jr shows, this resulted in greater mixing and 'cultural osmosis' than anywhere else in North America. 'Despite significant differences between cultures and official efforts to manipulate those differences,' Usner argues, frequent 'small-scale, face-to-face episodes of exchange' stymied notions of fundamental racial divisions between different peoples.[2]

The political and economic context was not overwhelmingly in favour of the Europeans and consequently local elites lacked the power held by their counterparts elsewhere in the South. Louisiana's most practical benefit to the Spanish was to serve as a base from which to attack the British. Taking advantage of Britain's preoccupation with the revolutionary war, Governor Bernardo de Galvez successfully reclaimed West Florida by the early 1780s. French and Spanish support for the Americans in their quest for independence from Great Britain was designed to put as much pressure as possible on their old imperial rival. Both powers also threatened British possessions in the Caribbean. In 1783, this aggressive policy paid off when the whole of Florida was ceded back to the Spanish after twenty years of British rule.

Louisiana continued to grow steadily and in the 1790s found not one but two staple plantation crops that would quickly concentrate the efforts of slaveholders and begin to rein in the flexibility that characterised the colonial period. French influence remained uppermost within the colony, boosted by the arrival of native French speakers expelled by the British from Acadia (present-day Nova Scotia, Canada) and by French planters fleeing the chaos of Saint Domingue in the 1790s. The latter group were very important, quickly realising that sugar could be grown west of New Orleans in the lower half of Louisiana. The slave trade reopened in the region and between 1796 and 1800 at least sixty plantations switched from tobacco and indigo to sugar production. Settlers also found the unusually rich alluvial soil on the banks of the Mississippi River to their liking. Short-staple cotton flourished in these conditions and the cotton gin was not only available in New Orleans but refined and improved versions were on sale from the mid-1790s. Just as southern Louisiana was becoming a sugar country, to the north cotton production soared. These twin developments became the foundation of slavery's expansion in the nineteenth century, as sugar and cotton injected new life into American slavery, themes that will be taken up in Chapter 5.[3]

In 1795, the Spanish-American Treaty of San Lorenzo (known as the Pinckney treaty in the US after its negotiator Thomas Pinckney) set the southern boundary at the 31st parallel. The agreement also gave American ships the right to sail the Mississippi and pass goods through New Orleans without paying duty. While diplomatically advantageous to the nation as a whole, few in the South were happy with an agreement that shored up the

Spanish position. Spanish territory remained a favoured destination for escaped slaves, and maroon colonies continued to grow in size and strength. Moreover, settlers west of the Appalachians relied on the Mississippi River to transport their goods. As long as the Mississippi remained in foreign hands, it constituted a potential obstacle to future development. Indian tribes in the Old Southwest also remained powerful and uncontrolled by weak Spanish government. The problem was not to remain one that concerned Spain for much longer, however. Under pressure from Napoleon, who was hoping to re-establish a French influence in North America, the Spanish secretly ceded Louisiana back to France in October 1800.

Thomas Jefferson, elected president in 1800, had long realised the strategic importance of New Orleans, as had many other Americans. Frightened at the prospect of a French revival, he sent James Monroe to Paris to negotiate for its purchase in April 1803. Unbeknown to the Americans, French plans for North America were changed after their failure to retake Saint Domingue and Napoleon saw a way to raise funds for European campaigns by selling the whole of Louisiana, not just New Orleans, to the United States. Jefferson had not envisaged such an unprecedented deal but was delighted when his negotiators agreed to it. Louisiana cost the United States $15,000,000 for 827,000 square miles (roughly three and a half cents an acre). While some Americans were alarmed by the acquisition of so much new territory, southerners, especially slaveholders, were delighted. Slavery could not expand north of the Ohio River under the terms of the 1787 Northwest Ordinance, so the Louisiana Purchase opened a vast expanse of fresh land to slaveholders. Jefferson considered this the making of an 'empire for liberty' but, as it turned out, the states carved out of the massive Louisiana territory became an empire for slavery. This acquisition would strengthen ideas of white cultural and racial supremacy in the South, and the nation as a whole, in the first third of the nineteenth century as attention focused on the various Indian tribes who stood in the way of future settlement.

NATIVE AMERICANS IN THE NEW REPUBLIC

Native Americans found their position gradually worsening in the latter half of the eighteenth century. For decades, Indians had conducted a delicate diplomacy, playing European rivals against one another to their advantage. Bitter experience had taught them that both settlers and the colonial powers encroached on Indian land, breaking numerous promises and agreements over the years, but that they could force concessions by strategically allying themselves with the different parties. With the withdrawal of the French from

North America in 1763, one less option was open to tribal leaders. Native Americans took sides in the American Revolution, the majority going with Great Britain as the lesser of two evils. Above all, they were anxious not to be left to face the colonists alone because Britain had at least made efforts to check white encroachment. This fear became a reality, however, when negotiations culminating in the Treaty of Paris took no account of Indian land rights, despite relations built up with the British over many years in some cases. The re-taking of Florida by Spain was scant consolation, for the Spanish were not nearly as strong or as committed to defending their territory in the American South. Creek leader Alexander McGillivray reflected ruefully that 'to find ourselves and country betrayed to our enemies and divided between the Spaniards and the Americans is cruel and ungenerous'.[4] Southern tribes were positioned ominously in the way of the expanding United States as slavery developed rapidly in the Old Southwest.

Nonetheless, Indian policy in the new nation sought 'expansion with honor', according to historian Robert F. Berkhofer, and seemingly all was not lost.[5] It was hoped that previous diplomatic mistakes might be avoided by placing the emphasis on the federal government to negotiate with Indian tribes. This was an important decision, for had individual states and territories unilaterally dealt with Indians, the outcome would almost certainly have led to greater bloodshed. (Under the terms of the Northwest Ordinance, western areas seeking to join the United States were territories until they reached a threshold of 60,000 inhabitants, at which point they could apply to become states). Indian–white relations in the early republic were always tense and the first decades of the nineteenth century witnessed a series of sporadic conflicts between whites and Indians in the Old Southwest. The federal government prevented blatant abuse of Indian rights and while only partially successful at least attempted to bring some measure of justice. An element of optimism was apparent in the American outlook. Perhaps the new nation might succeed where individual colonies had always failed: by successfully and fairly resolving the place of Native Americans in white society.

Leading American politicians took a positive view of the Indian capacity to assimilate. Reinvigorated by Enlightenment thinking portraying Indians in noble terms, the late eighteenth and early nineteenth centuries witnessed an upsurge in sympathy for the plight of the indigenous peoples. Such views were often tinged with a hint of jealousy at the supposedly pure and harmonious relationship Indians enjoyed with the land. Thomas Jefferson, in marked contrast to his observations of African Americans, suggested in 1785 'that the proofs of genius given by the Indians of N. America, place them on a level with whites in the same uncultivated state. . . . I believe the Indian then to be in body and mind equal to the white man. I have supposed the black man, in his present state, might not be so.'[6] Jefferson thought Indians capable of being educated in white ways and eventually assuming their place in American civilisation. Capability, however, was very different from acceptance. Jefferson was crystal clear that Native Americans should be treated justly, but was equally explicit that they must change traditional ways before becoming part of the republic. That meant abandoning hunting in favour of sedentary agriculture, speaking English, living in settled family units, becoming educated, adopting a democratic political system and embracing Christianity.

From the white perspective, the beauty of Jefferson's plan was that, as Indians gradually changed through the generations, land-hungry Americans would be the beneficiaries. 'While they are learning to do better on less land, our increasing numbers will be calling for more land,' stated Jefferson, 'and thus a coincidence of interests will be produced between those who have land to spare, and want other necessaries, and those who have such necessaries to spare, and want land.'[7] The Louisiana Purchase would allow Jefferson to carry out his plan. If tribes did not want to be assimilated, or proved incapable of so doing, they could now be removed beyond the Mississippi River. The federal government would oversee westward expansion to what they perceived to be the mutual benefit of both parties, giving Indians time to adjust.

The principle of gradual assimilation informed government policy in the early republic. A series of Trade and Intercourse Acts sought harmonious relations with tribes. Land purchases were to be negotiated, trading posts (or 'factories', as contemporaries called them) built on the frontier, an educational programme to be devised and white settlers to be firmly kept in check. Gradualists hoped that Indians would take the opportunities before them to become 'civilised' and eventually adjust to white values. Henry Knox, Secretary of War, stated in 1792 that his government offered the indigenous peoples 'all the blessings of civilized life, of teaching you to cultivate the earth, and raise corn; to raise oxen, sheep, and other domestic animals; to build comfortable houses, and to educate your children, so as ever to dwell upon the land'.[8]

Historians disagree as to whether these plans should be considered as good intentions, as a thinly disguised promotion of white supremacy, or simply as political rhetoric – they were probably a combination of all these elements. The American Revolution promoted an unshakeable belief in the superiority of the republic and the future greatness of the nation. A providential strain of thinking quickly became embedded in American nationalist discourse (indeed, such feelings had been there since the first arrival of Europeans in North America), and whites could not understand how other groups could turn down the chance of becoming part of American civilisation. This was God's chosen country. The plight of Native Americans became more urgent as the idea of the vanishing Indian grew in popularity. Partly based on the scientific theory of superior and inferior races, but also on empirical observations of the declining population since first contact, it was asserted that the Indian was actually in grave danger of dying out altogether, necessitating urgent action. It was also the case that states on the Atlantic seaboard had subjugated their Indian population many years beforehand. Those like Jefferson, as well as many New England supporters of Indian rights, had the luxury of holding such positive views because Native Americans had long ceased to be an inconvenience in their states.

THE RACIALISATION AND EXPULSION OF NATIVE AMERICANS

It did not really matter how well intentioned or fair the federal government believed itself to be in dealing with the indigenous population. A rising tide of popular feeling pointed to the demise of the Native American in one way or another. By the early 1800s, according to historian Alexander Saxton, the white outlook was set: 'Natural law required that bearers of advanced civilization replace or dominate primitive and savage peoples.'[9] The development of popular ideas of white cultural and racial superiority continued at a pace, and became bound up in the movement to extend the nation westward. Indians had usually been regarded in very different terms when compared with blacks, but evolving codes of white supremacy in the nineteenth century posited the natural inferiority of both as separate races. The 1810s and 1820s witnessed a new militancy about the place of Indians in the republic that was reflective of this changing mood. The racialising of Indians as irrevocably different had particular appeal in the South, despite the positive views of those like Jefferson. The phrenologist George Combe summed up the emerging view: 'the existing races of native American Indians show skulls inferior in their moral and intellectual development to those of the Anglo-Saxon race . . . morally and intellectually, these Indians are inferior to their Anglo-Saxon invaders, and have receded before them'.[10]

Southerners in the trans-Appalachian West had always displayed a much less sanguine view of Native Americans than was the case elsewhere. They held few nostalgic illusions about Indians or justice, and advocated a policy of immediate separation and removal. Native Americans stood in the way of expansion and were to be removed by any means possible. This outlook reflected the geographical proximity of whites and Indians as more and more settlers encroached on Indian lands – the 1820 census showed approximately a quarter of the nation's population living west of the Appalachians. Whereas considerable distances usually separated Indians and whites in the colonial period, this was not the case in the early nineteenth century, perhaps inevitably leading to confrontation. Most settlers displayed extremely low opinions of Indians, and even those who did not tended to agree with the majority: tribal land must be opened to white settlement. This pressure proved irresistible by the 1820s.

Born on the Carolina frontier and growing up in Tennessee, Andrew Jackson epitomised in thought and deed the archetypal southwesterner. Just before engaging his Tennessee militia in a bitter war against the Red Stick faction of the Creeks (1812–14), he described his enemies as 'savage bloodhounds' and 'blood thirsty barbarians'. Jackson himself acted savagely at Horseshoe Bend, Alabama, in retaliation for an earlier attack by the Red Sticks at Fort Mims. He urged his men to show no mercy and to 'teach the cannibals . . . that the thunder of our arms is more terrible than the Earth quakes of their Prophets, and that Heaven Dooms to inevitable destruction the wretch who Smiles at the torture he inflicts'.[11] In March 1814, Jackson's combined force of white militia, Creek and Cherokee killed 800 warriors in the bloodiest confrontation between Indians and European-Americans ever seen up to that point. Despite fighting with the aid of friendly Indian allies, Jackson demanded 2.2 million acres of tribal land at the conclusion of the hostilities. These actions were condemned by many back east, but made Jackson a hero in the Old Southwest. His reputation as an Indian-fighter helped to propel him to the White House later in his career. Jackson's popularity suggested that the vast majority of whites in the trans-Appalachian West and the Old Southwest thought along the same lines as he did. Indiscriminate killing perhaps went a little too far for the consciences of some, but if the Indian was dying anyway, it made little difference.

The irony was that southern tribes had already given up vast acreages of land. By 1810, the Cherokee had ceded approximately half of their territory to the United States, a chaotic process which proceeded as much by fraud as by legal negotiation. The decentralised nature of tribal leadership rarely gave individuals or even groups of individuals the right to make decisions for the whole tribe. Southern tribes, above all others, had also made fundamental changes to their traditional ways. Their economies quickly adapted to European needs, leading to joint collaboration in the lucrative fur trade, and in other pursuits, which brought political as well as economic rewards.

European cultural influences had a massive impact. Indeed, the so-called 'five civilised tribes' of the South, as contemporaries referred to the Creek, Cherokee, Choctaw, Chickasaw and Seminole, earned their name by assimilating numerous aspects of white society in their daily routines. Contrary to contemporary popular images, these tribes had lived in settled communities for centuries. But by the 1820s, many had also adopted a system of writing, practised mixed farming, sent children to school, were subject to a hierarchical political system, wore American clothes and converted to Christianity. The Cherokee even had an English-language newspaper.[12]

Slavery was also practised in various forms by southern tribes, creating much interest among historians as to whether Indian masters were more humane than white slaveholders. Treatment differed not only from tribe to tribe, but also between individual slaveholders, making generalisations difficult. Master–slave relations were, on the whole, less severe and more personable within tribal cultures that placed little emphasis on private ownership. The Seminole especially had a long tradition of incorporating blacks within their tribe. Even those held in bondage by the Seminole enjoyed liberties not accorded to slaves elsewhere. Slaves held by Indians were not always used in plantation agriculture and, if they were, cultivated cotton, so they were spared the harsh demands of growing rice and sugar. What can be stated with certainty is that slavery had less impact on Native American society than it did on white society. Numbers of slaves owned by Indians were but a tiny fraction of the 1.5 million in total recorded by the 1820 census. In 1832, just 162 Creeks out of a population of 21,762 owned slaves, less than 1 per cent of the tribe. The Cherokee were the largest slaveholders but still only 8 per cent of household heads owned slaves in 1835, just 1,592 bondspeople in total. 'Mixed bloods' (as those with Indian and European ancestry were known) were most likely to become planters. 'Although Cherokee planters required hard work from their bondsmen,' argues historian Theda Perdue, 'they probably treated their slaves much better on the average than did their white counterparts.'[13]

More convincing evidence of Indian assimilation is perhaps provided by their adoption of white racial views of blacks. This conversion was by no means absolute and remains controversial. Scholars today are wary of an older historical view of Indian hostility to blacks based on evidence from the late nineteenth and twentieth centuries. Proximity to whites in the early 1800s appears to have been the catalyst for the emergence of more prejudiced attitudes. Indians gradually took on board white racist views as a consequence of more frequent contact. Such views were also influenced by the changing social context – Native Americans regularly observed blacks as plantation slaves, subject to harsh conditions and arbitrary punishment, whereas before they had encountered them less frequently, and as runaways, as soldiers, or as the personal servants of white traders. As the bifurcated racial lines of the South hardened, Indians faced a decision as to whether they wanted to be classified as black or white. The strategic choice was to push for inclusion with whites. Historian James H. Merrell's analysis of the Catawba in South Carolina is instructive. In the antebellum period, the Catawba had to choose sides and Merrell argues that they 'cast their lot with the dominant culture and strengthened the barrier separating them from blacks by adopting white racial attitudes'.[14]

This extremely complex process needs much greater investigation. Racial categories were certainly used by Indians to their advantage on occasions. Indeed, it seems likely that native people embraced 'red' as a marker of skin colour in order to distinguish themselves clearly from both blacks and whites. Attitudes towards blacks probably did become progressively harsher in the antebellum period, but that does not mean that Indians accepted the scientific view of fixed races. For the vast majority of Indians, identity remained flexible and rooted in kinship and the matrilineal line, rather than determined by the concept of hereditary inheritance. It was culture, not race, that mattered most. With indigenous identity threatened by American cultural practices, most southern tribes became divided between 'traditionalists' and 'accommodationists'. The Red Stick faction of the Creek, for example, rejected European influences, one of the underlying causes of the Creek War. Accommodationists welcomed change. They often had substantial European heritage, coming from families of former white traders who took Indian wives and assimilated into tribal lifestyles.

Antebellum Americans believed that southern tribes were dominated by 'mixed blood' leaders by the 1820s. Theda Perdue argues skilfully that notions of biological racism played an important role in shaping and promoting such views. 'Mixed blood' leaders supposedly held considerable power and influence, being distinguished from the allegedly simpler, less cunning, 'pure' Indians in the minds of those like Andrew Jackson. Contemporary Americans evinced a deep mistrust of 'mixed bloods', blaming them for leading others astray in resisting white intentions. This contributed to a wider debate about the importance of maintaining pure racial stocks and of the dangers posed by hybrid peoples, or 'half-breeds' as the derogatory slur put it. As Perdue points out, many historians have taken such views at face value, portraying the 'mixed bloods' unfairly as promoting their own interests over those of their tribes. This pejorative characterisation of Indian leaders helped to disseminate and popularise racial thinking in the antebellum period, especially in the South, forging a critical link between race and power. 'Racial designations,' argues Perdue, 'became more than descriptors; white politicians invested them with political meanings that came to have important implications for Indians and non-Indians, that is for the South as a whole.'[15]

Whatever concessions Native Americans made, in terms of land or culture, had little effect. The bottom line was that southern tribes inhabited thousands of valuable acres in the heart of the cotton Black Belt, an extremely fertile expanse of territory stretching across Georgia, Alabama, Mississippi and Louisiana. If the cotton boom was to continue, white southerners reasoned, this land had to be taken. With the final removal of European powers from the Old Southwest in the 1810s, Indians faced the Americans alone. The War of 1812 between the United States and Great Britain came about in no small part because of continued friction and threatened British incursions in Florida and along the Gulf Coast. Andrew Jackson made his reputation by defeating the English decisively at New Orleans on 8 January 1815. Three years later, Jackson led an expedition into Spanish Florida pursuing Indian 'rebels', which played a part in finally persuading Spain to relinquish Florida. The Adams–Onís Treaty (1819) ceded Florida to the United States and also settled the border between Louisiana and Texas at the same time. Texas thus became the last major outpost of Spain, regarded by the Spanish as an essential buffer between American expansion and Mexico. Texas would not become part of the United States until 1845, nine years after winning independence from Spain.

When Mississippi and Alabama gained statehood, in 1817 and 1819 respectively, the pressure on southern tribes increased yet further. Federal policy in the 1820s became more coercive, decisively so following Andrew Jackson's victory in the presidential election of 1828. Georgia, Alabama and Mississippi immediately declared that Native Americans within their borders were subject to state laws and that they would no longer recognise tribal law or government. Indian lands were opened to white settlers and the goal of gradual assimilation was replaced by immediate exclusion. Jackson supported these measures, ignoring the Indians' historical and legal attachment to the land. The Indian Removal Act, passed on 28 May 1830, provided funds for the relocation of all remaining Native Americans west of the Mississippi, to reside in perpetuity in the so-called Indian Territory (present-day Oklahoma). Indians who refused to move would be subject to state laws and would not be entitled to federal protection. The Removal Act passed by the slimmest of margins, indicating that there was still some reluctance to force expulsion, but it made no difference.

In a last-ditch effort to ward off these measures, the Cherokee took their opposition to the Supreme Court. Two landmark cases, in which they used the American legal process to their own advantage, were a telling indication of how far they had became acquainted with the ways of white society. In *Cherokee Nation* v. *Georgia* (1831), John Ross argued that Georgia had no jurisdiction over Indians who had occupied the land for time immemorial. Chief Justice John Marshall's response was ambiguous, seeming to agree with the Cherokee leader's reasoning but denying the right of a 'domestic dependent nation' whose relationship with the United States was 'that of a ward to his guardian' to bring the case to the Supreme Court. In *Worcester* v. *Georgia*, a year later, Marshall unequivocally supported the Cherokee, interpreting tribes as 'distinct, independent political communities' entitled to federal protection and not subject to state law. Georgia's actions were 'repugnant to the constitution, treaties, and laws of the United States and ought, therefore, to be reversed and annulled'. Andrew Jackson's response was reportedly to say 'John Marshall has made his decision; now let him enforce it', exposing any pretence of justice as a sham. Those Indians remaining east of the Mississippi were forced to leave their homes.[16]

During the 1830s, the federal government worked hand-in-hand with state governments in a policy of forced removal akin to ethnic cleansing in the twentieth century. The Cherokee aptly called their 800-mile journey the 'Trail of Tears'. Of the 18,500 who set off in 1838, 4,000 lost their lives due to inadequate protection, a lack of provisions and appalling winter conditions. The Seminoles violently resisted in a guerrilla war (1835–42) costing around twenty million dollars. Others resisted in more subtle ways and some successfully survived the transition to American rule to become prominent slaveholders in Mississippi and Alabama. However, the majority simply resigned themselves to their fate, and set out for the Indian Territory.

The Old Southwest view of the Native American prevailed in the nation as a whole. Andrew Jackson's second annual address to Congress, in December 1830, asked who 'would prefer a country covered with forests and ranged by a few thousand savages to our extensive Republic, studded with cities, towns, and prosperous farms, embellished with all the improvements which art can devise or industry execute, occupied by more than 12,000,000 happy people, and filled with all the blessings of liberty, civilization, and religion?' Georgia senator John Forsyth stated more bluntly that Indians 'were a race not admitted to be equal to the rest of the community'. The expulsion of the Indians was a powerful statement of the inherent supremacy of whites above other races. As Theda Perdue observes, 'racism intensified throughout the nineteenth century, and while African

Americans were the primary victims of the violence that it engendered, Indian societies suffered almost irreparable harm'. The triangular process of identity formation noted by Winthrop Jordan in the colonial period had reached its conclusion. Indians had been removed and the vast majority of Africans permanently enslaved, leaving whites economically, politically and psychologically at the pinnacle of southern society. Native Americans continued to have a presence within the southern states, individually and in groups (living on land whites considered worthless unless they had negotiated an agreement), and some of them fought for the Confederacy in the Civil War. However, they would not collectively influence debates over race or territorial expansion to any great extent after this point. As Reginald Horsman contends, public opinion by the mid-nineteenth century 'had for the most part abandoned any belief in potential Indian equality', believing 'that American Indians were doomed because of their own inferiority and that their extinction would further world progress'. The removal of tribes from the South confirmed the racial supremacy, even destiny, of the white race in the southern white mind.[17]

A HERRENVOLK DEMOCRACY?

In the 1830s, the South arguably came of age as a fully functioning white supremacist society. That is, the southern economy, culture and society was fundamentally shaped by, and built upon, the enslavement of blacks and the privileging of whiteness. Many of the most obvious status difference between whites were removed, emphasising race above class in a way not apparent before. The strength and significance of white supremacy had grown inexorably with the development of the southern colonies, and in the late antebellum decades became tied to a powerful scientific racist discourse and to a democratic ideology assuaging class divisions. 'An omnipotent racism convinced all whites that only bondage enabled black and white to coexist without massive social trauma,' states a recent southern history textbook, making 'believable an ideology that placed all whites on an equal social and political level, despite sharp economic and social distinctions.' The authors cite a quotation from South Carolinian John C. Calhoun that neatly sums up this view: 'the two great divisions of society are not the rich and the poor, but white and black; and all the former, the poor as well as the rich, belong to the upper class, and are respected and treated as equals, if honest and industrious'. Borrowing a term associated with the sociologist Pierre L. van den Berghe, historian George M. Fredrickson describes this as 'Herrenvolk democracy'.[18]

Whiteness united southern men and muted class divisions, at least in the rhetoric of the planter elite. Gender was less obvious but equally crucial in fostering a sense of egalitarianism between male heads of households, whether they owned slaves or not – patriarchal control over wives and children was the bedrock of antebellum white male identity. Herrenvolk democracy was also ideologically underpinned in the antebellum period by the growing credibility of biological racism, which prevailed in the North as much as the South, as well as in Europe. The scientific explanation of superior and inferior races was not unchallenged, especially as it clashed with the scriptural proclamation of human equality before the eyes of God. Nonetheless, three important developments in the nineteenth century served to legitimate and disseminate doctrines of white racial superiority.

First, the American School of Ethnology emerged in the 1840s, and became increasingly prominent in the 1850s, presenting pseudo-scientific assertions of racial doctrine based on physical and historical evidence. Philadelphian Samuel George Morton was the key theorist of the American School. In *Crania Americana* (1839), he presented thirteen different measurements of human skulls 'proving' the existence of different races. Brain size supposedly reflected the hierarchy of the races, from the large brain of the superior Caucasian to the smallest brain of the inferior Negro. Morton provided a scientific response to the environmentalist Samuel Stanhope Smith's earlier argument that it was 'impossible' to distinguish races with any certainty. In his classic study of antebellum science, historian William Stanton observes that with the publication of *Crania Americana* 'impossibility became accomplished fact' and the environmentalist position rapidly lost credibility thereafter, as the scientific assertion of a fixed racial hierarchy rapidly gained acceptance.[19]

Dr Josiah Nott, from Mobile, Alabama, was the main propagandist of scientific racism. His chief contribution was to challenge the biblical interpretation of single creation and stress instead the separate creation of the races, a theory only implicit in Morton's work. Nott was a noted medical scientist whose investigations of yellow fever in his home town realised significant breakthroughs, but his research into human races was exaggerated, crude and lacked evidence. Nott realised that his main purpose was to defend and promote the southern cause. In 1854, with his collaborator George R. Gliddon, a native Briton who had provided Morton with many of his skull samples from his base in Egypt before coming to the United States, Nott put together an authoritative summary of the latest ethnographical research that became so popular it eventually ran into ten editions. *Types of Mankind* (1854) was 'the standard scientific explanation of racial origins and distinctiveness', according to historian Reginald Horsman.[20]

Scientists and intellectuals, as well as politicians and newspaper and journal editors, were heavily influenced by the work of the American School. Swiss-born zoologist Louis Agassiz, who took a position at Harvard University in 1846, was the most famous of many converts to the theory of polygenesis (multiple creation of the human race, rather than common descent from Adam and Eve). This was not a new idea. Historians, philosophers and scientists, from as early as the sixteenth century, had struggled to reconcile the idea of common descent with the very different physical types found around the globe. What the American School claimed to provide was 'scientific' proof. The idea of five main races – Caucasian, Ethiopian, Mongol, Malay and American (Indian) – gradually became the dominant paradigm, although there was great confusion and little consistency about how many races there were. Ideas of biological and cultural superiority fused together with westward expansion in the powerful concept of America's 'Manifest Destiny' to rule over the continent – an idea popularised during the war with Mexico (1846–48). Historian Reginald Horsman places a great emphasis on the way this conflict promoted a strong 'racial Anglo-Saxonism' in the late 1840s and 1850s.[21]

Despite considerable methodological defects, ethnography was a crucially important agent in the dissemination of racial ideology in the later antebellum period and beyond. The *Charleston Medical Journal* praised Morton's contribution when he died in 1851: 'the South should consider him as our benefactor, for aiding most materially in giving to the negro his true position as an inferior race'. Dr Samuel Cartwright, a Louisiana physician with an interest in the medical peculiarities, as he saw it, of blacks, privately admitted that the 'mission of Ethnology' was 'to vindicate the great truths on which the institutions of the South are founded'.[22] Historian Bruce Dain notes the inconsistencies in the logic of the American School, not only from a modern perspective, but also from the state of scientific knowledge in the 1800s. Despite such flaws and the self-serving approach of the ethnologists, these arguments were well received in the nineteenth century. 'Morton invented an apparently legitimate scientific language,' Dain notes, allegedly proving 'that racial groups stood in a hierarchy of value, with black people on the lowest rung.' Whereas considerable scientific doubt existed before publication of his work, after Morton 'race was a fixed entity and racial inferiority a fact'.[23]

Second, the abolitionist attack on the South became progressively fiercer, forcing a southern response that increasingly promoted a racial defence of slavery. William Lloyd Garrison, the most famous abolitionist, began publishing the *Liberator* newspaper in Boston in 1831. His first editorial set the tone of the abolitionist message: 'I am in earnest – I will not equivocate – I will not excuse – I will not retreat a single inch – AND I WILL BE HEARD.'[24] That uncompromising message bluntly stated that slaveholding was a sin and called for immediate emancipation. Garrison was supported by free blacks, philanthropists and wealthy reformers such as the Tappan brothers, who collectively formed the American Anti-Slavery Society in 1833. The rise of the abolitionist movement reflected complex religious, economic and humanitarian developments in the antebellum North and had strong links with Great Britain. Scholarly opinion is divided as to whether abolitionists were anti-racist as well as anti-slavery. Historian Paul Goodman argues that abolitionists were committed to fighting racial prejudice, regarding mankind to be born 'of one blood'.[25] Others portray abolitionists as sympathetic for paternal reasons, because they regarded blacks as innately different from, and usually inferior to, whites. Whatever the case, the abolitionists put severe pressure on the South, creating something of a siege mentality below the Mason–Dixon line by the 1850s.

A pro-slavery argument articulated by a cross section of elite southern society, including politicians, lawyers, physicians, scientists, writers, editors and clergymen, countered abolitionism. Drawing upon history, religion, science, economics and politics, pro-slavery spokesmen presented a comprehensive justification of the peculiar institution. Whereas some doubt had existed over the utility of bondage in the revolutionary era, slavery was presented as a positive good by the late antebellum period. The turning point for this view was the pivotal year of 1831. Nat Turner's Rebellion in Virginia that year had an intense impact on the white psyche, creating much panic, and reopened the debate about whether colonisation was the ideal solution to race relations after all. In 1832, the Virginia legislature conducted a vigorous discussion over slavery's future in which emancipation was a serious possibility, argues historian Alison Freehling.[26] The primarily non-slaveholding districts in western Virginia were not persuaded of the economic benefits of slavery, favouring internal improvements over the costs of policing the slave system. Planter interests prevailed in the end, not least because colonisation was shown to be a practical impossibility, and slavery's future in Virginia was secured.

Thus, the prospect of a viable anti-slavery movement in the Upper South was curtailed, as whites closed ranks behind an aggressive pro-slavery stance.[27] Any doubts over the place of slavery and blacks in southern society were ended in the wake of the Virginia debates. While recent scholarship has shown that antislavery feeling was not so firmly extinguished as once thought, remaining viable in parts of the Upper South, overwhelming numbers of white southerners regarded slavery as a natural and essential part of their world. Quaker Elmina Foster recalled growing up in North Carolina and sympathising with the situation of the slaves she saw, but 'brought up as I was in a slave holding neighborhood, accustomed to seeing slaves at work on all sides, in the fields, I supposed conditions to remain the same always, for slavery was a vast, far reaching thing, so deeply entrenched in society, it did not seem possible that it should ever be eradicated'.[28] The centrality of slavery made racist ideology all the more plausible. The concept of black inferiority stemmed almost naturally from slavery's entrenchment in the antebellum South. Moreover, while the North and Europe looked down on slavery, very few objections were raised challenging the logic of race.

Third, the Jacksonian period saw an unprecedented extension of the franchise to southern white males, going some way towards levelling class differences and encouraging the notion of white racial solidarity. 'A wave of political democratization swept the South' in the 1820s and 1830s, historian J. William Harris writes.[29] Southern states, especially those in the Lower South, entered the Union on an unprecedented democratic basis. The Gulf states in the Old Southwest had virtually no qualifications for political office based on property or tax requirements. Alabama's state constitution of 1819 recognised universal white male suffrage and elected officials. Arkansas adopted the same principles in 1836 and Mississippi changed its constitution in 1832, abolishing property qualifications, as did Louisiana in 1845. Florida and Texas both became states in 1845 on a democratic basis, although, as in Louisiana, political representation within state legislatures favoured slaveholding counties. At a time when the working classes in England were fighting extremely hard for political rights, the Lower South had some considerable justification for claiming white men to be equal in political terms.

Significantly, matters were different in older states. Virginia, North Carolina and South Carolina retained qualifications for voting and continued to appoint rather than elect officials, as elites successfully resisted drastic change (although some compromises were made). In fact, most Upper South states, which had been in existence for some considerable time by the mid-nineteenth century, were more structured and hierarchical than the frontier environment of the new southern states. For example, the so-called Natchez nabobs (planters in Natchez, Mississippi) were some of the richest men in the South, but they were typically just second- or third-generation and newly rich in comparison to their aristocratic counterparts in Virginia and South Carolina. Eighteenth-century deferential culture sat uneasily alongside nineteenth-century republican claims of equality between white men in the older southern states. Lowcountry planters especially were reluctant to concede any change in their exalted status and elite honour codes specifically excluded the lower classes. Powerful figures such as James Henry Hammond clearly looked down on their neighbours in private.[30] Divisions between plantation and upcountry areas were also more problematic in the Upper South, and by the 1850s relations were becoming increasingly fractious in some places.

CLASS, GENDER AND SOCIAL CONSENSUS IN THE OLD SOUTH

If the pro-slavery argument is to be believed, the South enjoyed unprecedented social consensus because blacks carried out the essential manual labour guaranteeing white equality. The notion of white racism bridging social, economic and political differences is a perennial and dominant theme of southern history, from U. B. Phillips to W. J. Cash's influential work identifying a 'proto-Dorian convention' creating a 'common brotherhood of white men', and more recent interpretations. Gender and class, however, complicate the idea of a dominant and unifying whiteness acting as a social glue binding whites together in the Old South. Some historians are sceptical of genuine white unity at all, while others suggest that this was not a unity generated primarily by race.[31]

Indeed, a careful reading of George Fredrickson's original discussion of Herrenvolk democracy suggests a more limited and polemical concept: 'it was not the *fact* of white equality that encouraged racial prejudice, but rather an ideology of equality maintained in the face of real inequalities,' he states. In this light, Herrenvolk democracy was a device to legitimate elite control and solicit the support of the lower classes by manipulating racial constructions.[32] Did southern whites accept a racism positing immutable physical and mental differences? Did non-slaveholding whites feel an affinity with slaveholders based upon their shared whiteness, assuaging economic divisions? Answers to these questions reveal more conflict than southern politicians would admit, and suggests that very careful attention must be paid both to local conditions and to regional differences, especially between the Upper and the Lower South.

Undeniably, slaveholding was the key to economic and social success in the Old South and planters enjoyed wealth, status and political power far beyond their small numbers. Approximately one in four southerners owned slaves in 1860. The South's total white population in 1860 was just over eight million, of whom 24 per cent were slaveholders. Of the 1.5 million heads of households in southern states, 385,000 owned slaves, although a crucial contrast needs emphasising: 37 per cent of families in the Lower South were slaveholding, compared to just 20 per cent in the Upper South. Approximately half of all slaveholders owned fewer than five slaves. Those with more than five slaves but less than twenty were 'middling' slaveholders. Only 12 per cent of slaveholders held twenty slaves or more, and thus qualified as planters, although there are grounds for differentiating between those with higher numbers of slaves. In his classic analysis of American slavery, for example, Kenneth M. Stampp found that only those with thirty slaves or more achieved 'maximum efficiency, the most complex economic organization, and the highest degree of specialization within their labor forces'. If the figure of fifty slaves is taken as a sign of elite status, then only 13,000 masters reached that threshold. Less than 1 per cent of slaveholding families – or 2,300 families – owned 100 or more slaves.[33]

Considering just how important slavery was to the South and the great influence that planters exerted, these figures seem surprising. Historian Eugene D. Genovese has long argued for the significance of planter hegemony. Elite planters, according to Genovese, convinced ordinary whites of slavery's benefits and its central importance to southern society. They steered the Old South towards a defence of slavery ultimately leading to civil war. Genovese suggests that 'so long as the yeomen accepted the existing master-slave relation as either something to aspire to or something peripheral to their own lives, they were led step by step into willing acceptance of a subordinate position in society . . . because they saw themselves as aspiring slaveholders or as nonslaveholding beneficiaries of a slaveholding world that constituted the only world they knew'.[34]

Were the three-quarters of whites who did not own slaves 'subordinate' to planters or were they happy to acquiesce to their rule in order to preserve white supremacy, not least because they saw slavery as being in their interests? While a somewhat crude division, non-elite southerners roughly divide into two groups: the majority were property-holding yeomen, the minority were property-less poor whites. The classic stereotype of the average yeoman farmer depicted him as hard-working, self-sufficient in foodstuffs and other items such as clothes, and largely independent of slavery and planters.[35]

This image has been much revised in the last two decades. No consensus has emerged as to a precise definition, but historians are agreed that the yeomen class owned their own farms, relied on family labour as well as small numbers of slaves (either bought or hired), and devoted considerable time to producing cash crops by the 1850s. Far from exclusively taking a cautious, 'safety-first' approach – concentrating on satisfying household needs before risking time and effort on producing for the market – yeomen were far more aggressively market-orientated than hitherto appreciated. At the same time, there were yeomen communities that were essentially pre-modern and traditional in orientation. Such communities were based on strong kin networks, had limited geographical mobility and were based on local, face-to-face exchange that proceeded by barter as much as by cash.[36]

Geography helps to explain this dichotomous view of yeomen. In general, yeomen migrants to states such as Mississippi and Louisiana were searching for better opportunities; by nature they were acquisitive, restless and anxious for upward mobility. Historian Bradley Bond found yeomen in the Mississippi piney-woods eager to produce and sell surplus goods. The ultimate aim of this 'strategy of accumulation' was to reach a position where they had enough land and resources to produce cotton and eventually purchase slaves. These yeomen were risk-takers whose decision to migrate to the western frontier was the result of frustration at the lack of opportunity available to them in the Upper South areas of their birth.[37]

Slavery and whiteness were very important to these men and the opportunity to join the slaveholding ranks was a major motivation. Politics in the Lower South states proceeded vigorously and yeomen rarely allowed planters to have things their own way. Historian Edward E. Baptist depicts social relations as anything but easy in Middle Florida, and consensus – in the sense that all whites agreed on the basic principles of slavery and white male supremacy – did not prevent an intense and enduring battle for power. Planters, yeomen and poor whites competed robustly with one another. Frontier society in the Lower South was essentially a compromise between planters wanting to re-establish old hierarchies and non-slaveholders unwilling to allow them to do so. Yeomen 'cooperated with planters to keep down those deemed less than manly,' Baptist argues, 'women and the poorest of whites, but above all, African Americans'.[38]

Non-slaveholders in the Upper South were less restless and, while becoming more heavily involved with the market economy in the 1850s, adhered to traditional ways more closely than their migrant peers. They valued their independence above all else and cherished and fiercely defended their political rights. Moreover, an important geographical distinction must be made between yeomen in the upcountry and those in plantation areas, especially in the Upper South. Upcountry yeomen, living in more sparsely populated locations with lower numbers of slaves and plantations, were indeed more concerned with 'safety-first' agriculture, although, as Lacy K. Ford shows in his study of the South Carolinian upcountry, once those needs were satisfied, they were prepared to grow small amounts of cotton for sale. Yeomen like this were largely left to their own devices by state governments. They were willing to comply with planter rule as long as it did not impinge on their community priorities.[39]

Yeomen in plantation districts, living side-by-side with planters and slave-holders, were far more likely to concentrate their efforts on producing cotton. They most fully shared planters' racist attitudes towards blacks and were strongly supportive of the institution of slavery. The contrast between slave and free was acute in the Black Belt and the Lowcountry, where whites were reminded daily of the liberty they enjoyed. White unity was essential in maintaining control over the large numbers of blacks. Geographical proximity also increased the hegemony of the large slaveholders. Yeomen had frequent contact with planters, particularly if they planted cotton, and planters might display a paternalistic concern for their neighbours in the processing, transportation and sale of cotton, which could lessen conflict. They shared common forms of worship and planters held annual barbecues designed to ensure constituency support. While some planters, especially those in the Lowcountry, resented having to hold such events, they provided regular public displays of white male equality.

Away from the plantation areas, with fewer blacks, slavery and race were not really critical issues. Indeed, the yeoman outlook in upcountry sections of the Upper South was probably best characterised as being ambivalent toward slavery. Historians David Brown and Harold D. Tallant argue that a residual anti-slavery feeling existed in Piedmont, North Carolina and in parts of Kentucky, respectively, and William W. Freehling suggests the same for sections of the whole Upper South.[40] These were areas in which slavery was not central to the local economy, and consequently support for the planter regime was by no means unqualified. It would be an exaggeration, though, to think that large numbers of ordinary southerners in the upcountry were anti-slavery. There were a few abolitionists like Hinton Rowan Helper and Cassius M. Clay, but the vast majority of yeomen were extremely apprehensive about the prospect of abolition. Most believed freed slaves to be an undesirable and uncontrollable problem, and this was where the racial argument about inferior African American character was most influential.

Slavery guaranteed stability. Although upcountry yeomen were not always convinced of the peculiar institution's benefits, they were not prepared to sanction its demise and feared the consequences of emancipation. 'Were you sitting as the Southern Yeomen are,' wrote Alabamian D. H. Hundley, 'would you be pleased to see four millions of inferior blacks suddenly raised from a position of vassalage, and placed upon an equality with yourselves?' Whether yeomen fully accepted the tenets of biological racism has yet to be proven. Southern evangelical churches eventually accommodated slavery, but they continued to stress the common origins of mankind and rejected the idea of separate creation. Sermons emphasised the virtues of duty and hierarchy, encouraging yeomen to accept their place in the social order. Myths like the Curse of Ham possibly served to popularise the idea of blacks as irrevocably different, thereby having the same effect as scientific racism while adhering to a biblical interpretation. Why did ordinary whites need scientific racism, though? The vast majority of blacks were slaves and therefore inferior, fully explaining their place in society. As historian Bill Cecil-Fronsman notes, while 'blacks stayed in their places, most common whites did little to abuse blacks and did not spend a good deal of time dwelling on the alleged shortcomings of their characters'.[41] The process by which scientific racism was disseminated at the lower levels of southern society needs far more attention.

Masculine identity was also critical. It was gender as much as race that served to unite yeomen with wealthier slaveholders, especially in places like the Lowcountry. Historian Stephanie McCurry makes the strongest case for social consensus being generated through common feelings of patriarchal domination: 'as freemen in a world of dependents,' McCurry writes, yeomen shared 'a definition of manhood rooted in the inviolability of the household, the command of dependents, and the public prerogatives manhood conferred'. This message was frequently voiced in popular politics and also in the evangelical pulpits. It was a Presbyterian minister, though, not a Baptist or a Methodist, who was probably the foremost proponent of the message of social conservatism and the notion of a hierarchically ordained world in which blacks and women occupied a similarly inferior plane. James Henley Thornwell asserted that the master–slave relationship was placed 'on the same foot with the other relations of life' and was sanctioned by the Bible. 'We find masters exhorted in the same connection with husbands, parents and magistrates,' Thornwell declared, and 'slaves exhorted in the same connection with wives, children and subjects.'[42]

The key to yeomen support of slavery, in short, was their acceptance of slavery's economic and social utility. Slavery had to serve their interests. Georgia yeoman Benton Miller's diary entry in 1858 is revealing: 'It is the first time that I ever planted cotton for myself. I am making a commencement in life.' Having made this commitment, Miller allied himself with the slaveholding regime, whether consciously or unconsciously. This suggests that the Herrenvolk thesis needs modifying to reflect a more utilitarian notion of whiteness. Support for the planter regime was contingent upon slavery's usefulness to the yeomen. Peter Kolchin argues that many non-slaveholding whites actually had 'an economic stake in slavery' through family ties or connections to the plantation economy.[43] Put together with slaveholders, this group comprised approximately half of all white southerners. Notions of racial superiority followed conveniently from shared interests, but race was hardly enough to unify all whites in its own right – gender was probably equally significant. Geography was also crucial, isolating pockets of discontent and ensuring that planter rule rarely impinged directly on the rights of upcountry yeomen.

Poor whites, on the other hand, had a very different relationship with both planters and slaves. Herrenvolk democracy applied only very loosely to them, as, unlike yeomen, their economic stake in southern society was minimal and their prospects uncertain. Non-slaveowning, non-land-owning and often illiterate whites stood at the margins of the antebellum South. Some of the most exciting new scholarship focuses on those at the bottom of the social hierarchy. Poor whites had frequent interaction with slaves and free blacks, on a variety of levels: social, economic, criminal, sexual and religious. At a time when middling southerners probably moved closer towards slaveholders, poor whites seemingly moved in the opposite direction. The autobiography of Edward Isham, a poor white from Georgia, provides a fascinating insight into this group's squalid, transient and violent lifestyle, which centred around the grog shop. Isham was friends with slaves, free blacks and Indians, had frequent sexual relationships with different women of all kind, and was even hired as a labourer by a free black. Historian Martha Hodes shows that consensual interracial relationships common in the colonial era continued in the antebellum period on a less frequent basis. They were not unnoticed or always condoned, but existed with a degree of flexibility and toleration previously unrecognised. Race relations at the bottom of the social scale were far less rigid and much more multifarious than the orthodox interpretation suggests.[44]

Primary evidence concerning poor whites is rare, hampering understanding of this elusive group, but some important points are clear. Historian Charles C. Bolton convincingly refutes Frank Owsley's myth of the omnipotent southern yeoman. Owsley suggested that the vast majority of non-slaveholding whites were relatively prosperous farmers, not the poor white 'trash' that visitors to the Old South regularly noted. Bolton, in a seminal work, however, estimates that between 30 and 50 per cent of all southern whites were actually landless in 1860, and the majority were poor whites who must be distinguished from yeomen.[45] This group, living in upcountry and plantation areas, was forced to rent land from, or work for, wealthier southerners, or live a bare subsistence lifestyle, and their economic prospects were getting worse in the 1850s, especially in the Upper South. Work available to them was usually temporary and could entail labouring side-by-side with the enslaved.

These impoverished circumstances encouraged poor whites and slaves to seek mutually advantageous opportunities. One of the most innovative areas of recent historical inquiry about the South considers the significance of the informal economy, which existed in the colonial and revolutionary period but was at its height by the late antebellum period. Slaves traded with whites in a whole host of goods and services, some of the items, such as bales of cotton, being illicitly obtained, and we need to know more about the role of poor whites in this enterprise.[46] It is very difficult to calculate the scale of the informal economy with any precision, in particular the numbers and status of whites involved. However, the large amounts of property and, in some cases, the considerable sums of cash accumulated by slaves in the 1850s was surely only achievable by forming illicit partnerships with whites at times. Alcohol, typically prohibited by slaveholders, could only be obtained in this way. The more wily planters bought their bondspeople's produce themselves and an important distinction must be made between the informal economy sanctioned and facilitated by the master and clandestine transactions undertaken without permission.

The widely held notion of an antagonistic relationship between poor whites and blacks, summed up by the title of the slave song 'Rather be a Nigger than a Poor White Man', has been overturned in recent studies. Violence was always a possibility in black–poor white relations, but was not necessarily motivated by racial concerns, as is often assumed, because brawling was a pervasive aspect of lower-class white culture in general. Slaves had a low opinion of some poor whites – especially overseers and non-slaveholders who took part in slave patrols organised to police plantations – but viewed others in far more positive terms. Indeed, shared deprivation seems to have encouraged closer interaction, not mutual hatred. Grog shops, brothels and gambling houses paid very little attention to the racial divide demarcated by elite southerners. Poor whites and blacks (slave and free) drank, stole, played cards, ran away and slept together. Racial barriers were not inconsequential in this world but, as historian Tim Lockley puts it, they constituted 'lines in the sand' that 'were impermanent, movable, and vulnerable'. Racism between poor whites and blacks was 'more virulent and extreme' after the Civil War, not before it.[47]

The ways in which racial boundaries actually functioned in the Old South were not necessarily the ways in which planters proclaimed that they did. The success of southern society was facilitated by economic opportunities provided by expansion into the south-west in the early nineteenth century, opportunities that were available to all white men. The process of Indian removal provided a powerful stimulus to the idea of white supremacy and came at a time when scientific racism was rapidly growing in credibility. These factors militated against class resentment, even though planters were far more wealthy and powerful than other groups. However, some scholars of the American South have pushed the idea of antebellum white racial consensus too far. In spite of the best efforts of Josiah Nott and his peers, the concept and meaning of race was often ambiguous. As historian Michael O'Brien reminds us, 'the unstable complexities of the word, *race,* makes it easy to misread many antebellum writings, the more so as Southerners themselves did not always know what they meant by the word'. Race could be used interchangeably with group, class and nation. It would not be universally understood in physiological terms until later in the nineteenth century.[48]

The Old South was never wholly unified on the grounds of race. Class and gender remained crucial components of southern identity. Upcountry yeomen (especially in the Upper South) and poor whites mostly lived in different worlds to planters and middling slaveholders. The former were fiercely protective of their rights and can hardly be described as acquiescing to planter rule. It is difficult to see how the latter fit into the consensus paradigm at all: poor whites were looked down on by both yeomen and planters. It was the plantation districts that most closely approximated the pro-slavery ideal of a white man's republic. Yeomen there more regularly rubbed shoulders with planters, especially if they grew cotton, and they played an active role in the political process. Moreover, shared mastery of the household and of dependents, whether slaves, women or children, encouraged powerful feelings of white male equality. Nonetheless, class tensions remained. The image of racial unity, if not harmony, projected by the southern elite conceals as much as it reveals about white society in the Old South.

Notes

1. Thomas N. Ingersoll, 'Free Blacks in a Slave Society: New Orleans, 1718–1812', *William and Mary Quarterly,* 48 (April 1991), pp. 173–200.
2. Daniel H. Usner, Jr, *Indians, Settlers, and Slaves in a Frontier Exchange Economy: The Lower Mississippi Valley Before 1783* ((Chapel Hill: University of North Carolina Press, 1992), pp. 277–8.

3. John Hebron Moore, *The Emergence of the Cotton Kingdom of the Old South-West* (Baton Rouge: Louisiana State University Press, 1988), pp. 1–17.
4. Alexander McGillivray, cited in Colin G. Calloway, *The American Revolution in Indian Country: Crisis and Diversity in Native American Communities* (Cambridge: Cambridge University Press, 1995), p. 276.
5. Robert F. Berkhofer, Jr, *The White Man's Indian: Images of the Indian From Columbus to the Present* (New York: Random House, 1975), p. 134.
6. Thomas Jefferson (1785), cited in Ronald T. Takaki, *Iron Cages: Race and Culture in Nineteenth-Century America* (New York: Knopf, 1979), p. 58.
7. Thomas Jefferson, cited in Philip Weeks, *Farewell, My Nation: The American Indian and the United States, 1820–1790* (Arlington Heights, IL: Harlan Davidson, 1990), p. 12.
8. Paul Prucha, *American Indian Policy in the Formative Years: The Indian Trade and Intercourse Acts, 1790–1834* (Cambridge, MA: Harvard University Press, 1962); Henry Knox (1792), cited in Reginald Horsman, *Race and Manifest Destiny: The Origins of Racial Anglo-Saxonism* (Cambridge, MA: Harvard University Press, 1981), p. 107.
9. Alexander Saxton, *The Rise and Fall of the White Republic: Class Politics and Mass Culture in Nineteenth-Century America* (London: Verso, 1990), p. 42.
10. George Combe (1841), cited in Horsman, *Race and Manifest Destiny,* pp. 58–9.
11. Andrew Jackson, cited in Takaki, *Iron Cages,* pp. 95–6.
12. For an excellent, succinct summary of these adaptations, see Theda Perdue, 'Indians in Southern History', in Frederick E. Hoxie and Peter Iverson (eds), *Indians in American History,* 2nd edition: (Wheeling: Harlan Davidson, 1998) pp. 121–39.
13. Daniel F. Littlefield, *Africans and Creeks: From the Colonial Period to the Civil War* (Westport, CT: Greenwood Press, 1979) pp. 254–9; Theda Perdue, *Slavery and the Evolution of Cherokee Society, 1540–1866* (Knoxville: University of Tennessee Press, 1979), p. 98.
14. James H. Merrell, 'The Racial Education of the Catawba Indians', *Journal of Southern History,* 50 (August 1984), p. 380.
15. Theda Perdue, *'Mixed Blood Indians': Racial Construction in the Early South* (Athens: University of Georgia Press, 2003), pp. 70–1.
16. Theda Perdue and Michael D. Green (eds), *The Cherokee Removal* (Boston, MA: Bedford/St. Martin's, 2005).
17. Andrew Jackson (1830), cited in Horsman, *Race and Manifest Destiny,* p. 202; John Forsyth, cited in Harry L. Watson, *Liberty and Power: The Politics of Jacksonian America* (New York: Noonday Press, 1990), p. 110; Perdue, *'Mixed Blood Indians',* pp. 97–8; Horsman, *Race and Manifest Destiny,* p. 207.
18. Thomas Terrill and William Cooper, Jr, *The American South: A History* (New York: McGraw-Hill, 1996), p. 262; George M. Fredrickson, *The Black Image in*

the White Mind: The Debate on Afro-American Character and Destiny, 1817–1914 (New York: Harper and Row, 1971), p. 61.

19. William Stanton, *The Leopard's Spots: Scientific Attitudes Towards Race in America, 1815–1859* (Chicago: University of Chicago Press, 1960), p. 33; Samuel George Morton, *Crania Americana; or, A Comparative View of the Skulls of Various Aboriginal Nations of North And South America . . .* (Philadelphia: J. Pennington, 1839).
20. Reginald Horsman, *Josiah Nott of Mobile: Southerner, Physician, and Racial Theorist* (Baton Rouge: Louisiana State University Press, 1987), p. 170; Josiah Nott and George R. Gliddon, *Types of Mankind: Or, Ethnological Researches . . .* (Philadelphia: Lippincott & Grambo, 1854).
21. Horsman, *Race and Manifest Destiny*, p. 208.
22. *Charleston Medical Journal*, cited in George Stocking, *Race, Culture and Evolution* (New York: Free Press, 1968), p. 144; Samuel Cartwright (1861), in Drew Faust (ed.), *The Ideology of Slavery* (Baton Rouge: Louisiana State University Press, 1981), p. 15.
23. Bruce Dain, *A Hideous Monster of the Mind: American Race Theory in the Early Republic* (Cambridge, MA: Harvard University Press, 2002), p. 198.
24. William Lloyd Garrison (1831), cited in William E. Cain (ed.), *William Lloyd Garrison and the Fight Against Slavery* (Boston, MA: Bedford/St. Martin's, 1995), p. 72.
25. Paul Goodman, *Of One Blood: Abolitionism and the Origins of Racial Equality* (Berkeley: University of California Press, 1998).
26. Alison Freehling, *Drift Toward Dissolution: The Virginia Slavery Debate of 1831–1832* (Baton Rouge: Louisiana State University Press, 1982).
27. Gordon E. Finnie, 'The Antislavery Movement in the Upper South before 1840', *Journal of Southern History*, 35 (August 1969), pp. 319–42.
28. Elmina Foster, cited in Bill Cecil-Fronsman, *Common Whites: Class and Culture in Antebellum North Carolina* (Lexington: University Press of Kentucky, 1992), p. 96.
29. J. William Harris, *The Making of the American South: A Short History, 1500–1877* (Oxford: Blackwell, 2006), p. 144.
30. Drew Gilpin Faust, *James Henry Hammond and the Old South: A Design for Mastery* (Baton Rouge: Louisiana State University Press, 1982).
31. U. B. Phillips, 'The Central Theme of Southern History', *American Historical Review*, 34 (October 1928), pp. 30–43; W. J. Cash, *The Mind of the South* (New York: Alfred A. Knopf, 1941), p. 62.
32. Fredrickson, *Black Image*, pp. 94–5.
33. John B. Boles, *Black Southerners, 1619–1869* (Lexington: The University Press of Kentucky, 2003), p. 75; James M. McPherson, *Battle Cry of Freedom: The Civil War Era* (New York: Oxford University Press, 1988), p. 255; Kenneth M. Stampp, *The Peculiar Institution: Slavery in the Ante-Bellum South* (New York: Vintage Books, 1956), p. 38.

34. Eugene Genovese and Elizabeth Fox-Genovese, *Fruits of Merchant Capital: Slavery and Bourgeois Property in the Rise and Expansion of Capitalism* (Oxford: Oxford University Press, 1983), p. 263.
35. Frank L. Owsley, *Plain Folk of the Old South* (Baton Rouge: Louisiana State University Press, 1949).
36. For more on the market revolution and the historiographical problem of defining yeomen and their position within the South's class structure, see Louis Billington and David Brown, 'Yeomen and Yankees Across the Mason–Dixon Line: A Different Perspective on the Antebellum North/South Divide?', in C. A. van Minnen and S. L. Hilton (eds), *Frontiers and Boundaries in U.S. History* (Amsterdam: VU University Press, 2004), pp. 101–16. See also Harry L. Watson, 'Slavery and Development in a Dual Economy: The South and the Market Revolution', in Melvyn Stokes and Steven Conway (eds), *The Market Revolution in America: Social, Political, and Religious Expressions, 1800–1860* (Charlottesville: University Press of Virginia, 1996), pp. 43–73.
37. Bradley G. Bond, 'Herders, Farmers and Markets on the Inner Frontier: The Mississippi Piney Woods, 1850–1860', in Samuel C. Hyde (ed.), *Plain Folk of the South Revisited* (Baton Rouge: Louisiana State University Press, 1997), pp. 73–99.
38. Edward E. Baptist, *Creating an Old South: Middle Florida's Plantation Frontier Before the Civil War* (Chapel Hill: University of North Carolina Press, 2002), p. 282.
39. Lacy K. Ford, *The Origins of Southern Radicalism: The South Carolina Upcountry 1800–1860* (New York: Oxford University Press, 1988).
40. David Brown, *Southern Outcast: Hinton Rowan Helper and The Impending Crisis of the South* (Baton Rouge: Louisiana State University Press, 2006); Harold D. Tallant, *Evil Necessity: Slavery and Political Culture in Antebellum Kentucky* (Lexington: University Press of Kentucky, 2003); William W. Freehling, *The South Vs. the South: How Anti-Confederate Southerners Shaped the Course of the Civil War* (New York: Oxford University Press, 2001).
41. D. H. Hundley, *Social Relations in our Southern States*, edited by William J. Cooper, Jr, (Baton Rouge: Louisiana State University Press, 1979), p. 219; Cecil-Fronsman, *Common Whites*, p. 81.
42. Stephanie McCurry, *Masters of Small Worlds: Yeoman Households, Gender Relations, and the Political Culture of the Antebellum South Carolina Low Country* (New York: Oxford University Press, 1995), pp. 304, 210–11.
43. J. William Harris, 'Portrait of a Small Slaveholder: The Journal of Benton Miller', *Georgia Historical Quarterly*, 74 (Spring 1990), p. 1; Peter Kolchin, *American Slavery, 1619–1877* (London: Penguin, 1993), pp. 180–1.
44. Scott P. Culclasure and Charles C. Bolton (eds), *The Confessions of Edward Isham: A Poor White Life of the Old South* (Athens: University of Georgia Press, 1998); Martha Hodes, *White Women, Black Men: Illicit Sex in the Nineteenth-Century South* (New Haven: Yale University Press, 1997).

45. Charles C. Bolton, *Poor Whites of the Antebellum South: Tenants and Laborers in Central North Carolina and Northeast Mississippi* (Durham, NC: Duke University Press, 1994), p. 5.
46. Jeff Forret, *Race Relations at the Margins: Slaves and Poor Whites in the Antebellum Southern* (Baton Rouge: Louisiana State University Press, 2006) promises to address this issue, but unfortunately was published too late for discussion here.
47. Timothy James Lockley, *Lines in the Sand: Race and Class in Lowcountry Georgia, 1750–1860* (Athens: University of Georgia Press, 2001), pp. 165, 168.
48. Michael O'Brien, *Conjectures of Order: Intellectual Life in the Old South, 1810–1860, Volume 1* (Chapel Hill: University of North Carolina Press, 2004), p. 250.

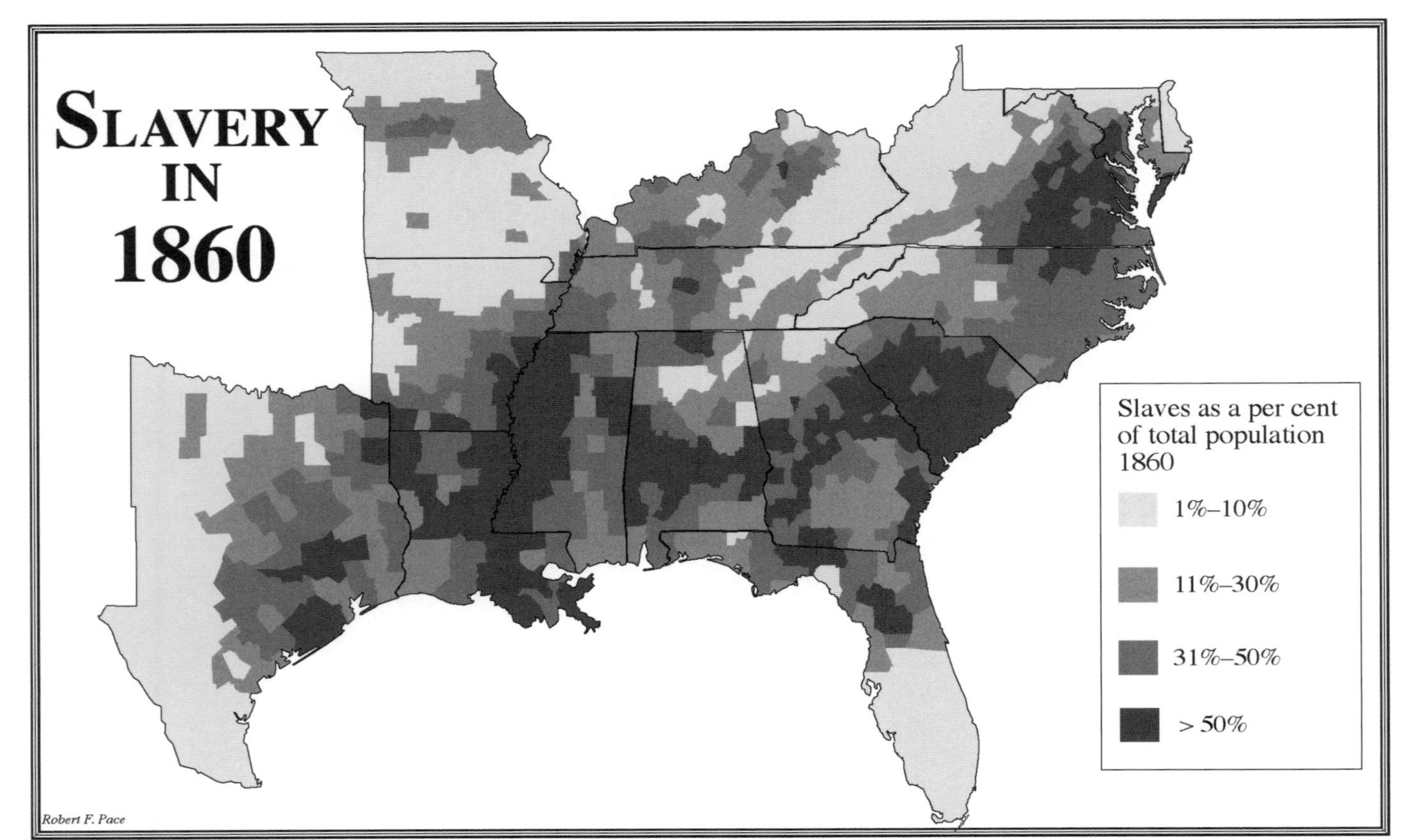
SLAVERY
IN
1860
Slaves as a per cent
of total population
1860
1%–10%
11%–30%
31%–50%
> 50%
Robert F. Pace

Chapter 5

THE PARADOXICAL INSTITUTION: ANTEBELLUM SLAVERY

Peter J. Parish describes southern slavery as 'the paradoxical institution' because 'its guiding principle was that slaves were property, but its everyday practice demonstrated the impossibility of living up to, or down to, that denial of the slave's humanity'.[1] African Americans did their very best to assert their agency in the face of overwhelming odds as the plantation system once again tightened its grip in the nineteenth century. Slaves sought to take advantage of the owner's reliance on their labour as far as they could. Some historians describe a paternalistic system of accommodation and resistance developing in the antebellum period; others see a distinctive variant of modern capitalism based on rewards and harsh punishments.

Slavery in the Old South was also paradoxical because of its exceptional diversity, as bondspeople laboured in a wide variety of settings. Like non-slaveholding whites, the lifestyles of the enslaved were heavily shaped by geographical and economic circumstances: the type of work and the size of plantation, as well as by regional variations such as those between the Upper and Lower South, and between plantation district and upcountry. At any one time, approximately three-quarters of slaves worked in the fields, but they were also blacksmiths, carpenters, carriage drivers, factory workers, boat hands, musicians, nurses, cooks, seamstresses and house servants. Moreover, the experience of field slaves was hardly monolithic. Cultivating the great staples of cotton, sugar, tobacco and rice demanded different types of skills, and planters grew other crops such as wheat and corn. Planters continually experimented with different work regimes in the hope of improving their harvest. They could do nothing about the vagaries of the weather or the changing of the seasons, however, and slaves carried out different tasks at different times of the year. Most plantations were hives of activity, providing for the many needs of the community, from basic food supplies to clothing and housing.

The antebellum white mind, however, generally failed to recognise African American diversity as blackness was synonymous with a servile condition. The dominant stereotype, both North and South, was of the black slave toiling in the hot sun. The connection between blackness and slavery was crucial in solidifying the doctrine of biological racism in the nineteenth century. To be sure, the ethnologists should not be discounted either, for their work conceptualised race in a powerful scientific discourse. The tentative rationalising of blacks as physically and mentally inferior to the white race that was apparent in the eighteenth century was decisively presented, and widely accepted, as fact by the mid-1800s. It is questionable how plausible such ideas would have been without the existence and indeed flourishing of slavery in the southern states. The African American view of race is exceedingly elusive. Nonetheless, black responses to scientific racism and the assertion of innate white supremacy and black inferiority must be considered in order to appreciate fully the dynamics of race in the antebellum South.

THE SECOND MIDDLE PASSAGE

The official closure of the international slave trade to the United States in 1808 precipitated a transformation in American slavery. Slaves moved from the Upper to the Lower South in huge numbers. The decline of tobacco in the Chesapeake and the subsequent switch to grain farming left a surplus of slaves coveted by traders for the high prices they fetched in the Southwest. The scale of this movement needs stressing. For many years, historians were uncertain exactly how many African Americans were 'sold down the river' (a phrase growing out of the forced displacement of slaves travelling by boat along the Mississippi River to be sold in New Orleans). The most recent view contends that the numbers involved in this trade were vast, overturning contemporary myths promoted by slaveholders (and the views of earlier historians) that only troublesome slaves were sold away while the majority migrated to the Southwest with their owners. Between 1820 and 1860, a minimum number of 875,000 slaves relocated from the Upper to the Lower South. Between 60 and 70 per cent were sold via the domestic slave trade, the rest migrating with owners or being sent to plantations owned by their master in the Deep South.[2]

Ira Berlin argues that the expansion of slavery in the antebellum period was no less than a second Middle Passage, 'a mighty torrent'. The migration generations, as Berlin calls them, faced as severe a test of their character and fortitude as the Africans taken for sale in the New World in the seventeenth and eighteenth centuries. A similar demographic profile united the migration generations with their forebears, as the young and the healthy were most sought after. Kinship ties were mostly ignored; a planter migrating from

Maryland was advised that 'it is better to buy *none in families,* but to *select only choice, first rate, young hands from 14 to 25 years of age,* (buying no children of aged negroes)'. The migration generations were torn from communities and settled routines in the Upper South to undertake an exhausting journey to an uncertain future in the Lower South. Berlin might exaggerate slightly here, but he persuasively suggests that pioneering slaves in the Deep South – Florida, Alabama, Mississippi and Louisiana – faced arduous, even perilous, conditions as they carved out new plantations in the wilderness.[3]

Slave trading was seasonal. The greatest demand from the Lower South came in the fall months, as planters used their profits to invest for the next year. Bondspeople sometimes travelled by boat, along the Mississippi or by sea from ports such as Norfolk, to New Orleans (and were later transported by rail), but the majority walked in organised groups called coffles. G. W. Featherstonhaugh, an English visitor to the South, witnessed about 300 slaves in 1843 bound for Natchez 'who had bivouacked the previous night *in chains* in the woods' and were getting ready for their continuing journey on the banks of the New River in Virginia. 'The female slaves were, some of them, sitting on logs of wood, whilst others were standing, and a great many little black children were warming themselves at the fires of the bivouac. In front of them all, and prepared for the march, stood, in double files, about two hundred male slaves, *manacled and chained to each other*.'[4] As ever, white southerners were fearful of large groups of slaves (although the average coffle was much smaller than the one Featherstonhaugh encountered) and those marching south were carefully supervised by white drivers. Chaining blacks together increased travelling time and exacerbated the physical exertion, as progress was made at a rate of approximately twenty miles a day. Traders would meander rather than go direct, picking up new recruits and supplies from farms and towns along the way. Most bondspeople were sold in the fall and winter months, so bad weather added to the already considerable hardships of a journey that proved fatal to many.

The first wave of the migration generations, already weakened by their journey, had to literally provide for themselves while the plantation took shape on the frontier in the early 1800s. Clearing the land was the first stage before any crops could be planted. Malarial diseases were a constant hazard in the new environment, especially as the prime locations were often situated in river bottoms infested with mosquitoes. Owners would rarely be present at this stage, hiring overseers in their place. They would also hire slaves, initially, for the most dangerous work rather than risk their own. A complex process of bargaining ensued as established work patterns were renegotiated. It was many years before garden plots were once again routinely allocated to slaves, something that had previously been common. The intensive labour needed to build plantations in the Lower South forced masters to push their slaves as hard as they could, often working seven days a week, which was resisted by the enslaved. It was some time before black drivers re-emerged in the cotton South as, at a stroke, the migration generations were torn from the plantation hierarchy that they were used to in the Upper South. Whether previously privileged or not, all slaves joined the rank and file in the Lower South. Masters and overseers directed operations, ensuring a furious pace was maintained. Ira Berlin suggests that master–slave relations were in a state of 'anarchy' at this point.[5] The opportunity to escape to the woods and the swamps, and also to Native American tribes, was taken by these first arrivals for relief from the punishing demands placed on them.

Gradually, though, order was established and communities became more stable as the frontier moved further west (where the pattern of master–slave confrontation was repeated in 'new' frontier settlements). Planters bought the best lands in prime locations and controlled fledgling government in the new states. This quickly enabled them to establish the legality of slavery in new territories and use the political process to aid in the expansion of the cotton kingdom. Yeomen and poor whites also followed, usually having to be content with plots in the upcountry. Nonetheless, the profits to be made by selling cotton were immense and white southerners enjoyed unprecedented opportunities no matter what their background, bringing new miseries for African Americans.

The threat, and the reality, of sale was a defining characteristic of the migration generations. Concentrating solely on the logistics of the domestic trade conceals the emotional trauma endured by the enslaved. All bondspeople dreaded being sold, but moving from the Upper to the Lower South was particularly frightening. The prospect of being taken from friends and family was bad enough, but faced with a choice of relocation within the same state (and hopefully a few miles away, as masters often sold to friends or to family members who lived close by) or the long journey to the Gulf states, there was no question which was preferable. Slaves not only feared working conditions in the Lower South, which had a reputation for being brutal, but they also knew they would effectively be leaving for ever. The chorus of a slave song from the 1830s captures that sense of foreboding:

> Old debble Lousy Anna,
> dat scarecrow fer po' nigger,
> Where de sugar cane grow to pine trees,
> An' de pine tree turns to sugar.[6]

These concerns were not misplaced: the unfavourable balance of males to females on sugar plantations, and the relentless physical exertion, made Louisiana particularly unattractive, as will be discussed in more detail below. Those lucky enough not to be sold were hardly unaffected. They continually had to pick up the pieces of broken families and communities.

Heart-wrenching stories are common in slave autobiographies, emphasising the instability of bondage: any slave could be sold at any time. Sources written by ex-slaves might be suspected of bias, as they were published to influence the public debate over slavery, sometimes with the help of abolitionists. The northern public was undoubtedly shocked by callous tales of the break-up of slave families, especially the sale of children from their mothers. There are too many other sources written by the southern elite, however, that suggest sale was a common practice, and despite strong paternalist rhetoric, many owners 'speculated' in slaves, selling when the price was high. The southern myth was that slave traders were Yankees and men of low character; the reality was that buying and selling was a regular activity.

Sale of family and friends was the worst predicament confronting those held in bondage. Frances Kemble, mistress on the Lowcountry plantation of Pierce Butler, was extremely distressed when a slave told her of the impending sale of her husband. Kemble's discomfort was nothing, though, in comparison to that of the male slave in question:

> Joe, the young man, poor Psyche's husband, raving almost in a state of frenzy, and in a voice broken with sobs and almost inarticulate with passion, reiterating his determination never to leave this plantation, never to go to Alabama, never to leave his old father and mother, his poor wife and children, and dashing his hat, which he was wringing like a cloth in his hands, upon the ground, he declared he would kill himself if he was compelled to follow Mr. K[ing].[7]

This was a scene repeated across the South during the antebellum period. Indeed, owners wanting to avoid problems would not tell slaves until the last minute that they, or their family members, were leaving. Sometimes it would only be after returning from the fields that the awful sale of a loved one was revealed.

Historian Walter Johnson, borrowing a term from escaped slave J. W. C. Pennington, writes of the '"chattel principle": any slave's identity might be disrupted as easily as a price could be set and a piece of paper passed from one hand to another'.[8] Not only was the threat of sale a constant; Johnson argues that slaves were encouraged to internalise the notion that they were commodities with a set price. Slave bodies were groomed and shaped to realise their maximum potential value on the market. From childhood, slaves were commodified in the eyes of owners who fed and exercised their property in the expectation of a high return. Males were prized for their physical prowess and encouraged to take part in athletic pursuits. Female beauty, usually associated with a lighter skin colour in the white mind, was deemed equally valuable, as was the potential for bearing children. Planters used terms such as 'choice', 'likely' and 'sound' as they cast their eyes over human merchandise.

The extent to which slaves actually internalised such identities, if any, is uncertain. William Dusinberre's bleak portrayal of slave life on rice plantations suggests that they did: 'Powerless, undervalued, despised, many slaves came to esteem themselves for some of the same qualities whites valued in them.' Dusinberre quotes Frances Kemble's comment that slave women had 'a most distinct and perfect knowledge of their value to their owners as property'. The commodification thesis emphasises that slavery was, fundamentally, the sale and possession of human bodies. Slaves could be bought to order by professional traders and delivered to buyers in the Lower South, but most were forced to endure the ignominy of the auction. Unlike the buying and selling of horses or cattle, however, potential buyers prodded and poked slaves, in the most intimate areas, seeking out imperfections and evidence of punishment that could make a difference of hundreds of dollars in price. In this way, slaveholders 'read' slave bodies, and by so doing violated private space in a way that would never have been allowed in free society – one of the less obvious but truly humiliating aspects of bondage. The emphasis on the physical was crucial. Reading an ethnological tract might have shaped ideas about race; frequent inspections in the slave pens, where slaveholders took pride in their 'knowledge' of the differing qualities of whiteness and blackness, was decisive. Race only makes sense in specific historical contexts. Walter Johnson is surely right in arguing that 'at no site was race more readily given daily shape than in the slave market'.[9]

THE CONTOURS OF ANTEBELLUM SLAVERY

The enslaved were primarily bought and sold for their labour. Admittedly, this was not the only reason for buying slaves, as cultural historians have recently emphasised. Light-skinned 'fancy' women were much sought after in the New Orleans slave markets to fulfil white sexual desires, for example. Sometimes troublesome slaves (identified by whipping scars on their backs) were deliberately bought in order to enhance slaveholder reputations as superior masters who could break the most recalcitrant bondsmen.[10] By far the greatest number of transactions, however, surely reflected the imperative of acquiring more 'hands', as slaveholders called them.

The geographical dispersal of slaves was determined by the differing soils and growing seasons of the South that favoured particular crops. Cotton was centred in the Black Belt stretching from Georgia through Alabama and Mississippi to Louisiana and, by the 1850s, Arkansas and Texas. Rice and indigo plantations continued to be profitable in the swampy, coastal areas of South Carolina and Georgia, while sugar thrived in southern Louisiana. Tobacco plantations were still found in Virginia, predominantly in the Piedmont, and also in North Carolina and Kentucky (where hemp flourished as well). Other staple crops such as corn, maize and wheat were grown on farms and plantations, the latter becoming the most important cash crop in parts of Virginia and North Carolina. Industrial slaves were predominately located in the Upper South and, by the 1850s, more and more slaves were 'hired' out in the region, granting some of them a 'quasi-free' status.

The experiences of slaves and slaveholders were different in the Upper and Lower South. There were far more slaves in the Lower South, generally considered by the antebellum era to be the states below North Carolina. In 1860, South Carolina and Mississippi were the only southern states with black majorities (57.2 per cent and 55.2 per cent of the respective populations being slave). Georgia (43.7 per cent), Florida (44 per cent), Alabama (45.1 per cent) and Louisiana (46.9 per cent) were not far behind, however. Most likely the frontier states of Texas (30.2 per cent) and Arkansas (25.5 per cent) would have eventually reached a slave population similar to that of the other Deep South states, had the Civil War not intervened. The *mentalité* of masters and slaves was that of a mature slave society, as defined by Ira Berlin in Chapter 1. Most slaves in the Lower South lived on large plantations (by American standards), which encouraged a strong African American culture and facilitated the growth of communities. The presence of large numbers of slaves fostered white solidarity, bridging the class divide between planter and non-slaveholder.

The eight states of the Upper South had nothing like the same concentration of bondspeople by 1860. About a third of North Carolina's and Virginia's population were enslaved, a quarter of Tennessee's, and a fifth of Kentucky's. The proportion of slaves in Maryland was just 12.7 per cent and in Missouri 9.7 per cent. A tiny 1.6 per cent of Delaware's population was enslaved. In parts of the Upper South, then, slavery seemed to be naturally declining, or had never really been that important, suggesting that slavery was in terminal decline in some places. Large numbers of free blacks in the Upper South added to this perception, as will be discussed below.

The distribution of slaves within each state was also uneven. In plantation areas, there were typically more slaves than whites. In the South Carolina and Georgia Lowcountry, in the Black Belt and on the lower banks of the Mississippi River, for example, the proportion of black to white reached as high as two-thirds. In Upper South states with sizeable slave populations, the peculiar institution was located in sub-regions such as eastern North Carolina and Virginia, and middle and western Tennessee. Slavery was not so economically important outside of these slaveholding sections. Planters in areas with the heaviest concentration of slaves would lead the South out of the Union in the secession crisis. South Carolina, Mississippi and Georgia produced nearly half the total cotton yield in 1860 and possessed a third of the total number of American slaves. It is unsurprising that they were the first, second and fourth southern states, respectively, to secede in 1860–61.

The vast majority of antebellum slaves – 1,815,000 out of a total number of 3,204,313 in 1850 – worked on cotton plantations. Short-staple cotton was the main export in the antebellum period, commanding consistently high prices in industrialising countries such as Great Britain, where textiles was a key industry. Between 1800 and 1860, cotton accounted for approximately half of the United States' total exports, boosting the northern economy as much as the southern, as the great shipping, insurance and finance companies were located in the North. Cotton, like tobacco, could be grown by small farmers, in contrast to sugar and rice that benefited from economies of scale necessitating large numbers of hands. In 1850, about 350,000 slaves cultivated tobacco, 150,000 sugar, 125,000 rice and 60,000 hemp.[11] Rice and sugar brought fabulous wealth to planters, who were some of the richest men in the world.

Completing and complicating this picture were free blacks, slaves in urban areas and industrial slaves, groups that tended to move closer towards one another during the antebellum period. There were 261,918 southern free blacks in 1860, overwhelmingly located in the Upper South and in southern cities, of which the vast majority traced their lineage to the post-revolutionary generation. Restrictions placed on free blacks in the early nineteenth century became more intensive over the decades. New laws made it difficult to be manumitted and remain within state and many civil rights, such as suffrage, were taken away. At the same time, free blacks were required to pay more tax, a move designed to encourage their migration out of the South. A small number of free blacks owned their own businesses, and an even smaller number were planters – a curious anomaly in the Old South. Some free blacks, mostly light-skinned, sought to distance themselves from the enslaved. The 'free people of color' in New Orleans had a long history of independence, were well educated and had strong links with elite white society, a legacy of the French and the Spanish. The exclusive Brown Fellowship Society in Charleston, largely composed of black slaveholders, refused membership to any African American formerly connected with slavery. Most southern free blacks, however, were poor and tried their best to be inconspicuous, not least because there was a constant danger of being kidnapped into slavery. They could not adopt the aggressive abolitionist stance of their northern counterparts. Covertly, though, they did what they could, forging links with the slave community (which usually included friends and family members) and harbouring runaways.[12]

There were perhaps 140,000 bondspeople in urban areas and 200,000 industrial slaves by the 1850s, although figures are unreliable. Urban slaves were often on lease from plantations and farms, and enjoyed something of a quasi-free status. This was especially true in the Upper South as plantation slavery declined. As a result, more and more bondspeople were hired out, and some even managed to agree to a yearly fee with their owners in return for their effective autonomy. It was once again possible for the most industrious and determined blacks to buy themselves and their kin out of bondage. Industrial slaves like Sam Williams at Buffalo Forge, Virginia, became so indispensable that dealings with their owner could hardly be described as typical of the master–slave relationship. American slavery proved highly adaptable; 'industrial capitalists could quite advantageously combine wage labor and slave labor', maintains historian T. Stephen Whitman.[13]

Recent studies of antebellum Richmond have confirmed what earlier works on Baltimore and New Orleans pointed towards: race relations in urban areas were fluid and anything but fixed. Lower-class districts housed an incredibly diverse population of slaves, free blacks, immigrants from many different European countries and northerners, in addition to non-elite southern whites. The judicial system struggled to define who was black and who was white in such circumstances. As was the case in the eighteenth century, it proved remarkably difficult to enforce the colour line in southern cities.[14]

Indeed, the contrast between the urban and rural South was immense by the antebellum period. Historian Jonathan Daniel Wells has recently suggested that a southern middle class emerged in the urban South by the 1850s. Professionals working outside of the plantation economy – 'storekeepers, bankers, clerks, teachers, doctors, editors, ministers, and their families' – sharing a distinctive reform agenda, made up as much as 10 per cent of the white male population, Wells asserts. It is too early to tell what impact this radical challenge to the planter–yeomen–poor white paradigm, outlined in the previous chapter, will have. It does serve to emphasise, however, that norms and practices thought to be universal across the antebellum South often played out very differently in the big cities.

WORK, CULTURE AND SOCIETY

Solomon Northup, a free black kidnapped into bondage in 1841, laboured on both cotton and sugar plantations, providing a good insight into the burdens endured by slaves in the Lower South. Cotton requires moderate rainfall, a long growing season and becomes extremely labour intensive at harvest time. From the sowing of seeds in April, to hoeing and thinning in the summer, to picking that began in late August, there was plenty to keep slaves occupied. The gang system was the norm on cotton plantations. Northup described how 'the overseer or driver follows the slaves on horseback with a whip'. Anyone failing to keep up with the fastest hoer leading from the front was punished: 'if one falls behind or is a moment idle, he is whipped'. Each slave was expected to work as hard as they could: 'When a new hand, one unaccustomed to the business, is sent for the first time into the field, he is whipped up smartly, and made for the day to pick as fast as he possibly can.' Having set a standard – the amount of cotton picked by each slave was weighed every night – anyone falling 'short' would receive a whipping. 'No matter how fatigued and weary he may be' leaving the fields, 'a slave never approaches the gin-house with his basket of cotton but with fear.' The working day usually lasted from first light to dusk, although at times Northup worked by moonlight. Some breaks were allowed during the day, but slaves did 'not dare to stop . . . until the order to halt is given by the driver'. Before being allowed to go to bed, daily chores had to be completed, such as feeding the animals, cutting wood and grinding corn.[15]

Northup considered himself to be a mediocre cotton picker but much more skilled with sugar. He was hired out by his owner to a sugar planter at a cost of $1 a day and 'held the lead row . . . leading a gang of from fifty to a hundred hands'. Planting commenced in January, as sugar had a longer growing season than cotton. Delicate precision was required, with three gangs working together. The first gang 'draws the cane from the rick, or stack, cutting the top and flags from the stalk'. The second gang placed the cane in the ground, putting 'two stalks side by side in such a manner that joints will occur'. The third gang covered the stalks to a 'depth of three inches.' After that, the fields were hoed at least three times, and the cane usually ripened by October. Sugar planters anxiously hoped to avoid frost which was potentially ruinous. Unlike cotton, sugar processing was more troublesome than its growing. The 'grinding season' from October to January was notorious for its intensity, as the cutting and transporting of cane to the mill had to be intricately synchronised to allow round-the-clock production. 'The carts in which the cane is brought from the field as fast as it is cut, are unloaded at the sides of the shed', wrote Northup, giving some idea of the murderous pace of activity. Slave children placed the cane onto the equivalent of a modern conveyer belt. Steam rollers squeezed the juice into boiling hot copper vats, making the refineries a particularly nasty environment. The juice was collected in a reservoir and processed through 'five filterers' to eliminate impurities. After boiling, it was collected in wooden coolers that allowed the molasses to escape through sieve bottoms, leaving, eventually, 'white or loaf sugar'.[16]

The close proximity of sugar planters to the New Orleans slave markets made it easier to purchase a predominately male labour force, and their ability to do so was critical. Sugar required large numbers of slaves who effectively worked all year round. Only the young, fit and preferably male could cope with sugar's physical demands. The American slave population naturally increased at a rate of approximately 25 per cent each decade of the antebellum period, but this was not the case on sugar plantations, where numbers actually decreased. Various factors explain this phenomenon. The ratio of men to women was extremely unfavourable in the cane world, being approximately two-thirds to a third among newly imported slaves.[17] This, combined with a gruelling labour process in a potentially lethal disease environment causing under-nourishment and ill-health, left the chances of successful conception, healthy pregnancies and the survival of infants much reduced. The dread slaves felt about Louisiana seems well founded, although slaves on the state's cotton plantations (north of sugar country) were not nearly so badly off, living and working in similar conditions to cotton slaves across the South. As historian Michael Tadman concludes, the 'plantation crop was the essential influence in determining patterns of natural increase and decrease . . . sugar planting systematically brought together a lethal combination of factors that persistently and almost inevitably produced natural decrease among slaves'.[18]

Such a depressing scenario begs the question why would slaveholders allow this to happen, when it was in their interests to maintain a healthy and productive workforce? Moreover, how were African Americans motivated to labour in such conditions – purely by the power of the lash? These important questions have concentrated the minds of historians for decades, particularly as there is near-unanimous agreement that accompanying the profound structural transformation of American slavery in the antebellum decades was an equally important psychological and emotional shift. Historian Willie Lee Rose terms it 'the Domestication of Domestic Slavery'. With the closing of the international slave trade and slavery's centrality confirmed after the Virginia emancipation debates of 1832, southern slaveholders elevated paternalism as the single most important explanation of their position and responsibilities. The paternalism argument was evident in the eighteenth century but reached its apogee in the nineteenth, as planters loudly proclaimed the better treatment of slaves. Bondspeople were recognised as individuals entitled to certain rights and expectations. The worst excesses of colonial slave codes were reformed, although this provided in practice but a small check on the coercive power of the owner. Indeed, paternalism was not something that really lay within the law at all – it was self-generated by individual slaveholders who prided themselves on rearing a contented work-force.[19]

Planter sources and pro-slavery tracts reject the idea of a coercive master–slave relationship, portraying the owner's role as one of Christian stewardship of the family, white and black. The introduction to *Cotton is King* (1860), probably the most important defence of slavery in the antebellum period, put it this way:

> Slavery is the duty and obligation of the slave to labor for the mutual benefit of both master and slave, under a warrant to the slave of protection, and a comfortable subsistence, under all circumstances. . . . The master, as the head of the system, has a right to the obedience and labor of the slave, but the slave has also his mutual rights in the master; the right of protection, the right of counsel and guidance, the right of subsistence, the right of care and attention in sickness and old age.

This statement nicely captures antebellum paternalism as projected by planters. Pro-slavery theorist Henry Hughes even used the term 'Warranteeism' in preference to slavery because American slaves were granted fundamental rights, he insisted, rights that were denied to other slaves in different times and different places. [20]

Planter rhetoric should not be taken at face value, though, and there are three differing but connected elements of antebellum paternalism. First, paternalism was master-class ideology – a set of ideas justifying the power and position of the elite that underpinned the southern defence of slavery. Second, it reflected the self-image of individual planters and slaveholders. Many slaveholders did believe that they 'cared for' their slaves, and the material conditions of slavery probably did improve in the antebellum era. It has even been suggested that the American 'slave diet was not only adequate, it actually exceeded modern (1964) recommended daily levels of the chief nutrients'.[21] The benefits applied unevenly, however. Sugar slaves lived in particularly arduous circumstances, as we have seen, and conditions in the rice fields were also generally considered to be worse than those on cotton plantations. Morality rates were higher for sugar and rice slaves, for example, when compared to cotton slaves. Even so, sugar and rice planters considered themselves no less paternal because their slaves died in greater numbers. The rice-planting Manigault family of South Carolina blamed slaves for their weak constitutions, believing 'that the morally and physically irresponsible brought sickness upon themselves'. Refusing to heed plentiful evidence to the contrary, notes historian Jeffrey Robert Young, 'the Manigaults continued to believe that African-American slaves were thriving under the benevolent guardianship of concerned lowcountry masters'.[22] Even though death stalked the cane and rice worlds, masters rarely held themselves accountable for it.

This kind of paternalism went further than just provisions, though. Masters attempted to control all aspects of bondage, from marriage to religion to morality, with ominous implications for the enslaved. Often mistaken for kindliness, the dynamics of paternalism incorporated punishment, duty and instruction as much as benevolence, reminiscent of the Victorian concept of 'spare the rod and spoil the child'. The plantation regime thus became more invasive as it simultaneously reformed its worst excesses. The African American was also permanently infantilised in the mind of the slaveholder. As Willie Lee Rose puts it, 'blacks were categorized as a special and different kind of humanity, as lesser humans in a dependency assumed to be perpetual'. Considered 'luckless, unfortunate barbarians' in the eighteenth century, they became 'children expected never to grow up' in the nineteenth, reinforcing the idea of an irrevocable racial divide between blacks and whites. Master–slave relations were predicated on racial superiority and inferiority. Travellers coming south of the Mason–Dixon line sometimes commented on the lack of racial hostility they found toward blacks but, as traveller E. R. Sullivan suggests, this was merely a difference in emphasis: 'in the South he is sometimes a pet dog, whereas in the North he is always a cur, kicked and booted on every occasion'.[23]

The third and most controversial element of antebellum southern paternalism is identified by Eugene D. Genovese as the reciprocal rights and privileges negotiated by owners and slaves as a natural function of the labour process. Masters broke down black solidarity by encouraging slaves to identify with their values, fostering a close relationship based on the dependence of each individual on the owner. This created 'a fragile bridge' between both sides, forcing the master to recognise slave humanity. The slave's labour was considered 'a legitimate return to their masters for protection', but this was not how slaves saw it.[24] What owners took as mutual obligations, slaves quickly assumed as rights. In return for their labour, slaves expected to be compensated in a variety of ways. This was not planter benevolence but the minimum that they deserved. Genovese depicts a dialectical process of accommodation and resistance. Slaves alternately did as they were told, if demands were considered legitimate, but were more obstinate over unfair requests. While outright resistance was rare, they would work poorly and slowly – leaving weeds in the ground, breaking tools, feigning illness, running away – pressurising masters to accede to their wishes, such as task work rather than gang. Owners resigned themselves to the fact that their bondspeople would not work diligently without constant supervision and the simultaneous use of rewards and punishments.

The debate over paternalism is inseparably linked to questions over the wider significance of the slave mode of production. Did the absence of wage labour and the failure to industrialise like the antebellum North make the Old South an essentially reactionary, pre-modern society, more reminiscent of the feudal Middle Ages than other nineteenth-century western societies? Or was slavery simply a peculiar form of capitalism, with southern planters just as acquisitive and 'modern' as their counterparts elsewhere? These two dichotomous views of the antebellum South have slugged it out for nearly half a century. Eugene D. Genovese, the chief protagonist in this debate as in so many others concerning the slave South, boldly stated in 1961 that planters had 'an aristocratic, antibourgeois spirit with values and mores that emphasized family and status, had its code of honor, aspired to luxury, leisure and accomplishment'. He did not dispute that planters intended to yield a profit, but insisted that they 'recoiled at the notion that profit is the goal of life'.[25] For the last half-century, Genovese has refined this interpretation, in conjunction with Elizabeth Fox-Genovese. He has become an elusive target for his critics, who tend to attack earlier, less subtle formulations.

In contrast, Robert William Fogel argues that antebellum slavery was a capitalist enterprise. Planters gathered economic intelligence, responded to price fluctuations and were primarily motivated by considerations of profit and loss in 'a flexible, highly developed form of capitalism'. A recent study of the South's wealthiest planters amplifies this view, showing just how widely the elite invested its money in a surprising variety of pursuits: 'large slaveholders, both in their economic motivation and behaviour and in their family and inheritance practices, exhibited values little different from their free-state counterparts'.[26] Fogel controversially portrays slaves as being imbued with the Protestant work ethic: they worked hard because they were rewarded for doing so. 'In the *Time on the Cross* version of slavery,' Peter J. Parish observes, 'the carrot largely replaces the stick, and the great emphasis is placed on the array of incentives offered to slaves.'[27] This position is not entirely at odds with that of Genovese, who in recent work accepts the growing commercial spirit and the planters' move towards modernity in the later antebellum decades. Genovese insists, though, that the basic master–slave relation was not capitalist.[28]

James Oakes squarely refutes Genovese, emphasising the backbone of southern society as acquisitive, middling slaveholders – not elite planters. Most significantly, Oakes interprets capitalism and paternalism as being at odds with one another: 'intense devotion to the capitalistic spirit of accumulation had done much to diminish the influence of paternalistic ideals within the slaveholding class. . . . This was the contradiction that rendered paternalism so anachronistic to the nineteenth-century South.'[29] Taking a slightly different tack, William Dusinberre is equally critical of Genovese, preferring a 'system of punishments, allowances, and privileges' to paternalism. Dusinberre insists that planters were overwhelmingly motivated by self-interest, not by benevolence, demanding as much labour as they possibly could while minimising slave resistance (or 'dissidence', as he calls it). Michael Tadman's 'key slaves' thesis is potentially the most devastating critique of paternalism. 'Key slaves' constituted a small number of relatively favoured bondspeople with whom the owner thought that he or she had close ties of mutual affection and respect. The owners' perception of how they treated 'key slaves' allowed slaveholders to think of themselves as benevolent paternalists. At the same time, however, this convenient notion allowed them to treat the mass of their slaves with indifference. In Tadman's view, paternalism was self-serving and selective.[30]

Without delving too far into the complexities of this debate, competing views often hinge on differing definitions of capitalism. Genovese argues that a fixed labour system was incompatible with the development of a free market and hence with fostering a truly capitalist ethos. Others – probably the majority of recent historians – do not regard free labour as being so important in defining capitalism and point towards the ruthless exploitation of the slave work-force and to strong signs of commercialisation, if not industrialisation, by the 1850s. Moreover, it is important to distinguish between slavery at the level of the individual plantation and slavery as a system at the macro level. Few slaveholders, if any, failed to display capitalistic practices in the daily running of their operations. In the long term, however, the southern economy was hostage to the price its agricultural staples fetched on the world market. There was comparatively little investment in the South's infrastructure or diversification of its economy. Profits were ploughed back into buying more land and more slaves, hardly typical of a fully functioning capitalist society.

The emerging historiographical picture is of an Old South more capitalist than not, which promises a more subtle view in the long run. Indeed, having to choose one position or the other is probably a false dichotomy. The slave economy was both capitalist and non-capitalist simultaneously. Mark M. Smith's stimulating analysis shows how clock time imported from the industrial North challenged, and in some cases superseded, the natural seasonal rhythms that had been used in plantation management for centuries. Rejecting James Oakes, Jeffrey Robert Young argues that paternalism and liberal capitalism were exceedingly compatible, not mutually exclusive. And a later work by Oakes modifies his earlier position, moving somewhat closer to the Genovesian interpretation.[31] Planters used capitalist business practices and, in that sense, were comparable to their northern counterparts. At the same time, their social values were anything but similar. Abundant evidence points towards the centrality of a strong male code of honour and a peculiar set of ethics that was out of place in the modern world, indicating a divide between the economic and social outlook of the southern elite. Moreover, the relationship between master and slave was hardly the same as that between worker and factory owner.

The Louisiana cane world provides the best example of the merging of capitalism with paternalism. Historian Richard Follett borrows the term 'market paternalism' to describe the management of sugar planters. As we have seen, sugar production was at the forefront of mechanisation during the antebellum period. The operation of expensive machinery required a level of expertise that granted slaves a bargaining tool, as did the need to process cane as quickly as possible to prevent rotting. Planters simply could not afford any stoppages during the grinding season, let alone anything more serious (and spiking the rollers had far more serious consequences than breaking a hoe). They needed all cogs in the plantation machine functioning efficiently, providing extra rations at peak periods and financial wages for overwork outside of normal hours: 'The reciprocity of paternalism provided business-conscious planters with an ideological vocabulary for negotiating a contractual relationship with the slaves that aided plantation productivity.'[32] While something of a victory for those held in bondage, the reality was that the sugar masters ensured the smooth running of their operations for a small sum. Slavery and capitalism were seemingly combined. Applying Tom Downey's assessment of the economy of the South Carolina interior to the antebellum South as a whole probably best captures the current majority view: the region was 'in transition from being a society with capitalist features toward becoming a capitalist society'.[33]

THE WORLD THE PLANTATION SLAVES MADE

Between 1800 and 1860, the American slave population grew from approximately 900,000 to four million. Interpreting the world created by these slaves has stimulated some of the finest scholarship, as well as some fierce historical arguments. Writing in reaction to an earlier generation that included Kenneth M. Stampp and Stanley M. Elkins, revisionist historians in the 1970s unequivocally emphasised the slaves' enduring capacity to carve out a rich and protective cultural environment that nurtured and sustained a durable antebellum slave community. A number of important books appeared in quick succession, including landmark texts by John W. Blassingame, Eugene D. Genovese, Herbert G. Gutman and Lawrence W. Levine.[34] All implicitly – and some explicitly – sought to overturn Elkins' depiction of slaves as psychologically damaged and mired in 'utter dependence and childlike attachment' to the master. 'Sambo, the typical plantation slave, was docile but irresponsible, loyal but lazy, humble but chronically given to lying and stealing,' wrote Elkins in a seminal interpretation. Kenneth Stampp had not gone to this extreme in his classic and still valuable *The Peculiar Institution*, but he also suggested that American slaves 'existed in a kind of cultural void'.[35]

By the early 1980s, even the most ill-informed student of American slavery could not fail to be aware of a seismic shift in interpretation. Using a rich collection of interviews with ex-slaves recorded in the 1930s (the Works Progress Administration slave narratives), as well as slave autobiographies, revisionist historians focused renewed attention on the slave family, and on slave religion and culture, and collectively portrayed a proud and powerful slave community. At the very moment that a new orthodoxy appeared to have been established, however, Peter Kolchin chided revisionists for pushing 'the argument too far by replacing the Sambo myth with one equally untenable – that of the idyllic slave community'. Kolchin signalled the beginning of a backlash continued by historians such as William Dusinberre, Michael Tadman and Walter Johnson.[36]

As with most historiographical debates, scholars do not always fit neatly into one school or another. Those writing in reaction to the 1970s scholarship – who might be called post-revisionists – recognise the significance of slave culture and the power of the master to restrict slave agency, seeking a delicate balance between the two. Much like the capitalism debate, elements of the revisionist and post-revisionist interpretation of slave life have been combined as, in Stephanie M. H. Camp's words, 'scholars of slavery now consciously explore the contradictory and paradoxical qualities in bondpeople's lives . . . the ways in which they were both agents and subjects, persons and property, and people who resisted and who accommodated – sometimes in the same act'.[37] At issue is the degree of autonomy and unity within the slave community by the late antebellum period.

'Community' is a slippery term with multiple connotations. The simple fact that bondsmen and bondswomen lived together does not necessarily mean that a group identity was developed, if that implies communality and consensus. Peter Kolchin's critique emphasises the harmful nature of southern paternalism – as slaveholders sought to control all aspects of bondspeople's lives – which contrasted starkly with Caribbean planters, who were generally absentee owners. Kolchin places American slavery in a comparative context, showing that southern plantations were significantly smaller than elsewhere, whether considering unfree labour in Russia, the West Indies or South America. In 1860, approximately a quarter of southern slaves lived on small farms with just one to nine slaves. Half lived on medium holdings of between ten and forty-nine, while the remaining quarter lived on large plantations of fifty or more, although figures vary between the Upper and Lower South (slaves were far more likely to be on large plantations in the Lower South).[38]

While size was a factor, virtually all slaves developed links with adjacent plantations, in both formal and informal ways. William Cullen Bryant witnessed a corn shucking ceremony at which 'the negroes dropped in from the neighbouring plantations'. This was a social gathering as much as a work party: the group of slaves 'began to strip the husks from the ears, singing with great glee as they worked, keeping time to the music, and now and then throwing in an extravagant burst of laughter'. Alcohol was also sometimes provided as slaves sang songs, told stories and exchanged their news. Whether those present were quite as happy as Bryant describes is questionable. While taking advantage of a valuable opportunity for camaraderie, these slaves were working out of hours for their masters. At the same time, some of the complex problems and frustrations experienced by the enslaved were confronted. The threat of sale, for example, was the subject of a song recited at the corn shucking:

Johnny come down de hollow.
Oh hollow!
Johnny come down de hollow.
Oh hollow!
De nigger-trader got me.

Oh hollow!
De speculator bought me.
Oh hollow!
I'm sold for silver dollars.
Oh hollow!
Boys, go catch de pony.
Oh hollow!
Bring him around the corner.
Oh hollow!
I'm goin' away to Georgia.
Oh hollow!
Boys, good-by forever!
Oh hollow![39]

Gatherings like these took place at Christmas and Easter, and at other ceremonies like funerals and weddings, but covert meetings were also held. The location of slave quarters away from the master's house granted some privacy, however precarious and limited by the threat of random inspections by overseer or owner. After dark, slaves stole away to the cover of the trees, or 'brush arbors', and it would be surprising if such meetings were not cross-plantation occurrences. In this way, links were forged beyond the confines of the immediate plantation.

The bedrock of the community was the slave family. Families suited both slaves and owners, even though there was no reason why slaveholders should automatically sanction them. Masters would probably argue that a sense of Christian duty compelled their actions. In truth, there were so many practical advantages that it would have been bizarre not to organise slaves in this way. A family was a convenient unit for distributing supplies and allocating living space. Raising children was also an urgent priority for slaveholders. While stories of slave breeding and 'stud' farms circulated in the antebellum era (stemming mostly from abolitionists), historians discount their existence. There is plenty of evidence, however, that owners tried to force slaves into relationships and offered incentives to those becoming pregnant. Women's bodies thus became tools used for both work and procreation, although bondswomen did not tamely accept this. As historian Stephanie M. H. Camp argues, 'the body, so personal, was also a political entity, a site of both domination and resistance'.[40]

Above all, the bond between husband and wife, and between parent and child, was manipulated by the owner. Slaves were far less likely to run away if they were members of families. Henry Bibb's autobiography provides a poignant example. While delighted to meet and fall in love, Bibb and his partner were afraid of a commitment that would compromise their hopes of escaping. Although he chose to marry and father a baby, Bibb was never truly happy despite the love that he felt, particularly as he 'could never look upon the dear child without being filled with sorry and fearful apprehensions, of being separated by slaveholders'. He eventually could not endure bondage any longer and successfully escaped but 'it required all the moral courage that I was master of to suppress my feelings while taking leave of my little family'. Just as distressing was the inability of males to protect their wives from punishment and rape by the overseer and owner (or his sons), which had a devastating effect. North Carolinian slave Moses Grandy explained how husbands would try to do their wives' work if they possibly could, hoping to save them 'from being flogged', but, because they could not always protect spouses, they preferred not to be in the same field at all. Worse, husbands might have to witness 'her taken home at night, stripped naked, and whipped before all the men'.[41]

This pressure undoubtedly took its toll. Historian Brenda E. Stevenson presents a disturbing picture of 'distress and discord' between spouses, and between parents and children, in Virginia that epitomises the post-revisionist position. The psychological strain caused by the owner's sexual abuse led some bondsmen to blame their wives and resort to violence. Stevenson argues that children were beaten in order to teach them the harsh lesson of absolute compliance considered vital in a plantation setting, where one word out of place might result in a whipping. The rape of slave women symbolised white male power and sent out a message to the whole community. Mulatto children were placed in a very difficult position, being a constant reminder of miscegenation, but were usually reared without reference to their paternity. All children learnt harshness and cruelty within slavery, according to Nell Irvin Painter: 'neglect was routine, abuse was rampant, and anger was to be suppressed', and thus 'the child abuse of slavery imposed enormous costs'. This interpretation highlights the damage caused by slavery to men, women and children, and it is certainly the case that the historiography has yet to come to terms with the full implications of white sexual abuse. Undeniably, though, the family added a critical dimension to the lives of the slaves, however fragile and dependent on the master's acquiescence it may be, as Painter acknowledges.[42]

A variety of family structures were found in the slave community and children had large groups of extended kin, sometimes but not always blood related, which helped to cope with forced separation. As many as one in three slave marriages ended by sale, but it was probably more unusual to separate mother from child. The nuclear family was the most common experience, even though fathers were not always present continuously. Emily West estimates that a third of slave marriages in antebellum South Carolina were 'abroad', involving partners from different plantations (and usually different owners), with fathers visiting when they could. Some scholars have questioned the effectiveness of such arrangements, but West concludes that they were usually as strong as marriages on the same plantation. This was crucial, given that the small size of cotton and tobacco plantations made finding partners difficult. West stresses the love and emotional attachment between spouses and their offspring in spite of the obvious problems they faced. Larry E. Hudson takes a similar view. On balance, John W. Blassingame's influential argument that the family was 'one of the most important survival mechanisms for the slave' remains credible, with the coda that the family was equally important for slaveholders. As Norrece T. Jones puts it, the slave family was 'the planters' most effective control mechanism', but simultaneously provided 'the greatest mitigation of the harshness and severity of bondage' for the enslaved.[43]

Parents provided a crucial emotional buffer for their children and, most importantly, trained them to survive slavery. Given that, between 1820 and 1860, a third of the American slave population was under ten years old, this was a vital service, although parenting was never easy or uncontested. Masters tried 'to teach boys and girls that they – not parents – headed the plantation household' from a very early age. Slave children undertook a wide variety of duties, taking on increased responsibilities as they became older. They usually assumed full responsibilities and were working in the fields between the ages of ten and twelve. Wilma King argues that childhood was stolen from slaves because of the work they were forced to do, but Marie Jenkins Schwartz presents a more complex picture. Each stage of childhood was marked by conflict between parents, children and owner over issues of housing, food, clothing, education, religion, courtship, marriage and work. Schwartz places the dynamics of slave childhood within the web of paternalistic relations. Harsh treatment of a child enraged the slave community and owners could expect a corresponding drop in the quality of work. Masters frequently interfered but parents resisted, Schwartz contends, exploiting their owner's desire for efficient labour and healthy children.[44]

If families formed the basic building block of the community, African American religion was the cement binding it together. The Baptists and Methodists, as well as the Catholic Church in the Southwest, converted significant numbers of enslaved men and women in the two decades before the Civil War. Slaveholders hoped that religion would make slaves more obedient, with mixed results. While some slaves dutifully attended white services on Sundays – indeed, they would dress up in their best clothes to mark the special occasion – the appeal of Christianity lay in the particular form that it took on the plantation, where it became fused with African cultural traditions. The formal style of service common in orthodox churches was abandoned in slave meetings that were sometimes sanctioned by the owner and sometimes held covertly. Black preachers stressed the freeing of the Israelites from bondage and other stories of retribution, justice and deliverance. They employed a call-and-response style, making the audience active participants. Dance and music were central features of the ceremony, releasing the pent-up frustration that slavery generated. If only for a moment, those held in bondage found themselves in a different realm, transcending the geographical constrictions of bondage that allowed little opportunity for movement. Probably most importantly, Christianity provided a set of moral values from a higher power, giving slaves a way of judging and evaluating their masters. Former slave Louis Hughes recalled that no matter 'what their troubles had been during the week – how much they had been lashed, the prayer meeting on Saturday evening never failed to be held'. Such gatherings 'were the joy and comfort of the slaves', and even non-believers 'were calm and thoughtful while in attendance'.[45]

Religion forms one part of what historian Lawrence W. Levine calls 'the sacred world of black slaves' that also included folk stories (the most famous being the Brer Rabbit tales), ghosts and spirits, herbal remedies and conjuring. Conjuring – the art of charms and spells that was strongest on the plantations of the Lowcountry and the Deep South – has been portrayed as incompatible with Christianity, and some slaves, including Frederick Douglass, proclaimed it to be superstitious ritual. However, as in many aspects of slave culture, Christianity and conjuring merged together to create a complex world view reflecting a fluid mixture of African, European and American elements. Conjuring provided a means of loosening the depressingly tight reins of bondage and, however unreliable it may have been, it made slaves feel that they were not powerless. As Sharla M. Fett illustrates, conjuring was also intimately connected to healing. Black doctors played an important role in the community, although the alternative service that they provided was not uncontested by owners: they 'wrestled continuously, and sometimes unsuccessfully, with slaveholders, overseers, and white doctors for their chance to pursue their own visions of health'.[46] Masters tried to subdue black influences in a constant struggle over the form and content of slave culture.

These varied elements encouraged the development of community and forged a supportive network and belief system, sustaining each individual slave while collectively drawing strength from the whole. Religious faith remained with slaves through the week, as spirituals were sung in the fields as often as they were in church. Although never fully autonomous from the master, slave culture provided essential breathing space – what historian Charles Joyner describes as 'African cultural grammars'.[47] Joyner's fine study of slavery in the South Carolina rice swamps highlights the richness of slave culture and the strong links forged by bondspeople, but is also explicit that this was regionally specific in that it reflected unique Lowcountry conditions such as the relative lack of owner interference, the large black community, the time afforded to slaves by the task system and the strong African influence retained by successive generations. It is erroneous to assume that this was replicated in precisely the same way across the diverse regions of the South.

Careful attention must be paid to local conditions, but all bondspeople were to an extent unified by the oppression and racism enshrined within the master–slave relationship. Mia Bay is the only historian to date to consider in detail how the enslaved thought about race, conceding that it 'is virtually impossible to map exactly how white racist ideology trickled down to the slaves'. Most problematic is distinguishing between responses to slavery and to racial ethnology, because the condition of servitude fundamentally shaped black understanding of their situation and attitudes toward whites. Race, slavery and colour were 'overlapping categories in a society where all slaves were black, and most blacks were slaves'. It is clear, though, that doctrines of scientific racism were largely unknown in the slave quarters. By contrast, nineteenth-century black ethnologists from the North contested accusations of Negro inferiority, although they rarely disputed the fundamental assertion of racial difference and thus unwittingly legitimised race as a concept. Slave folklore did not recognise the idea of individual races but stressed the inherent humanity of blacks and their inclusion in the great family of mankind. There was little or no connection made between the physicality of whites and the power they wielded, as the racial stereotyping of southern whites was largely absent among blacks. 'They ain't all just alike,' recalled one former bondsman. Above all, slaves rejected the master's tendency to consider them like animals, stressing that they had souls and were fundamentally similar to whites. 'Us ain't hogs or horses,' stated an ex-slave from Arkansas, 'us is human flesh.' Bay makes the important point that the lack of racial consciousness among the enslaved suggests that white racism 'was not the inevitable response of one physically different population to another', but was a self-serving explanation for 'the subordination of black people as the natural condition of the black race'.[48]

Shared oppression did not automatically encourage communality, and there were tensions, possibly even class divisions, within antebellum slavery.

An ex-slave from South Carolina recalled: 'De fust class was de house servants. Dese was de butler, de maids, de nurses, chambermaids, and de cooks. De nex' class was de carriage drivers and de gardeners, de carpenters, de barber, and de stable men. Then come de nex' class de wheelwright, wagoners, blacksmiths and slave foremen,' followed by 'de cow men and de niggers dat have care of de dogs.' There is limited evidence suggesting that house slaves felt themselves superior to the rank and file, though their experiences were unique in many ways. For personal servants, particularly the plantation mistress's maid, duty often called twenty-four hours a day in a claustrophobic relationship. Drivers were also caught between the master and the slave community, although recent scholarship suggests they used this position to help themselves, their families and other slaves as best they could. Indeed, it has been argued that the enslaved generally accorded the highest status to those who carried out services within the community and were not much concerned with jobs assigned by the slaveholder. Skilled slaves also had a slightly different experience. Blacksmiths and carpenters found on most plantations worked more at their own pace and received extra income by exploiting their skills, as did musicians or indeed any slave with a particular skill. With the increased accumulation of money and property within the quarters by the late antebellum period (via the informal economy), it would be surprising if there was not an element of jealousy and even petty thievery.[49]

Potentially the most significant division within the slave community is that of gender. Detailed studies of female slaves published in the 1980s stressed gender as an added burden on the shoulders of black women, discriminated against because of their race and sex. Nonetheless, Deborah Gray White and Jaqueline Jones argue, women generally coped well with the demands placed upon them. They worked extremely hard, as few, if any, gender concessions were made by slaveholders. Yet they also performed a critical role within the family and community, taking charge of domestic chores within the quarters, as well as having the primary responsibility for child-rearing. Patriarchy was much weaker in the slave quarters than in southern white society, it was pointed out. Bondsmen could not protect their wives from abuse or sale (although many tried), they had no legal privilege as males and their ability to provide for the family was circumscribed.

White in particular suggests that the slave family and community was more female-centred, or matrifocal, than previously recognised by revisionist historians who in the 1970s reasserted the importance of the slave father. The key relationship in this view was between mothers and their children, and more generally between bondswomen, as the 'supportive atmosphere of the female community' provided a 'buffer . . . against the depersonalizing regime of plantation work and the generally dehumanizing nature of slavery'. Brenda Stevenson's recent study of slavery in Loudon County, Virginia, builds on this interpretation with considerable sophistication. The constant outflow of males forced bondswomen to face the 'challenges of slave matrifocality' that 'inspired idealized traits of self-protection, self-reliance, and self-determination among many black women'. Older black women became repositories of authority and knowledge within the community, gaining respect by virtue of their long service.[50]

This reminds us of the dangers of generalising about the slave experience. The Upper South location of Loudon County was much more likely to have an outflow of males than slave communities elsewhere, especially by the late antebellum period. Gender relations described by Stevenson were not necessarily similar to those in South Carolina or Mississippi, just as the strength of slave culture or the extent of African influences varied from one plantation to another. The strengths and weaknesses of the slave community differed on a case-by-case basis, according to a variety of factors.

Nonetheless, there was common ground. All bondspeople were torn between the demands of the master and the wants of the community, between the work environment and the social environment of the quarters, and between the conflicting gendered expectations and actual roles of men and women. The permanent threat of sale and the intense commodification of slave bodies epitomised the experiences of the migration generations as slavery expanded considerably in the nineteenth century. An immense physical and psychological strain weighed heavily on African Americans yearning for freedom for themselves, their partners and their children. Slave communities, built on families, black Christianity, folklore and conjurism, coped as best they could, finding a measure of cultural autonomy that served to distance them from the control and interference of slaveholders. Historians remain divided as to how successful they were. Undeniably, though, the decisive action of the enslaved during the Civil War suggests stalwart resilience in the face of immense hardship and oppression, as will be discussed in Chapter 6. Antebellum racial ideology might have stressed African American inferiority, but the strength, endurance and intelligence of southern blacks made a nonsense of this claim.

Notes

1. Peter J. Parish, *Slavery: History and Historians* (New York: Harper & Row, 1989), p. 1.

2. Steven Deyle, *Carry Me Back: The Domestic Slave Trade in American Life* (New York: Oxford University Press, 2005), pp. 288–9. See also Michael Tadman, *Speculators and Slaves: Masters, Traders, and Slaves in the Old South* (Madison: University of Wisconsin Press, 1989).
3. Ira Berlin, *Generations of Captivity: A History of African-American Slaves* (Cambridge, MA: Harvard University Press, 2003), p. 163; Steven F. Miller, 'Plantation Labor Organization and Slave Life on the Cotton Frontier: The Alabama-Mississippi Black Belt, 1815–1840', in Ira Berlin and Phillip D. Morgan (eds), *Cultivation and Culture: Labor and the Shaping of Slave Life in the Americas* (Charlottesville: University of Virginia Press, 1993), p. 157.
4. G. W. Featherstonhaugh, *Excursions Through the Slave States*, 2 vols (New York, 1844), I, p. 119.
5. Berlin, *Generations of Captivity*, p. 175.
6. Michael Tadman, 'The Demographic Cost of Sugar: Debates on Slave Societies and Natural Increase in the Americas', *American Historical Review*, 105 (December 2000), p. 1548.
7. Frances Anne Kemble, *Journal of Residence on a Georgian Plantation in 1838–1839* (New York: Alfred A. Knopf, 1961), p. 136.
8. Walter Johnson, *Soul by Soul: Life Inside the Antebellum Slave Market* (Cambridge, MA: Harvard University Press, 1999), p. 19.
9. William Dusinberre, *Them Dark Days: Slavery in the American Rice Swamps* (New York: Oxford University Press, 1996), pp. 269–71; Johnson, *Soul by Soul*, p. 136.
10. Edward E. Baptist, '"Cuffy", "Fancy Maids" and "One-Eyed Men": Rape, Commodification, and the Domestic Slave Trade in the United States', *American Historical Review*, 106 (December 2001), pp. 1619–50; Johnson, *Soul by Soul*, pp. 78–116.
11. Parish, *Slavery*, p. 29.
12. Ira Berlin, *Slaves Without Masters: The Free Negro in the Antebellum South* (New York: Random House Inc., 1974); Larry Koger, *Black Slaveowners: Free Black Slave Masters in South Carolina, 1790–1860* ([1985] Columbia: University of South Carolina Press, 1995).
13. Charles B. Dew, *Bond of Iron: Master and Slave at Buffalo Forge* (New York: W. W. Norton, 1994); T. Stephen Whitman, *The Price of Freedom: Slavery and Manumission in Baltimore and Early National Maryland* (Lexington: University Press of Kentucky, 1997), p. 164.
14. Gregg D. Kimball, *American City, Southern Place: A Cultural History of Antebellum Richmond* (Athens: University of Georgia Press, 2000); Ira Berlin and Herbert G. Gutman, 'Natives and Immigrants, Free Men and Slaves: Urban Workingmen in the Antebellum South', *American Historical Review*, 88 (December 1983), pp. 1175–1200; D. C. Rousey, 'Aliens in the WASP Nest: Ethnocultural Diversity in the Antebellum Urban South', *Journal of American History*, 79 (June 1992), pp. 152–64; Jonathan Daniel Wells, *The Origins of the*

Southern Middle Class, 1800–1861, (Chapel Hill: University of North Carolina Press, 2004), p. 8.

15. Solomon Northup, *Twelve Years a Slave: Narrative of Solomon Northup* (New York, 1853) in Gilbert Osofsky, *Puttin' on Ole Massa* (New York: Harper & Row, 1969), pp. 314–15.
16. Ibid. pp. 339–41.
17. Richard Follet, *The Sugar Masters: Planters and Slaves in Louisiana's Cane World, 1820–1860* (Baton Rouge: Louisiana State University Press, 2005), p. 49.
18. Tadman, 'Demographic Cost of Sugar', p. 1536.
19. Willie Lee Rose, 'The Domestication of Domestic Slavery', in Rose, *Slavery and Freedom* (New York: Oxford University Press, 1982), pp. 18–36.
20. E. N. Elliott (ed.), *Cotton is King*, cited in Eugene D. Genovese, *Roll, Jordan, Roll: The World the Slaves Made* (New York: Pantheon, 1974), p. 76; Douglas Ambrose, *Henry Hughes and Proslavery Thought in the Old South* (Baton Rouge: Louisiana State University Press, 1996).
21. Robert William Fogel and Stanley L. Engerman, *Time on the Cross: The Economics of American Negro Slavery* (Boston, MA: Little, Brown and Company, 1974), p. 115.
22. Jeffrey Robert Young, 'Ideology and Death on a Savannah River Rice Plantation, 1835–1867: Paternalism Amidst "a Good Supply of Disease and Pain"', *Journal of Southern History*, 59 (November 1993), pp. 691, 693.
23. Rose, *Slavery and Freedom*, p. 25; Sir E. R. Sullivan, cited in Max Berger, *The British Traveller in America, 1836–1860* (New York: Columbia University Press, 1943), pp. 124–5.
24. Genovese, *Roll, Jordan, Roll*, p. 5.
25. Eugene D. Genovese, 'The Slave South: An Interpretation', *Science and Society*, 25 (December 1961), pp. 320–7.
26. Robert William Fogel, *Without Consent or Contract: The Rise and Fall of American Slavery* (New York: W. W. Norton, 1989), p. 64; William Kauffman Scarborough, *Masters of the Big House: Elite Slaveholders of the Mid-Nineteenth-Century South* (Baton Rouge: Louisiana State University Press, 2003), p. 409.
27. Parish, *Slavery*, p. 33.
28. Eugene D. Genovese, *The Slaveholders' Dilemma: Freedom and Progress in Southern Conservative Thought, 1820–1860* (Columbia: South Carolina University Press, 1992).
29. James Oakes, *The Ruling Race: A History of American Slaveholders* (New York: Alfred A. Knopf, 1982), p. 191.
30. Dusinberre, *Them Dark Days*, p. 202; Michael Tadman, 'Class and the Construction of "Race": White Racism in the American South', in Melvyn Stokes (ed.), *The State of US History* (Oxford: Berg, 2000). Tadman's 'key slave' thesis will be developed in a forthcoming book with the provisional title *On the Old Plantation: The Deceits of White Supremacy in the Slave South*.

31. Mark M. Smith, *Mastered by the Clock: Time, Slavery, and Freedom in the American South* (Chapel Hill: University of North Carolina Press, 1997); Jeffrey Robert Young, *Domesticating Slavery: The Master Class in Georgia and South Carolina, 1670–1837* (Chapel Hill: University of North Carolina Press, 1999); James Oakes, *Slavery and Freedom: An Interpretation of the Old South* (New York: Alfred A. Knopf, 1990).
32. Follet, *Sugar Masters*, pp. 155–6.
33. Tom Downey, *Planting a Capitalist South: Masters, Merchants, and Manufacturers in the Southern Interior, 1790–1860* (Baton Rouge: Louisiana State University Press, 2006), p. 227.
34. John W. Blassingame, *The Slave Community: Plantation Life in the Antebellum South* (New York: Oxford University Press, 1972); Genovese, *Roll, Jordan, Roll;* Herbert G. Gutman, *The Black Family in Slavery and Freedom, 1750–1925* (New York: Pantheon, 1976); Lawrence W. Levine, *Black Culture and Black Consciousness: Afro-American Folk Thought From Slavery to Freedom* (New York: Oxford University Press, 1977).
35. Stanley Elkins, *Slavery: A Problem in American Intellectual and Institutional Life* (Chicago: University of Chicago Press), p. 82; Kenneth M. Stampp, *The Peculiar Institution: Slavery in the Ante-Bellum South* (New York: Alfred A. Knopf, 1956), p. 364.
36. Peter Kolchin, 'Reevaluating the Antebellum Slave Community: A Comparative Perspective', *Journal of American History*, 70 (December 1983), p. 601.
37. Stephanie M. H. Camp, *Closer to Freedom: Enslaved Women and Everyday Resistance in the Plantation South* (Chapel Hill: University of North Carolina Press, 2004), p. 1.
38. Peter Kolchin, *American Slavery 1619–1877* (New York: Hill and Wang, 1993), pp. 101, 243; Peter Kolchin, *Unfree Labor: American Slavery and Russian Serfdom* (Cambridge, MA: Harvard University Press, 1987), pp. 195–241.
39. William Cullen Bryant (1850), cited in Roger D. Abrahams, *Singing the Master: The Emergence of African American Culture in the Plantation South* (New York: Pantheon, 1992), pp. 223–4.
40. Camp, *Closer to Freedom*, p. 62. See also Liese Perrin, 'Resisting Reproduction: Reconsidering Slave Contraception in the Old South', *Journal of American Studies*, 35 (August 2001), pp. 255–74.
41. Osofsky, (ed.), *Puttin' on Ole Massa*, pp. 81–2; Moses Grandy, *Narrative of the Life of Moses Grandy, Late a Slave in the United States of America*, edited by G. Thompson (London: Gilpin, 1843), pp. 27–8.
42. Brenda Stevenson, 'Distress and Discord in Virginia Slave Families, 1830–1860', in Carol Bleser (ed.), *In Joy and In Sorrow: Women, Family, and Marriage in the Victorian South, 1830–1900* (New York: Oxford University Press, 1991), pp. 101–24; Nell Irvin Painter, 'Soul Murder and Slavery:

Toward a Fully Loaded Cost Accounting', in Linda K. Kerber, Alice Kessler-Harris and Kathryn Kish Sklar (eds), *U.S. History as Women's History: New Feminist Essays* (Chapel Hill: University of North Carolina Press, 1995), p. 134.

43. Emily West, *Chains of Love: Slave Couples in Antebellum South Carolina* (Urbana: University of Illinois Press, 2004); Larry E. Hudson, Jr, *To Have and to Hold: Slave Work and Family Life in Antebellum South Carolina* (Athens: University of Georgia Press, 1997), pp. 141–76; John W. Blassingame, *The Slave Community: Plantation Life in the Antebellum South,* revised and enlarged edition (New York: Oxford University Press, 1979), p. 151; Norrece T. Jones, Jr, *Born a Child of Freedom, Yet a Slave: Mechanisms of Control and Strategies of Resistance in Antebellum South Carolina* (Wesleyan University Press, 1990), p. 37.
44. Marie Jenkins Schwartz, *Born in Bondage: Growing Up Enslaved in the Antebellum South* (Cambridge, MA: Harvard University Press, 2000), pp. 5, 77; Wilma King, *Stolen Childhood: Slave Youth in Nineteenth-Century America* (Bloomington: Indiana University Press, 1997), p. xx.
45. Louis Hughes, *Thirty Years a Slave: From Bondage to Freedom* (Milwaukee, WI: South Side, 1897), pp. 53–4.
46. Levine, *Black Culture,* pp. 3–80; Sharla M. Fett, *Working Cures: Healing, Health, and Power on Southern Slave Plantations* (Chapel Hill: University of North Carolina Press, 2002), pp. 6–7.
47. Charles Joyner, *Down by the Riverside: A South Carolina Slave Community* (Urbana: University of Illinois Press, 1984), p. 239.
48. Mia Bay, *The White Image in the Black Mind: African-American Ideas About White People, 1830–1925* (New York: Oxford University Press, 2000), pp. 142, 119–20, 176, 165.
49. Rosa Starke, cited in George Rawick (ed.), *The American Slave: A Composite Autobiography,* vol. 3 (South Carolina), Part 4, p. 148; William L. Van De Burg, *The Slave Drivers: Black Agricultural Labor Supervisors in the Antebellum South* (Westport, CT: Greenwood Press, 1979), pp. 115–16; John W. Blassingame, 'Status and Social Structure in the Slave Community: Evidence from New Sources', in Harry P. Owens (ed.), *Perspectives and Irony in American Slavery* (Jackson: University Press of Mississippi, 1976), pp. 137–51.
50. Deborah Gray White, *Ar'n't I a Woman? Female Slaves in the Plantation South* (New York: W. W. Norton, 1985), p. 131; Jaqueline Jones, *Labor of Love, Labor of Sorrow: Black Women, Work and the Family, from Slavery to the Present* (New York: Basic Books, 1985), pp. 11–43; Brenda E. Stevenson, *Life in Black and White: Family and Community in the Slave South* (New York: Oxford University Press, 1996), p. 234.

THE AMERICAN CIVIL WAR
CANADA
MAINE
MINNESOTA
WISCONSIN
MICHIGAN
VERMONT
NEW HAMPSHIRE
MASS.
NEW YORK
CONN.
RHODE ISLAND
IOWA
PENNSYLVANIA
NEW JERSEY
Gettysburg
ILLINOIS
INDIANA
OHIO
Antietam
DELAWARE
MARYLAND
Manassas
WEST VIRGINIA (1863)
Fredericksburg
Petersburg
MISSOURI
Perryville
KENTUCKY
VIRGINIA
Wilson's Creek
NORTH CAROLINA
Nashville
TENNESSEE
Prairie Grove
Shiloh
Chattanooga
ARKANSAS
Chickamauga
SOUTH CAROLINA
Atlantic Ocean
Atlanta
Fort Sumter
MISSISSIPPI
ALABAMA
GEORGIA
Savannah
Vicksburg
LOUISIANA
TEXAS
N
W
E
S
New Orleans
Gulf of Mexico
FLORIDA
Union States
Border Slave States (Union)
Confederate States
Major Battle Site
Miles 0
200
400
Kms 0
200
400
Robert F. Pace

Chapter 6

A FRAGILE FREEDOM: THE CIVIL WAR AND THE COLLAPSE OF SLAVERY

When Abraham Lincoln said in 1858 that 'a house divided against itself cannot stand', he expressed a widespread feeling that slavery and freedom could not continue to co-exist within the United States.[1] This did not make war inevitable – specific circumstances in 1860–61 triggered the secession of southern states. Even though numerous factors have been cited, however, very few professional historians would deny that slavery was the root cause of the American Civil War. The political problem posed by slavery in the antebellum period caused profound disagreements which eventually became insurmountable. Moderates in both the North and the South struggled desperately to hold the Union together in the 1850s, but with Abraham Lincoln's victory in the presidential election of 1860 that no longer seemed possible.

Slavery would also be critical to the conduct of the war, even though emancipation was not an official Union policy until well after the start of hostilities in April 1861. Modern warfare relied as much on industrial might as it did on soldiers in the field, and the distinctive agrarian character of the South placed it at a huge disadvantage in comparison with the North. Nonetheless, the South tried to make the best of what it had and bondspeople were put to many different tasks by the Confederates. In order to defeat the Confederacy, it became essential to destroy slavery. Secession was undertaken in order to protect slavery from the perceived threat of Lincoln's Republican Party, but ironically it eventually brought the destruction of the peculiar institution. The exigencies of four years of gruelling warfare placed a tremendous strain on southerners, testing the limits of social consensus as class and gender fault lines emerged prominently and divisively.

Freedom was not given to African Americans. Slaves flocking to Federal lines in their thousands not only helped to destroy the institution from within by destabilising the South, but simultaneously forced the Union to consider the controversial issue of emancipation and enlistment of African American soldiers. By taking charge of their own destinies, blacks compelled Abraham

Lincoln to take not only steps towards emancipation, but force whites in both the North and the South to reconsider prejudiced views and, in so doing, make a strong case for their inclusion as full citizens of the United States. Northern victory was only the beginning, however. How would the South adjust to the loss of an institution that had been the foundation of social, economic and political life for hundreds of years? Above all, how would race relations function in a South without the institution of bondage? The post-war era of Reconstruction was a period of major and far-reaching change, but ultimately one of continuity as well. As W. E. B. Du Bois poignantly put it: 'The slave went free; stood a brief moment in the sun; then moved back again toward slavery.'[2]

THE ROAD TO DISUNION

Westward expansion, on which both the success of the South and the nation as a whole depended, was a fundamental cause of tension between the slave and free states in the nineteenth century. As new territory was acquired in the West, Congress had to decide how it should be incorporated into the Union. Politicians tried to maintain a balance between the sections, especially as the growing numerical and industrial superiority of the North had political implications. A rapidly expanding population gave the North more seats in Congress, causing an imbalance which threatened to become overwhelming with millions of immigrants arriving in the 1840s and 1850s (nine out of ten residing above the Mason–Dixon Line). The issue of slavery's expansion into the West was an emotive and divisive problem throughout the antebellum period. Southerners considered it their right to take slaves into new territories, but northerners wanted to establish new western states on a free labour basis.

The Missouri Compromise of 1820 attempted to solve this problem by fixing the boundary between slave and free states at the line of 36° 30′, with Missouri admitted as a slave state even though it was north of that latitude. This left a delicate balance of eleven free states and eleven slave states, with slavery barred from western territory north of the line. Both major antebellum political parties, the Whigs and the Democrats, tried to keep slavery off the political agenda after this point, but gains from the Mexican War (1846–48) eventually made this impossible. Congressman David Wilmot, supported by a majority of his northern peers, proposed a bill keeping slavery out of the Southwest. Only a unanimous rejection by southern senators prevented passage of the Wilmot Proviso, emphasising just how precarious the political situation was by mid-century. Northern states had far more seats in the House of Representatives, where a state's representation was based on the size of its population. In the Senate, each state, regardless of population, had two members. Since the Senate could veto legislation from the House of Representatives, and there were fifteen free states and fifteen slave states by 1848, the South could effectively block congressional attacks on slavery. Admission of a new state would therefore disrupt the balance of power.

In a highly charged atmosphere, the influential southern statesman Henry Clay set out proposals designed to appease both sections. After considerable debate and revision, a series of measures were passed, collectively known as the Compromise of 1850. This placated the North and the South, at least for the time being, but signalled the growing polarisation of the United States. With politicians overwhelmingly acting on a sectional basis during the debates, maintaining inter-regional political parties was becoming very difficult. In a classic study, historian David M. Potter questions whether a compromise was achieved at all: 'a truce perhaps, an armistice, certainly a settlement, but not a true compromise'.[3]

A rapid turn of events in the 1850s saw sectional tension escalate to critical levels. Northern reaction to the 1850 Compromise was often hostile, as abolitionists and some politicians, to the anger of the white South, openly proclaimed their defiance of the strengthened Fugitive Slave Law. The Kansas-Nebraska Act, passed in May 1854, prompted a bitter struggle between pro- and anti-slavery supporters over the organisation of the vast territory west of Missouri and Iowa. Democrat Stephen A. Douglas hoped to avert conflict by allowing western settlers to decide for themselves over the issue of slavery when they applied to join the Union (a policy known as popular sovereignty). Douglas's initiative failed and 'bleeding Kansas' witnessed brutal fighting between those wanting to keep slavery out of the West and pro-slavery southerners. These clashes were repeated in a less violent but equally divisive way by an ongoing war of words in the 1850s over the peculiar institution and its place within the United States. Pressured by the problem of slavery, as well as by ethnic and cultural issues created by mass immigration, the Whigs imploded in the mid-1850s. The Republican Party emerged in their place, composed of a number of different interest groups who were generally committed to a free-soil policy of keeping slavery out of the West. The Supreme Court's Dred Scott decision in 1857 encouraged southerners to think that slavery could not be banned by legislative action because of personal property laws. John Brown's raid at the town of Harpers Ferry, Virginia, on 16 October 1859, attempting to initiate a full-scale slave revolt in the South, dramatically exemplified a decade in which the nation had effectively been split in two.

Whether the antebellum North and the South were essentially similar or different societies has been the focus of considerable scholarly debate, but what really counted was that millions of southerners placed sectional identity above fealty to the Union by 1860. Northerners also valued their section highly, contrasting it with the 'backward' South; but, as historian Susan-Mary Grant shows, northern nationalism was strongly attached to the idea of the Union.[4] This helps to explain why northerners were prepared to go to war, as only a tiny minority were fighting to end slavery. The majority of northerners were broadly anti-slavery, not abolitionist – they were opposed to slavery in principle and to its expansion, although were not willing to push for its immediate end in southern states – but they also accepted racial arguments about black inferiority and white supremacy, and feared that freed slaves might head to the northern states. Probably the most influential view promulgated by the Republicans attacked slavery indirectly. The free labour critique, a 'condemnation of the slave society of the South and glorification of the progress, opportunity, and individual freedom embodied in the "free society" of the North', was disseminated widely in newspapers and political speeches in the 1850s.[5] Slavery was presented as a barrier to continued progress, perpetuated by a minority of fanatical planters.

The South did not distinguish between these different positions, however. Any attack upon slavery was regarded as a fundamental affront to the whole southern way of life, as a siege mentality developed that galvanised a majority of yeomen as much as it did slaveholders. The bitter political confrontations of the 1850s boiled down to one issue: could slavery be guaranteed if the South remained within the Union?

This question became urgent in the wake of Abraham Lincoln's success in the presidential election of November 1860. Lincoln and the Republican Party had campaigned on a free-soil ticket that specifically left slavery alone in places where it already existed, and the Democrats remained in control of Congress and the Supreme Court. Despite this, southern fire-eaters (radical pro-slavery politicians) argued that southern liberty was in immediate danger. In the most recent study of secession, Manisha Sinha argues that the South Carolinian planter elite – men such as William H. Gist, William Porcher Miles, Robert Barnwell Rhett and Lawrence M. Keitt – and their allies across the Lower South share primary responsibility for engineering southern withdrawal. Their actions were 'the culmination of an influential political ideology of slavery and separatism' to which most slaveholders, large or small, adhered. Planters carried out an organised and highly effective campaign, silencing their critics by coercive means when necessary in the winter of 1860–61. Sinha argues that they wanted to overthrow Jacksonian democracy as much as protect the institution of slavery. The South Carolinian elite looked to secure its ruling class position from the threat democracy presented in a 'counterrevolution of slavery' that rejected egalitarian ideals in a 'reactionary and antidemocratic discourse'.[6]

One does not need to accept fully the controversial argument that southern elites rejected white male equality to appreciate the significant role played by the planter elite during the secession crisis. An increasingly strident defence of slavery and the white South was expounded between 1830 and 1861. From South Carolina Senator John C. Calhoun's idea of the concurrent minority and his vehement defence of states' rights, to the demand for federal protection of slavery in the territories, to debates about reopening the African slave trade, Lowcountry planters consistently led the way in pushing 'the idea of a southern nation'.[7] Drawing on fear, a sense of compromised honour and decades of ill-feeling between the North and the South, secession leaders used the prospect of racial amalgamation as their trump card in persuading southerners to opt for secession.

Whether southern non-slaveholders supported secession is the critical historiographical question. If the planters' primary unspoken fear was over the loyalty of their slaves, not far behind was a nagging doubt about the commitment of non-slaveholders. Hinton Rowan Helper, a yeoman from North Carolina, caused great alarm by publishing a book not only pointing out the deficiencies of slavery and the superiority of free labour, but directing non-slaveholding whites to overthrow the slaveholding regime. He even hinted that they might ally themselves with slaves to defeat the plantocracy. The Republican Party had used Helper's *The Impending Crisis of the South* as a campaign document in the summer of 1860, confirming (in the planters' view) its aggressive intent to undermine southern stability. Elite southerners were greatly concerned that Lincoln would use federal patronage to entice non-slaveholders into his party. D. H. Hamilton's remark of January 1860 that he 'mistrust[ed] our own people more than I fear all the efforts of the Abolitionists' summed up this feeling of insecurity.[8]

Michael P. Johnson's study of Georgia makes the most forceful case that 'the internal crisis of the South necessitated secession', as planters moved to head off the yeoman challenge, but scholarly opinion is divided. Indeed, two of the leading historians of this crucial period in southern history flatly disagree about the loyalties of the rank and file in the Lower South. Daniel Crofts states that 'it now appears beyond dispute that secession met with popular approval' in the Lower South, but J. William Harris contends that 'a majority of non-slaveholders were, in fact, opposed to immediate secession', pointing to a significant correlation between patterns of slaveholding within each state and the likelihood of voting in favour of secession.[9] Undeniably there was a wide spectrum of opinion. Those against immediate secession were dubbed 'cooperationists': some wanted to wait until the South was ready to leave en masse; 'ultimationists' wanted to present Lincoln with a list of demands guaranteeing slavery's protection; and conditional Unionists would only secede in wake of an overtly aggressive act on Lincoln's part. Some were clearly reluctant to leave the Union at all, but many within the cooperationist camp were just as adamant as immediatists that Republican ascendancy was a fatal blow to southern interests. They merely disagreed on how and when to secede.[10]

South Carolina's decisive action in calling a secession convention on 17 December 1860 averted the prospect of a general meeting of southern states that might have slowed momentum. Following this lead, Alabama, Mississippi, Georgia, Louisiana, Florida, and eventually Texas, also called conventions composed of elected representatives from each county. Secessionists were victorious at conventions held in January and February 1861, although the vote was not unanimous, as it had been in South Carolina, indicating, at the very least, significant opposition to immediate secession across the Lower South. Nonetheless, delegates from seven states met at Montgomery, Alabama, on 4 February 1861, to draw up a Confederate Constitution and choose a provisional president and vice-president. With the formation of the Confederacy, attention now turned to the position of the Upper South.

Unionist forces were much stronger in the Upper South, although there were a small number of fire-eaters, such as Virginian Edmund Ruffin, eager to join the seceding states. Slavery was not as economically critical there as it was in the Lower South, and Lincoln's election was not considered such a dire threat. Only Arkansas and Virginia actually held conventions (secession was defeated by a slim margin in the former and a larger one in the latter) before the passage of critical events at Fort Sumter which triggered the outbreak of civil war. At a convention that was to be held in Missouri, unionist delegates outnumbered their opponents by three to one. North Carolina and Tennessee voted against holding a convention, and Maryland, Delaware and Kentucky did not consider holding conventions at all. The Crittenden Compromise, proposed by Kentucky Senator John J. Crittenden in the spring of 1861, desperately sought to keep the Upper South within the Union. It called for the restoration of the Missouri Compromise, allowing slavery into western territory below the line of 36° 30′, as well as a constitutional amendment guaranteeing slavery where it already existed. The history of the South would have been dramatically different had this been successful, but there was little northern enthusiasm nor, crucially, the support of Abraham Lincoln for Crittenden's proposal.

The spark that ignited the Civil War – and delivered four states critical to the potential success of the Confederacy – occurred, appropriately enough, in Charleston, South Carolina. Fort Sumter was built on a man-made island in the centre of Charleston bay, and, as a federal installation occupied by northern troops, constituted a hostile presence in wake of South Carolina's secession. A delicate stand-off between Confederate authorities and Abraham Lincoln came to a head on 12 April 1861. Major Robert Anderson's repeated refusal to evacuate Fort Sumter was met by a fierce bombardment from Confederate batteries on the shore, commencing at 4.30 a.m., the opening shots in the American Civil War. Three days later, Lincoln, refusing to recognise the legality of secession, called for 75,000 volunteers to suppress what he called a rebellion.

Following Lincoln's request, a wave of secessionist fervour swept the Upper South. It had always been clear that any coercive measure to prevent southern states leaving would be decisively rejected by the Upper South, but few could have predicted how strong the reaction would be. Unionists were dismayed and could not prevent a popular surge toward the Confederacy. Virginia passed a secession ordinance on 17 April; North Carolina and Arkansas followed in May, while Tennessee was the last state to join the Confederacy in June. Four slaveholding border states remained loyal, although precariously so in the case of Kentucky and Missouri, where an intense internal struggle took place between pro-Union and pro-Confederate groups. Slavery in Maryland and Delaware had declined steadily in the nineteenth century, and the geographical proximity of both states to the North made it highly unlikely that they would secede. In the summer of 1861, eleven southern states stood side-by-side, rapidly mobilising their resources to fight for the right to build a separate slaveholding nation.

FAULT LINES WITHIN THE CONFEDERACY

In the heady excitement of the first months of the war, southerners rushed to form companies (based on recruits from individual counties), anxious for the chance to 'whip the Yankees'. The South had long celebrated its martial spirit, and men young and old rallied to the cause from a sense of honour, duty and masculine pride. It was also a chance for many to earn a regular wage and leave the farm for the first time. Everyone anticipated that the war would be extremely short, and soldiers on both sides worried that they might miss out – Jefferson Davis had to persuade colleagues that terms of service for initial recruits should be twelve, not six, months. This was a tragic underestimation of the duration of the American Civil War, which lasted four years and in many ways was the first modern war, a contest of industrial might and civilian morale as much as troops and generals. Southerners would be severely tested between 1861 and 1865, as fighting took place mostly in their territory and the Confederacy was subject to a northern naval blockade, hampering imports and exports.

Few worried about this in the summer of 1861. Disagreements over secession were somewhat assuaged because honour codes required southerners to rally to the defence of home and family, and adhere to the decision of the majority to go to war, as historian Bertram Wyatt-Brown emphasises. Virginian Robert E. Lee, for example, who had favoured the Union, refused to take command of the Federal Army in 1861 because he could not 'raise my hand against my relatives, my children, my home'. Lee eventually took charge of the Army of Northern Virginia in June 1862, and would be a crucial figure in formulating Confederate military strategy, and in bringing hope to southerners that they could defeat the North. Any negative or cautious thoughts were put aside, however, as southern men from many different backgrounds joined up.[11]

Lee's skill as a military commander had to compensate for a gross disparity of resources between the two sides. The North had an overwhelming superiority in terms of manpower and industrial and financial resources, although it took a long while to harness those advantages effectively. There were twenty-two million people in the Union states compared to nine million in the Confederacy, of whom more than a third were slaves. Southern manufacturing capacity in 1860 was just one-twelfth that of its opponents. Moreover, Confederate wealth was tied up in slaves and land. Southerners hoped for the intervention of foreign powers, particularly Great Britain and France, and believed that disrupting cotton exports might force international recognition. 'King Cotton' diplomacy had some merit, but no foreign country was prepared to recognise the Confederacy as long as it remained a slave power. President Jefferson Davis and his cabinet, located in Richmond, Virginia, had some major disadvantages to overcome. Having said that, the South could adopt a defensive-offensive strategy, protecting its extensive borders (the Confederacy was 750,000 square miles in total) while choosing to engage in morale-boosting, but potentially costly, offensive battles selectively. In hindsight, it is all too easy to assume that the superior Union forces would be victorious, but Confederate defeat was not inevitable. The South only had to force the enemy to give up and, at times, it appeared to be close to achieving this aim, most notably in the summer of 1864, when Lincoln faced great pressure to consider negotiating a peace or else risk losing the support of his party in a crucial presidential election year.

Geographical fault lines that had been apparent for decades – between the upcountry and plantation districts, and the Upper and Lower South – as well as latent class divisions would greatly, perhaps fatally, undermine the southern cause between 1861 and 1865. White racial consensus was severely strained by the exigencies of war, and scholars are bitterly divided as to the strength of commitment shown by lower-class whites. On one side, historians like Paul D. Escott, Wayne K. Durrill, and more recently David W. Williams, argue that class divisions seriously undermined the Confederate cause. On the other side, Gary W. Gallagher and William A. Blair argue for the strength of Confederate unity, citing war-weariness as the major problem. In this view, a loss of will to continue the fight must be distinguished from a lack of will to fight in the first place – the overwhelming majority of southerners showed remarkable loyalty and commitment to a conflict that demanded terrible sacrifices, argue Gallagher and Blair. This vigorous historiographical debate links the home front to the battlefield, hinging on different assessments of the strength of southern nationalism. Did the political hierarchy in Richmond convince southerners that the Confederacy was a nation, with core beliefs and a distinctive identity, not just a group of states seeking to defend slavery?[12]

President Jefferson Davis was the figurehead of the Confederacy, and as such was a crucial focal point of nascent southern nationalism. Strong political leadership is essential in wartime, but especially so in a fledgling nation trying to establish itself. Davis's reputation has risen somewhat in recent biographies, but he unquestionably found it difficult to instil a strong sense of loyalty and empathy, with himself or with the Confederate nation, and his performance pales in comparison to that of Abraham Lincoln. Davis's appointment of officials and generals was frequent and indecisive. He was also an austere and humourless man, who was difficult to work with, and these were not qualities that inspired the masses. The relationship between ordinary southerners and the Confederate government was strained.

In some ways, though, this was not Davis's fault. The Confederacy had been formed because personal liberty and independence were allegedly threatened by the Republicans. In order to mobilise resources against a superior foe, however, Davis simply had to act autocratically, imposing taxation, conscription and impressment of personal property and goods, requiring immense sacrifices of southerners. This affected the poorest members of society disproportionately, leading to the cry of 'rich man's war, poor man's fight'. Moreover, state governors, such as Joseph E. Brown of Georgia and Zebulon Vance of North Carolina, proved unwilling to comply with central requests, accusing Davis of acting despotically. In increasingly desperate circumstances, they kept precious resources for their states, and did not provide for the Confederacy as a whole. As the war continued, and demands became progressively more severe, many southerners tended to identify with their states rather than with Richmond.

Davis was not the only focus of southern nationalism, points out Gary W. Gallagher. He argues that military commanders, such as Robert E. Lee and Thomas 'Stonewall' Jackson, were as important – and far more successful – in inspiring the southern public and winning morale–boosting victories on the battlefield.[13] Gallagher is clearly right to stress that Confederate morale was connected to the ebb and flow of the war situation. It is equally clear, though, that non-slaveholding whites were not unanimously or unequivocally committed to the defence of slavery explicitly enshrined in the Confederate Constitution. 'Southern recruits waxed more eloquent about their intention to fight *against* slavery than *for* it,' writes historian James M. McPherson, 'that is, against their own enslavement by the North.' Yeomen were probably more persuaded by the need to preserve the existing racial order, especially after the North made emancipation a war aim in 1863. Their primary commitment, however, was defending family, home and community; in essence, this was the 'South' to them, and it overrode all other considerations. 'We are fighting for matters real and tangible . . . our property and our homes,' declared one Texas volunteer.[14] When ordinary southerners no longer saw their primary interests coinciding with those of the Confederacy, they began to rethink their commitment, and desertion increased steadily throughout the war, becoming a chronic problem in the later years.

Moreover, substantial numbers of non-slaveholders *never* saw their interests coinciding with those of the Confederacy. The westernmost counties of Virginia, containing few slaves, refused to accept secession and formed their own government, becoming the thirty-fifth state – West Virginia – on 20 June 1863. East Tennessee was dominated by Unionists, and across the southern upcountry bands of rebels were formed by groups who opposed the Confederacy for a variety of reasons. This emphasises that there were many varied southern war experiences. Vicious guerrilla warfare, for example, pitted southerner against southerner in a very different kind of conflict to the regular war. Historian William W. Freehling stresses how anti-Confederate southerners 'seriously compromised Confederate military manpower'. Two hundred thousand white southerners from the border states fought for the Union, compared to just 90,000 who fought for the Confederacy. One hundred thousand white southerners from the other Upper South states also joined the Union Army. Given that the Confederacy had a total number of

900,000 troops, these southerners, overwhelmingly non-slaveholders, would have made a crucial difference to the Confederate cause.[15]

Gender was another critical fault line within Confederacy. Over the last two decades, scholars have shown considerable interest in the lives of elite white women. In a pioneering analysis, Anne Firor Scott portrays the plantation mistress caught in a world in which she was expected to live up to unrealistic ideals of being the perfect wife and mother. Catherine Clinton went further, suggesting the elite woman was 'trapped within a system over which she had no control, one from which she had no means of escape'. For Clinton it was not the gendered ideal of womanhood that was the main problem, however difficult it was to live up to that expectation, but the demanding managerial role assumed by the plantation mistress without warning or preparation. Clinton effectively debunks the myth of the leisurely southern lady who, in fact, took on considerable responsibilites in overseeing the running of the household. Shared hardship perhaps bridged the racial divide at times, encouraging white and black women to identify with one another on the lines of gender. White women also had to cope with the sexual transgression of their husbands with female slaves, something which potentially alienated them from the slave system. Mary Boykin Chesnut famously wrote that 'Like the patriarchs of old our men live all in one house with their wives and their concubines . . . and every lady tells you who is the father of all the mulatto children in everybody's household, but those in her own she seems to think drop from the clouds, or pretends so to think.' Elizabeth Fox-Genovese, on the other hand, argues that elite women were beneficiaries, not victims, of the system. They might complain 'about slavery and sometimes about men', but this should not be misinterpreted to 'mean that they opposed slavery as a social system or even the prerogatives with which its class and race relations endowed men'. Fox-Genovese asserts that frustrations, such as those caused by their husbands' liaisons with female slaves, were taken out on black women, especially personal servants, negating the formation of sisterly bonds.[16]

The attitude of elite women toward slavery was critical, for the Confederacy's lack of numbers necessitated the support of all. Would plantation mistresses support a war to preserve slavery? The historical verdict is mixed. Women found themselves taking a greater role in the daily running of the plantation, and some took sole charge. This put them in a difficult and unfamiliar situation, because gender roles dictated that men controlled slaves. Women had to forget the qualities of submission, meekness and gentility that were the essence of antebellum femininity, especially when administering punishment, which was so integral to plantation management.

Historian Drew Faust suggests that elite women were at first extremely patriotic, but soon struggled to cope with the demands asked of them. The antebellum patriarchal bargain, in which women were subservient in return for male protection, was broken by the war. 'A practical pacifism born of exhaustion and despair was replacing the mood of romantic militarism that had earlier gripped elite women' from around 1863.[17]

If elite women struggled, there is no doubt that lower-class women, left to run the farm without husbands or sons, suffered even more. Southern farms quite simply relied on the labour of male family members. One woman implored the North Carolina governor to allow her son home after his term of service had ended. With 'no man person to protect or assist' her, and army wages not enough to cover basic family needs, 'I do not see how we are to get a living with out him,' she wrote. Notably, she had not told her son of these concerns, however, and emphasised her support for the Confederate cause.[18] As the draft was extended to include older and younger men, and everyday supplies became progressively more scarce, such feelings became more vocal and less conciliatory. It particularly rankled that the rich could hire substitutes and found various exemptions from service for their relatives. Bread riots in 1863 in the Confederate capital Richmond, and elsewhere, indicated that female support was eroding away. Although directed at shopkeepers and businessmen who were accused of hoarding and speculating to drive up prices, these protests registered significant discontent with the war itself.

The combination of elite despair and lower-class resentment became a highly destructive force. Large numbers of women withdrew their support from the Confederacy by refusing to allow their loved ones to continue fighting. Letters urged husbands and sons to return home. 'It may well be because of its women that the South lost the Civil War,' Faust argues. Not all concur with this view. Historians such as LeeAnn Whites and Jacqueline Glass Campbell argue that female support was more enduring, strengthened by hatred of the Federals who wrought death and destruction in the South. Some women were empowered by their new responsibilities.[19] The divergence of emphasis is partly explained by the focus of each historian on different parts of the Confederacy, suggesting that greater attention needs to be paid to the significance of intra-regional contrasts within the war-time South. As has been repeatedly emphasised, the South was not monolithic. Wars can elicit an extraordinary level of sacrifice from ordinary citizens and this was undoubtedly true of countless southerners in the American Civil War. At the same time, it is worth remembering that many were not in favour of secession in the first place. It is hardly surprising, then, that some regions and some groups of southerners took the 'rich man's war, poor man's fight' line when commitment to the Confederacy was heavily contingent in 1861.

A combination of internal factors such as dissent, morale, class and gender, and external factors such as military and political leadership, economics and demographics, led to Robert E. Lee's surrender at Appomattox Court House on 9 April 1865. However scholars choose to interpret Confederate society, it is difficult to deny that there were serious divisions within. As historian James L. Roark put it, planters realised that 'rather than standing astride a perfectly ordered, conservative slave society, they were shakily perched on an unstable social pyramid, with deep fissures only thinly papered over'.[20] The intensity of historiographical debate over how successfully these cracks were 'papered over' obscures the merits of the differing viewpoints. It is a false dichotomy to posit a timeless class antagonism or strains of war as competing and rival explanations of Confederate defeat – both were important factors which reinforced the other. Southern women found it difficult to adjust to their new responsibilities and surely, at times, wanted to return to the status quo, although enraged by attacks on hearth and home. Synthesising the rival positions will help to provide a more nuanced understanding of the Confederate experience.

THE FREEDOM GENERATION

From the very beginning, Frederick Douglass argued that slavery was inextricably linked to the war, both as a cause and as a significant factor in its eventual outcome. Indeed, the very future of the Union was at stake, he argued. The leading black spokesman of the mid-nineteenth century urged Lincoln to utilise African Americans in the fight against the Confederacy and, above all, to strive for emancipation. In so doing, the war would be ennobled – transformed from a dispute about states' rights to a moral crusade intent on freeing the largest slave population in the world; 'the destiny of the colored American, however this mighty war shall terminate; is the destiny of America,' he said in 1862. Douglass challenged the nation to live up to the ideal that all men are created equal: 'In the very extreme difference of color and feature of the negro and the Anglo-Saxon, shall be learned the highest ideas of sacredness of man and the fullness and protection of human brotherhood.' Harriet Tubman, another escaped slave, was more blunt: 'God won't let Massa Linkum beat de South till he do the right thing. . . . dis nigger can tell Massa Linkum how to save de money and de young men. He do it by setting de niggers free.'[21]

Northern free blacks, in conjunction with abolitionist groups and Radical Republicans like Charles Sumner, tried their best to force the issue of slavery and emancipation onto the Civil War agenda. Southern free blacks were placed in an awkward situation and some, most notably the free people of colour in New Orleans, initially sided with the Confederates for fear that doing otherwise might jeopardise their position. Long-established black militia units in Louisiana that had fought with the Spanish, the French, and with Andrew Jackson against the Indians, would eventually fight for the Union, however. Much more so than white Americans, African Americans in both the North and the South quickly grasped the importance of the Civil War for their future, and the opportunity it provided to challenge notions of inherent inferiority.

It was the actions of the enslaved that proved most decisive, however; to be precise, slaves in Confederate states. Blacks had always taken advantage of any relaxation of plantation security to steal away for a few hours, or longer periods if possible. There was no more unsettling experience than that of civil war. African Americans left the plantations in their thousands. Fully a month *before* the official outbreak of hostilities at Fort Sumter, eight slaves entered Fort Pickens, manned by Union soldiers in Florida, seeking their freedom. They were arrested and handed over to local authorities for return to their owners. There can be little doubt that this caught the whites involved – soldiers, officers, local officials, slaveholders – by surprise. Secession seemed to be a purely white affair, touching slaves only tangentially. These blacks were not only fully aware of the current political situation, but sought to exploit it to their advantage. Federal policy, hastily clarified in the difficult circumstances, stipulated that the property rights of loyal southerners would be respected by suppressing slave rebellion and returning fugitives.

Paying no attention to official pronouncements, three escapees coming to the federal garrison at Fort Monroe, Virginia, in late May 1861, forced General Benjamin F. Butler into making a difficult decision. Southerners claiming to be loyal slaveholders asked for their return under the terms of the Fugitive Slave Act. Butler, who had been a courtroom lawyer before the war, refused on the grounds that the slaves were being used to aid the Confederate cause. Describing them as 'contraband of war', he turned the slaveholders away empty-handed, just as he would have done had they asked for the return of guns or cannons, because he knew that these slaves were being used to build an artillery battery. Within seven days, Butler reported the arrival of many more bondspeople – he estimated their market value to be about $60,000 – and thousands more poured into camp that summer. In August 1861, the First Confiscation Act supported Butler's actions, declaring that any property used 'for insurrectionary purposes' could be confiscated. That same month, General John C. Frémont issued a proclamation freeing all slaves belonging to Confederate sympathisers in Missouri. Frightened of the effect this might have on the border states, Lincoln forced Frémont to rescind the order. Nonetheless, shortly afterwards Congress forbade soldiers to return fugitive slaves and, in July 1862, the Second Confiscation Act permitted the seizure of enemy property, setting slaves taken in this way 'forever free'. While only applying to disloyal masters, this was a significant step nonetheless. By arriving in such great numbers, the problem of what to do with escaped slaves went up the chain of command, from the soldier to the general, to the War Department, and ultimately to the president himself.

The effect of this mass defection was immense. Enslaved labour undergirded the Confederate war effort. Impressment (compulsory hiring) of slaves became increasingly common in the Confederacy, making up for a shortage of manpower. On the frontlines, bondspeople built fortifications, dug trenches and provided menial support. They also came with planters as personal servants. In the shipyards and armouries, they helped to make the weapons to sustain the Confederate armies. They repaired roads, bridges and railroads. On the plantations, their labour cultivated the food needed to feed soldiers and civilians. No matter how badly slaves worked, their labour allowed southern whites to join the army. By seizing slave property, Union forces turned one of their enemy's strongest assets into a weapon of their own.

Moreover, Union soldiers hired blacks to carry out many different tasks. Camps of contrabands were established in occupied parts of the South. In eastern North Carolina, for example, a supervisor of the poor described the various ways in which approximately ten thousand black men, women and children contributed. Former bondsmen 'built three first class earth work forts' in just four months. They 'loaded and discharged cargoes' from ships, 'served regularly as crews on about forty steamers' and laboured in 'the Quatermasters, Commissary and Ordnance offices'. Some were 'good carpenters, blacksmiths, coopers', who helped to build bridges among other things. More than fifty volunteers undertook 'the most important work' of scouting and spying, roving 'from thirty to three hundred miles within the enemy's lines'. The pay was eight dollars a month. 'The women and children supported themselves with but little aid from the government by washing, ironing, cooking, making pies, cakes &c. for the troops', and women working in 'hospitals received $4 a month, clothes and one ration'. Both the brawn and the brains of African Americans were utilised to defeat the Confederacy.[22]

Union forces were struck by the dignity and willingness to help of the escaped slaves, as well as their often shocking state of dress and health. The majority of white northerners had never encountered blacks, let alone slavery, and this came as something of a surprise. Union nurse Mary Livermore described contrabands boarding a Mississippi steamer as 'subdued, impassive, solemn, [with] hope and courage now lighting up their sable faces'. She also described the capture and eventual return of 'an intelligent contraband'. This individual had been a vital source of knowledge about the local environment and the movement of enemy troops, like countless other blacks during the course of the war. Union soldiers recaptured him at Baton Rouge. He had been given 150 lashes by the Confederates, and an iron collar had been fixed around his neck, which Livermore described in great detail: 'a round rod of iron, two inches in circumference, riveted together before and behind with two iron prongs one inch wide, three fourths of an inch thick, and twelve inches long, rising from each side directly outside the ears'.[23] Incidents such as this vividly highlighted the horrors of bondage, and were widely reported in letters back home, gradually influencing northern public opinion.

Slaveholders were as vigilant as they could be in policing the plantations at a time when thousands of white men left to fight. The most resourceful 'refugeed' their slaves to what they hoped were safe locations within the South, such as Texas, out of the way of the advancing Union Army. However, blacks in the Confederate interior, who found it very difficult to reach Federal lines, became increasingly recalcitrant. Working duties were contested more vehemently than ever before, as planters tried, with some difficulty, to ratchet up the level of performance in order to meet war demands. Depending on local circumstances, slaves simply refused to carry out tasks they had performed for decades, would run away more frequently, or would steal provisions and other items. Reports of slaves being wilfully disobedient, in a manner not seen before, were widespread. This problem grew to unmanageable levels as the war took its toll and supplies of food became scarce, especially as supervision of slaves was more likely to be left in hands of wounded or elderly men and women.

Where owners and overseers remained in control – Confederate legislation exempted one man from conscription for every twenty slaves – the problem was slightly alleviated. But the key to running a plantation was maintaining discipline and all struggled to do that in the unique circumstances of 1861–65. The brother of Confederate vice-president Alexander H. Stephens wrote how the situation in Georgia was becoming untenable as early as 1863: 'Our negro population are going to give us great trouble. They are becoming extensively corrupted.' Without the requisite numbers of whites to maintain security and discipline, 'slavery is already so undermined and demoralized as never to be of much use to us, even if we had peace and independence to day. The institution has received a terrible shock which is tending to its disintegration and ruin.'[24]

There is no clearer signal of the African American desire for freedom than the huge numbers of blacks leaving the plantations. Of three and a half million slaves in the Confederacy, somewhere between 500,000 and 700,000 escaped. Escape was hardly an easy option, especially as blacks had learnt to proceed with extreme caution over the years. Slaves risked severe punishments – and even death – by leaving, and state authorities took preventative measures as best they could. Thousands of Confederate troops were stationed on the front line, and the home guard patrolled most counties. Nonetheless, the vast majority of slaves left when the opportunity presented itself, and not just individuals but whole families. Geographical location was crucial – it was much easier to escape if the Federals were close by. Virginian slaves, for example, had far greater opportunities than their counterparts in the Black Belt. Despite the dramatic drain of bondspeople, historians usually accept W. E. B. Du Bois's famous characterisation that southern slaves took part in a 'general strike', rather than a mass uprising, during the war.[25]

A recent work by Stephen Hahn takes a different view, contending that southern blacks took part in one of the largest slave rebellions in history, which 'inspired the most sweeping revolution of the nineteenth century'. In a major interpretative reconceptualisation (the evidence he uses is well known), Hahn redefines the slave community as inherently political and suggests that the enslaved, although not having formal political rights, nonetheless came from a long political tradition. The slave community was a crucial conduit of culture and focus of social networks but, Hahn argues, it also fostered a collective political identity by selecting (political) leaders and dissecting the latest news about congressional debates between the Democrats and the Republicans. Blacks listened to white conversations, and rumour became a powerful weapon in the hands of the weak. Political news, such as Lincoln's victory, spread from one plantation to another, being 'open to continuous improvisation and embellishment, thereby activating and energizing (in effect politicizing) those who become involved in its circuits'. Rumour 'may be regarded as a form of popular political discourse', he contends. With this political tradition behind them, American slaves 'felt empowered to turn one rebellion into two: to turn a rebellion of their masters against the authority of the federal government into a rebellion of their own'.[26] About one in five slaves escaped during the war, surely demonstrating that blacks were not broken by the experience of bondage, no matter how its demands subdued their spirits.

POLITICAL EMANCIPATION AND RECONSTRUCTION

The will to make emancipation a primary objective was intimately linked to the events of the war and the successes, or more accurately reverses, of the Union Army. Whether this was the main reason behind the political abolition of slavery and the eventual enlistment of blacks is a matter of considerable historiographical debate. In hindsight, it seems logical, even straightforward. The centrality of slavery to the Confederacy was obvious; the willingness of blacks to leave, and the problems this posed the southern states, equally clear. Moreover, African Americans were not only content to aid the Union cause by offering the labour, but they also wanted to become soldiers. Ex-slaves in particular had a strong motivation to join the Federal Army. Most needed a wage, it is clear, but the overwhelming desire was to fight former owners and contribute to the destruction of a hated institution. Such action would help to erode the emasculating effects of slavery, as blacks regained their manhood, although it should be noted that not all felt this way – some distrusted the Federals as much as they did the Confederates.

What seems obvious today was far from clear at the time, because the subject of black soldiers was extremely controversial. The steps leading up to Lincoln's Emancipation Proclamation are well known. On 22 July 1862, Lincoln told his cabinet that he intended to announce a preliminary Emancipation Proclamation. He asked their advice, but indicated that he would not be dissuaded from this course of action. On 23 September, after choosing to view stalemate at the battle of Antietam as a Union success, Lincoln announced that all slaves within rebellious states on 1 January 1863 would be 'then, thenceforward, and forever free'. If he hoped that this might persuade some reluctant Confederates to return to the fold, he was disappointed. When the Emancipation Proclamation came into effect on 1 January 1863, slaves in rebel states were liberated 'as an act of justice, warranted by the Constitution, upon military necessity'. The border states and parts of the Confederacy under Union control, notably sections of Louisiana, Virginia and Tennessee, were exempt. Lincoln simultaneously called for the recruitment of slaves and free blacks into the Union Army. Black troops, led by white officers in segregated regiments, made their way to the front lines in large numbers during the summer of 1863. From that point, Lincoln campaigned for a constitutional amendment to abolish slavery, fearing that his executive order issued under the authority of 'war powers' could be overturned when hostilities ceased.

Few historical acts have aroused so much controversy as the Emancipation Proclamation, and interpreting Abraham Lincoln's motivation remains a fiercely contested scholarly pursuit. Critics can find plenty of ammunition to show that Lincoln was racist, and was reluctantly forced to accede to demands for emancipation because of the state of the war in 1862. In this view, slavery's demise was a strategic, not a moral, decision. In April 1861, Lincoln informed the Virginia secession convention that 'I have no purpose, directly or indirectly, to interfere with the institution of slavery in the States where it exists. I believe I have no lawful right to do so, and I have no inclination to do so.' As late as August 1862, he wrote Horace Greeley that his 'paramount objective in this struggle *is* to save the Union, and is *not* either to save or to destroy slavery'. These comments should not be taken out of context, though. Lincoln chose his response carefully in accord with the circumstances of the day. Any move to attack slavery might push the border states toward the Confederacy. There is no doubt that Lincoln was a longtime critic of slavery as an institution, feeling it to be morally wrong, economically damaging and politically contradictory in a democratic republic.[27]

Lincoln's views on slavery were more clear-cut than his racial views, which he guarded closely and which probably changed during the course of his career. Like other Whigs, such as Henry Clay, he believed in the organic nature of American society and the need for its various parts to function in harmony to avoid social conflict.[28] Echoing the views of Thomas Jefferson, Lincoln thought that blacks and whites would struggle to peacefully co-exist in the United States, and therefore supported colonisation. He endorsed this position in a meeting with black leaders at the White House in August 1862, and the Preliminary Emancipation Proclamation outlined 'effort[s] to colonize persons of African descent, with their consent, upon this continent or elsewhere'. However, the actual Emancipation Proclamation failed to mention colonisation, and Lincoln never returned to this subject again. Like most of his era, Lincoln probably believed whites were superior to blacks, but he was not a racist demagogue. For example, he refused to be drawn into a race-baiting debate with Stephen A. Douglas in 1858, while running for the US senate in Illinois. Lincoln's republican mentality defended the rights of all to be granted equal opportunities; whether blacks and whites were equally capable of taking advantage of those opportunities was probably not the critical issue for him.

The bitter argument between historians considering Lincoln 'the Great Emancipator' and those stressing the role the slaves played in claiming freedom for themselves has tended to generate more heat than light. A variety of motives lay behind emancipation and the arming of blacks. It was a strategic move, delivering troops at a crucial time when northern morale was at a low ebb. It dashed southern hopes of British or French intervention, one way in which the Confederacy believed it might win the war. The failure to abolish slavery in the border states was cautious, but Lincoln was concerned about the authority of the executive office to take this action in loyal areas. He urged the border states voluntarily to draw up emancipation plans, and bondspeople forced this issue themselves by leaving for other states where they could claim their freedom by joining the Federal Army. At the same time, emancipation was a highly risky stategy, potentially jeopardising Lincoln's chances of re-election in 1864. The New York City draft riot in July 1863, in which more than a hundred people were killed, was the most prominent of a number of disturbances in the North in 1863 caused by the introduction of conscription and by the fear of an influx of blacks to the North. 'A balanced appraisal,' concludes historian Peter Kolchin, 'recognizes the ways in which slaves prodded the Federal government to take decisive action against slavery, but also recognizes the centrality of this [Federal] action to the overthrow of slavery – in other words, sees the slaves both as subjects helping to make their own history *and* as objects of historical action.'[29]

The arming of black troops was a vitally important turning point of the war. Historian Joseph T. Glatthaar argues that African Americans 'did not win the war, but timely and extensive support from them contributed significantly and may have made the difference between a Union victory and a stalemate or defeat'.[30] Approximately 180,000 African Americans served in the Union Army (10 per cent of the total number of serving Union soldiers), 10,000 served in the navy, and tens of thousands more served as military labourers and agricultural workers in the Federally-occupied South. The majority of recruits to the Union army and navy– approximately 134,000 – were black southerners. African American soldiers fought a war on two fronts, against the forces of Confederate resistance and against the forces of racism within the Union Army which reinforced their second-class status. Generals were reluctant to put them in battle. Black regiments were badly under-resourced and suffered discriminatory pay: $10 a month, compared to $13 for whites. Some troops refused to take this wage, and Sergeant William Walker was executed for his protests.

In spite of these problems, black troops fought with distinction in every theatre of the war. On 27 May 1863, 200 members of the Louisiana Native Guards died in an assault on Port Hudson in Louisiana, and the unit also fought with distinction in the battle of Milliken's Bend, turning back a Confederate assault with furious bayonet charges. The 54th Massachusetts Infantry Regiment led a suicidal assault on the Confederate position at Fort Wagner, South Carolina, in July 1863. Their courage captured the popular imagination and served as a powerful message to those who doubted African

Americans. Shortly afterwards, Lincoln rebuked those proclaiming they 'will not fight to free negroes'. When the North was victorious, he observed, African American men will know 'that, with silent tongue, and clenched teeth, and steady eye, and well-poised bayonet, they have helped mankind on to this great consummation; while, I fear, there will be some white ones, unable to forget that, with malignant heart, and deceitful speech, they have strove to hinder it.' These actions were a powerful reminder of the equality of men, resoundingly answering in the affirmative the popular question asked by whites: 'Can they fight?'[31]

The strained relationship with regular troops gradually got better as whites witnessed black commitment on the battlefield. Not all soldiers changed their racist opinions; a minority continued to believe that the only positive result of the Emancipation Proclamation was that blacks were now dying in place of whites. The effect on other white troops was profound, however. As an Irish officer succinctly put it, 'I never believed in niggers before, but by Jasus, they are hell for fighting.'[32] This was vitally important in changing northern public opinion and advancing the cause of black citizenship to a level unimaginable in 1860.

Lincoln's party, stunned by his assassination on 14 April 1865, faced a daunting task in attempting to rebuild the South. If reeling from the economic and human cost of the Civil War and the humiliation of defeat was not bad enough, the very foundation of southern society had been taken away by the Thirteenth Amendment abolishing slavery. Reconstruction between 1865 and 1877 saw the South occupied by northern troops in five military districts. An unprecedented flurry of legislative activity took place. The Republican Party legally granted African Americans full civil and political rights by passing three amendments to the Constitution, and many legislative bills. These measures were taken despite the opposition of President Andrew Johnson and southern state governments passing Black Codes in 1865 and 1866 that acknowledged the end of slavery but severely restricted the rights of blacks. The end of the American Civil War marked the beginning of an internal conflict in the South, as the federal government, former planters, non-slaveholders, free blacks and ex-slaves struggled to define the terms of the peace. Social, economic and political relations had to be redefined in a society that was no longer ordered by slavery.

BLACK RECONSTRUCTION IN THE SOUTH

Black southerners were highly active in promoting their freedom. They demonstrated great enterprise individually and collectively in distancing themselves from their slave past and constructing a future founded on equality and opportunity. However, this proved to be a fragile freedom. Not only did the federal government fail to implement the reforms needed to provide freedmen and their families with the same opportunities as whites, but the violent reaction of former Confederates to the Reconstruction process severely curtailed black independence.

The most potent symbol to African Americans of their new-found freedom was land ownership. As independent farmers, they would attain not only economic autonomy, but also a sense of personal empowerment. Former slaves felt a sense of entitlement to possession of their own farmland, considering it just compensation for the centuries of unpaid labour that they and their ancestors had performed for white planters. 'We has a right to the land where we are located,' stated Bayley Wyatt. 'Our wives, our children, our husbands, has been sold over and over again to purchase the lands we now locate upon; for that reason we have a divine right to the land. And then didn't we clear the lands and raise the crops of corn, of cotton, of tobacco, of rice, of sugar, of everything?'[33]

African Americans anticipated that the property of former Confederates would be confiscated and redistributed as smallholdings. However, President Johnson restored land to its former owners on condition they pledge their loyalty to the federal government. Only in South Carolina did the state government attempt to redistribute the property of white planters. The Republican administration in South Carolina established a land commission empowered to purchase land and resell it on extended terms of credit to African Americans. By 1876, about 14,000 families had acquired their own homesteads under this scheme. Despite this initiative, no other state government took similar action to feed African American hunger for land. Some imposed high taxes on landed property in the expectation that it would render plantations increasingly unprofitable and force whites to sell parts of their estates to blacks at a reduced rate. The plan did not work.

In July 1866, Congress passed the Southern Homestead Act. The new law provided for the cheap sale of public lands to blacks and loyal whites in five states. However, much of the land was of poor quality, and the federal government failed to provide the financial assistance that prospective farmers needed to purchase tools, seeds and fertiliser. The result was that only 4,000 persons obtained land under the terms of the new law.

Why did the Republican Party not make a more concerted effort to facilitate African Americans' acquisition of land? Despite the hopes of Radical Republicans, most party members were not ideologically disposed to the reallocation of land to former slaves. They considered such a policy to be in contravention of their principle of minimum federal government intervention in the affairs of the states. Moreover, the confiscation of land conflicted with their belief in the inviolable right of the individual to own private property. Many Republicans further reasoned that the provision of land to African Americans would undermine their ability to become self-reliant members of a free society. This assertion rested on the flawed assumption that freedmen no longer faced the structural barriers that impeded their ability to live on equal terms with their former masters.

Unable to fulfil their ambition of becoming independent farmers, blacks reluctantly returned to work for their former masters. The Freedmen's Bureau, set up in March 1865 to provide food, medical supplies and guidance to ex-slaves, assumed responsibility for assisting freedmen in negotiating labour contracts and resolving disputes with white landlords. However, the Bureau often sided with white landowners in enforcing contracts that restricted autonomy and re-tied African Americans to the bonds of dependency. From this situation emerged the new system of sharecropping that became the dominant mode of rural labour relations for decades. The disastrous impact of this system is discussed in detail in Chapter 7. While sharecropping was a harsh reality for freedmen who had dreamed of becoming independent yeomen, it did demonstrate the ability of African Americans to secure at least some concessions from white planters. Under the new labour arrangements, black farmers attained some measure of independence. Their resistance to the gang system in particular ensured that they were able to work without constant supervision. Freedmen also used their ability to move from one plantation to another as a means of forcing white landowners to compete for their labour by offering them improved working conditions.

Black southerners attempted to assert their autonomy from whites in numerous other ways. One of the most important aspects of this drive for self-determination was the stabilisation of black family life. Despite the interfering efforts of former masters, African Americans attained a new sense of order and stability in their family lives. The immediate aftermath of the war witnessed countless reunions of family members separated during slavery, and a rush on the part of couples to legalise their marriages. One observer in Richmond poignantly described the arrival of blacks searching for their relatives: 'Aged women and grayhaired men journeyed to Virginia from far-off Georgia hoping to hear some word or, perchance, to meet sons and daughters whom they bade farewell at the auction block. Many had the good fortune to find those they sought, and their greetings were pathetic beyond description.'[34]

Freedom also reshaped the dynamic of gender relations in African American households. Black men and women emulated white social conventions in subscribing to the notion of separate gender spheres. Black men bore with pride their ability to become the sole economic provider for the household. Their decision to reduce their working hours, and the withdrawal of their wives and children from the labour force, afforded a new freedom from the relentless toil of slavery. According to historians Roger Ransom and Richard Sutch, southern blacks worked on a per capita basis between 28 per cent and 37 per cent fewer hours following their emancipation.[35] The removal of women and children from the fields was a source of great irritation to white planters, who resented the loss of their labour. Whites contemptuously accused African American women who refused to work in the fields of 'playing the lady'. What they perceived as a mark of black indolence was in reality an affirmation of black independence. As one freedwoman informed a northern journalist, under slavery she had 'to nus' my chil'n four times a day and pick two hundred pounds cotton besides'. Assessing the changes brought by emancipation, she concluded: 'I've a heap better time now'n I had when I was in bondage.'[36]

Historian Laura F. Edwards argues that ultimately, however, gender served to reinforce the racial inferiority of blacks. In asserting male authority in the household, black men served to re-state the importance of patriarchy within the South, an institution that ultimately stressed the superiority of *white* men over dependents, be they blacks, women or children. Moreover, because virtually all blacks had to rent land from white planters, their free status was compromised, placing them within the web of a different kind of dependent relationship to that of master and slave, but one which was dependent nonetheless. The 'very fact that African Americans labored for another saturated them with a dependence that freedom alone could never eliminate', observes Edwards.[37]

A concern for the future of their families also led freedmen to embrace new educational opportunities. Most blacks had been denied the opportunity to acquire even basic literacy. Education offered them the hope that they could better themselves and establish a status of equality with whites. By 1877, more than 600,000 black children had attended schools established by Republican state governments and the Freedmen's Bureau. Moreover, African Americans pooled their collective efforts to purchase land, construct schoolhouses and pay the salaries of teachers. According to one estimate, by 1870 blacks had raised more than $1 million to promote education. This commitment towards education brought substantial results. When slavery was abolished, 90 per cent of African Americans could not read or write; by 1880, the black illiteracy rate had decreased to 70 per cent. Relative to whites, African Americans still suffered from a chronic lack of formal education.

Nonetheless, a 200 per cent increase in black literacy in only fifteen years represented real progress.[38]

Reconstruction also witnessed the establishment of the first institutions of black higher education in the South, including Fisk University in Nashville, Tennessee; Hampton Institute in Virginia; and Tougaloo College in Jackson, Mississippi. Black education nonetheless faced an uncertain future by the 1870s, after the federal government terminated the Freedmen's Bureau and withdrew almost all support for public schooling. The decision to entrust control of public education to local and state government resulted in enormous inequality in the provision of schooling for black and white children during the Jim Crow era.

Advances in black education were emblematic of broader efforts to build an autonomous community free of white social and economic control. At the core of this community was the church. The denominations that attracted most black worshippers were the African Methodist Episcopal Church, the African Methodist Episcopal Zion Church and, above all, the Baptists. Churches were not only a source of spiritual inspiration, but were also central in nurturing secular growth. They provided the space for schools, meetings of mutual aid and fraternal societies, political assemblies and social gatherings.

A further core element of freedom as defined by African Americans was the right to vote. Southern blacks first became involved in electoral politics as a result of the Reconstruction Act of 1867, which empowered them to help select representatives to the state constitutional conventions; male suffrage was also encouraged by the Fourteenth Amendment. On 26 February 1869, Congress approved the Fifteenth Amendment, forbidding federal or state governments to withold the right to vote 'on account of race, color, or previous condition of servitude'. Despite stubborn resistance, the Amendment received ratification on 30 March 1870. Republican support for black suffrage was motivated by both high principle and partisan self-interest. In the face of militant opposition from southern Democrats to the Reconstruction process, many Republicans argued that the franchise was the surest means to protect the rights of freedmen. The narrow margin of victory attained by Ulysses S. Grant in the 1868 presidential election also encouraged party members to support black suffrage because these thousands of new black voters were likely to cast their ballots for the Republicans.

African Americans seized upon the opportunity to participate in electoral politics. They swelled the ranks of the Union League, an auxiliary of the Republican Party that promoted black voter registration and raised funds for the provision of medical care and construction of schools and churches. Not only did the freedmen vote; but many also attained election to public office.

The number of African Americans who served at a national level was relatively small: two senators, sixteen congressmen and not a single governor. However, blacks gained more substantial representation at the state and local level. During Reconstruction, more than 600 African Americans served in southern legislatures. While some of these office-holders were northerners, most were former slaves. There were nonetheless serious limitations to black political influence. Relative to their share of the southern population, African Americans were under-represented in state government. Those who did serve also suffered the condescension of white Republicans, who seldom recognised them as equals. Despite this, most black office-holders worked determinedly to protect and promote the rights of their people.

For a brief time, southern state governments were bi-racial coalitions of whites, including former southern Unionists and non-slaveholders, ex-slaves and free blacks. Northerners also headed south for various reasons, including self-interest, but also for philanthropic purposes and from a desire to remould the region in the image of the North. In the decades after Reconstruction, southerners would accuse these administrations of being incompetent and corrupt, a charge supported by historians in the first half of the twentieth century. This interpretation says more about the worsening racial climate in the late nineteenth century and early twentieth century than it does about the post-war period. Recent scholarship shows that the record of southern Republican state administrations – who reformed taxes and the judiciary system, built more schools and hospitals, outlawed discrimination and embarked on a process of economic redevelopment – was no worse than that of their counterparts in the North.

African Americans would not have long to enjoy the opportunities afforded by political participation. White southerners may have lost the war, but a dominant belief in the innate inferiority of blacks and the rule of white males had not been surrendered. Feeding off racism, white supremacy and the alleged 'need' to protect white women from the black man, former planters in a resurgent Democratic Party attempted to break Republican rule. The fledgling southern Republican Party actually enjoyed surprising success in attracting votes in places like the North Carolina Piedmont, where historian Karin L. Zipf argues lower-class whites 'rejected white supremacist rhetoric'. Similarly, Paul D. Escott notes 'that appeals to race consciousness were not working' and it took a vicious campaign of Ku Klux Klan violence between 1868 and 1872 to oust the Republicans from the Piedmont.[39]

In states with substantial white voting majorities, however, the Republicans found it difficult to stay in office. Where the balance of power could not be overturned at the ballot box, Democrats resorted to fraud, intimidation and violence, conducting a ruthless campaign to strip freedmen of their rights and return the South to white home rule. In this way, the latent ugliness of southern racism, which had been somewhat checked under a system of slavery that regulated white–black relations, was released. The paternal view of blacks as child-like and dependent was superseded by a more hostile white view of the dangerous threat posed by blacks, especially black men, which was used as a justification for much greater levels of violence and led to a wave of mass lynchings in the late nineteenth century. The important work of Diane Miller Sommerville shows that the white southern preoccupation with black male sexuality and the idea of the black rapist – on which so much violence was predicated – was a phenomenon of the post-bellum years. As historian Joel Williamson puts it, 'one of the great ironies of American history' is that emancipation simultaneously 'freed racism'.[40]

White southern opposition to Reconstruction assumed its most potent form in the Ku Klux Klan. Founded in Pulaski, Tennessee, in December 1865, the secret order was sworn to the restoration of white supremacist rule. Klansmen waged a campaign of violence against blacks and their white allies. Freedmen's Bureau agent General W. P. Carlin testified to the scale of Klan brutality: 'The colored people are leaving their homes, and are fleeing to the towns and large cities for protection. They say that it is impossible for them to work during the day and keep watching during the night, which is necessary for them to do, in order to save their lives.'[41] Klan terrorism persisted even after Grand Wizard Nathan Bedford Forrest announced the dissolution of the 'invisible empire' in January 1869.

Congress attempted to counteract white paramilitary violence through the Enforcement Acts of 1870–71 and the Ku Klux Klan Act of 1871. However, the legislation failed to secure the conviction of more than a few hundred Klansmen. Members of the hooded order perjured themselves in court to provide false alibis for their friends. Witnesses prepared to testify against the Klan were also intimidated into silence. Moreover, racial violence did not cease with the disbandment of the Klan. On 13 April 1873, a paramilitary organisation known as the White League massacred more than 100 African Americans in Colfax, Louisiana.

Racial violence was not the only factor contributing to the demise of Reconstruction. The economic depression that swept through the United States in 1873 forced the Republican Party to alter its political priorities. By then, the influence of Radicals within the party had waned as a result of the deaths of their principal spokespersons, Thaddeus Stevens and Charles Sumner. The party had also been torn apart by the defection of a splinter group named the Liberal Republicans. In 1872, this faction nominated

Horace Greeley as its presidential candidate on a platform calling for sectional reconciliation and the restoration of southern home rule. Greeley suffered a resounding defeat, but his campaign struck a chord and contributed to a resurgence of northern racism. The Democrats made substantial electoral gains in the 1874 elections and reclaimed the House of Representatives.

Ultimately, nagging doubts about black equality in the North undermined Reconstruction. A minority of Radical Republicans believed in integration, but the vast majority of their constituents, as well as the more numerous moderates in the party, accepted prevailing racist doctrines. Initial public euphoria and sympathy for the slave, augmented by the contribution of black military regiments in the Civil War, waned. Reconstruction reached its untimely end as a result of the disputed presidential election of 1876. The South accepted the election of Republican Rutherford B. Hayes in return for the removal of all federal troops from the region. Republican rule was over and the South had been 'redeemed' by the Democrats.

Historians are divided in their assessment of the successes and failures of Reconstruction. Some regard it as an abject failure, others that there was little more that the Republicans could have done. For the first time, but not the last, the federal government made a significant effort to enforce the civil rights of black southerners and change racial attitudes in the South. However, Republicans were trying to implement equality in a social order conditioned by centuries of slavery. Although legal measures could be passed, deeply ingrained attitudes proved far more difficult to change. The problem was exacerbated by an appalling economic situation, in which a return to cotton eventually proved fatal. For the freedmen, the so-called Compromise of 1877 constituted a surrender of the promises of emancipation and signalled the beginning of a new era in southern history, in which overt violence, institutional racism and the myth of the black rapist underpinned the resurgence of white supremacy. No matter how bad things became for black southerners, however, they never doubted the importance of slavery's abolition, even though Reconstruction was an 'unfinished revolution'.[42]

Notes

1. Michael P. Johnson (ed.), *Abraham Lincoln, Slavery, and the Civil War: Selected Writings and Speeches* (Boston, MA: Bedford/St. Martin's, 2001), p. 63.
2. W. E. B. Du Bois, *Black Reconstruction in America 1860-1880* ([1935] New York: Atheneum, 1979), p. 30.
3. David M. Potter, *The Impending Crisis, 1848-1861* (New York: Harper and Row, 1976), p. 113.

4. Susan-Mary Grant, *North Over South: Northern Nationalism and American Identity in the Antebellum Era* (Lawrence: University Press of Kansas, 2000).
5. Eric Foner, *Free Soil, Free Labor, Free Men: The Ideology of the Republican Party Before the Civil War* ([1970] New York: Oxford University Press, 1995), p. xxv.
6. Manisha Sinha, *The Counterrevolution of Slavery: Politics and Ideology in Antebellum South Carolina* (Chapel Hill: University of North Carolina Press, 2000), pp. 221, 7.
7. John McCardell, *The Idea of a Southern Nation: Southern Nationalists and Southern Nationalism, 1830–1860* (New York: W. W. Norton, 1979).
8. David Brown, *Southern Outcast: Hinton Rowan Helper and The Impending Crisis of the South* (Baton Rouge: Louisiana State University Press, 2006), pp. 170–5 (Hamilton quotation on p. 174).
9. Michael P. Johnson, *Toward a Patriarchal Republic: The Secession of Georgia* (Baton Rouge: Louisiana State University Press, 1977), p. 87; Daniel Crofts, 'And the War Came', in Lacy K. Ford (ed.), *A Companion to the Civil War and Reconstruction* (Oxford: Blackwell, 2005), pp. 186–7; J. William Harris, *The Making of the American South: A Short History, 1500–1877* (Oxford: Blackwell, 2006), p. 177.
10. James M. McPherson, *Battle Cry of Freedom: The Civil War Era* (New York: Oxford University Press, 1988), pp. 237–9.
11. Bertram Wyatt-Brown, *Yankee Saints and Southern Sinners* (Baton Rouge: Louisiana State University Press, 1985), pp. 183–212; Emory M. Thomas, *Robert E. Lee: A Biography* (New York: W. W. Norton, 1995), p. 188.
12. The key works in this debate are evaluated in James L. Roark, 'Behind the Lines: Confederate Economy and Society', in James M. McPherson and William J. Cooper, Jr (eds), *Writing the Civil War: The Quest to Understand* (Columbia: University of South Carolina Press, 1998), pp. 201–27.
13. Gary W. Gallagher, *The Confederate War* (Cambridge, MA: Harvard University Press, 1997), pp. 63–111.
14. James M. McPherson, *For Cause and Comrades: Why Men Fought in the Civil War* (New York: Oxford University Press, 1997), p. 21; James M. McPherson, *What They Fought For, 1861–1865* (Baton Rouge: Louisiana State University Press, 1994), p. 18.
15. William W. Freehling, *The South Vs. the South: How Anti-Confederate Southerners Shaped the Course of the Civil War* (New York: Oxford University Press, 2001), p. 61.
16. Anne Firor Scott, *The Southern Lady: From Pedestal to Politics, 1830–1930* (Chicago: University of Chicago Press, 1970); Catherine Clinton, *The Plantation Mistress* (New York: Pantheon Books, 1982), p. 34.; Mary Boykin Chesnut, diary entry (18 March 1861), in C. Vann Woodward (ed.), *Mary Chesnut's Civil War* (New Haven: Yale University Press, 1981), p. 29; Elizabeth Fox-Genovese, *Within the Plantation Household: Black and White Women of the Old South* (Chapel Hill: University of North Carolina Press, 1988), p. 338.

17. Drew Gilpin Faust, *Mothers of Invention: Women of the Slaveholding South in the American Civil War* (Chapel Hill: University of North Carolina Press, 1996), p. 239.
18. Mary Nye (1862), cited in Martin Crawford, *Ashe County's Civil War: Community and Society in the Appalachian South* (Charlottesville: University Press of Virginia, 2001), p. 101.
19. Drew Gilpin Faust, 'Altars of Sacrifice: Confederate Women and the Narratives of War', *Journal of American History,* 76 (March 1992), p. 1228; LeeAnn Whites, *The Civil War as a Crisis in Gender: Augusta, Georgia, 1860–1890* (Athens: University of Georgia Press, 1995); Jacqueline Glass Campbell, *When Sherman Marched North from the Sea: Resistance on the Confederate Home Front* (Chapel Hill: University of North Carolina Press, 2003).
20. James L. Roark, *Masters Without Slaves: Southern Planters in the Civil War and Reconstruction* (New York: W. W. Norton, 1977), p. 14.
21. Frederick Douglass, cited in Susan-Mary Grant, 'Fighting for Freedom: African-American Soldiers in the Civil War', in Susan-Mary Grant and Brian Holden Reid (eds), *The American Civil War: Explorations and Reconsiderations* (Harlow: Longman, 2000), p. 207; Harriet Tubman, cited in Darlene Clark Hine (ed.), *Black Women in American History. Vol. IV* (New York: Carlson, 1990), p. 1145.
22. Vincent Colyer (1863), cited in Ira Berlin et al. (eds) *Free at Last: A Documentary History of Slavery, Freedom, and the Civil War* (New York: The New Press, 1992), pp. 175–6.
23. Mary Livermore, *My Story of the War: A Woman's Narrative of Four Years Personal Experience as Nurse in the Union Army* ([1887] New York: Da Capo, 1995), pp. 242, 440.
24. Linton Stephens (1863), cited in J. William Harris, *Plain Folk and Gentry in a Slave Society: White Liberty and Black Slavery in Augusta's Hinterlands* (Middletown, CT: Wesleyan University Press, 1985), p. 167.
25. Du Bois, *Black Reconstruction,* pp. 55–83.
26. Steven Hahn, *A Nation Under Our Feet: Black Political Struggles in the Rural South From Slavery to the Great Migration* (Cambridge, MA: Harvard University Press, 2003), pp. 65, 57–8, 64.
27. Johnson (ed.), *Abraham Lincoln,* p. 205.
28. Daniel Walker Howe, *The Political Culture of the American Whigs* (Chicago: University of Chicago Press, 1979), pp. 263–98.
29. Peter Kolchin, 'Slavery and Freedom in the Civil War South', in McPherson and Cooper (eds), *Writing the Civil War,* p. 250. In this essay, Kolchin provides a lucid summary of the competing historiographical views.
30. Joseph T. Glatthaar, 'Black Glory: The African-American Role in Union Victory', in Gabor S. Boritt (ed.), *Why the Confederacy Lost* (New York: Oxford University Press, 1992), p. 138.

31. Abraham Lincoln (1863), cited in McPherson, *Battle Cry of Freedom*, p. 687.
32. 'Irish Democrat', cited in Dudley Taylor Cornish, *The Sable Arm: Black Troops in the Union Army, 1861–1865* ([1956] Lawrence: University Press of Kansas, 1987), p. 147.
33. Roy Finkenbine (ed.), *Sources of the African-American Past* (London: Longman, 1993), p. 88.
34. *New National Era*, 23 July, 1874, in Dorothy Sterling (ed.), *The Trouble They Seen: The Story of Reconstruction in the Words of African Americans* ([1976] New York: Da Capo Press, 1994), p. 216.
35. Roger L. Ransom and Richard Sutch, *One Kind of Freedom: The Economic Consequences of Emancipation* (Cambridge: Cambridge University Press, 1977), p. 6.
36. Jacqueline Jones, *Labor of Love, Labor of Sorrow: Black Women, Work, and the Family, From Slavery to the Present* (New York: Basic Books, 1985), p. 60.
37. Laura F. Edwards, *Gendered Strife and Confusion: The Political Culture of Reconstruction* (Urbana: University of Illinois Press, 1997), p. 79. See also Leslie A. Schwalm, *A Hard Fight for We: Women's Transition from Slavery to Freedom in South Carolina* (Urbana: University of Illinois Press, 1997).
38. James M. McPherson, *Abraham Lincoln and the Second American Revolution* (New York: Oxford University Press, 1991), pp. 16–17.
39. Karin L. Zipf, '"The Whites Shall Rule This Land or Die"': Gender, Race, and Class in North Carolina Reconstruction Politics', *Journal of Southern History*, 65 (August 1999), p. 529; Paul D. Escott, 'White Republicanism and Ku Klux Klan Terror: The North Carolina Piedmont During Reconstruction', in Jeffrey J. Crow, Paul D. Escott and Charles L. Flynn, Jr, (eds), *Race, Class and Politics in Southern History: Essays in Honor of Robert F. Durden* (Baton Rouge: Louisiana State University Press, 1989), p. 28.
40. Diane Miller Sommerville, *Rape and Race in the Nineteenth-Century South* (Chapel Hill: University of North Carolina Press, 2004); Joel Williamson, *The Crucible of Race: Black–White Relations in the American South Since Emancipation* (New York: Oxford University Press, 1984), p. 109.
41. Allen W. Trelease, *White Terror: The Ku Klux Klan Conspiracy and Southern Reconstruction* (Baton Rouge: Louisiana State University Press, 1971), p. 42.
42. Eric Foner, *Reconstruction: America's Unfinished Revolution* (New York: Harper and Row, 1988).

Chapter 7

'THE WHITE SUPREME': RACE RELATIONS IN THE JIM CROW SOUTH

For Anne Moody, as for so many African Americans, it was as a child that she experienced her first awakening of racial consciousness. From that moment, her world was changed for ever. The young Moody had come face-to-face with what it meant to be black in the southern states, and that sudden insight had left her frightened and bewildered. It occurred one Saturday in the 1940s, when Moody went to the local movie theatre in Centreville, Mississippi. When she saw some white children who lived on the same street, she ran into the theatre lobby to greet them. Suddenly, her mother was screaming and forcibly escorting her outside. Anne could not understand what was happening and started to cry. On the way home, her mother explained that African Americans were not allowed into the lobby, but had to use a side entrance that led them to the racially separated seats in the balcony. Eventually, Anne saw the white children again and they started playing as before. 'But things were not the same. I had never really thought of them as white before. Now all of a sudden they were white, and their whiteness made them better than me. I now realized that not only were they better than me because they were white, but everything they owned and everything connected with them was better than what was available to me.'[1]

The late nineteenth and early twentieth centuries witnessed the brutal imposition of a new system of white supremacist control in the southern states. Taking its name from a black-face minstrel character, Jim Crow represented, in the famous words of historian Rayford Logan, 'the nadir' of American race relations.[2] This chapter focuses on the origins and impact of Jim Crow. Southern whites instituted the system not only through their exploitation of the apparatus of state power, but also through unrelenting acts of violent lawlessness. Although southern ideologues represented it as the natural order of social relations between the races, Jim Crow was a politically strategic construction that reinforced the power of white patriarchy. It united white males otherwise divided by class by emphasising their shared racial superiority over African Americans. In emphasising the need of white men to protect against the supposed danger that African Americans posed to the social order, it also confined white women to a subordinate status. The repression of white women nonetheless could not compare with the suffering of southern blacks. Jim Crow represented an attempt to secure the total physical and psychological subordination of African Americans. Race subsumed all other aspects of African American identity in the minds of southern whites. No matter whether they were male or female, prosperous or poor, African Americans were perceived as being inherently incapable of claiming the full rights of citizenship. As Anne Moody testified, southern blacks were confronted by their second-class status in every aspect of their daily lives.

BLACK WORKING LIVES

At the dawn of the twentieth century, nine out of ten African Americans – approximately eight million men, women and children – lived and laboured in the former slaveholding states of the South. The overwhelming majority of southern blacks resided in rural areas. Although African Americans continued to work the soil, few owned it. In 1900, there were 707,364 black farmers in the South. Only a quarter of these farmers owned the land they cultivated. The rise in independent black farm-ownership represented substantial progress since the days of slavery. However, black landowners still suffered serious hardships. Their farms were usually small and situated outside of the richer cotton-growing region of the Black Belt. Those who made a success of their farms also became the focus of racial violence by resentful whites. From the late 1880s, for example, vigilantes known as Whitecaps launched a series of night rider attacks on prospering black farmers in Mississippi and Louisiana. For most rural blacks, there was not even the prospect of upward mobility into the landowning class. By 1920, tenant farmers still constituted three-quarters of the rural black workforce.[3]

While there was considerable diversity amongst the tenancy arrangements between white planters and black farmers, most African American families were tied to the sharecropping system that had arisen after the Civil War. Landlords supplied sharecroppers with the seed, fertiliser and tools needed to till the soil in return for half of their cotton or grain production. Black labourers became economically entrapped because of their reliance on landlords to maintain accounts and sell crops. Planters routinely cheated sharecroppers out of their share by falsifying the account books. No matter how hard they toiled or how high their crop yield, sharecroppers were told that they had barely broken even, or that they still had not repaid their loans.

With the passing of each year, many slipped deeper and deeper into debt. Sharecroppers were therefore forced to work another twelve months for the same landlord, a system that ensured planters a stable supply of cheap labour. As the black poet Langston Hughes ruefully observed:

When the cotton's picked
And the work is done
Boss man takes the money
And we get none[4]

With no source of income until the harvest, sharecroppers had to purchase necessities such as food and clothing on credit 'furnished' by the landlord or a local merchant. The cost of goods purchased on credit, plus interest, was deducted from labourers' wages at 'settlement time'. Furnishing merchants charged usurious rates of interest averaging between 35 and 60 per cent, which they dishonestly argued were necessary because of the high risk of offering credit to impoverished farmers dependent on a single crop.[5] As a result, many sharecroppers discovered that the sale of their share of cotton did not cover the amount they owed, so that they were forced to ask for further credit. Ernestine Wright, a black woman from Arkansas, recalled how the furnishing merchant refused to give her grandmother a receipt for the goods she purchased on credit. When it was time to settle the account, the merchant added numerous unsold items to the bill. Wright's grandmother made the mistake of challenging the merchant. 'He said, "What you doin', callin' me a liar?" Well, she didn't say no more because she knew very well if she admitted that she was calling him a liar, there might be some kind of race riot or something.'[6]

The enactment of crop lien laws strengthened the economic hold of merchants on sharecroppers. Under these laws, black labourers were obliged to sign a bond that gave the merchants from whom they received credit the first claim to sale of their crop. When the harvest did not cover what they owed, they were forced to secure credit for the following year, which tied them further into a state of economic dependence. The laws also allowed merchants to demand as a term of credit that sharecroppers cultivate cotton to the exclusion of other crops. This had a disastrous effect for two reasons. First, black families had less land on which to grow food, forcing them to make even more purchases on credit from the merchant. Indeed, the dependency on cotton rendered the entire southern economy, which had been largely self-sufficient in foodstuffs before the Civil War, reliant on outside resources. Second, sharecroppers became reliant upon a single crop that suffered constant price fluctuations as a result of market forces. The agricultural depression of the 1890s, precipitated by overproduction, had a particularly catastrophic impact. So too did the infectious spread of the boll weevil during the second decade of the twentieth century.

Some tenant farmers sought to escape the sharecropping system by pushing for payment of a fixed rent at the start of the year, which would ensure they had sole ownership of their crops and could not be cheated by the landlord. By 1900, almost half of black tenants paid fixed rather than share rents. Some sharecroppers also attempted to improve their situation by moving from one farm to another, sometimes with the consent of their landlord, sometimes without. The southern states attempted to restrict mobility through the enactment of new laws that made it a criminal offence for labourers not to fulfil the terms of a contract. Planters threatened black tenants not only with these laws, but also with physical violence to ensure they remained on the farm until their debts were repaid. Such forms of coercion turned tenant farmers into peons, bound in servitude to their landlord creditors. Throughout the late nineteenth and early twentieth centuries, millions of rural blacks remained trapped in a downward spiral of poverty and debt, victims of the tyrannical reign of King Cotton.

The poverty and insecurity of farming life induced an increasing number of African Americans to seek employment opportunities in the expanding industrial economy of the New South. Black men worked as wage labourers in the iron and steel mills of Alabama, and in the tobacco factories of North Carolina and Virginia. They mined for phosphate in South Carolina and Florida, and for coal in Alabama. The railroad, turpentine and lumber industries across the region also recruited thousands of African Americans. Some blacks worked full-time in industry, others supplemented the incomes of their families through seasonal work. Despite the apparent diversity of black labour, the industrial economy afforded only limited opportunities to African Americans. The largest industrial employers in the region, textile manufacturers, denied black men jobs on the basis that they would threaten the white women and girls already working on the factory floors. Those jobs available to African Americans were the dirtiest and most dangerous, as well as the most poorly paid. Blacks had little prospect of promotion to skilled and supervisory positions because of the protests of whites, who jealously and sometimes violently protected their privileged status within the workforce.

African Americans also migrated from the farms to the towns and cities in search of work. The only positions open to them were at the lowest end of the wage economy. Most black men were denied access to skilled trades and therefore worked as menial labourers. White employers legitimated this occupational segregation on the basis that blacks lacked the intelligence and enterprise to perform work that exercised brains rather than brawn. Those black labourers who were married seldom earned enough to support their wives, who were also forced to secure employment. The overwhelming majority of black female wage-earners worked as domestics and laundresses: 98 per cent in the case of Atlanta during the 1880s.[7]

A small black business and professional class did emerge in urban areas during the Jim Crow era. However, black businesses were scarce, and successful black businesses scarcer still. African American merchants were at a competitive disadvantage to their white counterparts. Many lacked basic skills in management and accounting, which were seldom included in the curricula of black schools and colleges. With only limited capital of their own, they were obliged to turn to white lenders who considered black businesses a high investment risk and therefore charged excessive interest rates. The tight financial constraints within which African American businesses were forced to operate meant that the goods they sold were often poorer in quality but higher in price than those offered by white competitors. Their commercial prospects were further restricted by the limited purchasing power of black customers. Attracting even their trade was difficult since black merchants could seldom afford to extend credit. African American leaders attempted to promote black businesses by appealing to the racial loyalties of black consumers. Although these 'buy black' campaigns influenced the buying habits of some African Americans, abstract racial politics could not compete with the imperative to provide families with food and clothing. In the caustic words of one scholar, impoverished manual labourers 'could not be expected to give a man ten cents for an eight cent pound of sugar and two cents for racial pride'.[8] Class tensions also undermined racial solidarity. Some poorer blacks resented the privileged economic and occupational status of black businessmen and refused to patronise their establishments. Blacks, it was said, believed that 'the white man's ice is colder than the black man's ice, his sugar is sweeter'.[9] The inevitable result was a high rate of failure among African American businesses. Those entrepreneurs who succeeded despite the odds still faced the risk of arousing violent retaliation by resentful whites.

LOSING THE VOTE

While African Americans suffered restricted economic opportunities, many of the rights and freedoms they had attained during Reconstruction were eroded with increasing speed during the late nineteenth century. The loss of the right to vote would leave African Americans completely vulnerable to the imposition of a new era of white supremacist rule.

The demise of Reconstruction did not result in a sudden and total loss of southern blacks' political rights. African Americans continued to vote and hold public office during the last quarter of the nineteenth century. Nonetheless, southern whites succeeded through a combination of fraud, intimidation and violence in impeding increasing numbers of African Americans from registering as voters. That process accelerated during the 1890s and 1900s, when one southern state after another approved constitutional reforms that systematically disfranchised African Americans.

Southern blacks were dispossessed of their political rights in reaction to the rise of independent political parties that challenged the hegemony of the white elite. These third parties constructed bi-racial coalitions as a means of securing electoral power, most successfully in the case of the Readjuster Party, which took control of the state government in Virginia between 1879 and 1883. The most potent threat to white elite power came in the form of the Populist insurgency of the 1890s. The Populist revolt raised the prospect of an inter-racial alliance of lower-class blacks and whites that would challenge the hegemony of the planter and industrial elite. Southern and western farmers faced financial ruin as a result of the agricultural depression that gripped the United States in the last decade of the nineteenth century. A combination of domestic overproduction and international competition resulted in the supply of farm crops outstripping demand. The resultant decline in commodity prices forced farmers to cultivate more crops in order to sustain the same levels of income. This in turn created larger crop surpluses, which pushed prices down still further. Thousands of farmers therefore became trapped in a downward spiral of debt, bankruptcy and foreclosure.

The desperation of farmers drove them to seek radical political solutions. In 1888, the protective associations founded across the region were integrated into a single organisation, the Southern Farmers' Alliance. The Alliance advocated numerous solutions to the agricultural crisis, including government reduction of crop acreage, the establishment of warehouses that would store crops until renewed demand raised prices, and the extension of loans at low interest rates. Confronted by the indifference and opposition of Democratic politicians, Alliance leaders launched a third party in 1892.

Black as well as white farmers supported the People's Party. African Americans already living on the margins of the southern economy had been pushed to the very edge by the collapse of cotton prices. The Colored Farmers' Alliance and Cooperative Union was established in the same year as the Southern Farmers' Alliance, and at its peak attracted a membership of more than one million. The People's Party attempted to mobilise this potential mass base of support by emphasising the common plight of black and white farmers. In the words of Populist leader Tom Watson: 'The colored tenant is in the same boat as the white tenant, the colored laborer with the white laborer and . . . the accident of color can make no difference in the interests of farmers, croppers and laborers'.[10] The People's Party also attempted to attract African American support by condemning lynching and the convict-lease system and permitting black representation on campaign committees and at nominating conventions.

Writing in the 1950s, historian C. Vann Woodward concluded that the Populists represented an idealistic alternative to white supremacy. Two decades later, scholars such as Lawrence Goodwyn and J. Morgan Kousser lent support to the this interpretation. However, other historians are more circumspect. As Barton C. Shaw, Greg Cantrell and D. Scott Barton have demonstrated, the alliance between black and white farmers was nonetheless an uneasy one. The racially inclusive stance taken by the People's Party was motivated more by economic and political expediency than by moral principle. Although the party championed social justice for African Americans, it completely refuted racial equality. Moreover, while the party sought to protect those blacks who supported its campaign, it ruthlessly terrorised and intimidated those who did not. African Americans also remained suspicious of white farmers whom they considered most responsible for the mob violence that was then spreading across the South.[11]

Nevertheless, the threat that black and white farmers would unite on the basis of their common class interests represented a serious challenge to Democratic hegemony. The ruling elite reacted with a cynical campaign to divide and conquer their opponents by exploiting the racism of ordinary whites. The fate of the Populist revolt in North Carolina offers a telling example. As a means of overthrowing incumbent office-holders, the Populists and Republicans entered into electoral pacts in which one party supported the other's candidates in return for a share of political power. This 'fusion' strategy swept North Carolina Democrats from office in the elections of 1894. Fusionists used their control of the state legislature to appoint numerous African Americans to public office. Four years later, Democrats launched a retaliatory campaign to reclaim the state from 'Negro domination'. The Democrats fired an incendiary rhetorical tirade against African Americans whom they claimed were using their political power as a means of attaining social equality. Particular emphasis was placed on the supposed sexual threat of black men towards white women. The words of one campaign song called on white men to defend the honour of their wives and daughters from the clutches of the black rapist:

'See their blanched and anxious faces,/Not their frail, but lovely forms/Rise, defend their spotless virtue/With your strong and manly arms'.[12] Although the campaign succeeded in restoring Democratic rule, it could not abate rising racial tensions, which spilled into violence in the city of Wilmington on 10 November 1898. The riot claimed the lives of twenty African Americans; a further 1,400 fled the city. Black and white Republican office-holders were intimidated into immediately resigning their offices. The Democrats used their renewed control over the state legislature to introduce a constitutional amendment in 1900 that systematically disfranchised African Americans.

North Carolina followed the lead of Mississippi, which in 1890 had become the first of the former Confederate states to call a constitutional convention for the purpose of eliminating black suffrage. Other states also amended their constitutions to disfranchise African American voters: South Carolina in 1895, Louisiana in 1898, Alabama and Virginia in 1902, and Georgia in 1908. As Michael Perman demonstrates in the most important recent study of the subject, the disfranchisement movement in each state emerged out of differing political calculations and accommodations between white interest groups.[13] In general, the principal forces that fuelled the disfranchisement of African Americans were the drive to defeat Populism and the resurgence of white racism. However, there was one further influential factor. Progressive reformers who campaigned to clean up the rampant corruption in local and state politics during the late nineteenth century attributed much of the problem to African Americans. In their opinion, the ignorance of the former slaves allowed them to play into the hands of manipulative politicians who bribed black voters with empty promises in order to secure election. By removing African Americans from the electoral rolls, the reformers believed they would strip these corrupt politicians of their power bases. The white political establishment was only too happy to oblige.

Since the Fifteenth Amendment prohibited the denial of the right to vote on the basis of race, the state constitutional conventions were forced to accomplish their aims through numerous acts of legal subterfuge. While the new restrictions they imposed on the right to vote made no explicit reference to race, there was a purposeful difference between their content and their intent. The means by which African Americans were compelled to secure their right to vote included the payment of poll taxes, the passing of literacy tests and providing proof of their residential status. Although African Americans challenged disfranchisement through court cases and political lobbying, their efforts failed. In 1898, the United States Supreme Court added further federal support to the imposition of white supremacist rule in the South when it upheld the new Mississippi state constitution.[14]

Particularly in the Black Belt, disfranchisement enabled the white political elite to minimise the electoral influence not only of blacks but also of poor whites. The elite found common purpose with progressive reformers who also sought to impose more order and efficiency on the electoral process by restricting the eligibility of lower-class voters. Nonetheless, poor whites were not the principal targets of the disfranchisement movement. The new state constitutions included a number of loopholes that allowed poor and illiterate whites to circumvent the restrictions imposed on black voters. These included the understanding clause, which allowed for an individual to qualify as a voter by explaining a section of the state constitution to the registrar. Poor whites were also assisted by the grandfather clause, which enabled them to register if they possessed an immediate relative who had voted in the elections of 1867. Despite this legal chicanery, the refusal of southern registrars to make exceptions for those who failed to pay the poll tax meant that thousands of poor whites saw their names removed from the electoral rolls. Between the 1880s and 1900s, the number of adult white males who voted in southern elections fell from two-thirds to one-third.[15] Many poorer whites failed to protect their political rights by taking advantage of the grandfather clause for reasons that remain unclear. Historians still need to provide a proper explanation for the apparently irrational participation of poor whites in their own disfranchisement.

The impact of disfranchisement on African Americans was still more pronounced. In 1896, there were 130,334 registered black voters in Louisiana. Within eight years, the figure had fallen to less than 1,400.[16] Although some southern blacks were still able to register under the new state constitutions, they were essentially excluded from electoral politics by the introduction of the white primary. The demise of Reconstruction instituted a system of one-party politics in the South controlled by the Democrats. During the late nineteenth century, the Republican Party turned its back on southern black voters, as it started to cultivate a new constituency among white voters in the West. Declining Republican influence in the South meant that the outcome of elections was determined less by contests between competing parties than by the nominating process of Democratic candidates. The implementation of the white primary prohibited blacks from this process, depriving them of their ability to secure the election of representative public officials. By 1901, the last black southern politician, George White of North Carolina, had left Congress. This loss of basic citizenship rights left African Americans powerless to withstand the floodtide of white racism.

THE RISE OF RACIAL SEGREGATION

Disfranchisement was one of several factors that set in motion the imposition of Jim Crow apartheid. The generations of black and white southerners born after the Civil War were strangers to each other, separated not only physically but also psychologically. Whites were threatened by what they saw as a black population unwilling to accept their subordinate status within white society. As journalist Ray Stannard Baker observed: 'Many Southerners look back wistfully to the faithful, simple, ignorant, obedient, cheerful, old plantation Negro and deplore his disappearance.'[17] The influx of African Americans into the cities created particularly acute tensions, as the newcomers asserted their rights to jobs and municipal services.

The collapse of the Populist uprising silenced public voices of support among southern whites for the fairer treatment of African Americans. A small number of whites had responded to the rising tide of southern racism by advocating greater protection of black civil rights. George Washington Cable asserted in *The Silent South*, published in 1885, that African Americans should be guaranteed equality before the law, although he resisted a direct challenge to segregation. New South business leaders who sought to expand the regional economy also contended that the persecution of African Americans inhibited the maintenance and growth of an essential labour force. Despite the pragmatism and circumspection of their arguments, these racial moderates suffered a furious public reaction. Cable, for instance, was forced to leave the South entirely and seek refuge in Massachusetts.

The rise of de jure segregation was further facilitated by the withdrawal of federal protection of southern blacks after the Compromise of 1877. In 1890 and 1891, Senate Republicans attempted to pass a bill sponsored by Henry Cabot Lodge of Massachusetts that would protect blacks' rights to vote by empowering the federal government with supervisory control of elections. The failure to enact the Force Bill, as it was named by white supremacist opponents, led to a total Republican retreat on racial matters. Southern blacks had been abandoned by the party of Lincoln the Great Emancipator. In a series of decisions that one historian has described as a 'legal counter-revolution', the United States Supreme Court also stripped African Americans of the rights they had attained during Reconstruction.[18] The right of southern states to self-determine their race relations was restored incrementally over the last quarter of the nineteenth century, starting with the *Slaughter-House Cases* of 1873, in which the Court ruled that the Fourteenth Amendment was not intended to 'transfer the security and protection' of civil rights 'from the states to the federal government'. Ten years later, the Court invalidated the 1875 Civil Rights Act, which had, at least in theory, provided for the racial integration of public transport and accommodations. The fate of African Americans was sealed by the *Plessy* v. *Ferguson* decision of 1896, which provided federal sanction to the new segregation laws enacted by southern legislatures.

The subordination of southern blacks also found intellectual support within the broader national discourse on race in the late nineteenth and early twentieth centuries. The late nineteenth century witnessed the emergence of a new era of radical racism that supplanted paternalistic notions about the essential humanity of blacks. Theories of biological racism such as Social Darwinism asserted that the innate depravity of African Americans rendered it impossible to integrate them into an egalitarian society. A characteristic text was *The Negro a Beast* by Charles Carroll, published in 1900, in which the author asserted that African Americans were more akin to apes than human beings. 'No Negro Civilization has ever appeared!' claimed Carroll. 'The White Man is preeminently the man of civilization. This is just what God created him to be.'[19] Southern whites were therefore able to legitimise segregation on the basis that blacks were a plague of crime, disease and immorality that threatened to contaminate the rest of the population unless physically confined.

The imperialist expansionism of the United States in the late nineteenth century added further intellectual force to the notion of an immutable racial hierarchy in which whites were at the top and blacks at the bottom. Some black leaders saw the Spanish-American War of 1898 as an opportunity for African Americans to re-establish their claim to full citizenship through patriotic service. Although black soldiers fought and died in the service of their country, the conflict further strengthened white supremacism. Northern and southern whites reconciled their sectional differences in recognition of the shared burden to protect and promote the less 'civilised' peoples of Cuba and the Philippines. The racialist rhetoric of the times legitimated ideas of the United States as a white republic, which in turn incited a series of violent assaults on black troops stationed in the South.

Whites on either side of the Mason–Dixon Line were singing from the same sheet on racial matters by the late nineteenth century: literally so, in the case of popular songs such as Edward Hogan's 1896 composition 'All Coons Look Alike to Me'. The nascent consumer culture of the United States also promoted popular conceptions of black inferiority. Commercial advertising made considerable use of coon iconography – the dark-skinned black with bulging eyeballs and thick lips turned up in an inane smile – to market everything from cigarettes to soap. Popular literature and theatre similarly perpetuated malicious stereotypes of African Americans. Racial supremacist fantasies fuelled the fiction of Thomas Dixon, best-selling author of *The Leopard's Spots* and *The Clansman*, published in 1902 and 1905 respectively. Dixon reflected and reinforced white southern cultural memories of Reconstruction with his romanticised portrait of the Ku Klux Klan liberating the region from the clutches of brutal and ignorant former slaves.

While all of these factors were important in providing a political context for the imposition of Jim Crow, there has been considerable debate as to exactly when racial segregation was established in the southern states. In his seminal study *The Strange Career of Jim Crow*, historian C. Vann Woodward asserted that the strict enforcement of a colour line separating the races did not occur until the late nineteenth and early twentieth centuries. According to Woodward, the intervening years between the abolition of slavery and the imposition of southern apartheid were characterised by the fluidity of race relations. *The Strange Career of Jim Crow* was written in response to the United States Supreme Court decision in *Brown* v. *Board of Education* that segregation in public schools was unconstitutional. Woodward sought to demonstrate that segregation was not, as many southern whites insisted, the natural order of race relations, with roots deep in the history of the region. On the contrary, segregation was a system of recent origin that instead of emerging organically was imposed on the southern states by the political elite. By reminding his readership of the 'forgotten alternatives' to segregation, Woodward attempted to encourage popular acceptance of racial change.[20]

Scholars soon took issue with the Woodward thesis. According to revisionists such as Richard Wade and Joel Williamson, Woodward placed undue emphasis on the use of law, or de jure segregation, to regulate race relations. Long before the law sanctioned the separation of the races, segregation had become the pervasive custom and practice across the South. De facto segregation was a pervasive phenomenon in southern cities during the antebellum era. Although it was not systematically enforced, the colour line had been re-established before the end of Reconstruction. The segregation laws of the late nineteenth and early twentieth centuries therefore did not create Jim Crow, but rather added institutional force to existing social practice.[21]

During the 1970s, historian Howard Rabinowitz added a new dimension to the debate on the origins of segregation. Rabinowitz asserted that both the supporters and opponents of the Woodward thesis had erred in believing that the only historical alternatives available to southerners had been integration or segregation. This dichotomy obscured a third alternative: exclusion. Rabinowitz contended that after the Civil War southern blacks were denied access to most public services. Hence, the choice they faced was whether to tolerate their continuing exclusion or to welcome the introduction of public facilities that were, at least in principle, separate but equal. African Americans tolerated segregation both as an improvement in their status and a means to establish their institutional autonomy from whites. Segregation was therefore not only imposed arbitrarily by whites, but also to some extent voluntarily by blacks.[22]

Although his interpretation of the origins of segregation was not the same, Rabinowitz re-established the point made by Woodward that Jim Crow represented a departure from the racial conditions of the past. Revisionist scholars such as Williamson claimed that there was a clear line of continuity to southern race relations in the nineteenth century, since the new segregation laws simply reinforced a system that was already in widespread practice. However, the rise of Jim Crow witnessed a new radicalisation of racial politics, as southern whites turned not only to the power of law but also the use of terrorist violence and intimidation as a means to enforce systematically their dominion over African Americans.

The legal imposition of the colour line first took effect in public transportation. Although blacks and whites shared the use of trains and streetcars more commonly than they did many other public facilities, racial arrangements lacked precise legal definition. In 1881, Tennessee introduced a state law that sanctioned segregated facilities in railroad cars. Between 1887 and 1894, all of the southern states (with the exception of Virginia and the Carolinas) had implemented similar measures. The railroads were only the beginning. During the late nineteenth and early twentieth centuries, the southern states enacted a rash of laws that mandated racial segregation in every aspect of public life. Jim Crow was not, however, a monolith. Segregation laws differed from state to state and from city to city. The general pattern was nonetheless the almost complete circumscription of black public behaviour. Blacks and whites were separated from the cradle to the grave. They were born in separate hospitals, lived in separate neighbourhoods, were educated in separate schools, worshipped in separate churches, ate in separate restaurants, used separate water fountains, and were buried in separate cemeteries. African Americans had to sit at the rear of streetcar trolleys and in the balconies of movie theatres. Some communities continued to prohibit blacks completely from public facilities, including libraries, parks and playgrounds.

African Americans protested the introduction of the new laws. However, in 1896 the United States Supreme Court dashed their hopes of reversing the legislative tide with its ruling in *Plessy* v. *Ferguson*. Homer Plessy, a prosperous Louisiana mulatto, had boarded a train run by the East Louisiana Railroad, only to be forcibly removed from the first-class car. Plessy filed a suit claiming that the law sanctioning separate accommodations in railroad cars violated his rights under the Fourteenth Amendment. The Supreme Court disagreed. By a margin of seven to one, it ruled that separate accommodations were permissible under the constitution, provided that they were of similar quality. The sole dissenter, John Harlan, was ironically a former slaveholder. 'Our Constitution is color-blind,' he chastised his fellow justices, and their approval of segregation laws therefore relegated blacks to a 'condition of legal inferiority'. 'In my opinion,' he asserted, 'the judgment this day rendered will, in time, prove to be quite as pernicious as the decision made by this tribunal in the Dred Scott Case.'[23]

SEPARATE AND UNEQUAL

The southern states responded to the Supreme Court decision by applying the doctrine of 'separate but equal' to all public spaces. However, there proved to be an enormous disparity between the principle and the practice of racial segregation. As African Americans would painfully come to realise, public facilities were separate but *un*equal.

The provision of medical care for African Americans was far inferior to that for whites. Social and economic deprivation produced serious health problems among the black community. Low wages led to restricted diets that lacked essential nutrients and rendered African Americans less immune to the diseases that spread through their neighbourhoods as a result of poor sanitation. Rural blacks had a life expectancy of only thirty-three years. One in every three of their children died before the age of ten.[24] Southern whites nonetheless refused to accept that environmental factors were the principal cause of the medical problems that beset the black community. Instead, they attributed high disease rates and premature deaths to what they believed to be the innate depravity of African Americans. As evidence, they pointed to the federal censuses of 1870 and 1890, which appeared to show a rapidly falling birth rate among blacks. So precipitous was the decline that many southern whites predicted the race would soon become extinct. The explanation offered for the dwindling black population was that emancipation had removed the civilising constraints that had protected bondsmen from their own degeneracy. Without the paternal care of white slave masters, African Americans had succumbed to self-destructive behaviour such as sexual licentiousness, alcoholism, and a disregard for basic standards of hygiene and nutrition. It was, southern whites insisted, this total absence of personal responsibility on the part of African Americans that caused the health crises within their communities. As one physician asserted: 'Virtue in the Negro race is like "angels" visits – few and far between.'[25] Attitudes such as this underlined the hopelessly under-resourced system of health care for African Americans. Black hospitals lacked essential staff, supplies and equipment. Moreover, most were situated far from the farming communities where most African Americans lived. Impoverished black farmers were often forced to turn for help in paying for medical fees to white landlords, whose goodwill could not be guaranteed.

Housing was as separate and unequal as health care. In rural areas, sharecroppers constructed their cabins not out of logs but rough boards that were seldom plastered for insulation. Without glass windows or screen doors, the cabins suffered from a lack of light and ventilation. Families crowded into small spaces that afforded little privacy. The black activist W. E. B. Du Bois painted a pathetic portrait of the homes of black farm labourers in Dougherty County, Georgia, at the start of the twentieth century: 'Within is a fire-place, black and smoky, and usually unsteady with age. A bed or two, a table, a wooden chest and a few chairs make up the furniture, while a stray show-bill or a newspaper decorate the walls.'[26] In urban areas, residential segregation confined African Americans to neighbourhoods that suffered from the lack of municipal services. A prosperous few could afford their own homes, with some of the conveniences of the nascent consumer culture. Nonetheless, most urban blacks lived on streets that were neither paved nor lit. Their homes were commonly small wooden-frame dwellings, for which they paid inflated rents. Without water and sewage systems or regular rubbish collections, black neighbourhoods became the breeding grounds for disease. Pauli Murray provided a description of black housing in Durham, North Carolina, remarkable for its similarity to the depiction of sharecropper cabins by Du Bois. While the black elite resided in neat cottages or bungalows, most African Americans 'lived in rented, unpainted two- or three-room shacks with no running water and only a pump in the yard. Their bare walls were pasted over with brown-colored rotogravure newspapers, which served as decoration and as covering for the cracks'.[27]

Restrictions on black education were also essential to the maintenance of white supremacist rule. Southern whites feared the potentially revolutionary consequences of an educated black population. Education, they believed, would breed black discontent. African Americans would come to expect more to life than their subordinate status within the southern hierarchy. Education therefore threatened equality between the races.

Confronted with this threat to the foundations of southern race and labour relations, southern state governments imposed strict controls on the allocation of public funds for black schools. In 1910, South Carolina, for instance, spent an average of only $5.95 per black pupil, compared with $40.68 for the average white pupil.[28] White officials also hired black principals and teachers as much for their deference to the racial order as their ability to educate and inspire their pupils. Black educators dared not risk their positions by extending their curricula beyond the industrial and agricultural education deemed sufficient for African Americans.

While blacks suffered limited educational opportunities across the South, conditions in rural schools were particularly poor. Black children had little or no access to public transport to and from school, but were instead forced to trek on foot. En route, many may have paused ruefully as they passed the local white school, which was closer to home but prohibited their admission. Nor once they reached their destination was there much reason to believe it had been worth the long journey. Without sufficient heat or ventilation, black schoolchildren shivered in the winter and sweated in the summer. The books from which they learned were torn and outdated. Adverse conditions acted as a disincentive to many of the more qualified black schoolteachers. As a result, rural educators were often poorly trained and, faced with low wages and an unfavourable working environment, lacked professional motivation. The economically dependent status of tenant and sharecropper families also had an impact on rural education. Schools were forced to close during the harvest season so that every hand was available to work in the fields. Throughout the rural South, the school year lasted less than six months; in some parts, it amounted to as little as two. In 1915, only 58 per cent of black school-age children in the region were enrolled in school at all, compared with 80 per cent of whites.[29] Willie Harrell, who grew up in a Mississippi sharecropping family, summarised the difficulties he and other black children faced in receiving a formal education. 'You had to walk seven or eight miles to the school. When it rained and you couldn't do nothing in the field or you couldn't do no other kind of work, that's when you had a chance to go to school, but as soon as the sun comes out and dry off, you in the field.' The limited education he received as a child left Harrell still functionally illiterate in adulthood.[30]

Jim Crow sought not only to restrict the physical spaces shared by the races, but also to regulate the public behaviour of African Americans towards whites. African Americans were expected to conform to an elaborate system of racial etiquette that reinforced their subordinate status within the social hierarchy. As Erleen Lindsay of Alabama observed, 'everybody knew where their place was and they stayed in their place'.[31] The rituals of deference that African Americans were forced to perform included approaching whites' homes by the back door, waiting in line at stores until whites were served, and stepping off the pavement to allow a white pedestrian to pass. Black parents taught their children from an early age how to comport themselves in front of whites. Pauli Murray recalled that she 'learned an intricate racial code listening to and watching the older members of my family'. What children like the young Murray were instructed was that it was not sufficient simply to observe these social rituals, but to do so with a seemingly cheerful compliance. Any behaviour that could be construed as a breach of racial etiquette – disagreeing with the opinion of a white person, or daring to look him straight in the eye – risked violent retaliation. The best strategy was therefore to minimise inter-racial contact as much as possible. Murray heeded the warnings of her worried parents: 'I learned to throw my eyes off focus whenever I passed a white person, so that I would not see the face or the expression.'[32]

While African Americans were forced to show a fawning deference to whites at all times, they themselves received little or no courtesies. Whites refrained from any action that might imply social equality between the races. They refused to address African Americans as 'Mr' or 'Mrs' regardless of how prominent their status might be within the black community. Instead, they referred to African Americans by their first names, or by such generic terms as 'boy', 'girl', 'uncle' or 'auntie'. Whites contributed in countless other ways to the daily humiliation and degradation of African Americans. As Evelyn Brooks Higginbotham argues, the racial identity of African Americans determined how whites treated them, regardless of their class status or gender. For instance, no African American woman, 'regardless of income, education, refinement, or character, enjoyed the status of a lady'. [33] When whites met blacks, they declined to shake their hands. When white men found themselves in the presence of standing black women, they remained seated. When white store owners served African Americans, they refused to allow them to sample their goods. Willie Harrell of Mississippi summed up the double standards of white southerners: 'Blacks couldn't look at no white. But whites could look at blacks all they wanted.'[34]

SOUTHERN JUSTICE

Southern blacks had little or no recourse to the law to protect themselves from the brutal imposition of white supremacist rule. In the assessment of one scholar, the victimisation of African Americans by the southern criminal justice system amounted to 'legal terrorism'.[35] White authorities attempted to restrict the personal mobility that urban spaces afforded to blacks through the enforcement of curfew laws. We do not have a proper account of how law enforcement officers policed the streets of southern communities during the Jim Crow era. It is nonetheless clear that African Americans suffered abuse, intimidation and disproportionate numbers of arrests at the hands of white policemen. In Atlanta during the 1880s, African Americans constituted 44 per cent of the population but 67 per cent of arrested persons.[36] The fate of those arrested was often predetermined. Southern courts routinely denied African Americans due process of law. Black defendants stood little chance of acquittal in courtrooms that were dominated by white judges, lawyers and juries. They also received tougher sentences than whites for the same offence. By contrast, whites who committed crimes against African Americans were seldom made to stand trial. The one means by which blacks could attempt to mitigate the harshness of the criminal justice system was to rely upon the support of a white patron, usually their employer, who could testify to their good character. Although the use of patronage might protect a black defendant from a particularly harsh sentence, it also strengthened the social order by reinforcing his dependency upon more powerful whites.

One of the most blatant elements of institutionalised racism within the southern justice system was the exploitation of black convict labour. Under the convict-lease system, private employers paid the state for the use of prison inmates as manual labourers. Most of these prisoners were black. At the start of the twentieth century, an estimated 20,000 to 30,000 African Americans, one in four of them children, were serving out sentences in convict-lease camps. In 1912, black prison labourers earned the state of Alabama around one million dollars. The low cost of convict labour made it highly attractive to private contractors. Southern courts conspired to supply the demand by sentencing African Americans convicted of minor offences such as vagrancy and petty theft to terms of hard labour. Planters paid the fines of convicted criminals and then forced them to work off their debt by picking cotton on their farms. Federal indifference facilitated the collusion of local authorities in this perpetuation of debt peonage. The United States Supreme Court took a piecemeal approach to the issue. In the cases of *Alonzo* v. *Bailey* (1911) and *U.S.* v. *Reynolds* (1914), the Court struck down state laws that enforced the peonage system in Alabama. However, similar legislation remained on the statute books of Georgia and Florida until the Second World War. Peonage conditions still operated in some rural areas as late as the 1960s.

The work performed by prisoners was long, arduous and intense. Inmates toiled as coal miners, swamp clearers and railroad construction workers, up to fourteen hours a day and six to seven days a week. Many died as a result of appalling working conditions or physical abuse by camp guards. One report on convict labourers by the Mississippi Board of Health concluded: 'Most of them have their backs cut in great wales, scars and blisters, some of the skin peeling off as a result of the severe beatings. They were lying there dying, so poor and emaciated that their bones almost came through their skin.'[37]

In 1904, Mississippi Governor James K. Vardaman attempted to eradicate the convict-lease system through the establishment of Parchman Farm. Vardaman believed that the railroad barons and plantation owners who contracted the labour of prison inmates had no interest in promoting their reformation, but only in bolstering their profits at the public expense. Parchman was therefore intended to improve the condition of black prisoners by instilling them with the habits of hard work and respect for white authority. However, the new prison proved to be as brutally repressive as the system it replaced. Parchman was a working plantation on which inmates toiled to produce cotton in a manner reminiscent of the old slave regime. Prison authorities pushed their labour force hard in pursuit of profit. Discipline was enforced through physical punishment. Most inmates formed an intimate acquaintance with 'Black Annie', the leather strap used to whip slow or insubordinate workers. Escape was not an option. Many of the guards were themselves convicts who stood to gain a complete pardon from the governor should they shoot an attempted fugitive. Penal institutions such as the Louisiana State Penitentiary in Angola and Sugar Land Prison in Texas ('the hell hole of the Brazos') were places of fear that haunted the thoughts of African Americans. It is no coincidence that the lamentations of black inmates, real and imagined, should form a sub-genre of the blues music that emerged out of the Mississippi Delta in the late nineteenth century. One of the most potent prison blues is 'Parchman Farm Blues' by former inmate Bukka White. White paints a vivid portrait of the punishing hours of physical labour performed by prisoners: 'We goes to work in the mornin' just at dawn of day/Just at the setting of the sun that's when the work is done'. Bewailing the fact that he 'sure wanna go back home', White offers solemn words of warning to his fellow African Americans: 'Oh, listen you men, I don't mean no harm/If you wanna do good you'd better stay off Parchman Farm'.[38]

No matter how powerful an instrument of racial control the criminal justice system was, whites still complained that the courts were too slow and unreliable in protecting their communities from black criminals. Accordingly, they took the law into their own hands. In one of the most famous anthems of black protest, Billie Holliday sang with a heartrending blend of grief and anger how 'Southern trees bear a strange fruit,/Blood on the leaves and blood at the root'.[39] The 'strange fruit' was the dead bodies of African American men and, occasionally, women who had been hanged by white lynch mobs. We will never know the precise number of black lynching victims. No statistics are available for the first two decades that followed emancipation, and thereafter the lack of a consistent definition of lynching causes difficulty in determining an accurate count. What we can be sure of is that the statistic commonly cited by scholars – 3,220 victims between 1880 and 1930 – is a conservative estimate.[40] The highest number of incidents occurred during the last decade of the nineteenth century. Between 1891 and 1901, the number of lynching victims never fell below one hundred per year. The epidemic of racial violence reached its pinnacle in 1892, when 230 people, 161 of them black, died at the hands of vigilantes.[41]

Lynching occurred most commonly in rural communities and small towns where the white community was seized with apprehension about the future. The agricultural depression of the 1890s precipitated a collapse in cotton prices, which in turn caused the failure of many family farms. Driven close to destitution, white farmers also had to contend with a more assertive black labour force that moved into their communities in search of employment in lumber camps and on large plantations. The sudden influx of these racial strangers fuelled white fears, which became embodied in the form of the black male rapist.

Sexual relations between black men and white women had been tolerated before the Civil War, but during Reconstruction came to be seen as a dangerous assertion of the freedmen's desire for social equality. Southern whites claimed that emancipation had eliminated the social restraints imposed on black males by slavery, resulting in their reversion to savagery. In an attempt to contain the threat of black male sexuality, the southern states tightened their legislative prohibition of miscegenation. Black men were made to fear that any interaction with white women – the slightest smile or look in the eye – would result in legal or extra-legal retaliation. One white woman interviewed in Atlanta by Ray Stannard Baker recalled how a black man had once hurriedly brushed against her as he walked out of a hallway onto the street: 'When he turned and found it was a white woman he had touched, such a look of abject terror and fear came into his face as I hope never again to see on a human countenance. He knew what it meant if I was frightened, called for help, and accused him of insulting or attacking me. He stood still a moment, then turned and ran down the street, dodging into the first alley he came to.'[42]

The patriarchal imperative to protect white women from the rapacious advances of black men became the pretext for lynching across the southern states. Lynching provided a means by which white men could assert their masculinity by fulfilling a protective role towards their womenfolk, who they claimed were under threat from black men. As historians including

Jacqueline Dowd Hall and Glenda Gilmore have shown, although the primary purpose of mob violence was to repress African Americans, it also fortified the dependency of white women on male protection. In the words of Hall, exploitation of fears of the black rapist 'served as a dramatization of hierarchical power relationships based both on gender and on race'.[43] Many white women appear to have accepted the need for men to secure their safety. As the white political activist Rebecca Latimer Felton asserted, 'if it takes lynching to protect woman's dearest possession from drunken, ravening human beasts, then I say lynch a thousand a week if it becomes necessary'.[44] The extra-legal execution of African Americans therefore reinforced traditional gender, as well as racial, hierarchies.

However, although whites rationalised the actions of the mob on the basis that their victims had sexually assaulted white women, there were other underlying causes of mob violence. Lynching provided landlords and merchants in the cotton belt with the means to impose social control over an increasingly mobile black labour force. Acts of racial terrorism increased during times of agricultural recession, when planters attempted to combat declining cotton prices through increased production.[45]

Lynching also served an important psychological imperative, strengthening the control of whites in uncertain times. The extra-legal torture and execution of African Americans became a communal ritual. Hundreds or even thousands of whites crossed class lines in a public expression of racial unity. Special trains were chartered, refreshments were sold, and body parts were pocketed as souvenirs. One of the most notorious spectacle lynchings occurred in Newnan, Georgia, on 23 April 1899, when a black labourer named Sam Hose was ceremoniously burned and dismembered before a crowd of two thousand spectators who had come to witness the Sunday afternoon entertainment. His knuckles were later displayed in the window of an Atlanta grocery store. Acts of violence, such as the lynching of Hose, offered not only amusement to curious onlookers, they also reaffirmed white racial hegemony. The symbolic function of lynching is illustrated by a postcard that depicted the corpses of five African Americans hanged in Sabine County, Texas, in June 1908. Under the photograph were the following words:

> The negro, now, by eternal grace,
> Must learn to stay in the negro's place.
> In the Sunny South, the Land of the Free,
> Let the WHITE SUPREME forever be.
> Let this a warning to all negroes be
> Or they'll suffer the fate of the DOGWOOD TREE.[46]

While lower-class whites were usually the ones who held the rope, their actions were publicly condoned by the supposedly more respectable members of southern society. Governor Cole Blease of South Carolina stated that, rather than use the power of his office to prevent the lynching of one 'nigger brute', he would have 'resigned the office' and 'led the mob myself'.[47] The failure or refusal of local and state authorities to intervene, even when a lynching had been publicised in advance, ensured that few mob leaders were indicted for their crimes. When grand juries did investigate acts of mob violence, they routinely concluded that the victim had died 'at the hands of persons unknown'.

The threat and reality of lynching deterred African Americans from daring to transgress the racial boundaries prescribed by whites. Much of the power of racial violence lay in its randomness. White mobs made little effort to determine the guilt or innocence of their victims, but instead indiscriminately targeted African Americans. No matter how watchful they were, southern blacks understood that they could become the victims of racial violence at any time, and without warning. Richard Wright, a black novelist who spent his formative years in Mississippi and Tennessee, described the incapacitating paralysis that this awareness caused: 'the white brutality that I had not seen was a more effective control of my behavior than that which I knew. The actual experience would have let me see the realistic outlines of what was really happening, but as long as it remained something terrible and yet remote, something whose horror and blood might descend upon me at any moment, I was compelled to give my entire imagination over to it, an act which blocked the springs of thought and feeling in me.'[48]

Although lynching was principally a small-town and rural phenomenon, African Americans in the cities had no immunity against the contagion of racial violence. Southern whites had since slavery times considered urban life antithetical to the social control of African Americans. The migration of rural labourers to the cities in the late nineteenth century compounded white fears. In July 1900, a riot broke out on the streets of New Orleans after an African American named Robert Charles shot dead two police officers and wounded a third while resisting arrest. Whites used the manhunt for Charles as an excuse to assault African Americans indiscriminately, murdering at least twelve and seriously injuring another sixty-seven. A mob estimated at 20,000 eventually laid siege to Charles's hiding place. The fugitive killed five whites and injured nineteen more before he was finally shot dead. Tensions had been building in the city for some time before the riot. Alarmist editorials in the local press deplored the failure of law enforcement officials to police the increasing number of young black males in city parks who 'lie in the grass, evidently waiting for the young maidens to pass them'.[49] Charles himself appeared to be the embodiment of Stagolee, the 'bad nigger' of blues legend, who mercilessly and with little motive shoots a man dead.[50]

Fear at the ease with which urban black males appeared to cross the colour line also fuelled the flames of a riot in Atlanta in 1906. In a situation that echoed the earlier incidents in New Orleans, the local press had exacerbated racial tensions by reporting that black men were carousing in saloons, drinking beer from bottles labelled with images of naked white women. On 22 September, reports circulated throughout the city that four black men in separate incidents had attempted to rape white women. Fearful of the threat that blacks posed to the social order, whites determined to reassert their authority. Thousands tore through the black district of the city, killing between twenty-five and forty African Americans.

BETWEEN BLACK AND WHITE

The strict demarcation of racial boundaries in the late nineteenth-century South had serious consequences not only for African Americans, but also for the small number of immigrant groups in the region. From the 1890s to the 1920s, the United States acted as a magnet that attracted millions of foreign migrants, especially from southern and eastern Europe. Only a fraction of these new arrivals established their homes in the South. In 1910, immigrants represented 20 per cent of the northern population, but only 2 per cent of all southerners.[51] There were numerous reasons why foreign persons chose not to settle in the South. First, the stagnant agricultural economy of the South offered fewer opportunities than did the expanding industrial and urban centres to the North. Second, the incursion of Federal troops into the South during the Civil War had instilled a strong hostility towards outsiders, a situation compounded by the ethnic homogeneity of the white population. Third, the relative absence of large urban areas meant there were few ethnic neighbourhoods to which new immigrants could move. Ethnic enclaves in northern cities acted as important cultural half-way houses that allowed foreign persons an opportunity to learn the language and customs of their adopted homeland before moving into the broader mainstream of American life.

The southern states did lure a small proportion of foreign settlers. Planters in states such as Louisiana and Mississippi recruited immigrants as an alternative labour force to African Americans, whom they believed had become lazy and insubordinate since their emancipation from slavery. Railroad companies and industrial entrepreneurs also saw foreign labour as a means to generate the economy of the New South.

Many white southerners nonetheless saw the settlement of new ethnic minorities as a threat to the social order, since their ambiguous racial status complicated the colour line. The imposition of a racial system based on a simple black/white binary provided whites with a clear sense of order and hierarchy during the troubled times of the late nineteenth century. However, the indeterminate racial identity of many immigrants challenged the certainties of the southern caste system. Southern whites responded to this situation in a manner that demonstrated their confusion over the place of ethnic minorities in the racial order. Their refusal to accept the new immigrants who arrived in the post-bellum era as white led them to classify them as black, despite the obvious differences in skin colour. During the late nineteenth and early twentieth centuries, school boards in Louisiana and Mississippi forced Sicilian and Chinese parents to send their children to black schools. In 1927, the US Supreme Court ruled in *Gong Lum* v. *Rice* that the board of trustees at a school in Bolivar County, Mississippi, could exclude a nine-year-old Chinese girl on the grounds that she was not white.[52]

When ethnic minorities transgressed racial boundaries, whites reacted with repressive violence. On 14 March 1891, vigilantes in New Orleans lynched eleven Sicilians accused of murdering the local chief of police. The leaders of the mob were local white business leaders who bitterly resented the success of Sicilian entrepreneurs in monopolising trade at the local docks, and conspired to remove their rivals by force.[53] In contrast to immigrant groups such as the Sicilians, who settled in the South only in the late nineteenth century, Jews could trace their roots in the region back to the colonial era. Their status as whites nonetheless remained precarious. On 17 August 1915, whites lynched Leo Frank, a Jewish factory manager from Atlanta falsely convicted of the rape and murder of a young female employee named Mary Phagan. The anti-Semitic rhetoric that surrounded the case demonstrated that many southern whites associated Jews with the social problems created with the rise of the new urban and industrial economy. The sexual assault and murder of Phagan symbolised to many the rapacious greed of Jewish employers and the powerlessness of men to protect their womenfolk from the vagaries of the factory system. Suspicions about the place of Jews within the racial hierarchy would re-emerge several decades later during the crisis over school desegregation.[54]

Jim Crow imposed an appalling burden on African Americans. It had taken only one generation for the expectations of the future aroused among the freedmen to be superseded by a sense of despair and fatalism. Poverty, prejudice and violence were the daily realities endured by southern blacks. While many African Americans succumbed to white supremacist rule, others formulated strategies that ensured the preservation of individual dignity and the cultural survival of their communities. Chapter 8 assesses the complex, and at times competing, means by which southern blacks attempted to withstand the worst excesses of white racism.

Notes

1. Anne Moody, *Coming of Age in Mississippi* (New York: Doubleday, 1968), pp. 33–4.
2. Rayford W. Logan, *The Negro in American Life and Thought: The Nadir, 1877–1901* (New York, 1954).
3. R. Douglas Hurt (ed.), *African American Life in the Rural South, 1900–1950* (Columbia and London: University of Missouri Press, 2003), pp. 1–2.
4. Langston Hughes, 'Share-Croppers', in *Selected Poems of Langston Hughes* (New York: Alfred A. Knopf, 1959), p. 165.
5. Roger L. Ransom and Richard Sutch, *One Kind of Freedom: The Economic Consequences of Emancipation* (Cambridge: Cambridge University Press, 1977).
6. *Field to Factory–Voices of the Great Migration: Recalling the African American Migration to the Northern Cities* (Smithsonian Folkways Recordings – SFW90005, 1994).
7. Tera W. Hunter, *To 'Joy My Freedom: Southern Black Women's Lives and Labors after the Civil War* (Cambridge, MA: Harvard University Press, 1997), p. 50.
8. J. H. Harmon, Jr, 'The Negro as a Local Business Man', *Journal of Negro History*, 14 (1929), p. 131.
9. Lester C. Lamon, *Black Tennesseans, 1900–1930* (Knoxville: University of Tennessee Press, 1977), p. 168.
10. Richard Wormser, *The Rise and Fall of Jim Crow* (New York: St. Martin's Press, 2003), p. 73.
11. C. Vann Woodward, *The Strange Career of Jim Crow*, 2nd edition, revised (New York: Oxford University Press, 1966); Lawrence Goodwyn, 'Populist Dreams and Negro Rights: East Texas as a Case Study', *American Historical Review*, 76 (1971), pp. 1435–56; J. Morgan Kousser, *The Shaping of Southern Politics: Suffrage Restriction and the Establishment of the One-Party South, 1880–1910* (New Haven and London: Yale University Press, 1974); Barton C. Shaw, *The Wool-Hat Boys: Georgia's Populist Party* (Baton Rouge: Louisiana State University Press, 1984); Greg Cantrell and D. Scott Barton, 'Texas Populists and the Failure of Biracial Politics', *Journal of Southern History*, 55 (1989), pp. 659–92.
12. Glenda Elizabeth Gilmore, *Gender and Jim Crow: Women and the Politics of White Supremacy in North Carolina, 1896–1920* (Chapel Hill and London: University of North Carolina Press, 1996), p. 91.

13. Michael Perman, *Struggle for Mastery: Disfranchisement in the South, 1888–1908* (Chapel Hill: University of North Carolina Press, 2001).
14. *Williams* v. *Mississippi*, 170 U.S. 213.
15. Edward L. Ayers, *The Promise of the New South: Life After Reconstruction* (New York and Oxford: Oxford University Press, 1992), p. 309.
16. Barbara Bair, 'Though Justice Sleeps, 1880–1900', in Robin D. G. Kelley and Earl Lewis (eds), *To Make Our World Anew: A History of African Americans* (New York and Oxford: Oxford University Press, 2000), p. 305.
17. Ray Stannard Baker, *Following the Color Line: American Negro Citizenship in the Progressive Era* (New York: Harper & Row, 1964), p. 44.
18. Harvard Sitkoff, *A New Deal for Blacks: The Emergence of Civil Rights as a National Issue* (New York: Oxford University Press, 1978), p. 5.
19. Charles A. Carroll, *The Negro a Beast* (St Louis, MO: American Book and Bible House, 1900).
20. Woodward, *The Strange Career of Jim Crow*.
21. Richard C. Wade, *Slavery in the Cities: The South, 1820–1860* (New York: Oxford University Press, 1964); Joel Williamson, *After Slavery: The Negro in South Carolina during Reconstruction, 1861–1877* (Chapel Hill: University of North Carolina Press, 1965).
22. Howard Rabinowitz, *Race Relations in the Urban South, 1865–1900* (New York: Oxford University Press, 1978).
23. *Plessy* v. *Ferguson*, 163 U.S. 537 (1896), Historical Documents, http://www.historicaldocuments.com/PlessyvFerguson.htm (accessed 18 August 2005).
24. Jacqueline Jones, *Labor of Love, Labor of Sorrow: Black Women, Work and the Family, From Slavery to the Present* (New York: Basic Books, 1985), pp. 91–2. Jones does not provide comparative data on mortality rates among rural whites.
25. James H. Jones, *Bad Blood: The Tuskegee Syphilis Experiment* (New York: Free Press, 1981), p. 25.
26. W. E. Burghardt Du Bois, 'The Negro As He Really Is', in Donald P. DeNevi and Doris A. Holmes (eds), *Racism at the Turn of the Century: Documentary Perspectives, 1870–1910* (San Rafael, CA: Leswing Press, 1973), p. 115.
27. Pauli Murray, *Song in a Weary Throat: An American Pilgrimage* (New York: Harper & Row, 1987), p. 23.
28. William H. Chafe, et al. (eds), *Remembering Jim Crow: African Americans Tell About Life in the Segregated South* (New York: New Press, 2001), p. 153.
29. James R. Grossman, 'A Chance to Make Good: 1900–1929', in Kelley and Lewis (eds), *To Make Our World Anew*, pp. 375–6.
30. Chafe, et al., *Remembering Jim Crow*, p. 40.
31. *Field to Factory*.
32. Murray, *Song in a Weary Throat*, pp. 31–2.

33. Evelyn Brooks Higginbotham, 'African-American Women's History and the Metalanguage of Race', *Signs*, 17 (1992), p. 261.
34. Chafe, et. al., *Remembering Jim Crow*, p. 40.
35. Lisa Lindquist Dorr, 'Black-on-White Rape and Retribution in Twentieth-Century Virginia: "Men, Even Negroes, Must Have Some Protection"', *Journal of Southern History*, 64 (November 2000), p. 716.
36. Hunter, *To 'Joy My Freedom*, p. 67.
37. Richard Wormser, *The Rise and Fall of Jim Crow* (New York: St. Martin's Press, 2003), p. 57.
38. The history of Parchman Farm is recounted in David M. Oshinsky, *'Worse Than Slavery': Parchman Farm and the Ordeal of Jim Crow Justice* (New York: Free Press, 1996). There are numerous collections of songs by and about black prisoners. One of the best, which features 'Parchman Farm Blues', is *Prison Blues* (Catfish Records–43247 11792).
39. The history of this song is recounted in David Margolick, *Strange Fruit: Billie Holiday, Café Society, and an Early Cry for Civil Rights* (Philadelphia and London: Running Press, 2000).
40. Christopher Waldrep, *The Many Faces of Judge Lynch: Extralegal Violence and Punishment in America* (New York and Basingstoke: Palgrave Macmillan, 2002).
41. 'Lynchings: By Year and Race', http://www.law.umkc.edu/faculty/projects/ftrials/shipp/lynchingyear.html (accessed 12 August 2005).
42. Baker, *Following the Color Line*, p. 8.
43. Jacquelyn Down Hall, *Revolt Against Chivalry: Jessie Daniel Ames and the Women's Campaign Against Lynching* (New York: Columbia University Press, 1979), quotation on p. 156; Gilmore, *Gender and Jim Crow*.
44. Joel Williamson, *A Rage for Order: Black – White Relations in the American South Since Emancipation* (New York and Oxford: Oxford University Press, 1986), p. 95.
45. Stewart E. Tolnay and E. M. Beck, *A Festival of Violence: An Analysis of Southern Lynchings, 1882–1930* (Urbana and Chicago: University of Illinois Press, 1992).
46. Leon F. Litwack, *Trouble in Mind: Black Southerners in the Age of Jim Crow* (New York: Alfred A. Knopf, 1998), p. 287.
47. *Birmingham News*, 13 November 1911.
48. Richard Wright, *Black Boy: A Record of Childhood and Youth* ([1945] Harlow, Longman, 1970), pp. 150–1. A similar sentiment is expressed in Murray, *Song in a Weary Throat*, p. 36.
49. Williamson, *A Rage for Order*, p. 137.
50. The musical history of Stagolee, and the real-life incident that inspired his tale, is the subject of Cecil Brown, *Stagolee Shot Billy* (Cambridge, MA: Harvard University Press, 2003).
51. Rowland T. Berthoff, 'Southern Attitudes Toward Immigration, 1865–1914', *Journal of Southern History*, 17 (1951), p. 342.

52. James W. Loewen, *The Mississippi Chinese: Between Black and White* ([1971] Prospect Heights, IL: Waveland Press, Inc., 1988), pp. 66–8.
53. Clive Webb, 'The Lynching of Sicilian Immigrants in the American South, 1886 to 1910', *American Nineteenth Century History,* 3 (Spring 2002), pp. 45–76.
54. Leonard Dinnerstein, *The Leo Frank Case* ([1968] Athens: University of Georgia Press, 1997).

Chapter 8

A WORLD OF THEIR OWN: BLACK CULTURE AND RESISTANCE

Confronted day in and day out with the realities of a society that denied them many of the basic rights of citizenship, it would have been no surprise if many southern blacks had succumbed to a fatalistic sense of hopelessness and despair. It is therefore all the more remarkable that during the racial nadir of the late nineteenth and early twentieth centuries, the African American community should have attained considerable cohesion and strength. Southern blacks could seldom challenge white supremacy for fear of invoking violent retaliation. As the author Richard Wright observed: 'They were strong and we were weak. Outright black rebellion could never win.'[1] Southern blacks nonetheless succeeded in working within the restrictions of a segregated society, constructing institutions that paralleled those of whites and catered to their own spiritual, intellectual, cultural and material needs. The system of social and economic control created by whites hence had the ironic effect of strengthening the vitality of the black community. Within its protective environment, southern blacks found the solace, support and inspiration needed to withstand the otherwise relentless discrimination they endured. In this sense, African Americans attempted to balance a twin existence between an outer world they could not control and an inner world of their own creation. The white Mississippi writer David Cohn attested to the skill with which they maintained this balance when he observed how the southern black moved in a realm 'of his own from which the white is jealously excluded; of which he knows nothing and cannot ever know'.[2]

Southern blacks created the institutional walls that to some extent shielded them from the external forces of white racism. Yet within those walls ran deep lines of fissure. The 'black community' did not share a consensus as to the best means by which to promote the interests of the race. On the contrary, bitter ideological and tactical disputes created intra-racial tension and conflict. This chapter assesses the numerous strategies of resistance pursued by southern blacks during this era, and in particular the incremental shift from a policy of racial accommodation to one of direct protest.

ACCOMMODATION AND PROTEST: BOOKER T. WASHINGTON AND W. E. B. DU BOIS

The man whom both blacks and whites recognised as the pre-eminent African American leader of the era was Booker T. Washington. Washington pursued a strategy of racial accommodation, conceding the fundamental reality of a white supremacist social order while working within its confines to promote the interests of his race. Although Washington was the dominant black spokesperson during these years, there were many African Americans who did not adhere to his political doctrine. These black activists, the most conspicuous of whom was W. E. B. Du Bois, took issue with the temporising approach of Washington. They disputed both the precise nature of the race problem and the solutions needed to resolve it.

Booker Talliaferro Washington was born in Franklin County, Virginia, on 5 April 1856, the son of a female slave and an unidentified white man. Washington spent the first nine years of his life in slavery. Following emancipation, he worked in the coal mines and salt furnaces of West Virginia. Between 1872 and 1875, Washington studied at the Hampton Institute in Virginia, an experience that shaped his personal and political outlook for the rest of his life. Hampton was founded by the white philanthropist and educator Samuel Chapman Armstrong, who believed that the progress of the black race depended on personal morality, hard work and an industrial education.

Inspired by this philosophy, Washington in 1881 founded and became the first principal of the Tuskegee Normal and Industrial Institute in Alabama. The curriculum at Tuskegee placed an emphasis on vocational skills at the expense of more academic disciplines. 'I believe most earnestly,' asserted Washington, 'that for years to come the education of the people of my race should be so directed that the greatest proportion of the mental strength of the masses will be brought to bear upon the every-day practical things of life, upon something that is needed to be done, and something which they will be permitted to do in the community in which they reside'.[3] Male students received technical training in such trades as farming, carpentry and printing, while female students were taught domestic skills including cooking, laundry work and sewing. Washington believed that the position of African Americans within southern society would be improved once they had proved to whites that they were loyal and proficient workers who performed an economically essential role. This, in turn, would increase white respect for

African Americans, resulting in the gradual improvement in race relations to the point when, ultimately, southern blacks would be able to obtain the full rights of citizenship. Washington therefore presented economic improvement as the panacea for the problems that afflicted his people. Nothing would prove a more positive advertisement to whites of the real and potential achievements of African Americans than their accumulation through hard work of increased material wealth. As Washington asserted: 'Every white man will respect the Negro who owns a two-story brick business block in the center of town and has five thousand dollars in the bank.'[4]

Washington most famously articulated his political philosophy in a speech delivered at the Cotton States and International Exposition in Atlanta on 18 September 1895. At a time of intense racial tension, Washington attempted to placate southern whites by stressing the limited aspirations of his people. His speech emphasised the loyalty of African Americans by painting a nostalgic portrait of slavery as a system based on mutual affection between bondsmen and masters, and disavowing Reconstruction as a misguided act of social and political engineering that impeded the natural evolution of race relations. 'The wisest among my race understand that the agitation of social equality is the extremest folly,' conceded Washington, 'and that progress in the enjoyment of all the privileges that will come to us will be the result of severe and constant struggle rather than of artificial forcing.' Washington painted a portrait of a southern society in which African Americans accepted the social separation of the races but still worked together with whites for their common economic prosperity: 'In all things that are purely social we can be as separate as the fingers, yet as the hand in all things essential to mutual progress.'[5]

The speech captured the popular imagination. With the death of Frederick Douglass earlier that year, Washington rose to the status of national leader of the black race. Published in 1901, his autobiography, *Up From Slavery*, presented its author as the embodiment of the virtues of personal industry, morality and hygiene by which African Americans would attain racial uplift.

Although Washington was the dominant political force within the black community during the late nineteenth and early twentieth centuries, his accommodationist strategy did not command universal support. Black politicians and newspaper editors in the northern states took particular issue with Washington, believing that his attempts at compromise amounted to a capitulation to white racism. In the words of William Monroe Trotter of the *Boston Guardian*: 'What man is a worse enemy to the race than a leader who looks with equanimity on the disfranchisement of his race in a country where other races have universal suffrage, by constitutions that make one rule for his race and another for the dominant race.'[6] The novelist Charles W. Chesnutt also believed that Washington's abnegation of black political rights constituted an act of racial betrayal: 'To try to read any good thing into these fraudulent Southern constitutions, or to accept them as an accomplished fact, is to condone a crime against one's race.'[7]

The most outspoken critic of Washington was William Edward Burghardt Du Bois. Du Bois was born on 23 February 1868 in Great Barrington, Massachusetts. A brilliant scholar, he received his undergraduate degree from Fisk University in Tennessee, before pursuing postgraduate study at Harvard and Berlin. Between 1894 and 1896, Du Bois taught classics at Wilberforce University, a black institution in Ohio. Having completed a sociological study of the black community of Philadelphia under the auspices of the University of Pennsylvania, in 1897 he assumed a teaching position at Atlanta University. During these early years, Du Bois enthusiastically endorsed the accommodationist tactics of Washington. He publicly defended the Atlanta Compromise from its detractors, contending that it 'might be the basis of a real settlement between whites and blacks in the South'.[8]

However, Du Bois became increasingly disaffected with what he saw as Washington's betrayal of the black race. One of the seminal moments that shaped his political apostasy was the lynching of Sam Hose in 1899. A carnival atmosphere surrounded the incident, with crowds travelling by specially chartered trains to witness Hose being tortured and burned, and to purchase his dismembered body parts as souvenirs. The sadistic brutality of the mob emphasised to Du Bois the futility of attempting to compromise with the forces of white racism.

In 1903, Du Bois published his seminal work *The Souls of Black Folk*. The book included an essay titled 'On Mr. Booker T. Washington and Others' that poured scorn on the philosophy of racial accommodationism. The essay did acknowledge that the rise of Washington to a status of political power and influence was 'the most striking thing in the history of the American Negro' since the demise of Reconstruction.[9] Yet it also ridiculed many of the fundamental principles of Washingtonian ideology, which, Du Bois claimed, was snared in a 'triple paradox'. First, Du Bois took issue with Washington for renouncing political rights in favour of economic progress. Without the vote, he insisted, southern blacks would be powerless to protect themselves from white oppression and maintain any advances they made as workers. Second, Du Bois insisted that it was impossible for Washington to promote racial pride while also encouraging his people to accept white social and political supremacy. Du Bois framed his criticism in gendered terms, arguing that Washington emasculated black men by forcing them to adopt a servile attitude towards whites. Third, Du Bois criticised the emphasis that Washington placed on industrial training at the expense of higher education. Without proper provision for the latter, he asserted, there would be no teachers to train the black masses in the skills promoted by Washington. Du Bois emphasised the need to nourish an intellectual elite, which he named the Talented Tenth, who would provide the leadership needed to advance the interests of African Americans.

The growing disaffection with Washington assumed institutional force in July 1905, when Du Bois organised a meeting of thirty African American leaders, at least six of them from the South, on the Canadian side of Niagara Falls. The delegates drafted a 'Declaration of Principles' that explicitly blamed white racism for the degraded status of blacks. In an uncompromising address to the second meeting of what had become known as the Niagara Movement, Du Bois criticised Washington for claiming that African Americans needed to improve their moral condition and economic status in order to attain the full rights of citizenship. On the contrary, they were entitled by their birthright as American citizens to the same freedom and opportunity as whites. 'We claim for ourselves every single right that belongs to a freeborn American, political, civil and social; and until we get these rights we will never cease to protest and to assail the ears of America.'[10] To this end, the Niagara Movement demanded the overthrow of racial segregation, the restoration of universal manhood suffrage, and equal educational and employment opportunities for African Americans.

The conflicting political philosophies of Washington and Du Bois reflected fundamental personal differences between the two men both in terms of their regional and class backgrounds. Where Washington was a southerner born in slavery, Du Bois was a northerner born into relative prosperity and had never experienced bondage. The need to survive in an environment of unrelenting white racism tempered the political attitude of Washington far more than it did that of Du Bois, encouraging the former to promote conciliation and the latter to encourage confrontation. The issue remains as to which one of the two men advocated the most appropriate strategy to further the interests of southern blacks.

Studies of Washington published during the 1970s and 1980s interpreted his accommodationist strategy as a failure that compounded the plight of African Americans. Writing in the wake of the civil rights movement, historians such as I. A. Newby and Louis Harlan measured Washington against the standard of more contemporary black leaders and found him severely wanting. This critical assessment of Washington continues to carry considerable weight among scholars. Most recently, Brian Kelly has emphasised the ideological limitations of accommodation, especially the naïve faith that

Washington placed in the free market economy.[11] However, there is no clear consensus about Washington. Adam Fairclough, for instance, has attempted to rehabilitate the reputation of Washington. His revisionist interpretation is more radical than that of other scholars who defend Washington on the grounds that accommodation was a necessary tactical retreat for African Americans at a time of unremitting racial hostility. According to Fairclough, there was a far greater line of continuity between the accommodationist tactics of Washington and the later direct action phase of black protest. Washington, he insists, 'laid the groundwork for the militant confrontation of the civil rights movement'.[12]

The reason why the debate on Washington should remain unresolved is that his contribution to protecting and promoting the interests of African Americans is profoundly ambiguous. Historians nonetheless agree on one essential point. Any critical assessment of the accommodationist strategy espoused by Washington must take into consideration the political constraints that southern whites imposed on black protest. As Neil McMillen asserts, analysis of black leadership during the Jim Crow era should be framed within the context of its 'feasible limits'.[13] During an era of unremitting racial animosity, African Americans had little option other than to pursue a policy of public appeasement. A more confrontational stand would have proved counter-productive since it risked incurring the retaliatory wrath of whites. The accommodationist strategy of Washington therefore represented a necessary political compromise. Washington assumed a compliant tone towards whites so that he could promote the material interests of his people. This represented a short-term response to a longer-term political objective. By pushing for racial reform within the restraints of a segregated society, he ultimately hoped to restore the full rights of citizenship to African Americans. The tactic met with some success, although its impact was complicated.

The policy of racial uplift espoused by Washington challenged the dominant racial discourse of the era. The story of how Washington rose from humble origins to attain enormous success and status demonstrated both to black and white readers the potential of his race. To African Americans, it instilled a sense of hope that they could emulate the example of Washington to better their individual and collective condition. To whites, Washington proved a capacity for self-improvement that repudiated popular 'scientific' notions that African Americans were inherently and irredeemably dull, violent and depraved.

One of the other most important contributions that Washington made was an improvement in the provision of black education. Washington transformed the Tuskegee campus from its ramshackle and poorly resourced origins into the flagship of black education in the South. By 1901, the Institute boasted more than one hundred faculty members and in excess of one thousand students.[14] Washington succeeded in securing white philanthropic support not only for his own institution, but also for the construction and improvement of black schools and colleges across the region. The Rosenwald Fund, for instance, between 1912 and 1932 provided for the construction of 4,977 schools in fifteen states.[15] Washington also channelled financial donations from white philanthropists into the improvement of black health care.

Despite these improvements, there remained enormous disparities in the provision of public education for white and black schoolchildren. Indeed, the emphasis that Washington placed on the limited educational aspirations of African Americans allowed whites to perpetuate a system of separate and unequal schools. The disparity in public spending on black and white schools increased over the course of the early twentieth century. Southern state legislatures also slashed the budgets of state-supported black colleges on the basis that their curricula exceeded the industrial education advocated by Washington. Although white charitable support did lead to the improvement of African American schools, it also trapped black educators in a dependent relationship with their benefactors. White school board members and superintendents imposed tight control on the content of courses taught in black schools, restricting the autonomy of teachers and students.

While these criticisms cannot be dismissed, it is important to remember the political circumstances in which Washington operated. The advances in black education that he oversaw are all the more impressive given that they occurred in a context of almost relentless white hostility towards black schooling. As outlined in the last chapter, southern whites worried that the education of African Americans would undermine their ability to control an otherwise compliant labour force. A little knowledge was a dangerous thing, since it planted seeds of discontent that could sprout into increased personal ambition. In the diplomatic words of Robert Moton, who succeeded Washington as principal of Tuskegee: 'there are many people who thoroughly believe in Negro education, but we must remember that there are also many honest, sincere white people who are still doubtful as to the wisdom of educating the colored man'.[16] Washington gave black education the institutional strength to weather the storm of white prejudice.

Washington was less successful with some of the other aspects of his political programme. It is difficult not to accept the evaluation of Kevern Verney that 'If the Tuskegeean's achievements during his lifetime were limited, it was not just because of the constraints imposed by American society, but also because of the boundaries for action set by Washington himself.'[17] The economic policies Washington espoused, for instance, were impractical and had the unintentional effect of impeding, rather than promoting, the racial advancement of African Americans. In his Atlanta Compromise address, Washington encouraged southern blacks not to seek employment opportunities elsewhere, but to 'Cast down your bucket where you are.' However, the South was far from being a land of unlimited economic possibilities, as represented by Washington. While the late nineteenth century witnessed an industrial revolution in the United States, the South remained relatively underdeveloped. By attempting to dissuade southern blacks from migrating to the North, Washington denied them the chance to secure improved wages and working conditions in the new industrial and manufacturing economy. Moreover, the industrial education he advocated did not provide the instruction African Americans needed to participate competitively in the southern economy. Tuskegee and other institutions that emulated its example trained students in artisanal trades at a time when the imposition of segregation had led to the displacement of thousands of skilled black craftsmen from the southern workforce. Although the New South economy opened doors to black labourers, the regimes in the steel mills and mining and lumbering camps were often brutal. In opposing unionisation, Washington undermined the ability of industrial labourers to protect themselves against the exploitative practices of employers.

Washington had a naïve trust in what he considered were the colour-blind dynamics of the market economy. He assumed that the system would ultimately reward those African Americans who worked hard enough. In his words: 'No race that has anything to contribute to the markets of the world is long in any degree ostracized.'[18] Such a belief underestimated the structural barriers that obstructed black economic progress. That African Americans did not possess equality of opportunity in a free market is illustrated by the limited impact of the National Negro Business League. Washington established the league in 1900 to promote black entrepreneurialism. Although the League succeeded in promoting black business enterprises across the country, African Americans remained at a competitive disadvantage to whites, as banks often refused them loans, forcing them to operate with limited capital. Washington's faith in free-market competition forced him to attribute the failure of many black businesses not to the system, but to the deficiencies of individual entrepreneurs. This created a culture of blame that may have unnecessarily handicapped black business initiative.

The relationships that Washington cultivated with successive presidential administrations also brought limited benefit to African Americans. In 1901, President Theodore Roosevelt invited Washington to attend a meeting at the

White House, an event that reinforced the latter's reputation as the 'progressive' black leader. However, the invitation also aroused the animus of white southerners, who were outraged that the executive should treat an African American on terms that implied social equality between the races. As Senator Ben Tillman of South Carolina asserted: 'The action of President Roosevelt in entertaining that nigger will necessitate our killing a thousand niggers in the South before they will learn their place again.'[19] The meeting between Washington and Roosevelt certainly had a powerful symbolic resonance for African Americans whose political stock had sunk to its lowest levels since Reconstruction.

However, in substantive terms it was of little significance. Washington had minimal influence over federal policy towards African Americans, a fact underlined by his failure to secure justice for black soldiers stationed in Brownsville, Texas. In 1906, the US Army assigned the First Battalion of the 25th Infantry Regiment to Fort Brown. The black troops suffered constant harassment and abuse from local whites. When an unidentified group of armed men shot two whites, killing one and wounding the other, the black soldiers came under suspicion, despite the fact that their officers insisted they had been in their barracks at the time of the incident. The soldiers were pressured to reveal who was responsible, but insisted they did not know. Confronted by what he considered a conspiracy of silence, President Roosevelt ordered the dishonourable discharge of 167 soldiers. Although Washington privately protested the action, he refrained from any public criticism and maintained his loyalty to the president. His efforts to persuade Roosevelt to moderate the language of a speech on mob violence also ended in failure. The president proceeded to inform Congress that the lynching of African Americans was a lesser crime than the raping of white women by black men. Washington had even less influence on the men who succeeded Roosevelt in the White House. William Taft ceased the appointment of African Americans to federal positions in the South, while Woodrow Wilson went still further. After decades of Republican hegemony, Wilson was significantly both a Democrat and a southerner. As president, he removed many African Americans from their positions within the federal bureaucracy and imposed tighter segregation. The actions of the executive reflected the hardening of white racial attitudes that occurred in American society around the time of the First World War.

Similar criticisms can be made of the way Washington attempted to promote the interests of African Americans by appealing to what he believed were the nobler instincts of white southerners. He believed that he had brokered a compromise between his own race and what he described as 'the best white people of the South'.[20] However, this was a serious miscalculation. By the late nineteenth century, the paternalistic attitudes of elite whites towards African Americans had been supplanted by a visceral racism. Southern blacks were stripped of their basic humanity and reduced to a status of bestiality. The middle ground that Washington thought he had established between the races was entirely eroded. Nothing more dramatically demonstrated his misplaced trust in whites than the rise in racial violence across the region. Washington had on occasion publicly condemned the violent persecution of his people. Yet he had also intensified the suffering of southern blacks by blaming them for bringing the lynch mobs down upon themselves. Washington attributed racial violence to the irresponsible behaviour of lower-class blacks, whose loose morals confirmed white stereotypes of African Americans as being dangerously degenerate. It was his hope that 'the idle element that lives by its wits without permanent or reliable occupation or place of abode is either reformed or gotten rid of in some manner. In most cases it is this element that furnishes the powder for these explosions.'[21] This assertion that the brutalities inflicted on African Americans were the result of their own personal deficiencies, rather than the bigotry of whites, provided sanction for the actions of the mob. The criticism of lower-class blacks by a middle-class leader also exposed one of the most serious fault lines within the African American community, an issue that will be explored in more detail later in this chapter.

The relentlessness of racial violence against African Americans eventually led Washington to reconsider his political position. The Atlanta race riot of 1906 in particular appears to have unsettled his faith in the politics of accommodationism. Despite his public disclaimers about black social and political rights, Washington had since the 1880s secretly sponsored lawsuits that contested numerous forms of racial discrimination, including disfranchisement, debt peonage and segregation on public transport. In the last decade of his life, his disillusionment with 'the best white people' led him to take a more openly confrontational stand against southern racism. Washington publicly confronted official tolerance of lynch law and segregation on railroads and streetcars. He also added his voice to the chorus of black protests against the racist film *The Birth of a Nation*. 'My View of the Segregation Laws', an article published after his premature death in November 1915, revealed his more militant political consciousness.

The accommodationist strategy with which Washington had persevered for more than three decades had become an anachronism by the time he died. However, he could not entirely abandon the policy of racial uplift that was the source of his personal power and prestige. In a still-powerful critique of Washington published in the 1960s, August Meier noted how, throughout his political career, he employed a system of patronage to reward those black leaders who supported him and punish those who did not. During the last decade of his life, he relied more and more on the power of the Tuskegee Machine to undermine the more militant black activists whose emergence challenged his dominance as the pre-eminent spokesperson for his race.[22] The Niagara Movement, having failed to mobilise mass support, had ceased to function by 1910. However, it laid the foundation for a new civil rights organisation, the National Association for the Advancement of Colored People (NAACP). Although its political power base in the southern states remained small, the establishment of the NAACP presaged a new era of black protest that would supplant the accommodationist strategy of Washington. Building on the revisionist interpretation of Adam Fairclough, some scholars argue that the legal challenges to segregation and discrimination made by Washington anticipated the political agenda of those civil rights organisations that succeeded him.[23] Had he lived longer, it is still not possible to see him colluding with these organisations to secure racial reform. On the contrary, his hostility towards those who threatened his political authority would have caused him to destabilise the incipient civil rights reform. In this sense, the torch of black political leadership passed on at just the right time.

ACTION, EVASION AND ESCAPE

In contrast to the public stoicism of accommodationist leaders such as Washington, some southern blacks were unable to contain their outrage at the imposition of Jim Crow apartheid and launched direct-action campaigns that challenged the new laws. These protests reflected the rise of a new generation of southern blacks, born after slavery, who did not share the same deferential attitudes towards whites as their parents. African Americans, both individually and collectively, used their economic power as consumers to pressure white businesses into easing their enforcement of the colour line. A case in point is the series of economic boycotts that blacks organised against segregated streetcars. African Americans in Georgia established a plan of political action that other communities would follow, conducting such protests in Atlanta in 1892, Augusta in 1898, and Savannah in 1899. The first decade of the twentieth century witnessed further boycotts in twenty-seven cities. These demonstrations of black disaffection took place despite white threats of violence and arrest. African Americans also threatened to withdraw their trade from white businesses as a means of securing improved service and protection against the sale of inferior products. Southern blacks additionally used the courts to contest racial segregation and discrimination. Black plaintiffs, for instance, filed suits against the states of Mississippi and Alabama in an attempt to reinstate their right to vote. While these acts of resistance have faded from popular memory, they demonstrate that half a century before the emergence of the civil rights movement, southern blacks were already engaged in direct protest against their second-class status.

Ultimately, most of these acts of resistance ended in failure. African Americans in some instances maintained their boycotts of segregated streetcars for months. In Augusta, the campaigners persisted in their efforts for three years. Despite their resilience, they still could not break the will of the streetcar companies or local authorities. Nor did the judicial system afford African Americans redress. Legal challenges to black disfranchisement suffered defeat when the US Supreme Court upheld the state constitutions of Mississippi and Alabama in 1898 and 1903 respectively. Yet the inability of African Americans to restrict the enforcement of white supremacy is attributable less to their lack of resolve than it is to the unremittingly hostile political climate in which they waged their protests.

Southern whites could not entirely silence black political dissent. The increasingly militant opposition of some African Americans to lynching is one illustration of this. Southern blacks were slow to launch a direct assault on mob violence. Many middle-class leaders shared the sentiment of Booker T. Washington that mobs only murdered those who had actually committed a criminal offence. The solution to lynching, in their opinion, rested in an improvement in the behaviour not of whites but of lowly and degenerate blacks, whose dissoluteness incited acts of retaliatory violence. These individuals needed to attain sufficient moral improvement as to place them beyond criminal suspicion. By contrast, some blacks, especially those of the labouring classes, took a more confrontational stand against white mobs, establishing armed self-defence committees. 'Get guns, Negroes!' exclaimed militant clergyman Henry McNeal Turner. 'Get guns, and may God give you good aim when you shoot.'[24] The sharp contrast between this statement and the accommodationist tone of many black leaders emphasises the fault lines that at times fractured black political unity.

The most outspoken anti-lynching activist was Ida B. Wells (later Wells-Barnett). Wells was born a slave in Holly Springs, Mississippi, on 16 July 1862. She initially pursued a teaching career, but became drawn into both journalism and community activism. Her first taste of notoriety came in 1884, when her refusal to vacate a segregated railroad car led to her forcible removal. Wells successfully sued the railroad company, although the Supreme Court later overturned the ruling. In 1889, Wells became co-owner and editor of the

Memphis Free Speech. Writing under the pseudonym 'Iola', she also wrote a nationally syndicated newspaper column in which she railed against the rising tide of white racism. Her public opposition to racial discrimination assumed a new intensity as a result of a brutal act of mob violence that occurred in March 1892. Black businessman Thomas Moss had established a grocery store that cut into the profits of a white competitor, who rallied a mob to run him out of the area. Moss and two of his friends, Calvin McDowell and Henry Stewart, armed themselves to protect the store. The men shot three intruders who attempted to force their way in. White panic led to the arrest of more than one hundred African Americans. However, even this did not abate the thirst for retribution. A mob seized Moss and his two friends from jail and shot them dead. Wells had a close personal relationship with Moss: she was godmother to his daughter. She responded to the lynching by publishing an impassioned indictment of racial violence. Her public demand for the arrest and conviction of the mob leaders aroused the ire of the white community. While she was away in Philadelphia, a mob ransacked the office of the *Free Speech* and burned it to the ground. Wells was forced into exile.

This dramatic turn of events only seems to have made Wells more determined to pursue her cause. In 1893 and 1894, she toured the United Kingdom in an attempt to impel international condemnation of American mob violence. By the late nineteenth century, diplomatic officials from numerous overseas governments had successfully lobbied Washington for the payment of indemnities to families of foreign nationals lynched in the United States. African Americans lacked similar institutional leverage to force a similar response from the federal government, though, and Wells's tour did not secure comparable political representation for her people. The British government had no right to make formal representations to Washington on behalf of African American victims of mob violence. Her actions nonetheless anticipated the efforts of later civil rights activists who attempted to use the court of international opinion, and in particular the United Nations, as a means of pressuring Washington to take a more interventionist role against racial violence and discrimination.

Wells also used the power of the printed word to assail lynching. She published a series of pamphlets that exposed not only the scale of mob violence against African Americans, but also the blatant falsehoods used by white southerners to rationalise these acts of barbarism. In 1892, Wells published the first of these pamphlets, entitled *Southern Horrors: Lynch Law in All Its Phases*. The year after her second tour of the United Kingdom saw the publication of a second pamphlet, *A Red Record*. The third and final pamphlet, *Mob Rule in New Orleans*, appeared in 1900.

These publications provided a powerful corrective to popular assumptions about racial violence. Wells used statistical data to demonstrate the scale of lynching in the southern states, and included explicit detail of many of the more shocking episodes. In establishing the geography of mob violence, she disproved the claim of lynching apologists that the shortcomings of the criminal justice system compelled citizens to take the law into their own hands to protect themselves against black criminals. On the contrary, she pointed out, lynching occurred in communities with fully functional law courts.

Wells further refuted the common assertion that lynching was necessary to protect white women against sexual assault by black men. Only a third of the lynching victims documented by Wells had been charged with rape; fewer still were actually guilty of the crime. Wells did not deny that there were sexual relations between white women and black men. However, she insisted that many of these liaisons were not only consensual but also initiated by the woman. It was only when these affairs suffered public exposure that the woman, fearful of the shame and loss of honour, accused her lover of rape. The claim that lynching was essential to defend white women from predatory black men was therefore nothing more than a figleaf that concealed the real motivations for mob violence. To 'excuse some of the most heinous crimes that ever stained the history of a country,' Wells concluded, 'the South is shielding itself behind the plausible screen of defending the honor of its women.'[25] Wells also asserted that the only 'crime' many lynching victims had committed was to transgress the racial boundaries imposed by white southerners, such as challenging an employer or, as was the case with Thomas Moss, establishing a successful business. The real criminals were not black men who raped white women, but white men who, with almost complete impunity, sexually violated black women. As Wells affirmed, 'even when punishment is meted out by law to white villains for this horrible crime, it is seldom or never that capital punishment is invoked'.[26]

Through her analysis of lynch law, Wells revealed the racial and sexual double standards of white southern males. White men failed to observe the strict social codes that they so ruthlessly enforced on others. Their lynching of African American men whom they accused of committing inter-racial rape concealed the fact that they themselves were the worst perpetrators of such a crime. Yet they rationalised their own behaviour by accusing the black women whom they sexually victimised of being licentious creatures with no sense of moral virtue. While making excuses for their own oversexed behaviour, they also suppressed the erotic impulses of white women by portraying them as chaste and in need of protection. Wells therefore demonstrated how the repressive nature of the southern white patriarchal order cut across racial and gender lines.

Although Wells launched a direct assault on southern racial violence, she did so from a position of relative safety outside the region. Most southern blacks understood that such outspoken attacks on white racism would endanger their lives and their livelihoods. The strategies they implemented to protest the system therefore assumed a less direct form.

Writing in the 1930s, social anthropologist John Dollard neatly summarised the social meaning of race in the southern states. 'Whiteness represents full personal dignity and full participation in American society,' he observed, whereas 'Blackness or darkness represents limitation and inferiority.'[27] It should not be surprising that, in such a repressive racial climate, some African Americans internalised the notion of their inherent deficiencies compared to whites. That some southern blacks embraced whiteness as a racial ideal is evident from the social hierarchies that they constructed within their communities, which elevated the status of those who possessed lighter skins. Black newspapers also contained numerous advertisements for consumer products such as hair straighteners and skin whiteners. Mississippi Delta bluesman Sam Chatman commented ironically on the racial self-hatred of some southern blacks in the song 'I Have to Paint My Face':

Say now when God made people
He done pretty well
But when he made a jet black nigger
He made them some hell[28]

According to African American author Richard Wright, many black southerners hated and resented whites, but were powerless to act upon their emotions. Therefore they took out their frustrations by turning violently on one another.[29]

Southern blacks nonetheless demonstrated considerable resilience in resisting their total subjugation. The racial etiquette of the Jim Crow South required African Americans to assume an obsequious public manner towards whites. Many whites discerned the outward behaviour of African Americans as an expression of their inner acceptance of the social order. This apparent acquiescence concealed what the historian Robin Kelley describes as a 'hidden transcript', a culture of political dissent that challenged white hegemony.[30] Evidence of this hidden transcript can be found in the stories, music and humour shared by southern blacks. Richard Wright wrote of a friend named Griggs who had mastered the art of dissembling. According to Griggs, the only way for African Americans to get good paid work was to adopt a fawning attitude towards white employers. However, no sooner had the boss turned his back than the seemingly sycophantic Griggs would slyly recite 'All these white folks dressed so fine/Their ass-holes smell just like mine'.[31]

The hidden transcript also appeared in public spaces controlled by whites, although in a less direct form. African American labourers occasionally mobilised in collective action against white employers, as in 1881, when black washerwomen in Atlanta organised a union and called a strike for improved wages. However, most black employees dared not risk direct confrontation with white bosses. Consequently, they drew on more artful forms of protest, such as stealing, feigning sickness or sabotaging tools and machinery. Southern blacks inherited their skill in the art of deception from earlier generations who, as slaves, had by numerous means succeeded in 'Puttin' On Ole Massa'.[32] When challenged about the supposed accidents that disrupted their working schedules, they used white prejudices to their own advantage by pretending ignorance. Domestic servants applied particularly subtle tactics of resistance that allowed them to maintain a discreet physical and psychological distance from employers. They accomplished this both by refusing to move into the homes of the people for whom they worked and, no matter how many confidences their employers shared with them, by revealing few of their own inner thoughts. A white woman in Atlanta informed Ray Stannard Baker that, although her cook had been in her service for nineteen years and was loved by the family, 'Susie never tells us a thing about her life or her friends, and we couldn't, if we tried, make her tell what goes on in the society she belongs to.'[33]

While the concept of the 'hidden transcript' provides an important reinterpretation of African American responses to white racism, it is necessary to sound a word of caution. Chapter 5 demonstrated how scholars such as Peter Kolchin have warned of the dangers of placing too much emphasis on the cohesion of the communities created by slaves or the strength of their resistance to the plantation system. Similarly, historians should not interpret every action by the African American labouring class as a surreptitious act of rebellion against the Jim Crow caste system. As Eric Arnesen observes, to do so is to risk 'creating a romanticized view of the black working class'.[34]

The most unusual means by which blacks attempted to improve their social and economic condition was to cross the colour line by pretending to be white. Racial passing was an urban phenomenon. It was also an option available to only the lightest-skinned African Americans. The issue is analysed in a number of fictional works from this era, including the 1900 novel *The House Behind the Cedars* by William C. Chesnutt. It is impossible to determine how many blacks successfully pursued this strategy, since it rested on the public erasure of their real racial identity. Although it was most commonly individuals who passed for white, occasionally couples and entire families transformed their social status. Some pretended to be white only at work, returning home each day to their black neighbourhoods. Others secured a complete and permanent change of racial identity. Although passing improved the status of individual African Americans, it represented a tacit acceptance on their part of the southern caste system.

Other African Americans pursued a more obvious means of escape from racial persecution. The economist Albert Hirschman asserts that people faced with declining personal circumstances and opportunities have three options. The first is to protest their situation through escape, the second is to stand and fight for reform, and the third is simply to accept the status quo. Hirschman refers to these three options respectively as 'Exit', 'Voice' and 'Loyalty'. Southern blacks frustrated at the failure of Reconstruction to fulfil its promises of economic freedom and the full rights of citizenship pursued these strategies in different measures. Some fatalistically accepted their status within the southern hierarchy. Others pursued tactics that ranged from racial accommodation to open resistance, in an attempt to improve the condition of their people. Still others calculated the risk of political protest and decided to seek physical escape from their misfortunes. As Hirschman maintains: 'Why raise your voice in contradiction and get yourself into trouble as long as you can always remove yourself entirely from any given environment should it become too unpleasant?'[35]

Black rural labourers routinely moved within county boundaries from one employer to another, in the hope of improving their working conditions. The search for better opportunities also drew increasing numbers of African Americans westward. Despite the introduction of anti-enticement laws intended to restrict the mobility of southern blacks, labour agents recruited thousands of workers from the south-eastern states to the expanding cotton economies of Arkansas, Mississippi, Louisiana and Texas. Some African Americans were so disillusioned with the racially restrictive practices of the South that they abandoned not only the region but also the United States.

During the 1870s, accelerating numbers of southern blacks migrated to Kansas. That trickle suddenly became a flood in 1879, as 25,000 African Americans caught 'Kansas Fever' and embarked on an exodus to the mid-western state. Some of the Exodusters turned back when they discovered that the federal government had not, as they hoped, provided steamships to transport them up the Mississippi River. Others reached their destination, only to be disappointed there. Nonetheless, those who remained in their adopted state demonstrated the determination of southern blacks to overcome the obstacles of white supremacist rule. Some African Americans believed that the only means to breach the barriers that impeded their progress was to emigrate. African Methodist Episcopal (AME) Bishop Henry McNeal Turner advocated black repatriation to Africa. Turner declared that emigration to the African state of Liberia offered an opportunity for African Americans to reclaim not only their liberties, but also the manhood that whites had taken from them. However, the dream of colonising Liberia was dashed by the hard realities of limited finances. The 'Exit' strategy pursued by some southern blacks nevertheless had a substantial demographic impact on the region. Between 1880 and 1910, the southern states experienced a net loss of more than half a million African Americans. It should also be noted that economic conditions led more than a million whites to leave during the same period.

A SOCIETY WITHIN A SOCIETY

Despite the lure of new opportunities in other parts of the country, most southern blacks chose to remain in the region of their birth. Denied access to many public facilities reserved for the exclusive use of whites, African Americans constructed their own autonomous institutions. The imposition of racial segregation therefore had the unintended effect of creating a greater sense of strength and cohesion within the black community, albeit one born out of adversity.

African Americans established informal and formal support networks that sustained their communities in the face of adversity. Rural families shared subsistence needs by offering the fruits of their labour to others who had suffered setbacks as a result of death or illness. Leroy Boyd remembered how black farming families in the Mississippi Delta relied on mutual assistance to support them through hard times. 'If you was a neighbor and you had got behind, my family would just go and help you [for] free. When we kill a hog, we'd share the meat. It wouldn't be no whole lot, but we'd send so-and-so a big mess of meat. They would do us the same way.'[36] Black women tobacco workers shared a similar sense of collective responsibility, raising money to support families affected by sickness or bereavement, and symbolically referring to one another as 'sister'. Laundresses in the towns and cities constructed comparable ties of kinship and co-dependence.[37]

The untiring effort of African Americans to maintain and improve their schools is one of the most potent expressions of community self-help. Black parents placed a great deal of faith in education as the means by which their children would attain a better life. As white journalist Ray Stannard Baker attested: 'They will submit to all sorts of inconveniences in order that their children may get an education.'[38] Some rural families saved sufficient money from their meagre incomes to pay for their children to stay with friends or relatives while they attended the better-financed urban schools. Others banded together to boost the schools in their own communities. The discriminatory allocation of public monies meant that African Americans paid taxes to support white schools from which their children were excluded. To improve conditions in their own under-resourced schools, black parents were therefore forced to 'second-tax' themselves, donating what they could in terms of time, money and labour. Reverend David Matthews recalled of his childhood in the Mississippi Delta how the local black community pooled their resources to keep their school open, even for a few more weeks. They 'would scrape up money or vegetables or milk, butter, eggs, flour, and those that had a little money would share a little money with the teachers, and the teachers who were interested in our plight would dedicate themselves to serving on a month or so because of the needs of the children and the interest of the parents'.[39]

Black schools, especially those in small towns and rural areas, often suffered from inferior facilities and poorly trained teachers. Despite these disadvantages, African American educators strove to instil a sense of personal ambition and racial pride in their students. The Association for the Study of Negro Life and History, established by Carter G. Woodson in 1915, fostered racial advancement by promoting the teaching of black cultural and political achievements. African Americans also held annual remembrance ceremonies that emphasised the nobility with which their race had risen above a historical burden of prejudice and oppression. Decoration Day venerated black veterans who had fought as Union soldiers during the Civil War to liberate their fellow African Americans from slavery. Emancipation Day honoured the living survivors of the old plantation system. In contrast to white celebrations of Confederate war heroes such as Robert E. Lee, African Americans observed the birthdays of political leaders who championed the cause of racial justice, such as Frederick Douglass and Abraham Lincoln. These acts of commemoration restored a historical record of black accomplishment that white schoolbooks had attempted to erase. The reconciliation of northern and southern whites during the late nineteenth century further marginalised blacks within American society. The construction of an alternative memory of the Civil War experience that celebrated their own achievement was therefore a source of psychological empowerment for African Americans. Celebration of the past also provided southern blacks with a renewed focus on the future. Just as earlier generations of African Americans had fought for the full rights of citizenship, so must the current one continue the struggle.

Southern blacks drew the comfort and strength needed to cope with the hardships of their daily lives from the church. In the aftermath of the Civil War, emancipated slaves established their own churches as a means to worship free of the controlling influence of their former masters. African Americans flocked in greatest numbers to the Baptist faith. In 1890, there were 1.3 million southern black Baptists. That same year, the AME Zion Church claimed 366,000 southern black congregants; the AME Church 310,000; and the Methodists 125,000.[40] Churches tended to both the spiritual and worldly needs of worshippers. The sermons preached by ministers provided African Americans with the solace that they would ultimately be delivered from the injustices suffered in their earthly lives. In the more immediate term, services provided an outlet for cultural expression, an occasion to socialise, and an opportunity to share concerns and information. Erleen Lindsay of Alabama affirmed that the church 'was the survival of the people because, out of the church, that's where everybody gathered on a Sunday to fellowship and find out what was going on and around'.[41] The church also provided institutional co-ordination for charitable work within the community, such as raising funds to improve schools or feeding indigent families. Its protective environment moreover furnished a safe space for political meetings. The church was therefore the emotional and material fulcrum around which the lives of many southern blacks turned. In the words of Clifton Taulbert, it was 'more than an institution, it was the very heart of our lives'.[42]

The most energetic contributions to church activities often came from female congregants, many of whom were inspired by the spirit of volunteer activism to join the ranks of the women's club movement. The most influential body within this movement was the National Association of Colored Women, established in 1896 under the presidency of Mary Church Terrell. By the 1920s, the organisation boasted a membership of more than 100,000, drawn mainly from the ranks of the black urban elite. Its principal purpose, represented by the motto 'Lifting as We Climb', was to improve the social and economic condition of lower-class blacks as a means of raising the collective status of the entire race. Association activists provided material support such as food, clothing and medical care to needy families. They also attempted to promote the upward mobility of the lower classes in the longer term by teaching them the habits of thrift, chastity and temperance. This emphasis on personal respectability challenged prevailing stereotypes of African Americans as being innately dirty, depraved and irresponsible. Black men also performed important charitable work. Fraternal orders such as the

Masons and Odd Fellows established mutual aid schemes that offered support to members affected by misfortune. The network of black clubs, mutual aid societies and fraternal orders not only offered material support to African Americans, but also afforded their members opportunities otherwise denied them by whites to acquire political skills, experience and leadership.

The efforts of middle-class African Americans to uplift the less socially and economically mobile members of their race were also a source of tension within the black community. The rhetoric of many middle-class reformers represented the South as a meritocratic society in which race was no obstacle to individual advancement. Accordingly, they attributed the failure of many working-class blacks to improve their condition to individual weakness rather than structural inequalities. A case in point is Robert Moton of Tuskegee, who ascribed the lowly status of many southern blacks to the 'ignorance, shiftlessness, disease, inefficiency, and crime' that 'are still prevalent among our people'.[43] This onus on individual responsibility led in some instances to black leaders insisting that the solution to racial prejudice rested not in social protest but in improvements in personal conduct and hygiene. As T. V. Gibbs asserted, the surest means by which African Americans would gain greater social acceptance was to comport themselves in a more civilised manner. Such criticisms of the lower classes to some extent reflected the acceptance of white cultural values by the lighter-skinned persons who made up most of the black middle class. According to Gibbs: 'When our people as a mass learn to ride in railway cars without eating water melons, fat meat, and peanuts, throwing the rinds on the floor; when our women leave their snuff sticks, greasy bundles and uncouth manners at home, railroad discriminations will abate much of their injustice.'[44]

Working-class blacks in turn resented those self-appointed moral guardians who attempted to reform and regulate their habits and behaviour. Middle-class reformers, for instance, assailed the dance halls and juke joints frequented by working-class blacks as places of sin and depravity. They despaired that the conspicuous consumption of alcohol and sexually charged dances performed by patrons undermined their ability to instil a stronger sense of moral responsibility among their people. One black minister in Virginia described the eroticised dancing at these venues in condemnatory terms that also betrayed a troubled sense of excitement: 'Look at the young girl or some one's wife borne around the room in the arms of a man; his arms are drawn around her waist; her swelling bosom rests against his; her limbs are tangled with his; her head rests against his face; her bare neck reflecting the soft mellow light of the chandelier, while the passions are raging like a furnace of fire.'[45] Those African Americans who patronised such establishments had an altogether more positive interpretation of their experiences. To them, the dance halls provided an opportunity for personal expression uninhibited by the watchful eyes of whites. Dressing up and dancing in the company of friends, they attained a momentary transcendence from the restrictions and hardships of their daily lives. Black leaders therefore did not always command the support of those people whose interests they claimed to represent.

Many of the songs performed by black musicians contained potent observations about the trials and tribulations of African Americans in the southern states. This is especially true of the blues, which emerged from the small towns and rural areas of the Deep South in the late nineteenth century. The blues drew upon the call-and-response form of the work songs and field hollers of slaves in the antebellum South, the vocal lines being emulated instrumentally by the sound of the guitar. Although the songs performed by blues artists were personal meditations on the individual suffering of the musician, many also resonated powerfully with the broader group experience of southern blacks. The perils and uncertainties of life in a society where African Americans were exposed to indiscrimate acts of racial violence resonates powerfully in the lyrics to songs such as 'Hellhound on My Trail' by Robert Johnson, or 'Down the Dirt Road Blues' by Charley Patton:

> Every day seem like murder here
> (My God I'm no sheriff)
> Every day seem like murder here
> I'm gonna leave tomorrow, I know you don't bid my care.[46]

It is a remarkable testimony to the cultural strength of the black community that it should have created so many new musical forms during the Jim Crow era. The roots of blues and ragtime rested in the soil of the rural South, while the streets of cities such as New Orleans gave rise to jazz.

When black protesters took to the streets during the civil rights revolution of the 1950s and 1960s, they drew strength from a growing consensus of national and international support for the cause of racial equality. By contrast, the earlier generations of southern blacks that lived during the late nineteenth and early twentieth centuries faced the hostile forces of white racism alone. Despite these adverse circumstances, African Americans demonstrated considerable resilience. Albeit with limited success, they devised and implemented many of the tactics later used to break down the barriers of racial segregation. One of the most important shifts in the historiography of southern race relations is the increasing emphasis that scholars now place on the continuity of black protest. As William Chafe has recently stated, the community activism of southern blacks during the Jim Crow era laid the foundations for the future civil rights movement. In his words: 'It is easy to define one period as a time of accommodation and another as an era of protest. But using such labels can obscure the more important truth that the black experience in America has been one of constant struggle.'[47] The civil rights activists of the mid-twentieth century did not therefore emerge out of a historical vacuum, but rather drew upon a broader tradition of black political protest. That tradition continued through the era of the two world wars, when southern blacks would have to respond to a complicated series of setbacks and opportunities.

Notes

1. Richard Wright, *Black Boy: A Record of Childhood and Youth* ([1945], Harlow: Longman, 1970), p. 221.
2. James C. Cobb, *The Most Southern Place on Earth: The Mississippi Delta and the Roots of Regional Identity* (New York and Oxford: Oxford University Press, 1992), p. 173.
3. Booker T. Washington, 'Industrial Education for the Negro', in Booker T. Washington, et al., *The Negro Problem* (Amherst, NY: Humanity Books, 2003), p. 17.
4. Louis R. Harlan and Raymond W. Smock (eds), *The Booker T. Washington Papers*, 13 vols (Urbana: University of Illinois Press, 1972–84), 3: p. 373.
5. The complete text of the address can be found in Booker T. Washington, *Up From Slavery* (New York: Penguin, 1986), pp. 218–25. The quotations are taken from pp. 223 and 221.
6. August Meier, Elliott Rudwick and Francis L. Broderick (eds), *Black Protest Thought in the Twentieth Century* (Indianapolis, IN: Bobbs-Merill, 1971), pp. 32–3.
7. Charles W. Chesnutt, 'The Disfranchisement of the Negro', in Washington, et al., *The Negro Problem*, p. 111.
8. Mark Bauerlein, 'Washington, Du Bois, and the Black Future', *Wilson Quarterly*, 28 (Autumn 2004), p. 77.
9. W. E. B. Du Bois, *The Souls of Black Folk* (New York: Penguin, 1989), p. 36.
10. David Levering Lewis, *W. E. B. Du Bois: Biography of a Race, 1868–1919* (New York: Henry Holt, 1993), p. 330.
11. I. A. Newby, *Black Carolinians: A History of Blacks in South Carolina from 1895 to 1968* (Columbia: University of South Carolina Press, 1973); Louis R. Harlan, *Booker T. Washington: The Making of a Black Leader, 1856–1901* (New York: Oxford University Press, 1972) and *Booker T. Washington: The Wizard of Tuskegee, 1901–1915* (New York: Oxford University Press, 1983); Brian Kelly,

Race, Class, and Power in the Alabama Coalfields, 1908–1921 (Urbana: University of Illinois Press, 2001).

12. Adam Fairclough, *Better Day Coming: Blacks and Equality, 1890–2000* (New York: Penguin, 2002), quotation on p. xiii.
13. Neil R. McMillen, *Dark Journey: Black Mississippians in the Age of Jim Crow* (Urbana and Chicago: University of Illinois Press, 1990), p. 287.
14. Manning Marable, *Black Leadership* (New York: Columbia University Press, 1998), p. 28.
15. Beverly Jones, 'Rosenwald Schools', in John C. Inscoe (ed.), *The New Georgia Encyclopedia*, http://www.georgiaencyclopedia.org/nge/Artcile.jsp?id=h-1113 (accessed 12 February 2006).
16. Robert Russa Moton, *Finding a Way Out* (London: T. Fisher Unwin, 1920), p. 217.
17. Kevern Verney, *The Art of the Possible: Booker T. Washington and Black Leadership in the United States, 1881–1925* (New York and London: Routledge, 2001), p. 46.
18. Marable, *Black Leadership*, p. 33.
19. Stephen Kantrowitz, *Ben Tillman & the Reconstruction of White Supremacy* (Chapel Hill: University of North Carolina Press, 2000), p. 259.
20. Leon F. Litwack, *Trouble in Mind: Black Southerners in the Age of Jim Crow* (New York: Alfred A. Knopf, 1998), p. 354.
21. Cary Wintz, *African-American Political Thought, 1890–1930* (Armonk, NY: M. E. Sharpe, 1996), pp. 67–8.
22. August Meier, *Negro Thought in America, 1880–1915: Radical Ideologies in the Age of Booker T. Washington* (Ann Arbor: University of Michigan Press, 1963).
23. See, for example, Robert J. Norrell, *The House I Live In: Race in the American Century* (New York: Oxford University Press, 2005), p. 63.
24. Christopher Waldrep, *The Many Faces of Judge Lynch: Extralegal Violence and Punishment in America* (New York: Palgrave Macmillan, 2002), p. 124.
25. Ida B. Wells, *Southern Horrors: Lynch Law in All Its Phases* (1892), in Jacqueline Jones Royster (ed.), *Southern Horrors and Other Writings: The Anti-Lynching Campaign of Ida B. Wells, 1892–1900* (Boston, MA: Bedford Books, 1997), p. 61.
26. Wells, *A Red Record* (1895), in ibid., p. 130.
27. John Dollard, *Caste and Class in a Southern Town* (Garden City, NY: Doubleday & Company, 1957), p. 69.
28. Various Artists, *I Have to Paint My Face: A Collection of Mississippi Blues* (Arhoolie – F1005).
29. Wright, *Black Boy*, p. 222.
30. Robin D. G. Kelley, '"We Are Not What We Seem": Rethinking Black Working-Class Opposition in the Jim Crow South', *Journal of American History*, 80 (June 1993), pp. 75–112.
31. Wright, *Black Boy*, p. 162.

32. Gilbert Osofsky, *Puttin' On Ole Massa: The Slave Narratives of Henry Bibb, William Wells Brown, and Solomon Northup* (New York: Harper and Row, 1969).
33. Ray Stannard Baker, *Following the Color Line: American Negro Citizenship in the Progressive Era* (New York: Harper & Row, 1964), p. 39.
34. Eric Arnesen, 'Up From Exclusion: Black and White Workers, Race, and the State of Labor History', *Reviews in American History*, 26 (1993), p. 160.
35. Albert O. Hirschman, *Exit, Voice, and Loyalty: Responses to Decline in Firms, Organizations, and States* (Cambridge, MA: Harvard University Press, 1970). Quotation, p. 108.
36. William H. Chafe, et al. (eds), *Remembering Jim Crow: African Americans Tell About Life in the Segregated South* (New York: New Press, 2001), p. 123.
37. Kelley, '"We Are Not What We Seem"', p. 98; Tera W. Hunter, *To 'Joy My Freedom: Southern Black Women's Lives and Labors after the Civil War* (Cambridge, MA: Harvard University Press, 1997), p. 62.
38. Baker, *Following the Color Line*, p. 53.
39. Chafe, et al., *Remembering Jim Crow*, p. 108.
40. Edward L. Ayers, *The Promise of the New South: Life After Reconstruction* (New York and Oxford: Oxford University Press, 1992), p. 160.
41. *Field to Factory: Voices of the Great Migration: Recalling the African American Migration to the Northern Cities* (Smithsonian Folkways Recordings – SFSP90005, 1994).
42. Clifton Taulbert, *Once Upon a Time When We Were Colored* (Tulsa, OK: Council Oak Books, 1989), p. 91.
43. Moton, *Finding a Way Out*, p. 217.
44. Paul Ortiz, '"Eat Your Bread without Butter, but Pay Your Poll Tax!": Roots of the African American Voter Registration Movement in Florida, 1919–1920', in Charles Payne and Adam Green (eds), *Time Longer Than Rope: A Century of African American Activism* (New York and London: New York University Press, 2003), p. 206.
45. Hunter, *To 'Joy My Freedom*, p. 175.
46. Charley Patton, *Founder of the Delta Blues* (Yazoo L–1020, 1970).
47. William H. Chafe, '"The Gods Bring Threads to Webs Begun"', *Journal of American History*, 86 (2000), pp. 1531–2.

Chapter 9

THE CHALLENGE OF REFORM: THE SOUTH IN THE ERA OF THE WORLD WARS

On the eve of American intervention in the First World War, the South seemed to be a land suspended in time. In contrast to the urban and industrial North, the political and economic landscape of the southern states remained much as it had for decades. The old agrarian order still dominated the region. Southerners cultivated the land much as their ancestors had done, concentrating their labour on one staple crop, cotton. Whites also continued to assert their racial supremacy over African Americans, not only through the force of law but also through mob violence. The prospect of a New South, no longer reliant on cotton but instead integrated into the national industrial economy, had receded by the time the United States belatedly intervened in the war.

However, during the era of the world wars the American South underwent sudden changes that unsettled its social, political and economic foundations. Although the Jim Crow system absorbed much of the impact, the cumulative effect of these changes was to establish the preconditions for the civil rights revolution of the 1950s and 1960s. The exigencies of the Great Depression and the Second World War resulted in federal intervention in southern affairs on a scale not seen since Reconstruction. Such actions undermined the traditional pattern of rural labour relations, leading thousands of African American farmers to abandon the land, some heading north while others resettled in the rapidly expanding urban and industrial centres of the South. The influx of these rural migrants to southern towns and cities created problems for the continued maintenance of racial segregation. Federal intervention also raised hopes among African Americans of their future inclusion as full citizens of the United States, just as it raised fears among the white elite at the loss of their autonomous control of the region. By the time the military conflict of the Second World War came to an end, a new set of battle-lines had begun to emerge in the southern states between a black race animated by a sense of political entitlement and a white conservative opposition determined to resist reform.

A WAR FOR DEMOCRACY?

The First World War had a complicated impact upon southern race relations. African Americans became increasingly aware of the disparity between the democratic rhetoric of the Wilson administration and the persistence of racial oppression in their daily lives. Of particular importance to this process of politicisation were the experiences of black soldiers who served overseas and saw in the more racially tolerant cultures of other countries the possibility for an amelioration of the conditions they endured back home. The war therefore imbued African Americans with a stronger determination to push for greater social and political inclusion. The wartime migration of southern blacks to work in the northern defence industries also disrupted the traditional pattern of labour relations in the region. Migration benefited not only those blacks who moved out of the South in search of new opportunities, but also those who remained behind. Southern blacks used the reliance of their white employers on a diminishing labour supply to negotiate improvements in wages and working conditions. However, whites met these challenges to their power and authority with an array of repressive legal and extra-legal measures. The post-war years were therefore a time of escalating political violence.

Three years after the outbreak of hostilities in Europe, on 6 April 1917, the United States declared war on Germany. President Woodrow Wilson appealed to the consciences of an isolationist American public by declaring the conflict a 'War for Democracy'. African Americans enthusiastically rallied around the flag. W. E. B. Du Bois published an editorial in the NAACP publication *The Crisis* that encouraged his people to set aside their racial grievances and 'Close Ranks' with white Americans in common cause against the enemy. The editorial was in part influenced by concern that the authorities would interpret criticism of the war effort as an act of treason. Government officials accused *The Crisis* of being a German propaganda tool because it spread political dissent among African Americans; but what also motivated Du Bois was the more idealistic expectation that the United States would live up to the idealistic rhetoric of the president by turning the fight into a war for democracy at home as well as abroad. The federal government would, he hoped, reward the patriotic sacrifice of African Americans by restoring their civil rights. Tuskegee principal Robert Moton expressed similar optimism. Sent by President Wilson to assess the situation of black soldiers stationed in France, Moton also had the opportunity to address white troops. He impressed on them the need to recognise the contribution that African Americans had made to military victory by resolving, on their return home, 'to see that these black men and the twelve millions of people whom they represent in our great country, who have stood so loyally by you and America in peace and in war, shall have a fair and absolutely equal chance with every other American citizen, along every line'.[1]

More than 400,000 African Americans performed military service during the First World War. Blacks nonetheless found themselves fighting for a country that failed to recognise their contribution to the war effort. Draft boards discriminated against blacks, denying them exemptions while allowing whites to evade military conscription. The US Army also practised a policy of strict racial segregation, confining black troops to one of four separate, and more poorly resourced, units. In the southern states, African American soldiers also suffered at the hands of white civilians affronted by the sight of uniformed black men. Simmering tensions between black troops and white civilians reached boiling point at Camp Logan in Houston, Texas. African American soldiers who travelled into the city endured restricted access to public facilities and persistent harassment from the local police. On 23 August 1917, police assaulted a black soldier for interfering with the arrest of an African American woman. A black military policeman sent to investigate the situation also suffered a beating and arrest. More than one hundred black troops mutinied and marched on the city. An armed confrontation between the soldiers and the police resulted in the deaths of sixteen whites and four blacks. A military court found 110 soldiers guilty of participating in the riot, sentencing 63 of them to life in prison and hanging another 19 more.

During the Civil War, African Americans in the Union Army had endured much discrimination, including unequal pay, restricted opportunities for promotion and disproportionate assignment to manual labour rather than combat. Half a century later, the military had done little to improve the condition of black troops. Although African Americans did serve overseas, the army seldom entrusted them with the responsibility of combat, restricting them instead to menial labour roles. The army, for instance, assigned less than a fifth of the black troops sent to France to combat duties. Despite their expectations, the country for which African American soldiers were prepared to sacrifice their lives repaid them with betrayal.

THE GREAT MIGRATION

Although the First World War afforded African American soldiers little chance to fight for freedom on foreign battlefields, back home black civilians experienced new opportunities. Most southern blacks had since emancipation suffered restricted mobility as a result of their economic dependency on white landlords. While some relocated from rural areas to the towns and cities, the best that most could hope for was to move from farm to farm in search of better working conditions. Some southern blacks, like the slaves who considered escape from the plantations of the Old South, looked northwards and dreamed of a Promised Land where they would be delivered from their oppression. The black author Richard Wright was one of those dreamers. In his words: 'The North symbolised to me all that I had not felt and seen; it had no relation whatever to what actually existed. Yet, by imagining a place where everything was possible, I kept hope alive in me.'[2] It was nonetheless beyond the means of most southern blacks to turn the dream of escape into reality. Few possessed the necessary financial resources or the friends and relatives in the North who could have facilitated their resettlement. Even if they had the skills needed to work in northern industry, which most did not, the racially exclusionary practices of white employers would have restricted their ability to make a living. These obstacles meant that, between 1890 and 1910, only about 200,000 of the ten million African Americans in the South moved out of the region.[3]

The slow flow of black migration turned to a sudden flood during the war. Between 1910 and 1920, more than half a million southern blacks abandoned the region for northern and western cities. That decade represented only the start of a demographic phenomenon known as the Great Migration. By 1930, the number of southern blacks who had relocated from their homeland had risen to more than 1.5 million. Migration within the South also increased. During the decades from 1890 to 1930 the number of southern blacks living in urban areas rose from 17 to 33 per cent.

Racial discrimination alone cannot account for the Great Migration. Since the demise of Reconstruction, southern blacks had suffered decades of repression without deciding to leave the region. What stimulated out-migration was instead a number of factors that simultaneously pushed blacks out of the South and pulled them towards the North. The most important of the push factors was a series of natural disasters that afflicted the southern rural economy, causing economic ruin to black and white farmers. No force was more destructive than the boll weevil, a cotton-eating insect that spread eastwards from Texas in the 1890s. Blues musician Charley Patton mused on how this infestation drove thousands of farmers out of the South in the song 'Mississippi Bo Weavil Blues':

> Well I saw the bo weavil Lord a circle Lordie in the air, Lordie!
> The next time I seed him he had his family there, Lordie!
> Bo weavil left Texas Lord, he bid me 'Fare thee well, Lordie![4]

Black farmers driven from the land by the spread of the boll weevil found new employment opportunities in the industrial economy of the North. The First World War disrupted the flow of cheap foreign workers who had turned the wheels of the northern factory system. Labour shortages threatened the production targets of employers, forcing them to launch recruitment drives for black labour. Southern blacks were also lured northwards by the *Chicago Defender*. Under the editorship of Robert S. Abbot, the newspaper contrasted the restricted economic opportunities and racial violence of the southern states with the richer economic prospects and full rights of citizenship it claimed migrants would find in the North. Such rhetoric belied the racial realities of life above the Mason–Dixon Line. Black migrants discovered all too soon that racism was a pervasive force not only in the South but across the entire United States. Social and economic discrimination restricted many African Americans to poorly paid manual labour and the grim confines of inner city ghettos. As Richard Wright observed, his image of the North was little more than an illusion. Despite these limitations, to most black migrants the northern states represented a substantial improvement on the conditions they had endured in the South.

Although the Great Migration was not an explicit act of political protest, the exodus of hundreds of thousands of African Americans threatened to destabilise labour relations and the social order of the South. Some whites welcomed black migration as a means of improving conditions in the region, since it removed what they considered economically inefficient and politically discontented African Americans. Others were alarmed at the potential loss of a cheap labour force, which they attempted to counteract through a series of measures intended to restrict black mobility. Southern legislatures introduced anti-enticement laws that made it an offence for northern labour agents to recruit black workers without a licence. Blacks found in the vicinity of railway stations were arrested for vagrancy. Some communities also suppressed circulation of the *Chicago Defender* because of its promotion of black migration.

When these coercive tactics failed to stem the flow of black migrants, whites were forced to offer more positive incentives. Southern newspapers launched a counter-propaganda campaign that attempted to dispel the reality of a declining agricultural economy and promote the region as a place of untapped economic opportunity. The *Memphis Commercial Appeal*, for instance, ran the following headline:

> SOUTH IS BETTER FOR NEGRO, SAY MISSISSIPPIANS
> COLORED PEOPLE FOUND PROSPEROUS AND HAPPY[5]

As was the case when slaves abandoned plantations during the Civil War, white planters suffered delusions about the contentment of black farmers, failing to understand why they should want to leave for the North. These efforts to induce African Americans to remain in the South appear to have been motivated more by economic necessity than by a paternalistic impulse to protect and promote the welfare of black labourers. Whatever the motivation, white alarm at the diminishing labour supply worked to the advantage of those African Americans who remained in the South, as they were able to push for lower rents or increased wages as a guarantee of their continued loyalty. Many of these concessions proved only temporary. The easing of labour shortages after the war led to the restoration of old patterns of labour relations. Indeed, the years that followed the Armistice witnessed a brutal restoration of white supremacist control in all areas of public life.

RADICALISM AND REACTION

The wartime experiences of many southern blacks stirred a new commitment to challenge white supremacist rule. Black workers became embroiled in a series of strikes that affected southern industries. The more militant racial consciousness of many southern blacks also resulted in a substantial increase in the membership of civil rights organisations. In 1914, the NAACP had only three branches in the entire South. Five years later, a recruiting drive by field secretary James Weldon Johnson had contributed to the establishment of a further 128 branches, more than 40 per cent of the national total. The NAACP also scored its first success in challenging the legal foundation of Jim Crow in 1917, when the Supreme Court ruled a residential segregation law in Louisville, Kentucky, unconstitutional.[6] While the NAACP enlisted most of its members from the urban middle classes, the disaffection of many African Americans in small towns and rural areas led to their mobilisation in support of the black nationalist Marcus Garvey. During the 1920s, the South accounted for half the branches of Garvey's United Negro Improvement Association. However, the organisation imploded after federal authorities deported its leader from the United States in 1927.

Whites demonstrated their determination to suppress black dissent during the war. Planters used their influence in local and state government to ensure the enactment of 'work or fight' ordinances that allowed them to maintain control of black labourers by restricting their mobility. Landowners also used other forms of legal coercion. Black workers exempted from military service had their status overturned by draft boards when they dared to challenge the authority of landlords. Planters also imposed restrictions on the leisure time of tenant farmers.

Race relations deteriorated further in the aftermath of the war, when whites responded to rising black unrest with brutal retaliatory violence. During the war, some white soldiers allegedly mailed their army pistols home so their families could protect themselves against an increasingly assertive black population.[7] White men eventually returned home determined to demonstrate that, despite black expectations, the war had done nothing to change southern race relations. Black veterans became particular targets. Service overseas exposed African American soldiers to the more racially permissible cultures of countries such as France. This imbued them with a determination after their demobilisation from the army to challenge the restrictions of their own society. Whites met this resistance with repressive violence. On 4 April 1919, a mob in Blakely, Georgia, beat Private William Little to death after he refused to remove his military uniform.[8]

White southerners were not exceptional in their use of force to suppress mounting black expectations. Racial violence erupted across the United States in 1919, the bloodshed leading black activists to refers to the months from May to October as the 'Red Summer'. The worst outbreak occurred in Chicago, where a riot led to the deaths of twenty-three blacks and fifteen whites. The Chicago riot attested to the racial tensions stirred in northern communities by the sudden influx of thousands of black southern migrants, with resultant overcrowding and competition for municipal services.

In the South, the determination of whites to restore their control over a restless black population resulted in a series of racial disorders during the Red Summer. Riots erupted in Charleston, South Carolina, on 10 May; in Longview, Texas, on 10 July; and in Knoxville, Tennessee, on 30 and 31 August. The bloodiest incident of racial violence occurred in the rural community of Elaine, Arkansas. On 30 September 1919, black cotton farmers gathered at a local church. They came not to worship, but to co-ordinate their opposition to white planters who cheated them out of their share of the profits from their crops. The labourers organised themselves into the Progressive Farmers and Household Union of America, and resolved to use the services of a white lawyer to secure a settlement with their landlords. However, the optimism of the meeting was shattered when armed whites surrounded the church and opened fire. One white died and another suffered serious injury in the resulting exchange of gunshots. A posse comprising federal troops and hundreds of white vigilantes pursued the fleeing black activists. By the time order had been restored, at least twenty-five blacks and five whites were dead. The posse arrested hundreds of African Americans, whom they released once they had consented to return to work on terms dictated by their landlords. Twelve union members, tortured to confess or testify against one another, stood trial for murder. It took only minutes for their guilt to be determined and a sentence of death handed down. After four years, the NAACP eventually secured the overturning of their convictions. The flames of racial violence nonetheless continued to flare into the early 1920s. On New Year's Day 1923, a mob pursuing a rapist tore into the black township of Rosewood in Florida, murdering seventeen members of the community and forcing the others to flee as they set fire to buildings. Political repression moreover impacted on civil rights organisations such as the NAACP, depleting their membership base and driving them underground.

The post-war years also witnessed the rebirth of the Ku Klux Klan. On Thanksgiving Eve 1915, William J. Simmons, a former itinerant preacher and insurance salesman, resurrected the Invisible Empire at a cross-burning ceremony on Stone Mountain, Georgia. Simmons was in part inspired by the motion picture epic *The Birth of a Nation,* and its heroic depiction of the Reconstruction-era Klan rescuing white women from the rapacious clutches of former slaves. Historians have labelled the politics of the Klan 'reactionary populism'. A study of the Klan in Athens, Georgia, shows that it recruited its members from the lower middle classes, whose social and economic status was threatened from above by a concentration of wealth in the hands of a small elite, and from below by a militant labour force. Another analysis of the Klan in Alabama similarly demonstrates that its members were ordinary white citizens attempting to reclaim political power from the economic elite of planters and industrialists who exerted a stranglehold on state politics. Although, in both instances, Klansmen had legitimate grievances about their precarious economic and political position, they took their anger out on racial and ethnic minorities whom they scapegoated as the source of their troubles. In Alabama, the Klan launched a terrorist campaign that made it the 'single factor most responsible for breeding an atmosphere of unrestrained mob violence in the state'.[9]

Despite the determination of most whites to restore the ancien regime, the post-war era did offer African Americans some hope for future racial reform. One illustration of this is the tentative collaboration between black activists and white liberals. The Commission on Interracial Cooperation emerged out of a series of meetings between black and white ministers alarmed at the racial violence that had coursed through the country during the Red Summer. Under the directorship of Will W. Alexander, the commission campaigned for the elimination of lynching and the improvement of black health, education and living conditions. However, there were limitations to its commitment to racial liberalism. The Commission sought only to improve standards for African Americans within the existing structure of racial segregation. It therefore accepted the subordinate status of blacks within the social, political and economic hierarchy. This meant a refusal to support the re-enfranchisement of African Americans. Moreover, its conviction that the responsibility to control mob violence rested with local and state authorities led it to oppose federal legislation to outlaw lynching. This was also true of the Association of Southern Women for the Prevention of Lynching, founded under the leadership of Jessie Daniel Ames in 1930. Despite its name, the Commission on Interracial Cooperation was primarily composed of paternalistic whites who possessed little faith that African Americans themselves had the ability to improve their condition. Their influence on other southern whites also remained minimal.

THE GREAT DEPRESSION AND THE NEW DEAL

On Wednesday, 23 October 1929, brokers on the New York Stock Exchange, acting on the orders of their customers, suddenly offered for sale millions of shares of stocks. The following day, a sense of panic swept through the Stock Exchange as the sale of shares caused a precipitous fall in prices. Within five hours, stocks suffered a $10 billion decline in their market value. The financial collapse led commentators to describe that day as Black Thursday. Stock prices stabilised for a few days. Then, on Tuesday, 29 October, brokers unloaded sixteen million unwanted shares onto the market. There followed another swift and steep fall in stock market prices. At the end of the year, the loss in stock values totalled $40 billion. The causes of economic collapse need not be elaborated on in detail, but included increases in manufactured output that far outstripped domestic consumer demand, resulting in an undue reliance on diminishing export markets; reckless speculation on the stock market; and an unstable banking system. The confident forecasts of politicians and economists of a rapid re-stabilisation of the financial system proved hopelessly inaccurate. By the early 1930s, the United States was in the midst of the worst depression in its history.

The declining southern economy could do little to withstand the impact of the Great Depression. In 1938, the federal government released a 'Report on Economic Conditions in the South', accompanied by a letter from President Roosevelt identifyng the region as 'the Nation's No.1 economic problem'.[10] The Great Depression cut across class and racial lines in the South. However, it brought disproportionate economic ruin to African Americans, especially those in rural areas. Cotton prices declined precipitously from eighteen cents per pound in 1929 to less than six cents by 1933. More than two-thirds of black cotton farmers failed to turn a profit on their crops. The fortunate ones broke even; the less fortunate fell further into debt. Rural blacks also suffered from the increasing mechanisation of southern agriculture, which obviated the need for planters to retain manual labourers. The absence of rural relief programmes meant that there was no safety net for those African Americans who lost their livelihoods. Confronted by the diminishing opportunities afforded by the agricultural economy, tens of thousands of rural blacks abandoned the land. Between 1930 and 1933, the number of black sharecroppers in the southern states dwindled from 392,000 to 300,000.

The reluctance of the Hoover administration to abandon the traditional laissez faire attitude of the federal government towards the economy undermined its ability to effect recovery. By 1932, the American electorate pinned its hopes on a man who promised federal activism on an unprecedented scale to combat the crisis. 'I pledge you, I pledge myself,' asserted Franklin Delano Roosevelt in his acceptance speech at the Democratic convention, 'to a new deal for the American people.' The New Deal had a complicated impact on the social, political and economic structures of the South. On one hand, the racially discriminatory allocation of federal resources reinforced existing patterns of white power and privilege. Yet, on the other hand, the expansion of federal power into the South simultaneously contested the hegemony of the white elites who controlled the region, and raised hopes for African Americans that the national government would at last recognise their full rights of citizenship.

Despite the official non-discriminatory policy of New Deal agencies, southern blacks did not receive their fair share of federal government support. The cause of the problem was the reliance of the Roosevelt administration on state and local officials to administer relief and recovery programmes. This owed in part to the reluctance of the president to establish the centralised bureaucratic infrastructure needed for federal officials in Washington to oversee the implementation of New Deal reforms. In the South, the decision to place the responsibility for distributing federal government largesse in the hands of local and state authorities perpetuated the system of white supremacist power. The racial prejudice of white officials resulted in their restricting the allocation of federal resources to African Americans. Although aware of the racial bias of southern authorities, Roosevelt did not attempt to challenge them. To do so could risk a backlash from southern politicians, fatally weakening congressional support for key recovery measures. Southern Democrats controlled more than half the committee chairmanships in Congress, empowering them with the ability to make or break New Deal reforms. A confrontation with them over racial issues was hence too much of a risk for a Roosevelt administration that considered economic recovery its top priority. As William Leuchtenburg observes: 'Roosevelt had good reason to suppose that if he insisted on civil rights legislation, he not only would fail to get it, but also would imperil hopes for others measures, many of which benefited blacks.'[11]

New Deal agencies therefore often failed to protect African Americans from racial discrimination. One illustration of this is the Agricultural Adjustment Administration (AAA). Since the First World War, overproduction had caused a collapse in cotton prices, a situation that became even more acute as the depression started to bite. The AAA provided subsidies to farmers to reduce the amount of cotton land under production in an attempt to create a crop shortage that would push prices up. This scheme relied on planters to distribute the appropriate portion of the subsidies to the sharecroppers and tenant farmers whose land was no longer under the plough. However, many landlords seized the opportunity to cheat black labourers out of their due share. The failure of federal officials to pay subsidies directly to sharecroppers and tenant farmers stemmed from their concern that planters would interpret this as a challenge to their power. However, the fraudulent behaviour of landlords forced a change of policy. The AAA continued to send cheques to planters, but made them out in the names of specific employees. This still did not prevent some planters from threatening their labourers into signing the cheques over to them. Many planters also used the revenue they received from the AAA to purchase machinery that rendered manual labourers dispensable. Thousands of African Americans therefore suffered eviction. During the planting and harvest seasons, when landlords needed additional labour, they used their influence over local relief administrators to remove African Americans from the welfare rolls. This created a labour surplus that allowed planters to hire workers for low wages. Discrimination within the Resettlement and Farm Security Administrations also resulted in many black farmers having their applications for federal loans denied.

The desperate situation in the countryside drove increasing numbers of blacks into the towns and cities. However, opportunities there were no less limited. Unemployment led whites who otherwise would refuse to perform menial labour to wrench such jobs away from blacks. By 1932, almost 50 per cent of African Americans in southern cities were out of work. Unemployed blacks who turned for help to federal relief programmes also suffered discrimination at the hands of local authorities. Even when African Americans did receive welfare, the amount was less than that paid to whites. White officials defended this by arguing that the lower living standards of blacks allowed them to survive on less money.

Blacks suffered further bias from the National Industrial Recovery Act of June 1933. The act established the National Recovery Administration (NRA), which attempted to stabilise American industry by encouraging business leaders to adopt new codes of practice that restricted production and established maximum hours and minimum wages for workers. Section 7a of the act also guaranteed workers the right to collective bargaining through a union of their choice. Although the new law promoted the interests of many workers, it excluded domestic servants and unskilled labourers from its provisions. This meant that more than 60 per cent of black wage-earners received none of the protections included in the new industrial codes. When the Supreme Court ruled section 7a unconstitutional in 1935, Congress re-established the right to collective bargaining through the Wagner Labor Relations Act. However, this too omitted agricultural workers and domestic servants. Those African American labourers included under the provisions of New Deal legislation also failed to receive proper safeguards. Rather than pay blacks the same wages as whites, employers simply fired them. The failure of the New Deal to protect the rights of African American workers led many to claim with a combination of ruefulness and anger that NRA stood for 'Negroes Rarely Allowed'.

Racial discrimination restricted blacks from benefiting from other New Deal initiatives. The Social Security Act of 1935 also excluded agricultural labourers and domestic servants, leading NAACP lawyer Charles Houston to observe that the legislation was 'like a sieve with holes just big enough for the majority of Negroes to fall through'.[12] African Americans also suffered restrictions on their access to work relief programmes such as the Civilian Conservation Corps (CCC) and Works Progress Administration (WPA). The exclusion of African Americans from New Deal reforms was epitomised by the Tennessee Valley Authority (TVA). Established in May 1933, the TVA attempted to promote economic improvement in an impoverished southern region through the generation of electric power and tighter flood control. In a powerful critique of the institutionalised racism of the New Deal, historian Nancy L. Grant has detailed how blacks endured discrimination in the hiring and promotion of workers on construction projects, limitations on their access to new housing, and exclusion from model farm programmes.[13]

Roosevelt also failed to use the New Deal as a means to gain greater social justice for African Americans. A case in point is his failure to support legislation that would have made lynching a federal offence. The NAACP relentlessly lobbied Washington for the enactment of such a law. In 1921, it secured the agreement of Republican Congressman Leonidas C. Dyer to sponsor a bill that passed through the House of Representatives, but was defeated in the Senate. The publicity created by the NAACP campaign nonetheless contributed to a decline in mob violence during the 1920s. Although southern authorities had succeeded in containing the plague of lynching, they could not prevent a renewed outbreak. The Depression fuelled further violence against African Americans, as whites sought a scapegoat for their economic woes. One of the worst incidents occurred on 26 October 1934, when a mob seized an African American murder suspect named Claude Neal from an Alabama jail and transported him across state lines to Marianna, Florida, where he was tortured and then hanged. The NAACP used the incident to press for federal intervention against lynch mobs. An anti-lynching bill introduced to Congress in 1936 suffered the same fate as the legislation sponsored by Representative Dyer, securing the support of the House of Representatives but suffering defeat at the hands of a southern filibuster in the Senate. The refusal of the president to endorse the bill strengthened the hand of its opponents and ensured its failure. Roosevelt insisted that his first priority must be economic renewal. He could not therefore offer his support for anti-lynching legislation for fear it would stir a southern backlash against more pressing recovery measures. As he informed Walter White of the NAACP: 'If I come out for the anti-lynching bill they will block every bill I ask Congress to pass. I just can't take that risk.'[14]

The New Deal therefore did little during its early years to alleviate the economic condition of African Americans. By entrusting the responsibility for administering welfare and recovery programmes to local and state authorities, the Roosevelt administration allowed federal agencies to perpetuate regional patterns of segregation and discrimination. No wonder that many African Americans believed that they were less beneficiaries of a New Deal than casualties of the same Old Deal.

The failure of Republican and Democratic administrations to address the needs of impoverished southern blacks provided the political left with an opportunity to recruit discontented sharecroppers and tenant farmers to its cause. In 1928, the Sixth World Congress of the Communist International issued a resolution stating that blacks should be entitled to the right to self-determination in those areas where they represented a majority of the population. The Communist Party affirmed its commitment to racial equality four years later, when it nominated an African American, James W. Ford, as its vice-presidential candidate. Nothing associated the Communists more with the cause of African Americans than their involvement in the Scottsboro affair. On 2 March 1931, a fight broke out between black and white youths aboard a freight train travelling through Alabama. Thrown from the train, the humiliated whites went straight to the local sheriff. A posse apprehended nine blacks after the train had stopped in the town of Paint Rock. With the young men were two white women, Ruby Bates and Victoria Price, who claimed the blacks had sexually assaulted them. The absence of any forensic evidence to support their accusation did not stop a court from convicting eight of the youths of rape, and sentencing them to death. The Communist Party responded to this miscarriage of justice by organising protest demonstrations across the country. Its International Labor Defense took up the case, fighting a protracted legal battle that eventually secured the release of the defendants. The Communist Party used a similar twin strategy to secure the acquittal of Angelo Herndon, a black coal miner convicted in 1932 of inciting an insurrection after he led a bi-racial demonstration of unemployed workers.

At a more grassroots level, Communists also mobilised rural blacks to form unions in an effort to secure fairer treatment from white landlords. Their recruitment drive met with considerable success. By 1934, for instance, some 3,000 black farmers had joined the Alabama Sharecroppers Union. Few could claim to understand, or be interested in, the intricacies of Marxist doctrine. What they did comprehend was that the union offered them an organised means to fight back against their exploitation. As Ned Cobb explained of his decision to join: 'Well, it was many conditions that called for such a organization as that. Niggers had to get back and get back quick when the white man spoke. Had to be humble and submissive under em. My people needed a protection so long, so long.'[15] Socialists also attempted to unite black and white farmers across racial lines. In 1934, they formed the inter-racial Southern Tenant Farmers' Union near Tyronza, Arkansas, which attempted to fight the eviction of rural labourers caused by the AAA.

Despite its efforts to enlist the support of southern blacks, the left ultimately failed to mobilise a mass protest movement. The secular materialism of Marxist ideology was at odds with the Christian faith of most southern blacks. Many African Americans also suspected Communists of being political opportunists who were more interested in using blacks to promote their own cause than in combating Jim Crow. Moreover, the strength of white opposition to Communism persuaded most African Americans to steer wide of the movement. Those blacks who did become members of Communist organisations ran the risk of being arrested, beaten or murdered. Planters and their cronies in the local police used brute force to repress the sharecropper unions established in Alabama and Louisiana. Although he remained loyal to his union, Ned Cobb affirmed that 'niggers was scared, niggers was scared, that's telling the truth. White folks in this country didn't allow niggers to have no organization, no secret meetings.'[16]

During the early 1930s, most southern blacks therefore shared a sense of disappointment and despair. It was not until the re-election of Franklin Roosevelt in 1936 that they regained their faith in the future. The second Roosevelt administration made a more concerted effort to include African Americans in New Deal relief and recovery measures. Despite continued discrimination, the number of African Americans who benefited from federal government support increased, as did the amount of money they received, either in terms of wages or welfare.

Several factors account for this shift in policy. The first factor was the influence of southern liberals – such as Will Alexander at the Farm Security Administration, and Clark Foreman and Aubrey Williams at the National Youth Administration – who used their leadership of New Deal agencies to guarantee greater inclusion of African Americans. The second factor was the appointment of black federal officials, who provided African Americans with a more representative voice in government. Among the most prominent members of the 'Black Cabinet' of advisers were Mary McLeod Bethune of the National Youth Administration and Robert C. Weaver of the Department of the Interior. Although these officials had little direct role in formulating policy, they did use their influence to ensure the more racially equitable distribution of many New Deal programmes. The third factor was the mounting importance of the black vote. As the thousands of black southern migrants flooding into northern cities started to exercise their new rights as voters, they formed powerful electoral blocs that could determine the outcome of local and national elections.

The 1936 presidential contest demonstrated the importance of the northern black vote in building and sustaining a New Deal electoral coalition. That election witnessed African Americans abandoning their traditional political loyalty to the Republicans in favour of the Democratic Party. The electoral realignment of African Americans had its roots in their mounting sense of betrayal at the hands of 'the party of Lincoln'. During the late nineteenth and early twentieth centuries, the Republicans had done little to protest the disfranchisement of southern blacks. When women won the right to vote under the Nineteenth Amendment to the US Constitution in 1920, the Republicans also failed to defend black females who attempted to register on the electoral rolls. Instead, they resorted to blatantly racist appeals in an attempt to woo white women voters. Black disillusionment with the Republicans had therefore set in long before the Great Depression. Almost two-thirds of black voters cast their ballots in support of Herbert Hoover in 1932. However, their motivation was less an enthusiasm for the Republican candidate than scepticism about his Democratic opponent, who had no proven record on race relations. The benefits blacks gained from the New Deal nonetheless encouraged them to break from the Republicans. In the 1936 election, Roosevelt received 76 per cent of the northern black vote.[17]

These political forces influenced the direction of New Deal policy towards a greater inclusion of African Americans. From 1936, the Roosevelt administration made an increasingly substantial commitment to the cause of racial egalitarianism. The First Lady, Eleanor Roosevelt, became particularly associated with the promotion of black civil rights. Mrs Roosevelt attracted infamy among many southern whites, not least after her attendance at the inaugural meeting of the liberal Southern Conference for Human Welfare at Birmingham, Alabama, in 1938. In protest at a local ordinance that outlawed the integration of public assemblies, the First Lady defiantly sat in the aisle that separated black and white delegates.

That the wife of the president should take such action was of powerful symbolic importance to African Americans. Yet the New Deal also brought more substantive benefits to blacks whose lives were devastated by the depression.

Writing in the 1960s, historians such as Barton J. Bernstein, Paul Conkin and John Salmond criticised the New Deal for its failure to effect fundamental reform of the social and economic infrastructure of the United States. One aspect of the supposed conservatism of the New Deal was the reluctance of federal officials to confront racial inequality and injustice. In the estimation of Bernstein, 'Never would Roosevelt expend political capital in an assault upon the American caste system.'[18]

While they accept some of these criticisms, scholars writing more recently are more positive in their assessment of the role that the New Deal performed in improving the conditions of African Americans. Although the amount of federal assistance received by southern blacks did not meet their full needs, New Deal measures sustained many families who otherwise faced starvation. Despite the persistence of discrimination in the administration of its programmes, the New Deal represented the most substantial effort made by the federal government since Reconstruction to protect the needs and promote the interests of African Americans. Historian Tony Badger affirms that 'While New Deal agencies may have discriminated against blacks in the South, they provided blacks with greater assistance than they had ever received before, especially from state government.'[19] Following the Second New Deal, African Americans gained greater access to relief and recovery programmes. The Public Works Administration invested more than $40 million in the construction and renovation of black schools, libraries and hospitals. 'P.W.A, you the best ol' friend I ever seen,' sang bluesman Jimmy Gordon. 'Since the job ain't hard and the boss ain't mean.'[20] African Americans also received more than 50 per cent of federally-subsidised housing units in the South. Southern blacks moreover secured an increasing share of the job opportunities provided by public works programmes such as the CCC. Racism nevertheless continued to restrict black participation in such programmes: blacks employed by the CCC worked in segregated units and were routinely denied access to training opportunities or promotion to supervisory positions. In desperate times, public works programmes nonetheless provided unemployed blacks with a means to earn a regular income and regain their self-respect. By 1939, almost 200,000 African Americans had worked in the CCC.[21] Despite the persistence of discrimination in the administration of its programmes, the New Deal represented the most substantial effort made by the federal government since Reconstruction to protect the needs and promote the interests of African Americans.

African Americans also gained greater acceptance in the cultural mainstream during the 1930s. In 1939, the Daughters of the American Revolution (DAR) refused to allow the black contralto Marion Anderson to sing at Constitution Hall in Washington, DC. Eleanor Roosevelt resigned from the DAR in protest, and sponsored a concert by Anderson at the Lincoln Memorial attended by 75,000 people. Joe Louis, the son of sharecropping parents from Alabama, became the boxing world heavyweight champion when he knocked out Jim Braddock in the eighth round of a title fight on 22 June 1937. Boxing played a powerful symbolic role in the imaginations of many black people. In contrast to the structural disadvantages and social discrimination that precluded blacks from competing with whites in the larger society, a contest in the ring pitted man against man. Outside of the ring, Louis assumed the compliant and non-controversial role expected by white society. However, he was a different man when he donned his gloves. When Louis bested his white opponents, it allowed his black supporters by implication to believe that they too were landing a blow against their white oppressors. Black author Maya Angelou recalls how African Americans in her hometown of Stamps, Arkansas, crowded around a radio in a local store to hear Louis fight. In the moment of his victory, they attained a transcendent belief 'that we were the strongest people in the world'.[22] On 22 June 1938, Louis defeated the German Max Schmeling to regain the world title. White as well as black Americans shared in the celebration of a symbolic triumph of American democracy over German fascism.

The radicalisation of federal government policy during the New Deal was as welcome to blacks as it was alarming to whites. Although Bernstein and

Conkin dismiss what they describe as the empty rhetoric of New Deal officials on race matters, most scholars now recognise that African Americans drew strength and inspiration from a federal government that for the first time in more than half a century expressed a public commitment to equality of opportunity. What critics of the New Deal misunderstand, according to Doug McAdam, 'is the dramatic symbolic contrast between these actions and those of earlier administrations'.[23] In urban areas, where there were greater opportunities for political mobilisation, southern blacks responded to the racially inclusive policies of the Roosevelt administration by attempting to register as Democrats. Some succeeded. In Atlanta, for instance, the number of African Americans on the electoral rolls more than doubled between 1936 and 1939, from 1,000 to 2,100.[24] The longer-term impact of black electoral realignment is explored later in this book.

Conversely, the New Deal also contributed to the declining influence of southern politicians within the Democratic Party. Since Reconstruction, no Democratic presidential candidate could hope to secure the White House without a plurality of the ballots cast by white southerners. However, such was the strength of the coalition Roosevelt constructed in support of his New Deal policies that it carried him to victory in 1932, and again in 1936, without the need of a single southern electoral college vote. The election of northern Democrats also tipped the balance of power away from southern members of the party in Congress. Their influence further declined following the removal in 1936 of the two-thirds vote needed to secure the nomination of candidates at the Democratic Party convention, a device that traditionally provided southerners with veto power over who ran for the presidency, and on what platform.

Southern Democrats had initially been enthusiastic supporters of the New Deal. Although some feared its centralisation of federal power, they recognised the importance of recovery programmes in providing a source of credit or income to their constituents. During the late 1930s, southern Democrats nonetheless reacted with increasing hostility to the rise of more liberal northern forces within the party. They denounced New Deal measures intended to promote the interests of workers as an infringement on the rights of private employers to regulate labour relations, and resisted the inclusion of African Americans in relief and recovery programmes as a surreptitious attempt to promote racial equality. The support of many northern Democrats for the abolition of the poll tax and federal protection from lynching provided an even more direct challenge to white supremacist rule. In the words of Senator Ellison Smith of South Carolina, who walked out of the 1936 convention: 'The doors of the white man's party have been thrown open to snare the Negro vote in the North. Political equality means social equality, and social equality means intermarriage, and that means mongrelizing of the American race.'[25]

Pushed into open rebellion against their own party, southern Democrats established a bipartisan coalition with conservative Republicans in an attempt to undermine New Deal reform. Following the attack on Pearl Harbor in December 1941, President Roosevelt became reliant on congressional support to sustain the war effort, a situation that the coalition used to its political advantage. Conservatives launched a counter-attack on the New Deal that disabled some of the more racially progressive agencies such as the Farm Security Administration and National Youth Administration. This breach within the ranks of the Democratic Party had profound implications for the future. The ascendancy of northern liberalism within the ranks of the party during the 1930s later facilitated its support of the African American freedom struggle. Yet, as we will also see, the fratricidal conflict between the northern and southern wings of the party caused it incalculable electoral damage.

THE SECOND WORLD WAR AND THE RISING WIND OF CHANGE

The forces of change that first stirred during the New Deal swept through the southern states with gathering speed during The Second World War. Although the war did not fundamentally transform the social, political and economic structure of the region, it did induce many African Americans to question the status quo. The dissonance between the idealistic rhetoric of the war effort and the lived realities of southern blacks resulted in a new political radicalism. By the end of the war, African Americans across the region had mobilised in unprecedented numbers to push for reform.

Having seen their expectations shattered after the First World War, many African Americans were deeply suspicious of government propaganda encouraging military intervention. Black leaders assumed an isolationist attitude, depicting the European conflict as a 'white man's war' in which their people had little part to play. African American newspapers emphasised the hypocrisy of whites who criticised the racial policies of the Nazi regime in Germany while condoning the repression of their own black citizenry. According to the *Richmond Planet*: 'We manage by erosion or denial of law to disfranchise a greater proportion of the American electorate on account of race and color than Hitler does on account of race and creed'.[26] After the Japanese had bombed Pearl Harbor on 7 December 1941, African Americans nonetheless answered the call to arms, convinced that their patriotism must strengthen their claim to full citizenship.

The federal government facilitated the recruitment of black soldiers through the Selective Training and Service Act of 1940. This act authorised the enlistment and military instruction of all males aged between eighteen and thirty-six, regardless of race. Black men could serve their country, but only on a segregated basis: the military resisted its use as a 'sociological laboratory' for manufacturing social change and maintained a strict policy of racial separation.[27] African Americans suffered total exclusion from some sections of the armed forces. The Air Corps, Coast Guard and Marines all denied admission to black servicemen, while the Navy accepted them only as messmen. Racial quotas also limited the number of black female recruits. While more than 6,000 African American women joined the Women's Army Corps, restrictions meant that only 500 served as military nurses during the war.

Although the protests of civil rights leaders emphasised the discriminatory policies of the military, this did not discourage more than one million African Americans from joining its ranks. Almost half of them served overseas in the European, Pacific and Mediterranean theatres of war. Despite their contribution to the war effort, black service men and women endured persistent discrimination. The army not only maintained its policy of segregation, but also confined many black soldiers to non-combat duties. African American troops dug ditches, built bridges, washed dirty laundry, cooked and served meals – performed almost every function within the army, in short, other than fight. As late as 1943, more than four out of every five black servicemen remained stationed at home in menial labour roles. African Americans also faced little prospect of promotion through the ranks. By 1945, blacks represented less than 2 per cent of all army officers. African American women endured both racism and sexual harassment from white soldiers. One woman wrote despairingly of the abuse suffered by a black unit of the Women's Army Corps stationed in Camp Forrest, Tennessee: 'I guess there isn't anything that can be done about it. It has been reported to the N.A.A.C.P. already, one girl had guts enough to write a letter. She is being punished.'[28]

African American soldiers suffered further abuse from white civilians. About 80 per cent of black servicemen received their training at southern army bases. For many of these enlisted men, it was their first experience of the Jim Crow caste system. Not having been born and bred in the region, they were less willing to accept the restrictions imposed on their autonomy. Black soldiers bristled at having to travel to and from military bases aboard segregated buses and streetcars, and at their being denied access to many recreational facilities because of the colour of their skin. Nor did their uniforms protect them from harassment and abuse by local whites. Tensions between black troops and white civilians often turned to open conflict. In

April 1941, a band of whites bound and hanged black private Felix Hall near Fort Benning in Georgia. Nine months later, in January 1942, white police officers launched an unprovoked attack on black soldiers in Alexandria, Louisiana. Their actions incited a riot that led to the deaths of twenty-eight blacks and the arrest of a further three thousand. Other racial disturbances erupted at army bases across the South. Nothing symbolised the lack of respect accorded to African American soldiers more than their being denied admission to facilities that accepted the patronage of German prisoners of war. The impact on black morale could be severe. 'Why I ask you,' wrote one soldier, 'do we have to fight on the home front for our lives then go across seas and fight again?'[29]

A combination of black protest and military necessity eventually resulted in some improvements to the condition of African American service men and women. The Air Force authorised the training of black fighter pilots, albeit on segregated bases such as the one established at the Tuskegee Institute. In 1944, the Navy removed restrictions on black men performing sea duties and admitted black women to the WAVES (Women Accepted for Volunteer Emergency Service). The persistence of racism within the ranks nonetheless had an important influence in politicising many African Americans, who became embittered by the failure of the United States to honour its own democratic ideals. Similar issues made an impact on the racial consciousness of African Americans on the home front.

The Second World War accelerated the process of change that had undermined the traditional plantation economy of the South since the 1930s. During that decade, a combination of reduced acreage and increased mechanisation had resulted in the displacement of sharecropping and tenant families who now formed a surplus pool of cheap seasonal labour. American military intervention in the war caused a further transformation of rural labour relations. The enlistment of thousands of able-bodied white men in the armed forces created job shortages in the defence industries. As the demands of wartime production increased, so the labour deficit became more acute. African Americans therefore abandoned the farms and plantations in pursuit of new employment opportunities in factories and shipyards. Some moved to the areas of rapid urbanisation within the South, such as the coastal cities of Mobile, Alabama and Norfolk, Virginia. Others deserted the region altogether, resettling in the northern and western states. Black out-migration had maintained a steady momentum since the First World War. The number of African Americans leaving the South nonetheless escalated enormously after 1941. During the Second World War, more than one million southern blacks moved north.

Black migration drained the pool of cheap labour on which white planters relied. This represented a sudden loss of the traditional control that white employers had over black workers. The role of the federal government in facilitating black migration compounded their sense of disempowerment. At the outset of the war, federal agencies perpetuated the racial discrimination practised by the New Deal programmes of the preceding decade. African Americans who applied for positions in the war industries were denied jobs and industrial training. However, when labour shortages started to threaten production levels, the federal government reluctantly started to recruit black workers. From April 1942, the War Manpower Commission ordered the United States Employment Service to procure southern blacks for work in the northern and western defence industries. Federal intervention in the labour market met with strong resistance from southern white employers who resented their loss of power over the black rural workforce. Planters applied numerous legal and extra-legal measures in an attempt to restrict the mobility of black labourers, including 'work or fight' ordinances similar to those enacted during the First World War.

The opposition of white southerners to the Fair Employment Practices Committee (FEPC) further illustrates their determination to restrict the economic opportunities of African Americans. In January 1941, black union leader A. Philip Randolph launched the March on Washington Movement. Randolph threatened to lead a demonstration of mass civil disobedience in the nation's capital unless the federal government integrated the armed forces and improved employment opportunities for African Americans in the defence industries. The threat of a march by 100,000 black demonstrators was too much for President Roosevelt. On 25 June, he issued Executive Order 8802, which authorised the establishment of the FEPC, a federal agency charged with the responsibility to investigate complaints of racial discrimination within the defence industries. The March on Washington Movement represented the first occasion when the threat of direct action by African Americans had forced direct concessions from the federal government, a tactic that would be utilised to full effect by the civil rights movement during the 1960s.

However, the FEPC represented more of a symbolic than a substantial victory. The Roosevelt administration undermined the agency from the outset by failing to empower it with any enforcement mechanisms. Moreover, the FEPC encountered fierce hostility from white southerners, who interpreted it as an insidious attempt by the federal government to interfere with their political autonomy. As Alabama governor Frank Dixon asserted: 'the present emergency should not be used as a pretext to bring about the abolition of the color lines in the South'.[30] The FEPC ultimately did little to promote fairer opportunities for African Americans. Not only were many southern blacks too intimidated to file complaints against defence contractors, but the FEPC also upheld the position of the plaintiff in only a fifth of the cases that it did hear. Even then, its decisions met with vehement and, at times, violent opposition. The strength of white southern resistance became clear in May 1943, when violence broke out at the shipyard in Mobile, Alabama. Under pressure from the FEPC, the Alabama Dry Dock and Shipbuilding Company reluctantly appointed twelve black welders. White workers responded by randomly assaulting African Americans and then walking off the job. By the time the company secured a compromise settlement, 160,000 man-hours had been lost. The Second World War precipitated a rapid transformation of the southern economy, as the cities supplanted the countryside and African Americans abandoned their old positions as domestic servants and farm hands. However, the reaction of southern whites also showed how virulent their resistance to black economic progress remained.

White working-class prejudice also impeded the efforts of labour leaders to promote inter-racial unionism during the war. From the late 1930s, union leaders attempted to unite black and white workers on common class lines in an effort to strengthen their negotiating hand with employers. The grassroots recruitment drives of unions affiliated with the Congress of Industrial Organizations scored considerable success in mobilising black workers, including rubber-plant employees in Memphis, Tennessee, and tobacco workers in Winston-Salem, North Carolina. The local branch of the Food, Tobacco, Agricultural and Allied Workers Union in Winston-Salem also promoted the broader political interests of African Americans through such initiatives as citizenship classes and voter registration campaigns. White labourers accepted the recruitment of blacks because it acted to their own advantage, strengthening the ability of unions to secure improved wages and working conditions. However, the racism of many whites also minimised the prospects for a fully inter-racial working-class movement that could challenge the southern caste system. In Memphis, for instance, white union members accepted the recruitment of African Americans but refused to treat them as social equals. Union meetings remained segregated and positions on the executive committee were restricted mostly to whites.[31]

The experience of wartime prejudice and discrimination emboldened rather than undermined black aspirations. Many African Americans came through the Second World War with a sharpened racial consciousness. Those who performed military service were perhaps most acutely aware of the double standards of a country that encouraged African Americans to fight and die in defence of democracy abroad, but denied them the same basic rights and freedoms at home. As had been the case during the First World War, black soldiers who served overseas also encountered societies more racially tolerant than their own. Countries such as France welcomed African American troops as liberating heroes, accepting their social interaction with the white civilian population. Such treatment belied the notion that Jim Crow represented the natural order of relations between the races and emboldened black soldiers to push for reform when they returned home.

African American veterans formed the vanguard of new recruits who swelled the ranks of the civil rights movement during and after the Second World War. In contrast to the First World War, blacks were less inclined to 'Close Ranks' and defer the fight for greater social and political inclusion. A painful awareness of the hypocrisy of American war aims led them to mobilise in unprecedented numbers for their civil rights and liberties. In the title of a 1945 book, Walter White of the NAACP described this new political militancy as *A Rising Wind*.[32] The restlessness of African Americans on the home front fuelled the anxieties of southern whites. Rumours circulated that discontented blacks were secretly conspiring to launch a racial insurrection against their employers. In Memphis, for instance, whites worried that black insurgents were busily buying cartons of guns and ammunitions from mail order catalogues. Across the South, black domestic servants were said to be joining secret societies inspired by Mrs Roosevelt. Known as Eleanor Clubs, these allegedly plotted to liberate their membership from working in white households, and reportedly their alleged motto was 'A white woman in every kitchen by 1943'.[33] Although these reports proved unfounded, they demonstrate the mood of racial unrest to which the war gave rise.

African Americans may not have been stockpiling arms in preparation for a revolutionary assault on white supremacist rule, but they were organising politically. Many supported the 'Double V' campaign of the *Pittsburgh Courier*, which called on blacks to fight for democracy on two fronts, at home as well as abroad. The NAACP also experienced a political renaissance. Between 1940 and 1945, its membership increased from 50,556 to 450,000, and its number of branches from 355 to 1,073. Significantly, three-quarters of these new branches were in the South, showing that the organisation had broadened its support beyond its traditional base among northern middle-class urbanites. Among the many black veterans recruited by the NAACP during these years were future leaders of the civil rights movement, including Mississippians Medgar Evers, Aaron Henry and Amzie Moore. The scale of black political mobilisation has led to the historian Richard Dalfiume describing the Second World War as 'The Forgotten Years of the Negro Revolution'.[34]

The war also nurtured increasing bi-racial collaboration between black activists and white liberals. On 20 October 1942, black leaders from across the South convened in Durham, North Carolina, to draft a statement on race relations. The signatories to the statement, popularly known as the Durham Manifesto, asserted that they were 'fundamentally opposed to the principle and practice of compulsory segregation in our American society'. In April 1943, white moderates assembled in Atlanta to issue a resolution endorsing the manifesto. This in turn led to a meeting of black and white representatives in Richmond, Virginia, on 16 June 1943. That meeting led not only to a further statement in support of the Durham Manifesto, but also the decision to establish a new inter-racial organisation, the Southern Regional Council. Despite these developments, the relationship between black activists and white racial progressives remained tentative. Although the black leaders who signed the Durham Manifesto denounced segregation, their need to enlist the support of white moderates led them to insert the caveat that it was 'both sensible and timely' to concentrate on specific areas of discrimination rather than mounting a direct assault on Jim Crow. Most white moderates accepted the immutability of segregation and sought only to give greater practical meaning to the concept of separate but equal. Their aversion to federal interference in southern affairs and hostility to the more militant stance of northern black activists further underlined the ideological and tactical differences between themselves and African American leaders.[35]

Despite the increasing political mobilisation of southern blacks, historian Harvard Sitkoff also cautions against overestimating the importance of the war in transforming the scale and contour of civil rights protest. He points out that the need for African Americans to maintain their patriotic credentials, coupled with the persistently repressive political climate, precluded racial demonstrations in the Deep South during wartime. The black press also preferred to stress the political loyalty of African Americans rather than push for radical reform.[36]

It is the case that most black activists eschewed the direct-action tactics of the March on Washington Movement, and instead maintained their emphasis on challenging Jim Crow through the courts. Although blacks did not mobilise in collective resistance to racial segregation, individual acts of protest did increase during the war. During 1941–42, the police in Birmingham, Alabama, investigated fifty-five incidents in which black passengers defied segregation ordinances on local buses. Moreover, while direct action remained relatively rare, this did not prevent a renewed NAACP successfully litigating against discriminatory racial practices. Its most important legal victory came in April 1944, when, in the case of *Smith* v. *Allwright,* the US Supreme Court outlawed the white primary. Since the end of Reconstruction, the southern states had been a one-party region ruled by the Democrats. Success in the primary contest that determined Democratic candidates for public office virtually guaranteed victory in the general election. The exclusion of African Americans from primaries therefore denied them any active role in the democratic process. *Smith* v. *Allwright* had a substantial impact in re-empowering black electors. At the time of the decision, the number of southern blacks registered to vote was a mere 200,000, less than 5 per cent of a possible total of more than four million. Within eight years, that number had risen to 20 per cent.[37]

The Supreme Court decision also established an important precedent for future political action by the federal government to promote black civil rights. In June 1946, the court struck a further blow against de jure discrimination when it ruled segregation on interstate busing unconstitutional in the case of *Morgan* v. *Commonwealth of Virginia*. The institutional support of the court strengthened the legal campaign of the NAACP against all aspects of segregation in public life. Less than a decade after the war, in 1954, the court would act as a catalyst for a new era of civil rights activism when it outlawed segregation in public schools. The war also witnessed the emergence of a 'new brand of liberalism' that placed racial reform at the centre of its political agenda.[38] Northern liberals saw southern racism as an anachronism that undermined fundamental American ideals and values, such as freedom and democracy. Therefore they sought to remould the South in their image of an idealised nation. In particular, they hoped to reintegrate African Americans into the democratic process by securing the restoration of their political rights. The support of northern liberals would also prove decisive in the civil rights struggle during the post-war era.

The advances made by African Americans during the Second World War instilled a new sense of optimism that the forces of racial progressivism could transform the South. This sentiment was articulated by the Swedish economist Gunnar Myrdal, whose influential study *An American Dilemma* was published in 1944. Myrdal claimed that the war had made white Americans more conscious of the contradiction between their egalitarian ideals and the reality of racial inequality. He concluded enthusiastically that 'There is bound to be a redefinition of the Negro's status in America as a result of this War.'[39]

However, there were reasons to doubt the liberal optimism of Myrdal. Tempering the prospects for political change was the reaction of southern whites, who simultaneously feared the new militancy among African

Americans and resented increasing federal interference in local and state race relations. The white southern backlash frustrated the efforts of reformers. Revolts by southern senators, for instance, led to the defeat of an anti-poll tax bill in 1944, and the slashing of the FEPC budget the following year. The determination of white southerners to resist reform resulted in a wave of repressive violence that swept through the region in the immediate aftermath of the war. On 25 February 1946, police in Columbia, Tennessee, arrested two African Americans following an altercation with a white store clerk. Local whites interpreted the incident as a symptom of the threatening new assertiveness of African Americans. As a mob gathered around the local courthouse, blacks armed themselves in defence of their neighbourhood. The shooting of four white police officers sent into the black section of town resulted in the arrival of state highway patrolmen who, along with local whites, ransacked stores and arrested more than one hundred African Americans. Two of the prisoners were shot dead while in police custody. The Columbia riot was a potent reminder that, whatever advances African Americans had made during the war, the freedoms for which many had fought and died abroad still eluded them at home.

Notes

1. Robert Russa Moton, *Finding a Way Out* (London: T. Fisher Unwin, 1920), p. 264.
2. Richard Wright, *Black Boy: A Record of Childhood and Youth* ([1945] Harlow, Longman, 1970), p. 147.
3. Adam Fairclough, *Better Day Coming: Blacks and Equality, 1890–2000* (New York: Penguin, 2001), p. 89.
4. Charley Patton, *Founder of the Delta Blues* (Yazoo L–1020, 1970).
5. Nicholas Lemann, *The Promised Land: The Great Black Migration and How it Changed America* (New York: Alfred A. Knopf, 1991), p. 17.
6. *Buchanan* v. *Warley*, 245 U.S. 60 (1917).
7. John Dollard, *Caste and Class in a Southern Town* (Garden City, NY: Doubleday & Company, 1957), p. 42.
8. *Chicago Defender*, 5 April 1919.
9. Nancy MacLean, *Behind the Mask of Chivalry: The Making of the Second Ku Klux Klan* (New York: Oxford University Press, 1994); Glenn Feldman, *Politics, Society, and the Klan in Alabama, 1915–1949* (Tuscaloosa: University of Alabama Press, 1999). The quotation is from Feldman, p. 73.
10. David L. Carlton and Peter A. Coclanis (eds), *Confronting Southern Poverty in the Great Depression: The Report on Economic Conditions of the South with Related Documents* (Boston, MA: Bedford/St. Martin's, 1996).

11. William E. Leuchtenburg, *The White House Looks South: Franklin D. Roosevelt, Harry S. Truman, Lyndon B. Johnson* (Baton Rouge: Louisiana State University Press, 2005), p. 58.
12. Ira Katznelson, *When Affirmative Action Was White: An Untold History of Racial Inequality in Twentieth-Century America* (New York: W. W. Norton & Company, 2005), p. 43.
13. Nancy L. Grant, *TVA and Black Americans: Planning for the Status Quo* (Philadelphia: Temple University Press, 1990).
14. Harvard Sitkoff, 'The Impact of the New Deal on Black Southerners', in James C. Cobb and Michael V. Namorato (eds), *The New Deal and the South* (Jackson: University Press of Mississippi, 1984), p. 118.
15. Theodore Rosengarten, *All God's Dangers: The Life of Nate Shaw* (New York: Alfred A. Knopf, 1974), p. 299.
16. Ibid., p. 297.
17. Anthony J. Badger, *The New Deal: The Depression Years, 1933–1940* (Houndmills, Basingstoke and London: Macmillan, 1989), p. 251.
18. Barton J. Bernstein, 'The New Deal: The Conservative Achievements of Liberal Reform', in Melvyn Dubofsky (ed.), *The New Deal: Conflicting Interpretations and Shifting Perspectives* (New York and London: Garland, 1992), p. 15; Paul K. Conkin, *The New Deal* (London: Routledge, 1968), p. 75; John A. Salmond, *The Civilian Conservation Corps, 1933–1942: A New Deal Case Study* (Durham, NC: Duke University Press, 1967).
19. Badger, *The New Deal*, p. 253.
20. Jimmy Gordon, 'Don't Take Away My PWA', quoted in Paul Oliver, *Blues Fell This Morning: Meaning in the Blues* (Cambridge: Cambridge University Press, 1994), p. 36.
21. Sitkoff, 'Impact of the New Deal', p. 126.
22. Maya Angelou, *I Know Why the Caged Bird Sings* ([1969] London: Virago, 1984), p. 132.
23. Doug McAdam, *Political Process and the Development of Black Insurgency, 1930–1970* (Chicago: University of Chicago Press, 1982), pp. 108–9.
24. Harvard Sitkoff, *A New Deal for Blacks: The Emergence of Civil Rights as a National Issue* (New York: Oxford University Press, 1978), p. 233.
25. Ibid., p. 109.
26. *Richmond Planet*, 23 April 1938.
27. Neil A. Wynn, *The Afro-American and the Second World War* (New York and London: Holmes & Meier, 1993), p. 24.
28. Phillip McGuire, *Taps for a Jim Crow Army: Letters from Black Soldiers in World War II* (Santa Barbara, CA: ABC-Clio, 1983), p. 26.
29. Ibid., p. 183.
30. Charles D. Chamberlain, *Manpower and Race in the American South during World War II* (Athens: University of Georgia Press, 2003), p. 57.
31. Robert Korstad and Nelson Lichtenstein, 'Opportunities Found and Lost:

Labor, Radicals, and the Early Civil Rights Movement', *Journal of American History*, 75 (December 1988), pp. 786–811; Michael Honey, 'Industrial Unionism and Racial Justice in Memphis', in Robert H. Zieger (ed.), *Organized Labor in the Twentieth-Century South* (Knoxville: University of Tennessee Press, 1991), pp. 135–57.

32. Walter F. White, *A Rising Wind* (Garden City, NY: Doubleday, Doran & Company, 1945).
33. Howard W. Odum, *Race and Rumors of Race: The American South in the Early Forties* ([1943] Baltimore: Johns Hopkins University Press, 1997), p. 73.
34. Steve Estes, *I Am A Man! Race, Manhood, and the Civil Rights Movement* (Chapel Hill: University of North Carolina Press, 2005), p. 36; Richard M. Dalfiume, 'The Forgotten Years of the Negro Revolution', *Journal of American History*, 55 (1968), pp. 90–106.
35. John Egerton, *Speak Now Against the Day: The Generation Before the Civil Rights Movement in the South* (New York: Alfred A. Knopf, 1994), pp. 303–12. Quotations on p. 306.
36. Harvard Sitkoff, 'African American Militancy in the World War II South: Another Perspective', in Neil R. McMillen (ed.), *Remaking Dixie: The Impact of World War II on the American South* (Jackson: University Press of Mississippi, 1997), pp. 70–92.
37. Adam Fairclough, *To Redeem the Soul of America: The Southern Christian Leadership Conference and Martin Luther King, Jr.* (Athens and London: University of Georgia Press, 1987), p. 15.
38. Bryant Simon, 'Race Reactions: African American Organizing, Liberalism, and White Working-Class Politics in Postwar South Carolina', in Jane Dailey, Glenda Elizabeth Gilmore and Bryant Simon (eds), *Jumpin' Jim Crow: Southern Politics from Civil War to Civil Rights* (Princeton, NJ, and Oxford: Princeton University Press, 2000), pp. 242–3.
39. Gunnar Myrdal, *An American Dilemma: The Negro Problem and Modern Democracy* (New York: Harper and Row, 1944), p. 997.

Chapter 10

MODERATES AND MILITANTS: THE STRUGGLE FOR THE WHITE SOUTH

On 17 May 1954, the United States Supreme Court issued the ruling that millions of Americans – black and white, northern and southern – had been awaiting with enormous expectation. It had taken seventeen months for the Court to reach its decision in the case of *Brown* v. *Board of Education*. The central issue before the Court was whether racial segregation in public schools deprived black children of the same standard of education as whites. Reading from the bench, Chief Justice Earl Warren concluded that 'in the field of public education the doctrine of "separate but equal" has no place. Separate educational facilities are inherently unequal.'[1]

The *Brown* decision has attracted considerable debate among scholars. Some celebrate it as the decisive breakthrough in the struggle for racial equality; others discredit it as a flawed ruling that actually proved counter-productive to change. This chapter assesses the relative merits of both sides in the debate. It measures the impact of the Court decision by analysing the scale and momentum of racial reform in the southern states during the years immediately before and after *Brown*. In particular, it focuses on the political struggle between the forces of racial moderation and racial militancy as a means of determining whether change could have been accomplished peacefully from within the region or whether it had to be enforced from outside by the federal government.

THE TRUMAN ADMINISTRATION AND CIVIL RIGHTS

One of the most promising aspects of post-war change was the more activist role of the federal government on civil rights matters. During more than a dozen years in the White House, Franklin Roosevelt had resisted any direct advocacy of black civil rights, principally out of a concern not to alienate southern congressional support. The man who succeeded him as president, Harry S. Truman, associated his administration much more conspicuously with the cause of racial equality. Truman offered more than rhetorical commitment to civil rights. Many historians believe that Truman broadened and deepened the commitment of the federal government to promote full rights of citizenship for African Americans. His administration oversaw some important changes, particularly the desegregation of the armed services. However, the administration did not fulfil the expectations it aroused among African Americans. The conservative political reaction created by the emerging Cold War, the responsibility for which lay in part with Truman himself, undermined racial progress in the late 1940s and early 1950s.

African Americans initially placed little trust in the new president as a champion of civil rights reform. As a senator, he had established a relatively progressive record on racial issues, a position that was owed in part to the importance of the black vote in his home state of Missouri. Yet he framed his belief in fairer opportunities for blacks strictly within the context of separate but equal. Southern conservatives had sufficient confidence in his support of racial segregation to endorse his nomination for vice-president in 1944.

However, a number of forces influenced Truman to take a more progressive stand on civil rights. During and immediately after the war, race became a matter that no politician could choose to ignore. One factor that helped to push the problem to the centre of political discourse was the publication in 1944 of *An American Dilemma,* a monumental study of race relations in the United States by the Swedish economist Gunnar Myrdal. The book exposed in extensive detail the depth and breadth of racial prejudice in American society, forcing policy makers to address the problem. A second factor was the publication in the American press of the stark images of concentration camp survivors, which caused a reassessment of racial fanaticism closer to home. Most historians accept that the promotion of racial equality was, as Robert H. Ferrell puts it, an 'emotional matter' for Truman.[2] However, it is an overemphasis to state, as does Michael R. Gardner, that the president acted only on humanitarian impulses. Self-interest and political expediency were as important as enlightened principle in motivating governmental activism on the race issue.[3] The emerging Cold War acted as a third factor that induced the federal government to take a more sensitive approach towards southern racism. White repression of blacks provided the Soviet Union with political ammunition, allowing it to discredit the claim of the United States to act as leader of the free world and thereby win influence among non-aligned nations. The administration therefore needed to take action in order to restore the delicate strategic balance between the United States and its ideological enemy. As historian Mary Dudziak affirms: 'The need to address international criticism gave the federal government an incentive to promote social change at home.[4] The fourth factor that influenced Truman was also rooted in political pragmatism. His administration needed to appease African American voters, whose influence on electoral politics had increased substantially because of black wartime migration to northern cities. In 1946, the Republicans won a landslide in the mid-term congressional elections, a victory in part owed to northern black voters who had started to drift away from the Democrats. Truman had to regain the support of the black electorate if he was to have any chance of securing his election in 1948.

All of these factors conditioned the response of the Truman administration to the wave of racial violence that swept through the southern states in the aftermath of the Second World War. As was discussed in the previous chapter, the war had a profound impact on African Americans, instilling many with a strong determination to push for their civil rights and liberties. Black veterans believed that, by serving their country in its time of need, they were morally entitled to full citizenship. On their return home from the war, they pressed this claim by co-ordinating voter registration drives that added unprecedented numbers of African Americans to the electoral rolls. In 1946 alone, veterans' organisations in Georgia spearheaded a campaign that resulted in the registration of between 135,000 and 150,000 blacks.[5] The following year, black veterans successfully led a challenge to the right of the notoriously racist Mississippi politician Theodore Bilbo to take his seat in the US Senate. Represented by the NAACP, they accused the senator of using intimidation and obstructionism to prevent blacks from voting. Suspended from office pending an investigation, Bilbo died before the Senate could make a permanent decision.

Confronted by the political assertiveness of African Americans, southern whites launched a brutal counter-attack. Between June 1945 and September 1946, there were at least fifty-six separate racial assaults on southern blacks. The riot in Columbia, Tennessee, was the worst, but by no means the only, occurrence of its kind. In August 1946, for instance, a mob of 2,000 whites ran amok through the streets of Athens, Alabama, injuring as many as one hundred African Americans. It took a combination of state guardsmen and police from across the state to restore order. The catalyst for this disturbance was the effort of black veterans to mobilise black voters. African American servicemen were also the principal target in acts of individual violence. One of the most shocking of these incidents occurred on 13 February 1946 in Batesburg, South Carolina. A black veteran named Isaac Woodard, still in uniform, was travelling home by bus from Camp Gordon in Georgia to New York City. A dispute between Woodard and the driver led to the arrival of the local police, who set about the black soldier with unrestrained force. Woodard suffered blows to the face that left him permanently blinded. On 25 July 1946, another black veteran, Roger Malcolm, was murdered along with three other African Americans in Monroe, Georgia. Responsibility for the crime rested with the Ku Klux Klan, resurrected by whites after the war as a means to repress black militancy. The resuscitation of the Klan conformed to a recurrent pattern in southern history. In times of racial instability – such as the assertion of black militancy during and after the Second World War, and the political flux created by the Supreme Court decision outlawing school segregation – white militants revived the Hooded Empire in an attempt to reassert the old order.

Truman faced considerable political pressure to secure the prosecution of those responsible for these crimes, and to take preventive measures against any further outbreaks of racial violence. In August 1946, representatives from forty religious, professional, veterans and civil rights organisations convened to form the National Emergency Committee Against Mob Violence. When members of the committee met with the president the following month, it was clear that he had not understood the scale of southern lawlessness. At the same time, Truman expressed genuine moral revulsion at the acts of barbarism committed against black veterans. 'My God!' Truman exclaimed to Walter White of the NAACP. 'I had no idea it was as terrible as that! We've got to do something!'[6]

The president was true to his word. On 5 December 1946, Truman issued Executive Order 9808, which established a President's Committee on Civil Rights. The membership of the committee consisted of representatives from a supposed cross-section of the American populace – including two businessmen, two labour leaders, two white southerners, two blacks, two women, two Jews and two Catholics – which led to it being described as 'Noah's Ark'. Its chairman was the head of the General Electric Corporation, Charles E. Wilson. The committee released its report on 29 October 1947. *To Secure These Rights* established a radical agenda for governmental reform of race relations. Its recommendations included federal legislation against lynching and police brutality, abolition of the poll tax, and the establishment of a permanent commission on civil rights. The report also concluded that 'The separate but equal doctrine is inconsistent with the fundamental equalitarianism of the American way of life in that it marks groups with the brand of inferior status.' Accordingly, it advocated 'the elimination of segregation, based on race, color, creed, or national origin' from interstate transportation, health care, housing, education and the armed forces.[7]

To Secure These Rights committed Truman to the civil rights cause in a way that Roosevelt had assiduously avoided. In addition to those factors previously cited, one further consideration influenced his response to the report.

Truman faced the prospect of a third-party challenge in the forthcoming presidential election. The Progressive Party, led by former vice-president Henry Wallace, threatened to establish a coalition of African Americans, white liberals and trade unionists that would erode the Democratic vote. Truman needed to establish his credentials as an exponent of black civil rights in order to counter this electoral threat. His advisors assured him that he could pursue this strategy without seriously alienating the white southern support also essential to his campaign.

On 2 February 1948, Truman delivered a 'Special Message to the Congress on Civil Rights'. While the address endorsed many of the recommendations made in *To Secure These Rights*, it fell conspicuously short of calling for the eradication of racial segregation, except as it related to interstate transportation. Nor was there any realistic prospect of a conservative-controlled Congress implementing the president's legislative proposal. Nevertheless, the speech was unprecedented in publicly binding a presidential administration to the pursuit of racial equality. Truman further asserted his commitment to civil rights when he issued two executive orders on 26 July 1948, one of which established a Fair Employment Board to remove racial discrimination from the civilian federal service, and the other that led to the gradual desegregation of the armed services.

Attention now turned to the race for the White House. Truman's advisors had determined that black voters were essential to the success of his campaign, but that their loyalties were by no means certain. Nonetheless, his efforts to woo the wavering black electorate were not without risk, since it threatened to incur the wrath of white southerners. How serious that risk was would soon become clear.

THE DIXIECRAT REVOLT

Southern Democrats reacted to the civil rights initiatives of the Truman administration with anger and alarm. Senator Tom Connally of Texas denounced the president's special message as 'a lynching of the Constitution'. His Mississippi colleague James Eastland demonstrated a similar flair for hyperbole, insisting that the speech showed 'that organized mongrel minorities control the government' and intended to use its power 'to Harlemise the country'.[8] Tensions between southern and northern Democrats came to a head at the party convention held in Philadelphia in July 1948. When southerners tried and failed to soften the strong civil rights plank adopted as part of the party platform, all of the Mississippi delegates and half of those from Alabama stormed out of the convention. With the exception of a small number of party loyalists, the remaining southern delegates attempted unsuccessfully to secure the nomination of Senator Richard Russell of Georgia. Southern dissenters reconvened in Birmingham, Alabama, where they established the breakaway States' Rights Democratic Party. Its members nominated Senator Strom Thurmond of South Carolina and Governor Fielding Wright of Mississippi as their respective presidential and vice-presidential candidates. To symbolise their opposition to federal interference in southern race relations, the members of the new party prominently displayed the Confederate battle flag, a clear attempt to use memories of the past to evoke support for a present cause.

The supporters of the States' Rights Democratic Party (or 'Dixiecrats') did not believe that they could win the presidential election, but they did hope to influence its outcome. Securing the 127 electoral college votes of the southern states would ensure that neither the Republican nor the Democratic presidential candidate could win an overall majority. With the election thrown into the House of Representatives, the Dixiecrats would use their position as power brokers to demand concessions on the civil rights issue in return for their support.

However, the southern electorate proved reluctant to abandon their traditional loyalty to the Democratic Party. The Thurmond – Wright ticket won only four southern states: Alabama, Mississippi, Louisiana and South Carolina. Moreover, these were all states where the ballot papers listed the Dixiecrat candidates as the regular Democratic Party nominees. Why had the southern electorate proved so reluctant to board the Dixiecrat bandwagon? Part of the reason rested with the Dixecrats themselves. Party members did not share a clear consensus on such issues as the centrality of race to their campaign. While some appealed to moderate opinion by framing their opposition to Washington within the strict context of states' rights, others resorted to racial demagoguery. Yet, even with a more united front, the Dixiecrats would have struggled to win over southern voters. During the New Deal and the Second World War, the South had benefited substantially from the investment and recovery programmes of the federal government. Increases in income and employment opportunities helped to assuage popular fears about federal interference in the region. The transition from a rural to an urban and industrial economy had a particularly important impact. Business leaders in the new metropolitan centres understood that northern capital was essential to sustain economic growth. The Dixiecrat campaign threatened to dissuade potential investors through its militant assertion of southern autonomy. Thurmond, for instance, threatened that the federal government was attempting to enforce on the region a 'federal police state' that 'would force life on each hamlet in America to conform to a Washington patter'.[9] The entrepreneurial and professional classes therefore mobilised in opposition to a campaign that they feared could bring ruin to the nascent urban economy. Perhaps the most important failure of the Dixiecrats was their inability to recruit many conservatives, most of whom were still dedicated to the Democratic Party and considered it better to challenge its civil rights policies from within rather than from without. As Virginia attorney general J. Lindsay Almond asserted: 'The only sane and constructive course to follow is to remain in the house of our fathers – even though the roof leaks, and there be bats in the belfry, rats in the pantry, a cockroach waltz in the kitchen and skunks in the parlor.'[10]

The strategy of internal dissent advocated by Almond proved more successful than the Dixiecrat campaign in stifling civil rights reform. Although Harry Truman had defied the odds to defeat the Republican candidate Thomas Dewey, he had little control over a Congress still dominated by a conservative coalition of southern Democrats and northern Republicans. Moreover, the escalating Cold War caused the president to prioritise foreign policy, specifically the containment of international Communism, to which he had committed the United States in the Truman Doctrine of March 1947. Truman therefore refused to risk his limited political capital on civil rights reform. He did little to stop southerners defeating efforts to abolish the poll tax and establish a permanent Fair Employment Practices Committee.

Despite its failure, the Dixiecrat revolt also had important repercussions for the future. First, it represented the start of a longer-term process of Democratic Party decline in the South. As we will see in the Conclusion, southern opposition to the racial policies of the national party would contribute to a significant electoral realignment within the region, which emerged as a Republican stronghold. Second, the Dixiecrat revolt delineated the battle-lines in the civil rights struggles of the 1950s and 1960s. Most of the support for the Dixiecrats – like the loudest calls for secession almost a century earlier – came from the Black Belt, the plantation counties where whites were a minority of the population. It was there that the decline in the traditional rural economy and the increasing politicisation of African Americans most threatened the hegemonic control of whites. That sense of threat became more acute with the rise of the civil rights movement, and it was within the Black Belt that the forces of massive resistance against racial change would gain their greatest strength.

THE RED SCARE AND THE BLACK STRUGGLE

By the early 1950s, the onset of the Cold War chilled political enthusiasm for civil rights reform. In February 1950, Wisconsin senator Joseph McCarthy proclaimed to a credulous audience that he possessed the names of fifty-seven State Department officials who were members of the American Communist Party. Four months later, the United States became embroiled in the Korean War. The need for unity in a time of national crisis created a stifling conformism that silenced criticisms of domestic race relations. In the South, the winds of change that had swept through the region thinned to the barest whisper.

Historian Michael Klarman asserts that the years between the end of the Second World War and the *Brown* decision saw the election across the South of racially moderate politicians who worked to effect gradual reform of race relations. According to Klarman, the ruling was actually counter-productive, since it provoked a political backlash that undermined this process of change. The Supreme Court would, he concludes, have eased southern white acceptance of racial reform by focusing on a less emotionally charged issue than school desegregation, such as voting rights or public transportation.[11]

The problem with this interpretation is that overstates the political influence of racial moderates who had, by the time of the ruling, done little to ameliorate Jim Crow practices. It is the case that the late 1940s witnessed the rise to power of southern politicians who espoused a grassroots populism that cut across racial lines. Moderates occupied the governor's mansion in many states, including Gordon Browning in Tennessee, Jim Folsom in Alabama, Earl Long in Louisiana and Sid McMath in Arkansas. The new breed of southern political leaders also included a number of senators, including Albert Gore and Estes Kefauver of Tennessee, and Lister Hill and James Sparkman of Alabama.

Despite the emergence of this new generation of racially moderate politicians, there remained little prospect that serious change could be accomplished from within the South rather than having to be imposed from without. Although the moderates constructed electoral coalitions that included African American voters, most still believed it possible to accommodate black needs within the existing framework of racial segregation. Few of them cultivated personal contacts with their black constituents, but rather maintained a paternalistic attitude towards them. Their opposition to federal intervention on the race issue acted as a further obstacle to reform. Even had southern moderates possessed the will to push for change, they did not possess the way. The political influence of liberal politicians remained limited in the post-war South. As John Egerton confirms, 'the rebellious and reactionary segregationist mind-set was still the rule, not the exception'.[12] The conservative reaction fuelled by the onset of the Cold War resulted in the election of many politicians sworn to the preservation of the racial status quo.

Despite the failure of the Dixiecrats to influence the outcome of the presidential election, racial conservatives continued to win power at the local and state level during the late 1940s and early 1950s. A roll-call of the men elected to southern governorships during these years includes such reactionaries as John S. Battle of Virginia, James F. Byrnes of South Carolina, Robert F. Kennon of Louisiana, Allan Shivers of Texas and Herman Talmadge of Georgia.

Moreover, many of the moderate politicians who had come to power after the war maintained their offices only by moving to the right on the race issue. Those who failed to adhere to the doctrinaire line of white supremacy suffered damage to their personal reputations, as well as defeat at the polls. The ousting of New Deal liberals such as Senators Frank Porter Graham of North Carolina and Claude Pepper of Florida are cases in point. Graham had stirred considerable resentment in his native state because of his serving on President Truman's Committee on Civil Rights. He nonetheless held what seemed an insurmountable electoral lead in the 1950 North Carolina senatorial race – that was, until his opponents launched a renewed line of attack that accused him of promoting miscegenation, and predicted racial warfare if he won. Graham's adversaries also explicitly linked racial equality with the threat of internal subversion by claiming that he was a Communist sympathiser. Conservatives used a similar strategy of character assassination to discredit and defeat Claude Pepper.

To return to a theme from the previous chapter, some historians have alternatively asserted that the Cold War shattered the prospects of a grassroots alliance between civil rights organisations and trade unions. The principal proponents of this interpretation are Robert Korstad and Nelson Lichtenstein, who suggest that the 1930s and 1940s witnessed the emergence of a nascent inter-racial alliance rooted in the common economic interests of working-class whites and blacks.[13] There is some support for this claim. The Cold War did curtail the efforts of the union movement to promote bi-racial unionism in the South. In May 1946, the Congress of Industrial Organizations (CIO) launched a southern recruitment drive named 'Operation Dixie'. Cold War tensions had a powerful impact on the campaign, which struggled to gather momentum and had within three years ground to a complete halt. Southern employers manipulated popular fears about Communism by claiming that union organisers were instruments of a Soviet plot to overthrow white rule and mongrelise the races. These accusations provided the pretext for the police to intimidate, assault and arrest CIO activists. Anti-Communist forces within the CIO itself also fatally weakened the commitment of the union movement to the recruitment of southern black workers. CIO leaders feared that their political opponents would use the red scare to smear the union movement and undermine its mobilisation of white rank-and-file workers. The situation became acute after Congress passed the Taft-Hartley Act in 1947, which compelled unions to file affidavits declaring that none of their officers was a Communist. The CIO reacted to political pressure by expelling eleven unions that refused to comply with the law. This purge stripped the CIO of some of its most racially progressive members, undermining the institutional strength of civil rights unionism.

Yet this does not prove that the Cold War undermined an inter-racial alliance of union workers that could have challenged Jim Crow practices. As historians including Alan Draper, Bruce Nelson and Robert J. Norrell observe, irrespective of the repressive political climate of the Cold War, the strength of white prejudice among white union members inhibited the prospects of a proletarian rebellion against racial segregation. In the words of Norrell, the failure of inter-racial unionism was due 'in equal, if not greater, measure, to the militant white supremacy of many southern workers'. As illustration of this, during the era of massive resistance the Ku Klux Klan enlisted many of its recruits from the industrial unions of cities such as Atlanta and Birmingham.[14]

The early Cold War was also a time of political retrenchment for southern liberals. Since the late 1930s, the leading liberal organisation in the region had been the Southern Conference for Human Welfare (SCHW). Destabilised by declining funds and a loss of direction, the SCHW completely imploded in 1948 under pressure from the House Un-American Activities Committee, which accused it of being a Communist front. Its offshoot, the Southern Conference Educational Fund, struggled to survive an investigation by the Senate Committee on Internal Security.

Although the reactionary mood of the times retarded the advance of southern liberalism, it is also the case that many white moderates still lacked a moral commitment to abolishing Jim Crow. The Southern Regional Council did issue a statement in December 1951 that segregation was 'a cruel and needless penalty on the human spirit', but there was nonetheless a lack of consensus among southern liberals in support of social equality between the races. Some moderates continued to restrict their reformism to securing practical implementation of separate but equal public facilities. What distinguished these moderates from the conservatives who started to equalise schools in the 1950s was that they were motivated more by humanitarian impulses than by a pragmatic response to the threat of federal interference. Even those southern whites who advocated the removal of racial barriers believed it better to promote a policy of gradual voluntarism rather than federal coercion. In the opinion of Hodding Carter: 'Any abrupt Federal effort to end segregation as it is practised in the South today would not only be foredoomed to failure but would also dangerously impair the present progressive adjustments between the races.'[15] The emphasis on indigenous change showed how out of touch moderates were with the aspirations of civil rights activists. It entrusted responsibility for determining the scale and speed of desegregation entirely to southern whites, most of whom resisted surrendering their social and economic privileges.

The pursuit of suspected political subversives also caused the NAACP to assume a more establishmentarian line. Threatened with accusations that it was a political instrument of the Soviet Union, the organisation made a conspicuous effort to emphasise its patriotic credentials. In 1950, it officially banned Communists from its membership.

On the eve of the *Brown* decision, the forces of reaction therefore still exerted a stranglehold over the southern states. Many white southerners were prepared to resist reform by whatever means necessary. The early 1950s witnessed a renewed outburst of racial violence. According to the Southern Regional Council, white terrorists bombed the homes of forty black families during 1951 and 1952. One of the victims was Harry T. Moore, state director of the Florida NAACP, killed by a bomb planted under his house by Klansmen on Christmas Day 1951. It was an ominous portent of the conflict still to come.

BROWN V. *BOARD OF EDUCATION*

Although the anti-Communist witch-hunt forced civil rights activists on the defensive, the Cold War in some respects strengthened the cause of racial equality. The delicately poised balance between the competing superpowers provided civil rights organisations with considerable political leverage over Washington. NAACP leaders in particular emphasised the inconsistency between the claims of the United States to act as the defender of the free world and the persistence of racial oppression within its own borders. They stressed to the federal government that the country could suffer irreparable damage to its international prestige unless it reconciled the disparity between its democratic ideals and its racial practices. The United States could especially not afford to risk alienating the peoples of newly independent nations in Africa and Asia, for whose political allegiance it was in open competition with the Soviet Union. To avert such a situation, asserted black political scientist Ralph Bunche, 'freedom and justice must begin at home'.[16] The sensitivity of the federal government on this issue influenced its decision to file *amicus curiae* briefs in support of NAACP legal challenges to segregation.

By the early 1950s, the legal attack launched by the NAACP had succeeded in breaching the outer defences of Jim Crow. The principal legal strategist of the NAACP was Charles H. Houston, who served as its special counsel from 1934. Houston feared that a direct challenge to segregation would fail. He therefore attempted to use the *Plessy* v. *Ferguson* precedent to force southern states to provide educational facilities that were separate but equal. The cost of improving black schools would prove so prohibitive as to force southern authorities to abandon segregation or face economic ruin. In an attempt to build momentum behind the campaign, Houston focused initially not on public schools, but on the less contentious area of graduate education.

The strategy reaped substantial rewards. Three decisions handed down by the Supreme Court on the same day in June 1950 dented the principle of separate but equal. In *Henderson* v. *United States*, the Court ruled that the segregation of railway dining cars violated the Interstate Commerce Act. The Court also determined in the case of *Sweatt* v. *Painter* that the University of Texas must admit a black applicant to its law school. A separate law school for blacks established by the university, which consisted of part-time faculty teaching in three small basement rooms, could not in the opinion of the Court offer the same education as that available to white students. In *McLaurin* v. *Oklahoma State Regents*, the Court further decided that the University of Oklahoma could not admit a student to its doctoral programme, but then insist on seating him separately from white students.

Although the *Sweatt* and *McLaurin* decisions concerned only higher education, southern politicians conceded that it was just a matter of time before they faced a legal challenge to the segregated public school system. As Charles Houston had anticipated, they attempted to pre-empt such action by equalising educational provisions for black and white pupils. Governor James Byrnes of South Carolina conceded that 'To meet this situation we are forced to do now what we should have been doing for the last fifty years.' This assessment led the southern states to invest eight times the amount of money in black schools in 1951–52 than they did in 1939–40.[17] However, it was too little, too late. Decades of chronic underfunding had created an enormous disparity between black and white schools that could not instantly be resolved.

The legal challenge that southern authorities sought to avert came in the form of a series of suits filed by the NAACP on behalf of black parents in the District of Columbia and the states of Delaware, Kansas, Louisiana, South Carolina and Virginia. In December 1952, the Supreme Court heard arguments in five of the cases under the consolidated title of *Brown* v. *Board of Education*. On 17 May 1954, Chief Justice Earl Warren issued a unanimous decision in support of the plaintiffs. According to the Court, the maintenance of a dual school system deprived black students of the equal protection of the law guaranteed by the Fourteenth Amendment. The racial separation of schoolchildren also carried with it an implication of black inferiority that caused irreparable psychological damage. 'In the field of public education,' affirmed Warren, 'the doctrine of separate but equal has no place. Separate educational facilities are inherently unequal.'[18]

African Americans were ecstatic in their response to the decision. The *Richmond Afro-American* ran a cartoon that represented the ruling as an atomic bomb because of the strength of its impact; the *New York Amsterdam News* editorialised that it was 'the greatest victory for the Negro people since the Emancipation Proclamation'.[19] Although the decision related to public schools, many blacks saw it as the thin end of a wedge that the courts would drive through all racially restrictive barriers. In the assessment of Charles Johnson: 'If segregation is unconstitutional in educational institutions, it is no less so in other aspects of our national life.'[20]

The response of southern whites to the Supreme Court ruling ran the spectrum from positive endorsement to outspoken opposition. Mississippi State Supreme Court judge Tom P. Brady articulated the anger and resentment of whites in the Deep South in a speech that branded the day of the *Brown* decision 'Black Monday'. Brady expressed the fears of miscegenation that were fundamental to white resistance of racial integration. In apocalyptic terms, he prophesied the destruction of the white race that would result from intimate contact with blacks: 'Whenever and wherever the white man has drunk the cup of black hemlock, whenever and wherever his blood has been infused with the blood of the negro, the white man, his intellect and his culture have died.'[21] There was nonetheless no clear consensus among white southerners. The gubernatorial elections of 1954 demonstrate this. Although opposition to the ruling led to the election of conservatives such as Marvin Griffin in Georgia and George Bell Timmerman, Jr in South Carolina, in other parts of the South moderate politicians won the day over their reactionary opponents. Whites in the Upper South reacted with particular circumspection to the Supreme Court decision. While many opposed the principle of integration, they reluctantly accepted that the preservation of law and order compelled compliance. School desegregation occurred without incident in 1955 and 1956 in parts of Arkansas, Kentucky and Texas.

However, the miscalculation of the Supreme Court turned white southerners from a position of defence to one of offence. It took the Court a further twelve months after its initial ruling to issue an implementation decree. On 31 May 1955, the Court resolved what course of action southern authorities should take in the decision known as *Brown II*. Ironically, the Court's pronouncement caused greater obfuscation than clarification. In one of the most controversial phrases in American legal history, the Court determined only that school boards should act with 'all deliberate speed' to implement desegregation. The Court also failed to establish by what standard to measure that a school system was 'racially nondiscriminatory'. Instead, it entrusted to federal district and appeals courts the responsibility of devising an appropriate solution.[22]

The NAACP responded to *Brown II* by filing hundreds of lawsuits against school boards across the South to force them into compliance. Southern whites responded to this aggression by mobilising in mass opposition. Their resistance postponed implementation of school desegregation in some instances for months, in others for years. A decade after the Supreme Court decision, less than 2 per cent of black schoolchildren in the southern states attended desegregated schools. In the Deep South, the numbers were so small as to be barely worth counting: 0.007 per cent in Alabama, 0.004 per cent in South Carolina, and not a single child in Mississippi.[23] A cartoon in the *New York Times* encapsulated the strength of white resistance, picturing an animated scroll that contained the Supreme Court decision attempting unsuccessfully to push through a steel-padlocked door labelled 'THE SOUTH'.[24]

MASSIVE RESISTANCE

Opinion polls conducted during the 1950s showed that about eight out of ten southern whites opposed school desegregation. That statistic included the entire region: in the core states of the Deep South, the proportion was more than nine out of ten.[25] Southern political leaders mobilised this popular discontent into a campaign of what Virginia Senator Harry F. Byrd called 'massive resistance'. The pursuit of this policy turned much of the southern states into a battleground in the years that immediately followed the *Brown* decision.

There has been a recent resurgence of interest in white southern opposition to desegregation. Historian Charles Eagles observes that the scholarship on the civil rights movement until recently suffered from 'asymmetry', because it focused almost entirely on black protesters and their white liberal allies. However, scholars now understand that it is impossible to assess the significance of the civil rights movement without understanding the nature of the opposition that it faced.[26]

At the spearhead of southern resistance were the White Citizens' Councils. Founded by Mississippian Robert Patterson in July 1954, the councils claimed at their peak a membership of 250,000. The councils drew much of their support in the cities from the white working class, but in the small towns and rural communities from the middle class. The recruitment of middle-class support was a deliberate strategy intended to present an image of political respectability. The councils attempted to promote the legitimacy of their opposition to the *Brown* decision by disavowing violent resistance of the law and demagogic appeals to white prejudice. That meant distancing themselves from the Ku Klux Klan and a host of other extremist groups established in opposition to desegregation. Instead, the councils tried to appeal to issues of high political principle by framing their arguments within the strict doctrine of states' rights. According to the councils, the Supreme Court had no authority to overturn the precedent established in *Plessy* that individual states had the right to practise Jim Crow policies. *Brown* was, in their view, a 'sociologically-based decision' with no foundation in law. A cartoon in one of the councils' publications encapsulated this sentiment by depicting an imperious Earl Warren, resplendent in crown and robes, banging his gavel as he proclaims 'I HAVE SPOKEN!'[27]

Although the councils claimed to represent the forces of respectable opposition to the Supreme Court, in practice they employed tactics that set them outside the law, using economic intimidation in particular to repress black political protest. African Americans who attempted to register as voters, or to enrol their children at white schools, lost their jobs or had their loans called in by white merchants who refused them further credit. The councils also coerced many white moderates into becoming members by threatening social, economic and physical reprisals if they failed to join. Council leader Roy Harris adopted an aggressive posture towards those who did not publicly resist desegregation when he told one audience: 'If you're a white man, then it's time to stand up with us, or black your face and get on the other side.'[28]

Southern politicians such as Harris were a conspicuous presence within the ranks of the Citizens' Council. Confronted by the federal assault on state autonomy, the political leadership of the South closed ranks. One of the most important factors facilitating segregationist resistance was that after the Second World War electoral reapportionment did not keep pace with urban growth. The lack of proportionate representation for metropolitan centres meant that racially moderate city voters had less influence over elections than did their more militant rural and small-town counterparts. The politicians who represented the South at a state and national level were therefore predominantly hard-line opponents of reform. Although the metropolitan centres challenged the hegemony of rural areas, they did not gain proportionate power until after 1962, when the Supreme Court outlawed malapportionment in *Baker* v. *Carr*. Another significant factor that influenced the capitulation to political extremism was the reluctance of moderate politicians to support desegregation. Their reticence allowed the reactionaries to seize the political initiative. Historian Tony Badger argues that the ability of moderates to retain public office during the desegregation crisis shows that they over-estimated the strength of popular support for massive resistance. Moreover, these politicians lacked the same commitment towards reform that the reactionaries had towards maintaining racial segregation.[29]

The political paralysis of many southern moderates is apparent from their reaction to the Southern Manifesto. In March 1956, more than one hundred members of the House and Senate added their names to a 'Declaration of Constitutional Principles'. The Southern Manifesto, as the statement was otherwise known, protested the 'unwarranted exercise of power' by the Supreme Court, and pledged the signatories to use every legal means to resist school desegregation. Moderate politicians who did not support a policy of massive resistance nonetheless appended their signatures to the document for fear that they would otherwise suffer a backlash from their constituents. As Alabama congressman Carl Elliott recalled: 'You were either with them or against them. And if you were against them, you were gone.'[30] The only southern senators who did not sign were Lyndon Johnson of Texas, and Estes Kefauver and Albert Gore of Tennessee, all of whom had ambitions for the presidency that would suffer if they were associated with sectional prejudice.

Southern legislatures also used and abused the power of law to circumvent the Supreme Court decision. In reaction to the *Brown* ruling, state governments enacted nearly 500 laws intended to obstruct school desegregation. In the words of James Kilpatrick of the *Richmond News Leader*: 'if one remedial law is ruled invalid, then let us try another; and if the second is ruled invalid, then let us enact a third'.[31] Kilpatrick was a leading advocate of interposition, the nineteenth-century concept that individual states may veto federal laws that infringe upon their rights. By the middle of 1957, eight southern states had passed interposition resolutions in an attempt to resist implementation of school desegregation. Southern law-makers enacted numerous other measures to resist the Supreme Court. This included 'pupil placement' legislation, which allowed local districts to assign students to schools according to complicated criteria that made no explicit mention of race but were clearly intended to maintain segregation. State legislatures also threatened to withhold funds from schools that complied with federal court orders to admit black students, and approved payment of tuition grants to white parents who removed their children from desegregated schools. Federal courts also facilitated the drift towards token and gradual compliance with the *Brown* decision by approving the cautious implementation plans of southern school boards.

Southern authorities in addition took ruthless measures to repress the NAACP, which stood almost alone in its struggle to secure school desegregation. State prosecutors in some instances forced the organisation to surrender its membership lists, exposing those peoples whose names appeared in the public domain to intimidation and violence. When the Alabama NAACP declined to submit the identities of its members, state authorities retaliated by banning the organisation. By December 1957, the NAACP had lost 39,000 southern members, and the organisation was spending more time and money protecting itself against public attack than on campaigning for desegregation.[32]

One of the most common tactics used to discredit the NAACP, and other civil rights organisations, was to accuse them of being Communist fronts. White southerners needed both intellectually and emotionally to believe that blacks were content with their place in society, and that responsibility for the civil rights movement must therefore rest with 'outside agitators'. This term was coded language for Communists, many of whom white southerners also believed to be Jewish. Despite the efforts of massive-resistance leaders to dissociate themselves from crude racial bigotry, anti-Semitism was never far from the surface of segregationist discourse.[33] To secure evidence for their smear campaign against civil rights activists, state legislatures established their own investigative agencies. The first and most infamous of these agencies was the Mississippi State Sovereignty Commission, founded in 1956. As Jeff Woods has demonstrated, one of the most insidious aspects of the state investigative agencies is that they received a constant flow of information from the Federal Bureau of Investigation. FBI director J. Edgar Hoover not only opposed the civil rights movement, he also suspected that anyone who supported it was a Communist. The actions of the FBI emphasise the complex relationship of the federal government to racial reform: while the Supreme Court championed its cause, the Bureau did its utmost to destroy it.[34]

Segregationists may have possessed the political machinery with which to resist desegregation but, according to one scholar, they did not have the force of intellectual and cultural argument to rally popular support for their cause. David Chappell asserts that the tone of segregationist rhetoric was indecisive and defensive. The leaders of the massive resistance movement sought to maintain their respectability by abstaining from crude emotional appeals to white racism. However, they could not construct an alternative line of reasoning with the resonance to mobilise grassroots resistance to the *Brown* decision. During the antebellum era, slaveholders had asserted that the peculiar institution was a 'positive good' for blacks as well as whites. By contrast, segregationists couched their language in negative terms. Their arguments emphasised the faults of their enemies – the Supreme Court had usurped its constitutional authority; northern critics of the South were hypocrites who ignored the poverty and violence in their own inner cities – rather than the virtues of racial segregation. In particular, claims Chappell, segregationists failed to enlist the intellectual and institutional support of the churches for Jim Crow. Black church leaders used the power of the pulpit to imbue ordinary African Americans with a sense of divine purpose in combating racism. White clergymen made far less effort to bestow a sense of cultural legitimacy on the segregationist cause.[35]

There is some substance to this interpretation. Only a small number of southern white clergymen claimed biblical sanction for segregation. Moreover, religious organisations such as the Southern Baptist Convention and the Southern Presbyterian General Assembly issued resolutions that endorsed desegregation. However, although only a small number of ministers forcefully defended segregation, fewer still spoke out against it. There was also tension between church leaders and ordinary laypersons over the use of Christian theology to legitimate Jim Crow. As Jane Dailey has demonstrated, many devout white southerners drew on religious doctrine to rationalise their opposition to racial integration. Fearing that the Supreme Court decision would lead to miscegenation, they turned to the Bible for evidence that racial amalgamation defied the will of God and would result in divine retribution. The punishment of Sodom and Gomorrah, and the destruction of the Tower of Babel, demonstrated to these believers that miscegenation was a sin. In the words of one lay official: 'I believe that the Lord would have made us all one color if he had intended that we be one race.'[36] When ministers failed to affirm the convictions of their congregations, pressure forced them from their pulpits. Although the number of clergymen fired for their racial apostasy is unknown, impressionistic estimates are high. What is perhaps most significant is that white southerners did not unite around religion as a legitimate defence of segregation. Whether or not the fractiousness of segregationist opposition was the crucial factor in the downfall of Jim Crow is still open to debate.

What is more certain is that supporters of massive resistance were rather disingenuous in claiming to oppose mob violence. Southern politicians insisted that they acted within the strict boundaries of the law in resisting desegregation. Their defiance of federal authority nonetheless contributed to a political climate that encouraged acts of mob intimidation and racial terrorism. The refusal of elected officials to respect the law of the land, their threats of interposition, and their disavowal of responsibility for the violence they claimed would occur in reaction to federal enforcement of desegregation emboldened white extremists to believe they could act with impunity in brutally repressing black civil rights. Between 1 January 1955 and 1 January 1959, 225 incidents of anti-civil rights violence occurred across the South.[37]

Much of the violence focused on educational institutions that attempted to admit black students. In February 1956, the University of Alabama admitted its first African American student, Autherine Lucy, under federal court order. On only her second day, a mob drove Lucy from the campus, and the university board of trustees decided to suspend her 'for her own safety'. When Lucy accused the university of encouraging mob rule, the trustees permanently expelled her.

Court orders to desegregate schools also precipitated violent unrest, much of it notably in Upper South states that had initially responded with restraint towards the Supreme Court decision. On 1 September 1956, Tennessee Governor Frank Clement ordered 600 National Guardsmen to restore calm in the small town of Clinton. Inspired by an itinerant segregationist named John Kasper, whites had taken to the streets in violent protest at the desegregation of the local high school. Occasional outbreaks continued to occur after the troops had been withdrawn. Nonetheless, in May 1957, Clinton became the first southern community in which a black student, Bobby Cain, graduated from a formerly white high school. Within days of the Clinton disorder, on 4 September 1956, a mob of 500 whites barred the admission of nine black students to a high school in the mining town of Sturgis in western Kentucky. Whites affirmed their determination to resist desegregation by roaming threateningly through the local black neighbourhood. Governor A. B. Chandler dispatched more than 200 National Guardsmen to the town in an attempt to restore order. He also sent an armed force of 500 guardsmen to Clay, a community eleven miles south of Sturgis. The civic leadership of the town had united with the school board in opposing the admission of two black children, Jimmy and Theresa Gordon, to a white elementary school. When the children entered the school under the protection of the guardsmen, Mayor Herman Clark announced a boycott by whites. By the end of the first school week, only seven of the seventeen teachers and three of the 590 pupils turned up for classes.

The incidents in Clay and Sturgis also emphasised how segregationists used the threat of economic reprisals to intimidate blacks. In Sturgis, the local mining company warned the fathers of the black children that they would lose their jobs unless they withdrew them from the school; in Clay, a white employer similarly threatened to fire James Gordon from his position as a car mechanic. Local merchants also exploited the fact that the Gordons were too poor to afford indoor plumbing by refusing to supply them with water. White resistance nonetheless soon waned. On 24 September, state attorney general

Jo Ferguson ordered the resegregation of the schools on a technicality. Three days later, federal judge Henry Brooks overturned the decision and ordered the schools to desegregate by the start of the following academic year.[38]

LEADING FROM THE BACK: THE EISENHOWER ADMINISTRATION

Responsibility for these racial disturbances rested foremost with the racist demagogues who stirred southern whites into open revolt against desegregation. However, it is also important to stress that the failure of the federal government to enforce the *Brown* decision gave implicit sanction to segregationists. The silence of the White House encouraged southern mobs to believe that they could act with impunity in resisting the implementation of court orders.

In 1952, Republican Dwight D. Eisenhower succeeded Harry Truman as President of the United States. The scholarly consensus is that the Eisenhower administration failed to comprehend the moral imperative to promote racial reform. Even those historians such as Stephen Ambrose, who are otherwise well-disposed towards the presidency of Dwight Eisenhower, accept that he did not provide appropriate leadership on civil rights issues. Eisenhower used neither his prestige as a military hero nor his authority as president to push for compliance with the Supreme Court decision. Moreover, many scholars claim that his vacillating position contributed to the very conflict over racial integration that he had hoped to avoid. In the assessment of Robert F. Burk, Eisenhower 'could never bring himself to recognize that civil rights represented a cause on which delay, compromise, and accommodation with the racial segregationists was neither morally right nor politically possible in the long run'.[39] His reluctance to act stemmed from a number of considerations. Eisenhower had a narrow interpretation of the powers of the executive branch of government. He did not believe that the White House had the authority to intervene in the internal jurisdiction of the states. To do so would be to risk political retaliation that could provoke a constitutional crisis. Rather than arbitrarily impose desegregation, the president insisted that it was more prudent to cultivate a change in white southern opinion that would lead to its eventual acceptance. This emphasis on gradualism also reflected the fact that Eisenhower was a native Texan more attuned to the sensitivities of white rather than black southerners. The president privately disapproved of the *Brown* decision, later claiming that his appointment of Earl Warren as Chief Justice was 'the biggest damn fool mistake' he ever made. Eisenhower further understood that his advocacy of states' rights afforded potential electoral advantages. In a clear demonstration of the continued disaffection of many white southerners with the Democratic Party, in the 1952 election Eisenhower had won the states of Florida, Virginia and Texas. He also received the endorsement of a number of southern Democrats, including governors Allan Shivers of Texas and James Byrnes of South Carolina. Eisenhower therefore emphasised the importance of states' rights as a means of making further inroads into the South and strengthening his re-election campaign of 1956.

Eisenhower pursued a policy of silence in the hope that it would defuse potential conflict. However, his efforts to maintain neutrality on the race issue fuelled the very crisis he tried to avert. The reluctance of the president to provide moral leadership to the nation motivated southern politicians to take measures in wanton disobedience of federal law. In August 1956, Texas governor Allan Shivers deployed state troopers to prevent the admissions of black students to a high school in Mansfield. When black activists appealed to Eisenhower, he insisted that he did not have the constitutional authority to intervene. In reality, he did not want to alienate a political ally whose endorsement he wanted for his re-election campaign. The failure of the president to assert the power of the federal government strengthened the determination of other southern politicians to resist court orders mandating school desegregation. This situation reached its pinnacle in the confrontation between the federal government and Arkansas governor Orval Faubus.

The local school board in the city of Little Rock had reacted promptly to the *Brown* decision by announcing its intention to implement desegregation. In May 1955, superintendent of schools Virgil T. Blossom issued a programme for the phased enrolment of black students to formerly white institutions. The programme honoured the letter rather than the spirit of the law. Not only did it restrict desegregation to one school, it also imposed a rigorous selection process that reduced the number of blacks who successfully applied for a transfer. The Blossom plan also emphasised the importance of class as well as race in shaping the policy of southern authorities towards school desegregation. Blossom selected Central High School for the admission of nine black students in the autumn of 1957. However, he made no provision to desegregate the newly constructed Hall High School, situated in an affluent and lily-white section of the city. This decision aroused the bitter resentment of working-class whites, who claimed with considerable justification that local elites had conspired to escape the burden of desegregation by imposing it on ordinary people. It was in this escalating crisis that Governor Faubus stepped centre-stage.

Faubus had come to power in 1954 with a progressive campaign that eschewed traditional race-baiting tactics. However, when he ran for re-election two years later, he faced a strong challenge from a hard-line segregationist who accused him of being soft on the race issue. The campaign convinced Faubus that he would need to reaffirm his white supremacist credentials with voters, if he were to win election to a third term. This political opportunism led the governor to take the decision on the day before the schools opened to call out the National Guard and order them to surround Central High. On the first day of classes, the nine black students due to attend classes at the school remained at home. They tried the following morning to enter Central High, but the guardsmen blocked their entrance. Eisenhower then intervened by inviting Faubus to a meeting at the White House, securing what he thought was a commitment from the governor not to cause further obstruction. A federal court then issued an injunction against further interference with the desegregation of the school by Arkansas state officials. Faubus complied by removing the guard. On Monday, 23 September 1957, a mob gathered outside Central High, chorusing 'Two, four, six, eight, we ain't gonna integrate'. Although the black students made a discreet entrance to the school through a side door, word soon reached the mob that they were inside the building. The resulting pandemonium caused the black teenagers to be withdrawn from the school for their own safety. Faubus, whose defiance had done so much to stir the violent animosities of local whites, was conveniently out of town at the time.

Eisenhower reacted to the spiralling chaos in Little Rock by federalising the Arkansas National Guard and dispatching more than 1,000 paratroopers from the 101st Airborne Division to restore order. This belated demonstration of federal force led to the readmission of the black students, who, despite persistent intimidation and abuse from some of their white classmates, saw through the rest of the school year at Central High. The use of troops nonetheless had a complicated impact on the desegregation issue. Eisenhower acted in part out of a sense of personal betrayal by Faubus, who had reneged on his promise not to interfere with the admission of the black students. His failure to face down a challenge from a southern governor would also have inflicted damage on the power and prestige of the executive office. Eisenhower further understood that the violence in Little Rock provided propaganda for the Soviet Union, which would waste little opportunity in 'telling the world of the "racial terror" in the United States'. The one factor that was not important was the moral principle of racial equality. Eisenhower insisted that his purpose in deploying troops was not to accelerate the desegregation process, but simply to restore law and order. As he later observed in his memoirs: 'If the day comes when we can obey the orders of our courts only *when we personally approve of them*, the end of the American system, as we know it, will not be far off.' The president also insisted that his actions would not set a precedent for further military action against recalcitrant southern communities.[40]

The military action taken by the Eisenhower administration did not secure a permanent solution to the school situation in Little Rock. In September 1958, the Supreme Court ruled in *Cooper* v. *Aaron* that the school board must implement desegregation without further delay. Refusing to surrender, Faubus signed new legislation that closed the high schools.

The deployment of armed troops in Little Rock nonetheless undermined the unanimity of white southern opposition to desegregation. On the one hand, the use of federal force provided militant segregationists with political ammunition. White supremacist organisations such as the Citizens' Council drew parallels between federal intervention in Little Rock and the use by the Soviet Union of armed troops a year earlier to crush the Hungarian uprising. The threat of totalitarianism, they asserted, was much closer to home than most Americans realised.

On the other hand, the flexing of federal muscle in Little Rock persuaded many moderate white southerners of the futility of interposition. To understand the position of these racial moderates, it is important to consider the economic transformation of the South during the Second World War. Federal investment led to massive expansion of the industrial and manufacturing sectors of the economy, and in turn the rise of a new white suburban middle class. Although these business people and professionals opposed desegregation in principle, they recognised that uncompromising resistance could prove counter-productive. The racial disorder that coursed through cities such as Little Rock risked deterring the investment of northern capital on which the economy of the New South relied. Racial moderates therefore acted out of an enlightened self-interest in pushing for the peaceful acceptance of school desegregation. Pressure from business leaders and parents' groups concerned at the threat to their children's education resulted in the reopening of Little Rock's high schools in September 1959.

A similar resolution of the desegregation issue occurred in Virginia. In September 1958, Governor J. Lindsay Almond had resisted a federal court order by closing nine schools in Warren County, Charlottesville and Norfolk. However, the local business establishment, fearing that the adverse publicity would lead to a potential loss of investment, forcefully opposed the decision. Public criticism led Almond to repudiate his support of massive resistance. When federal and state courts ruled the school closures unconstitutional in January 1959, the governor reopened them under a policy of local option that allowed for token desegregation.

Determined to avert the disruption that had damaged the reputations of Little Rock and Virginia, city leaders in other parts of the South implemented a policy of minimum compliance with court-ordered integration. The tone of southern authorities was more one of resignation than of rejoicing. Georgia governor Carl E. Sanders candidly admitted that local and state officials acted less out of moral commitment to racial reform than a pragmatic concern to protect the social order and economic stability of their communities. 'I am a segregationist,' proclaimed Sanders, 'but I am not a damned fool.'[41]

Not all racial moderates learned the lesson of Little Rock. City leaders in New Orleans failed in the fall of 1960 to take the pro-active role that would have facilitated the peaceful implementation of school desegregation. Their temporising allowed extremists to seize the political initiative. Thousands took to the streets in violent protest at the transfer of a six-year-old black girl to a white elementary school. There were also, as late as the mid-1960s, many members of the conservative old guard who considered it possible to resist what other white southerners considered was inevitable. On 14 January 1963, Alabama governor George Wallace used his inaugural address to proclaim his commitment to 'Segregation now – segregation tomorrow – segregation forever!'[42]

The grandstanding of demagogues owed much to the irresolution of both racial moderates and the Eisenhower and later Kennedy administrations. We will consider the civil rights record of the Kennedy administration in Chapter 11. Here it is important to stress that the failure of the Eisenhower administration to establish a clear line of policy on civil rights also undermined its efforts to increase black voter registration. Although the president claimed he had no jurisdiction to enforce school desegregation, the US Constitution explicitly entrusted responsibility for the protection of voting rights to the federal government. In 1957, the administration secured the passage of a Civil Rights Act that empowered the Justice Department to file suit against registrars who discriminated against African Americans and established a Commission on Civil Rights to assess allegations of racial bias. The act was the first federal civil rights law since Reconstruction, and therefore of considerable symbolic importance. However, in practical terms, it did little to increase the number of southern blacks on the electoral rolls. Conservative opponents of the law secured an amendment that allowed for the jury trial of defendants accused of obstructing black voter registration. Since most southern juries were composed exclusively of whites, the prospects of securing a conviction in such cases were poor. The emasculation of the new law owed much to the equivocation of the president. Eisenhower conceded at one press conference that 'I was reading part of that bill this morning, and there were certain phrases I didn't completely understand.'[43] The failure of the president to exert more pressure for the passage of the bill empowered southern congressmen to push for modifications that undermined its practical impact. Although the Eisenhower administration won congressional support for another Civil Rights Act in 1960, it made little more impression on the problem of black disfranchisement. The two laws contributed in total to only a 3 per cent increase in the number of African Americans registered as voters.

One scholar has claimed that Eisenhower practised a 'hidden-hand presidency', operating behind the scenes to push for peaceful improvements in American society.[44] On the issue of civil rights at least, the hand of the president was not only hidden; it was not there at all. Martin Luther King used an elaborate metaphor to describe the apparent inability of the president to grasp either the scale or moral urgency of the racial situation: 'His conservatism was fixed and rigid, and any evil defacing the nation had to be extracted bit by bit with a tweezer because the surgeon's knife was an instrument too radical to touch this best of all societies.'[45]

By the early 1960s, the metropolitan centres of the Sunbelt had started to supersede the Black Belt as the primary force in southern politics. This shift in power undermined the traditionally uncompromising support of the white South for Jim Crow practices. However, the transition proved far from smooth, with small-town and rural conservatives fighting a sustained rearguard action against racial reform. Some scholars propose that a smoother process of change could have occurred had the Supreme Court not selected the emotive issue of school desegregation as the target for its assault on southern apartheid. It is tempting to see in the scenes of violent disorder that accompanied the admission of black students to white campuses evidence that *Brown* retarded rather than advanced southern race relations. Southern authorities had started to make improvements to black educational facilities, albeit on a segregated basis, before the Supreme Court decision. There are nonetheless two reasons why this interpretation is unpersuasive. First, it overestimates the political influence of white moderates before *Brown*. Only when the policy of massive resistance proved politically bankrupt did moderates gain the strength and determination to push for minimum compliance with court desegregation mandates. Second, it underestimates the importance of the decision as a catalyst to *black* political activism. In the assessment of Martin Luther King, the ruling 'brought hope to millions of disinherited Negroes who had formerly dared only to dream of freedom'.[46] It was this new sense of hope that in part inspired Rosa Parks to launch a new phase of black protest when she refused to surrender her bus seat to a white passenger on a cold December day in Montgomery, Alabama.

Notes

1. *Brown* v. *Board of Education*, 347 U.S. 483 (1954).
2. Robert H. Ferrell, *Harry S. Truman and the Modern Presidency* (Boston, MA: Little, Brown and Company, 1983), p. 97. See also the evaluation of William E. Leuchtenburg that Truman's commitment to civil rights reflected his 'maturing convictions' (William E. Leuchtenburg, *The White House Looks South: Franklin D. Roosevelt, Harry S. Truman, Lyndon B. Johnson* (Baton Rouge: Louisiana State University Press, 2005), p. 170.
3. Michael R. Gardner, *Harry Truman and Civil Rights: Moral Courage and Political Risks* (Carbondale and Edwardsville: Southern Illinois University Press, 2002).
4. Mary L. Dudziak, *Cold War Civil Rights: Race and the Image of American Democracy* (Princeton, NJ, and Oxford: Princeton University Press, 2000), p. 12.
5. Jennifer E. Brooks, 'Winning the Peace: Georgia Veterans and the Struggle to Define the Political Legacy of World War II', *Journal of Southern History*, 66 (August 2000), p. 571.
6. Kari Fredrickson, *The Dixiecrat Revolt and the End of the Solid South, 1932–1968* (Chapel Hill and London: University of North Carolina Press, 2001), p. 57.
7. Steven F. Lawson (ed.), *To Secure These Rights: The Report of President Harry S. Truman's Committee on Civil Rights* (Boston, MA, and New York: Bedford/St. Martin's, 2004), p. 30; Numan V. Bartley, *The New South 1945–1980: The Story of the South's Modernization* (Baton Rouge: Louisiana State University Press, 1995), p. 77.
8. John Egerton, *Speak Now Against the Day: The Generation Before the Civil Rights Movement in the South* (New York: Alfred A. Knopf, 1994), p. 476; Bartley, *New South*, p. 82.
9. Fredrickson, *Dixiecrat Revolt*, p. 7
10. David R. Goldfield, *Promised Land: The South Since 1945* (Arlington Heights, IL: Harlan Davidson, 1987), p. 56.
11. Michael J. Klarman, 'How *Brown* Changed Race Relations: The Backlash Thesis', *Journal of American History*, 81 (June 1994), pp. 81–118. See also Gerald N. Rosenberg, *The Hollow Hope: Can Courts Bring About Social Change?* (Chicago: University of Chicago Press, 1991).
12. Egerton, *Speak Now Against the Day*, p. 521.
13. Robert Korstad and Nelson Lichtenstein, 'Opportunities Found and Lost: Labor, Radicals, and the Early Civil Rights Movement', *Journal of American History*, 75 (1988), pp. 786–811. See also Steve Rosswurm (ed.), *The CIO's Left-Led Unions* (New Brunswick, NJ: Rutgers University Press, 1992).

14. Bruce Nelson, *Divided We Stand: American Workers and the Struggle for Black Equality* (Princeton, NJ: Princeton University Press, 2001); Alan Draper, *Conflict of Interests: Organized Labor and the Civil Rights Movement in the South, 1954–1968* (Ithaca, NY: ILR Press, 1994); Robert J. Norrell, 'Caste in Steel: Jim Crow Careers in Birmingham, Alabama', *Journal of Southern History*, 73 (1986), p. 691.
15. Hodding Carter, *Southern Legacy* (Baton Rouge: Louisiana State University Press, 1950), pp. 89–90.
16. Jonathan Rosenberg, *How Far the Promised Land? World Affairs and the American Civil Rights Movement from the First World War to Vietnam* (Princeton, NJ: Princeton University Press, 2006), p. 188.
17. C. Vann Woodward, *The Strange Career of Jim Crow* (New York: Oxford University Press, third revised edition, 1974), pp. 145–6.
18. *Brown* v. *Board of Education*.
19. 'A Supreme Court Bomb!', *Richmond Afro-American*, 22 May 1954: *New York Amsterdam News*, 22 May 1954.
20. James T. Patterson, Brown *v.* Board of Education*: A Civil Rights Milestone and Its Troubled Legacy* (New York: Oxford University Press, 2001), p. 71.
21. Judge Tom P. Brady, *Black Monday* (Winona, MS: Association of Citizens' Councils, 1955).
22. *Brown* v. *Board of Education*, 349 U.S. 294 (1955).
23. Martin Gilbert, *The Dent Atlas of American History* (London: Dent, 1993), p. 105.
24. *New York Times*, 9 December 1956.
25. Numan V. Bartley, *The Rise of Massive Resistance: Race and Politics in the South During the 1950s* (Baton Rouge: Louisiana State University Press, 1969), pp. 13–14.
26. Charles W. Eagles, 'Toward New Histories of the Civil Rights Era', *Journal of Southern History*, 66 (2000), p. 842. For more information on the recent literature on massive resistance, see the Guide to Further Reading at the end of this book.
27. William D. Workman, Jr, *The Case for the South* (New York: Devin-Adair, 1960), p. 33; *The Citizens' Council*, April 1956.
28. Draper, *Conflict of Interests:* p. 18.
29. Tony Badger, 'Southerners Who Refused to Sign the Southern Manifesto', *Historical Journal*, 42 (June 1999), pp. 517–34; Tony Badger, '"The Forerunner of Our Opposition": Arkansas and the Southern Manifesto of 1956', *Arkansas Historical Quarterly*, 56 (Autumn 1997), pp. 353–60.
30. Carl Elliott, Sr and Michael D'Orso, *The Cost of Courage: The Journey of an American Congressman* (New York: Doubleday, 1992), p. 181.
31. John Bartlow Martin, *The Deep South Says "Never"* (New York: Ballantine Books, 1957), pp. 11–12.
32. John A. Morsell, Assistant to Executive Secretary, to Frank T. Simpson, State Civil Rights Commission, Connecticut, 6 December, 1957, Papers of the

NAACP, Part 20: White Resistance and Reprisals, 1956–1965, Reel 8: Group III, Series A, Administrative File, frames 365–6.
33. Clive Webb, *Fight Against Fear: Southern Jews and Black Civil Rights* (Athens: University of Georgia Press, 2001), pp. 43–68.
34. Jeff Woods, *Black Struggle, Red Scare: Segregation and Anti-Communism in the South, 1948–1968* (Baton Rouge: Louisiana State University Press, 2004), pp. 85–95.
35. David L. Chappell, *A Stone of Hope: Prophetic Religion and the Death of Jim Crow* (Chapel Hill: University of North Carolina Press, 2004).
36. Jane Dailey, 'Sex, Segregation and the Sacred after *Brown*', *Journal of American History*, 91 (June 2004), p. 134.
37. Michal R. Belknap, *Federal Law and Southern Order: Racial Violence and Constitutional Conflict* (Athens: University of Georgia Press, 1987), pp. 28–9.
38. *Time*, 17 September 1956; *Chicago Defender*, 22 September 1956; *Southern School News*, October 1956.
39. Stephen E. Ambrose, *Eisenhower, Vol. 2: The President, 1952–1969* (London: Allen and Unwin, 1984); Robert F. Burk, *Dwight D. Eisenhower: Hero and Politician* (Boston, MA: Twayne Publishers, 1986), p. 160.
40. Dwight D. Eisenhower, *The White House Years, Volume 2: Waging Peace, 1956–1961* (London: Heinemann, 1966), pp. 171, 175.
41. Bartley, *New South*, p. 256.
42. David R. Goldfield, *Black, White, and Southern: Race Relations and Southern Culture, 1940s to the Present* (Baton Rouge and London: Louisiana State University Press, 1990), p. 115.
43. Chester J. Pach, Jr and Elmo Richardson, *The Presidency of Dwight D. Eisenhower* (Lawrence: University of Kansas Press, revised edition, 1991), p. 148.
44. Fred I. Greenstein, *The Hidden-Hand Presidency: Eisenhower as Leader* (New York: Basic Books, 1982).
45. Stephen B. Oates, *Let the Trumpet Sound: A Life of Martin Luther King, Jr.* (New York: Harper & Row, 1982), p. 134.
46. James C. Cobb, *The* Brown *Decision, Jim Crow, & Southern Identity* (Athens: University of Georgia Press, 2005), p. 48.

Chapter 11

'WE SHALL OVERCOME': THE CIVIL RIGHTS MOVEMENT

By the mid-1960s, direct action protest by southern blacks had succeeded in dismantling the legal structure of segregation. It is important to stress that the civil rights movement did not appear out of a vacuum. As previous chapters demonstrated, southern blacks had mobilised with increasing force against white supremacy since the New Deal era. Historians have in recent years moved their analysis of the civil rights movement beyond the national leadership to grassroots activism at the local and state level. These studies have demonstrated that there was considerable continuity between the litigation-oriented era of the 1930s and 1940s and the later direct action phase of protest in the 1950s and 1960s. This has in turn led to a reassessment of the chronology of black activism. Scholars refer to 'The Long Civil Rights Movement', which started earlier and ended later than conventional narratives that cover only the years from 1954 to 1968. [1]

Academic interest in the historical foundations of the movement has allowed us to understand how it drew strength from social networks and institutional resources developed over many decades. The civil rights protests of the late 1950s and 1960s were nonetheless unprecedented both in terms of the mass participation of black protesters and the confrontational nature of their tactics. In the past, African Americans had attempted to promote incremental reform within the confines of segregation; now they launched a direct assault on the system itself. This chapter assesses the reasons for the success of the civil rights movement in destroying de jure segregation. It focuses in particular on how black activists created the public pressure that forced an often reluctant federal government to enact measures that finally toppled Jim Crow. The success of the movement owed not only to national leaders like Martin Luther King, Jr, but also to the efforts of thousands of ordinary people operating at a local level.

THE MONTGOMERY BUS BOYCOTT

Although the civil rights movement must be situated within a longer tradition of black protest, the era of mass direct action that started with the Montgomery bus boycott represented a new and more decisive phase. African Americans represented 70 per cent of all passengers on Montgomery buses. Their experiences were a daily reminder of their degraded status within the southern caste system. Alabama law reserved the front ten seats on a bus for white passengers and the back ten seats for blacks. Blacks could occupy the middle seats only so long as a white person was not left standing. Moreover, although blacks boarded the bus at the front in order to pay their fares, they then had to re-board at the back in order to take their seats. It was not uncommon for the bus to have already pulled away by the time they reached the rear door, leaving them stranded on the kerb.

Black activists had been waiting for an appropriate test case to challenge segregation on city buses. On 2 March 1955, a black high school student named Claudette Colvin had been arrested for refusing to surrender her seat to a white passenger. However, Colvin had physically resisted arrest, and as a result been charged with assault and battery as well as breaching segregation laws. She was also, despite being unmarried, expecting a baby. Colvin would therefore have been exposed to a ruthless assault on her character had she taken the stand in a test case. What was needed was a defendant with unimpeachable credentials. It was the arrest of Rosa Parks on Thursday, 1 December 1955 that provided community activists with the person they needed. Parks was a seamstress by profession, but she was also a seasoned political campaigner who had joined the NAACP in 1943 and served as the secretary of the local chapter. A few months before her arrest she had attended a workshop on desegregation at the Highlander Folk School in Tennessee.

The arrest of Parks acted as the catalyst for local blacks to boycott the buses. A number of individuals played a particularly important role in rallying the community. It is important to emphasise that these activists drew strength from the social networks they had helped to construct through years of campaigning to improve racial conditions in the city. The success of the boycott owed much to the political mobilisation of African Americans during the preceding decade. As historian Stewart Burns states, although Martin Luther King was the publicly identifiable figurehead of the boycott, he 'acted within a broad structure of grassroots leadership that had been preparing the ground for black community mobilization long before he arrived' in Montgomery.[2] NAACP leader Edgar Daniel Nixon planned a mass meeting in support of the boycott, and recruited reluctant black ministers to help promote the campaign. Nixon was a seasoned activist who used his connections as a member of the Brotherhood of Sleeping Car Porters, the trade union headed by A. Philip Randolph, to secure crucial financial support for the boycott. Jo Ann Robinson, a professor at Alabama State College, led the 300 members of the Women's Political Council (WPC) to print and distribute handbills publicising the boycott. Robinson had founded the WPC in 1949. In the years immediately prior to the boycott, the WPC tirelessly promoted such issues as black voter registration. The experience, organisational strength and personal contacts that WPC members attained during this time helped to facilitate their later mobilisation of the black community during the boycott. While men predominantly held leadership positions within the civil rights movement, female activists such as the members of the WPC formed its organisational backbone. Although slow to recognise the contribution of women both to the Montgomery bus boycott and to the broader movement, historians now emphasise the integral role they performed in organising and sustaining black protest.

On Monday, 5 December, black leaders established the Montgomery Improvement Association (MIA) to co-ordinate the boycott, and selected as its president a 26-year-old minister named Martin Luther King, Jr. That night King addressed a mass meeting at the Holt Street Baptist Church. The meeting ended with a resolution to continue the boycott until the demands of the MIA were met. What the MIA wanted was not the elimination of segregation, but rather improvements within the existing system: courteous treatment by white drivers, the employment of African American drivers on routes that travelled through black neighbourhoods, and the seating of passengers on a first-come, first-served basis. Despite these relatively modest demands, negotiations with bus company representatives and city council leaders broke down almost immediately. What had started out as a one-day protest now escalated into the most sustained campaign for racial reform in southern history.

The outcome of the boycott owed in some measure to the miscalculations of white authorities. City leaders pursued a policy of uncompromising resistance in reaction to black demands. The refusal of white authorities to offer any concession to the MIA stemmed from their fear that it would embolden blacks to launch further challenges to the colour line. In a demonstration of their determination to withstand such pressure, the members of the city commission joined the ranks of the White Citizens' Council. Local whites emulated their leaders, doubling the membership of the organisation from 6,000 to 12,000 in the early months of 1956. When they realised that they had seriously underestimated the resolve of the black community, whites also embarked on a campaign of intimidation and violence. White bosses dismissed black workers, and police officers harassed and arrested the drivers who had formed a car pool to transport black passengers around the city. On 26 January 1956, King was arrested for speeding. Four days later, dynamite exploded outside the homes of King and Nixon. Less than a month later, a federal grand jury indicted the leaders of the boycott.

Southern whites had long used such tactics to repress black political protest. However, the attempt to intimidate the black people of Montgomery proved disastrously counter-productive. Not only did it harden the will of blacks to stay off the buses, it also induced them to radicalise their demands and push for complete desegregation. With the support of the NAACP, the MIA filed a lawsuit to contest the segregation laws in federal court. The reaction of white authorities in Montgomery contrasted with that of city leaders in the Louisiana state capitol of Baton Rouge, who two years earlier resolved a similar boycott after only one week by negotiating a compromise that maintained segregation. That the tactics of Montgomery whites strengthened rather than weakened the boycott is illustrated by the indictment of MIA leaders. Whites believed that the indicted men would either submit feebly to the authorities or flee into hiding. Instead, in a public expression of their tenacity, the boycott leaders proudly marched to the police station, where they were met by a crowd of cheering supporters. The spirited resistance of black activists to white persecution also attracted international publicity, almost all of it favourable to their cause. Media coverage of the campaign provided crucial moral and financial support. Within a week of the indictments, MIA coffers had been flooded with an additional $12,000 in donations.

Despite the unrelenting opposition of whites, blacks sustained their boycott of the bus system for another nine months. In June 1956, a federal court in the case of *Browder* v. *Gayle* ruled segregation on city and state buses unconstitutional. White authorities still refused to accept surrender, and applied for an injunction against the car pool. However, it was too late. In November, the Supreme Court upheld the federal court decision. On 20 December, its ruling finally went into effect, and the triumphant MIA declared the end of the boycott.

Yet amid the chorus of cheers could be heard a dissenting voice that doubted the significance of the boycott. The NAACP, resentful that the MIA had not ceded to its authority, insisted with some justification that the desegregation of the buses owed less to the pressure of economic protest than its own litigation strategy. Nor did the boycott stimulate a mass movement of black protest across the South. Even in Montgomery, the MIA failed to build on the momentum created by the success of the campaign to push for the desegregation of other public facilities. The boycott was nonetheless important in a number of respects.

First, the media attention it attracted publicised to the world that blacks had not only a legal but a moral entitlement to be treated the same as whites. Second, the boycott demonstrated to blacks themselves that they could, through the power of collective action, overcome the racial terror of whites that had repressed them for so long. In practical terms, the accomplishments of the campaign may have been modest, but in psychological terms they were of immeasurable importance. White authorities had assumed at the outset that African Americans did not possess the determination or resources to sustain a long-term political protest. 'Come the first rainy day,' predicted Mayor William Gayle, 'and the Negroes will be back on the buses.'[3] Montgomery blacks proved him wrong. For more than a year, the boycott by black passengers remained more than 90 per cent effective. As Stewart Burns observes, the maintenance of the boycott owed to 'ordinary people acting in extraordinary ways'.[4] A disproportionate number of these foot soldiers were black women who drew upon a tradition of female activism within their churches. At the grassroots of the campaign, it was women who swelled the attendance of mass meetings, raised financial support and led by example in refraining from boarding the buses.

Third, the boycott elevated Martin Luther King to a position of international prominence as the pre-eminent civil rights leader of his generation. Despite his initial reluctance to lead the MIA, King had from the moment he addressed the audience at the Holt Street Baptist Church imposed his inspirational authority on the campaign. His speech claimed the moral high ground for blacks by contrasting their peaceful form of protest with the economic intimidation and terrorist violence of the White Citizens' Council and Ku Klux Klan. It also instilled the campaign with a sense of historical purpose guided by higher spiritual powers. King transformed the meaning of the boycott from a parochial struggle over segregated buses to a holy crusade that would benefit all mankind. '[W]hen the history books are written in the future, somebody will have to say "There lived a race of people, black people, fleecy locks and black complexion, of people who had the moral courage to stand up for their rights." And thereby they injected a new meaning into the veins of history and of civilization.'[5] The reaction of King to the bombing of his home reinforced his moral authority. When King returned from a mass meeting to the house, he was met by an angry throng of blacks, many of whom were armed and unwilling to comply with the orders of the police that they disperse. King succeeded in calming the crowd and averting any retributive violence. His asking of forgiveness for the bombers emphasised the courage and dignity of a black movement underpinned by Christian principles. 'I want it to be known the length and breadth of this land that if I am stopped this movement will not stop. If I am stopped our work will not stop. For what we are doing is right. What we are doing is just. And God is with us.'[6]

Following the success of the boycott, in February 1957 King founded the Southern Christian Leadership Conference (SCLC). However, the organisation initially floundered. It relied far too much on the inspirational leadership of King and his fellow ministers at the expense of a proper administrative infrastructure. The most startling illustration of this is the fact that the SCLC had only three members of staff: executive director Ella Baker and two secretaries. Baker was responsible for organising the principal SCLC campaign of the late 1950s, the Crusade for Citizenship. Ambitiously intended to register three million black voters, the campaign, as King later admitted, had barely scratched the surface of black disfranchisement. These years were nonetheless of great significance in terms of King's intellectual growth. In particular, the civil rights leader deepened his philosophical understanding of non-violent direct action. His visit to India in 1959, as a special guest of Prime Minister Jawaharlal Nehru, allowed him an opportunity to discuss Gandhian principles with some of the late Indian leader's disciples. Even so, it was a mounting sense of frustration on the part of a younger generation of black activists at the failure of older movement leaders like King to secure swifter and more widespread reform that led them to seize the political initiative at the dawn of the next decade.

THE STUDENT SIT-INS

On 1 February 1960, four black students from North Carolina A&T College in Greensboro sat down at the lunch counter in the downtown Woolworth's store and refused to leave when they were denied service. The following day, the four students – Ezell Blair, Franklin McCain, Joseph McNeil and David Richmond – returned. Only now, they were accompanied by twenty-three of their fellow classmates. By the end of the week, there were more than 300 student protesters.

The sit-in was not a new tactic. Scholars, such as Robert Weisbrot, who start their narrative of the civil rights movement with the sit-ins construct a false periodisation of history that ignores the continuity of black protest that occurred over the course of many decades.[7] The sit-in tactic had been pioneered by the Congress of Racial Equality (CORE) during the 1940s. In 1958, the NAACP Youth Council launched similar demonstrations in Oklahoma and Kansas; the following year, CORE revived its use of the sit-in at a lunch counter in Miami. The sit-ins of 1960 did nonetheless represent an important shift in black political action. None of the earlier protests had taken place in the heartland of the Jim Crow South, nor had they attracted national publicity. By contrast, the sit-ins of 1960 spread rapidly from Greensboro across the southern states. By April, seventy-eight communities had been affected by demonstrations involving 70,000 student activists, 3,000 of whom were arrested.

While the tactic was not new, the sit-ins also represented the start of a more militant phase in black activism. Although a boycott of buses could cause white transit authorities economic ruin, it was not possible for blacks to withdraw financial support from a business that refused to serve them. A more confrontational strategy was therefore needed to demonstrate the discriminatory exclusion of blacks. The readiness with which the students exposed themselves to the risk of violence and arrest also set the sit-ins apart from the bus boycotts of the 1950s. White authorities had long used the threat of imprisonment as a means of silencing black dissent. For many middle-class students, incarceration in a police cell risked not only physical endangerment but also personal disgrace. During the course of the demonstrations, the students not only overcame their fears of arrest but, in the words of John Lewis, learned to wear it as a 'badge of honor'.[8] The new-found confidence of southern black youth was exuberantly expressed in the protest songs they composed in response to their experiences. One of the most amusing of these anthems sardonically warned demonstrators 'You better leave segregation alone' because whites 'love segregation like a hound dog love a bone'.[9] The strength of the students' belief in the moral rightness of their cause is also testimony to the diminishing intellectual and cultural power of ideas about a natural racial hierarchy and the inability of blacks to interact on an equal basis with whites.

Although the sit-ins took the older black political leadership by surprise, most supported the campaign. While a small number of black college presidents succumbed to white political pressure and expelled student leaders, others refused to take disciplinary action. The NAACP Legal Defense and Educational Fund also offered to represent arrested students. Demonstrators in addition enlisted white support not only from northerners who organised boycotts of local branches of stores such as Woolworth's, but also from a small number of southern students who broke ranks to join the movement. Even some segregationists candidly admitted their admiration for the dignity with which the students endured beatings and abuse by white mobs. Newspaper editor James Kilpatrick contrasted 'the colored students, in coats, white shirts, ties' with the white hoodlums 'come to heckle, a ragtail rabble, slack-jawed, black-jacketed, grinning fit to kill'.[10]

The sit-ins had a substantial impact on the struggle for racial equality. In the Deep South, where resistance to racial reform remained most determined, the sit-ins failed to secure the desegregation of lunch counters, as white authorities launched a repressive crackdown on the demonstrators. However, in the more moderate Upper South the students successfully forced white businesses to integrate their facilities. The sit-ins were also important in another respect. In April 1960, 126 student delegates from across the southern states met at Shaw University in Raleigh, North Carolina, to discuss how to build on the political momentum created by the protests. The conference was sponsored by the SCLC, and King was the keynote speaker. When the delegates decided to establish a new organisation to co-ordinate their campaigning, they nonetheless chose not to affiliate it with the SCLC. The reason for this owed much to the influence of SCLC executive director Ella Baker, who had become disillusioned with what she believed was the undue reliance of the organisation on the cult of personality that surrounded King. Baker encouraged the students not to emulate the 'leader-centered group pattern of organization', but instead to develop a more democratic 'group-centered leadership'.[11] The delegates responded by establishing the autonomous Student Nonviolent Coordinating Committee (SNCC, commonly pronounced 'Snick'), a temporary organisation that assumed permanent status after a meeting in Atlanta six months later. The democratic ethos of SNCC led to a loose chain of command that offered young activists a more participatory voice in the protest movement. Despite the infamous remark of SNCC president Stokely Carmichael that the best position for women within the movement was prone, sexism was not as endemic as in other civil rights organisations, and female activists attained a prominent status.

The emphasis on non-violence in the name of the new organisation owed less to the influence of King than of James Lawson. A black Methodist minister based in Nashville, Lawson had been imprisoned because of his conscientious objection to the Korean War, and had later worked in India as a missionary, where he studied the teachings of Mohandas Gandhi. At the time of the sit-ins, he worked as a field secretary of the Fellowship of Reconciliation. Lawson had a profound influence on a number of student leaders whom he trained in non-violence at workshops held in Nashville. Among them were such prominent activists as James Bevel, John Lewis and Diane Nash, all of whom would help shape the character and direction of civil rights protest in the 1960s. Delegates at the Raleigh meeting adopted a statement of purpose authored by Lawson that declared: 'We affirm the philosophical or religious ideal of nonviolence as the foundation of our purpose, the pre-supposition of our faith, and the manner of our action.'[12] Despite the statement, there were many within the ranks of SNCC who accepted non-violence not as a philosophy of life but simply as a political strategy. They were therefore willing to embrace non-violence only so long as it secured political gains for the movement, and refused to rule out the use of self-defence in those circumstances where it did not. Over the next few years, the limitations of their support would be exposed by the brute force inflicted by white racists on SNCC field workers.

There was a clearer consensus among members that direct action was the most appropriate means to combat white racism. In contrast to the conciliatory tone of the SCLC, SNCC did not conceal its contempt for the litigation strategy of the NAACP, which it unduly criticised as hopelessly anachronistic. The formation of SNCC therefore revealed the fault lines within the movement that would in time split it wide open.

THE FREEDOM RIDES AND THE KENNEDY ADMINISTRATION

The promotion of black civil rights was not a priority for the Kennedy administration. As a presidential candidate, Kennedy had attempted to establish his credentials as a champion of the cause by securing the release from prison of Martin Luther King. The SCLC leader had been reluctantly persuaded by SNCC activists to participate in a sit-in at a lunch counter in downtown Atlanta. On 19 October 1960, police arrested fifty-two demonstrators, including King, who was sentenced to four months' hard labour at the Reidsville state prison. Kennedy's liberal advisors sensed an opportunity to promote his candidacy to black voters. They persuaded him to communicate his support for King by telephoning his distressed wife, Coretta. Kennedy's brother Robert, who had initially opposed intervening in the case because it would alienate white southern voters, eventually negotiated with the judge for the release of the imprisoned civil rights leader. The plan proved decisive: black voters helped to secure Kennedy a narrow victory over Republican candidate Richard Nixon in the November election.

African Americans therefore had high expectations that Kennedy would prove more pro-active on civil rights than had Eisenhower. However, they were soon to be bitterly disappointed. Kennedy was constrained by his failure to secure a popular mandate. He had defeated Nixon by only 112,000 votes, or 0.2 per cent of all ballots cast. To secure approval of new legislation, the president needed the support of conservative southern Democrats who controlled most of the important congressional committees. The introduction of a civil rights law would alienate exactly these politicians, who would use their power as committee chairmen to thwart passage of his other legislative proposals.

Many historians nonetheless conclude that the president could have overcome legislative opposition. Despite the positive evaluations of scholars such as Irving Bernstein and James Giglio, most historians are critical of the civil rights record of the Kennedy administration.[13] In particular, they stress that one of the most serious obstacles to federal action on the race issue was Kennedy himself. In a similar manner to some biographers of Eisenhower, a number of historians who are otherwise sympathetic towards Kennedy criticise his timid and compromising approach to civil rights. Robert Dallek, for instance, claims that Kennedy could have taken the moral high ground by pushing for a civil rights bill from the outset of his presidency. His failure to do so, he concludes, demonstrated both an underestimation of northern popular support for congressional action on civil rights and an overestimation of the strength of white southern opposition.[14] Other writers are even more damning in their assessment of the Kennedy administration. The title of the most recent study of the president's civil rights record states that he was nothing more than a 'Bystander' who watched events unravel from the distance of the White House. According to the author, Nick Bryant, Kennedy only took decisive action when forced to resolve racial crises that his own prevarication had helped to create.[15] As Bryant and others point out, Kennedy simply did not perceive civil rights as a political priority. On the contrary, he focused his attention far more on an aggressive foreign policy against the Soviet Union. In his inaugural address of January 1961, the newly-elected president had made no mention of the problem of racial discrimination, or how he intended to deal with it. Instead, he had used the occasion to prioritise his commitment to contain the spread of international Communism. As Robert Weisbrot observes, for Kennedy 'the challenge to democracy was symbolized far more by the Red hammer and sickle than by a white hood and burning cross'.[16]

Civil rights activists understood that more direct action was needed to force the hand of the Kennedy administration. They drew inspiration from a campaign that had occurred in the wake of the Second World War. In April 1947, the Congress of Racial Equality sent eight black and eight white activists on a Journey of Reconciliation. The activists travelled aboard buses through the Upper South in a test of the recent Supreme Court decision in *Morgan* v. *Virginia* outlawing segregation on interstate transport. Although they failed to force the compliance of southern authorities, their protest strategy provided a model for future action. In 1960, the Supreme Court ruled in *Boynton* v. *Virginia* that segregation on interstate transportation was unconstitutional. The following May, CORE launched a campaign to pressure the Kennedy administration into enforcing the decision. Under the leadership of James Farmer, thirteen activists set out aboard two buses on a Freedom Ride from Washington, DC to New Orleans.

Other than an attack by white youths in Rock Hill, South Carolina, the riders encountered relatively minor resistance as they travelled through the Upper South. Their luck did not last. As the first bus approached Anniston, Alabama, a white mob forced it to stop and then slashed its tyres. Although the bus pulled away, it soon ground to a complete halt. A bomb thrown through one of its windows exploded as the riders scrambled for cover. The mob then boarded the second bus and inflicted a furious beating on the other riders. Bruised but unbowed, the CORE activists continued on to Birmingham. Police Commissioner Eugene Connor had prepared for the arrival of the buses by withdrawing his officers and allowing Klansmen an opportunity to assault the riders. Unable to secure a driver who would transport them to Montgomery, most of the activists decided to abandon their plans and fly to New Orleans. SNCC activists from Nashville nonetheless resolved to continue the Freedom Rides. Attorney General Robert Kennedy negotiated with bus company officials to provide the riders with transportation, and convinced Alabama governor John Patterson to afford them police protection. However, when the bus reached Montgomery, the police stood on the sidelines as a mob assaulted the riders. Justice Department official John Siegenthaler, who had been sent to secure the protection of the activists, was himself beaten senseless by the mob. Whites then surrounded the First Baptist Church, where black activists including Martin Luther King had gathered to welcome the riders. Confronted by the threat of anarchic violence, Robert Kennedy pressured a reluctant Governor Patterson to order the Alabama National Guard to escort those trapped inside the church to safety.

The reaction of the Kennedy administration to the Freedom Rides exposed its lack of moral commitment to the civil rights cause. In many respects, the use of troops paralleled the response of President Eisenhower to the Little Rock crisis. On both occasions, the administration needed to reassert its authority over recalcitrant southern authorities or risk humiliation, and to repair the damage caused by domestic racial violence to the international reputation of the United States. At the time of the Freedom Rides, President Kennedy was preparing for a summit meeting in Vienna with Soviet premier Nikita Khrushchev. He feared that his Cold War adversary would use the violence in Alabama to demonstrate the hypocrisy of American claims to leadership of the free world, and to portray Kennedy himself as a weak politician who could not maintain law and order. It was these pragmatic considerations, more than any principled recognition of the Freedom Riders' cause, that led the administration to intervene. Reluctantly forced to side with the activists, Kennedy nonetheless confided that 'this whole thing and the people behind it were a giant pain in the ass'.[17]

The refusal of the administration to recognise the legitimacy of the campaign also determined its reaction when the riders announced they would travel on to Mississippi. Robert Kennedy secured an agreement with Mississippi senator James Eastland to protect the physical safety of the riders, but also to arrest them for violating segregation laws. He also attempted to avert a repeat of the violence that had occurred in Alabama by negotiating with movement leaders for a 'cooling-off period'. Far from acceding to the appeals of the federal government, black activists organised a Freedom Ride Coordinating Committee that sent riders from across the country to Mississippi. During the summer of 1961, police arrested 328 activists at the bus terminal in the state capital of Jackson, and incarcerated them in the notorious Parchman Farm.

Despite this cold indifference on the part of federal officials towards the fate of the demonstrators, the Freedom Rides were an important victory for the civil rights movement. The reaction of the Kennedy administration to the Freedom Rides demonstrated that it was more concerned with the preservation of law and order than the promotion of civil rights. Nonetheless, the relentless pressure created by the campaign forced the administration to take positive action. Robert Kennedy pushed the Interstate Commerce Commission to issue an order effective from 1 November 1961 that prohibited segregation in interstate travel. Despite some resistance in the Deep South, black activists succeeded over the following months in enforcing desegregation of the public transport system. The Freedom Rides were also crucial in restoring the fortunes of CORE, which now emerged as one of the most important forces within the civil rights coalition.

Determined to avert further racial violence, the Kennedy administration attempted to steer the civil rights movement away from direct action and towards voter registration. In April 1962, it launched the Voter Education Project (VEP), which provided direct funding from northern philanthropic organisations for civil rights groups to register blacks on the electoral rolls. All of the main civil rights organisations participated in the VEP. Despite their scepticism about the motivations of the Kennedy administration, SNCC and CORE enthusiastically launched voter registration drives in the small-town and rural areas of the Deep South, where black disfranchisement was at its most pervasive.

In July 1961, SNCC activist Robert Moses answered an invitation from local NAACP leader C. C. Bryant to initiate a registration campaign in McComb, Mississippi. Moses and other SNCC staff members suffered abuse and beatings at the hands of white racists. On 25 September, black farmer Herbert Lee, who had attempted to register to vote, was shot dead. A white jury acquitted the man responsible for his murder, state representative E. H. Hurst, on the grounds that he had acted in self-defence. SNCC activists were infuriated at the failure of the federal government to fulfil its commitment to protect civil rights workers and voter applicants from racial intimidation and violence. The Justice Department insisted that it did not have the jurisdiction to intervene in matters of state policing. However, in many instances it was the police themselves who were responsible for the assaults on movement activists. The failure of federal authorities to ensure the physical safety of voter registration workers severely curtailed the impact of the VEP. In 1962 and 1963, the VEP provided $50,000 in support of voter registration drives in Mississippi. However, the repressive violence of white racists meant that less than 4,000 new black voters were enrolled across the entire state; almost ten times that number still remained unregistered.[18]

The failure of the Kennedy administration to protect black activists in Mississippi owed to the unwillingness of the president to alienate influential southern politicians. This reluctance to take a more confrontational stance on civil rights resulted, in at least one instance, in death and disorder. In September 1962, Governor Ross Barnett rallied white opposition to the enrolment of a black student named James Meredith at the University of Mississippi. Robert Kennedy attempted to secure an agreement that would entrust responsibility for law and order with Barnett, while allowing him to maintain his reputation among segregationists. While the negotiations dragged on, demagogues seized the initiative. When Meredith arrived on campus under the escort of federal marshals, white protesters went on the rampage. The riot resulted in the deaths of two people and the wounding of another 375, twenty-eight of them with gunshot injuries.

DECAY AND REBIRTH: THE ALBANY AND BIRMINGHAM CAMPAIGNS

Frustrated at the political caution of the Kennedy administration, the SCLC attempted to pressure the federal government into implementing civil rights reform. The failure and success of this strategy was dramatised by the campaigns in Albany and Birmingham.

As part of its efforts to mobilise small-town and rural blacks in the Deep South, SNCC sent its activists into the Black Belt of Georgia. In October 1961, SNCC activists Cordell Reagon and Charles Sherrod started to mobilise the black community of Albany, in the south-western part of the state. The two men recruited black youths to a series of workshops on non-violent direct action, and then launched a sit-in of the local bus station. In November, community leaders formed the Albany Movement and elected Dr William G. Anderson as their president. During the next several weeks, the Albany Movement organised a series of mass meetings, protest marches and economic boycotts of white businesses. The demonstrations led to the arrest of more than 500 activists.

When city authorities proved reluctant to reach a settlement, Anderson called on Martin Luther King to offer his support for the protesters. Although SNCC staff feared that the arrival of the SCLC would undermine their efforts to foster a grassroots movement in Albany, they understood that King would attract the national publicity needed to pressure white officials. On 15 December, King received a rapturous response when he addressed an audience at the Shiloh Baptist Church. When city leaders still refused to negotiate, he and Ralph Abernathy led a march in which they and more than 250 other demonstrators were arrested. The Kennedy administration, anxious to avert negative publicity, pressured local authorities to secure a settlement with the protesters. Negotiations between the two sides resulted in an agreement from the Albany Movement to suspend demonstrations in return for the formation of a bi-racial committee to address its demands. King and Abernathy, who had vowed to rally support by remaining in jail, posted bond and withdrew from Albany. In their absence, the city authorities reneged on their agreement. Not until the SCLC leaders returned for sentencing in July 1962 did the Albany Movement renew mass protests.

Despite the success of the Albany Movement in mobilising community activism, the campaign collapsed amid bitter recrimination between its members. Numerous forces conspired to frustrate the campaign. One of the most important obstacles with which the Albany Movement had to contend was the wily chief of police, Laurie Pritchett. Pritchett had read King's memoir of the Montgomery bus boycott, *Stride Toward Freedom,* and this enabled him to anticipate his opponent's tactics. King attempted to highlight the plight of local blacks by precipitating a dramatic conflict between the protesters and the police. By ordering his men to use the utmost restraint in arresting black activists, Pritchett succeeded in preserving community order and removing the threat of federal intervention. He also frustrated the efforts of protesters to publicise their cause by filling local jails. The chief of police averted this situation by securing the use of alternative facilities in surrounding counties. He even clandestinely arranged for King to have his bond paid, forcing a reluctant and embarrassed civil rights leader to leave prison.

The carefully co-ordinated response of white authorities contrasted with the personal and political schisms that undermined the unity of black protesters. Tensions and rivalries between the various civil rights organisations destabilised the Albany Movement from the outset. The NAACP refused to support it because it had been established by SNCC activists whom it accused of irresponsible radicalism. SNCC activists in turn welcomed the publicity that the participation of the SCLC attracted, but resented the assumption of authority by King and his lieutenants. The mounting suspicion and mistrust of SNCC members towards the imperious attitude of the SCLC would later lead to bitter feuding that destabilised not only a specific campaign but the movement itself. In Albany, the divisiveness of black leaders weakened their ability to maintain morale and discipline within the ranks. On 24 July 1962, black youths communicated their mounting anger and frustration by throwing bricks and bottles at the police. Pritchett exploited the opportunity to compare the unruliness of the movement with the discipline of his own officers. 'See them non-violent rocks?' he sarcastically asked reporters.[19]

It might have been possible for the Albany Movement to surmount some of these problems had it more carefully planned the campaign. King intended neither to lead the protests nor to be imprisoned. However, he allowed the wave of enthusiasm that greeted his speech at the Shiloh Baptist Church to sweep him along without knowing where it headed. King was simply not prepared to lead the protests. The Albany Movement also launched its campaign without collecting the money needed to post bond for imprisoned protesters. Nor did it select an appropriate focus for its campaign, instead launching a diffuse assault on segregation in all aspects of public life. It has also been asserted that the invitation from Anderson to King was a miscalculation, since city leaders were already on the point of reaching a settlement. The presence of the SCLC leader led the Albany Movement to increase its demands, which in turn stiffened the resistance of white officials.[20] By August 1962, nine months of demonstrations had done nothing to breach the defences of Jim Crow in Albany. King cut his losses and abandoned the community. Although the Albany Movement continued throughout the 1960s to campaign for racial reform, it never fully regained momentum.

The civil rights movement faced an uncertain future after the failure of the Albany campaign. Internal dissent mounted, with some activists expressing their disillusionment with both the tactics of the SCLC and the leadership of

Martin Luther King. No issue weighed more heavily on the minds of activists than their inability to force federal government intervention in Albany. The refusal of the Kennedy administration to take sides in the dispute had doomed the protests to defeat. What the movement needed was a demonstration of the moral urgency of the race issue that would push it to the top of the domestic political agenda. That breakthrough came as a result of an audacious campaign by the SCLC in the notoriously racist city of Birmingham, Alabama.

Birmingham had the reputation of being the most segregated city in the United States. A strong recruiting ground for the Ku Klux Klan, its violently repressive political climate had earned it the bleak sobriquet 'Bombingham'. The principal force of racial terror was Commissioner of Public Safety Eugene 'Bull' Connor, who used his command of the police to intimidate, assault and arrest those who dared promote reform. Yet it was precisely because of its appalling reputation that Birmingham was chosen as the target of the SCLC campaign. As Birmingham activist Reverend Fred Shuttlesworth asserted: 'If you can break the back of segregation in Birmingham, Alabama, then you can break the back of segregation all over the nation.'[21]

Unlike Albany, the SCLC started the Birmingham campaign with several advantages. King was not properly prepared for the Albany campaign and as a result could not impose complete control over a divided local movement. The SCLC leader established a clearer line of authority in Birmingham. He benefited in particular from close strategic planning with the aforementioned Reverend Shuttlesworth, head of the Alabama Christian Movement for Human Rights, a local SCLC affiliate. In Albany, King had fought against a unified front from the white power structure. By contrast, with an imminent mayoral election, the white community in Birmingham was split between those who supported the extremist Bull Connor and others who backed the moderate Albert Boutwell. The Albany Movement had also suffered from a failure to define clearly its objectives. King now understood that a broad-based assault on segregation could result in a lack of strategic focus. In Birmingham, he therefore directed his efforts on a more clearly defined goal: the desegregation of downtown stores.

Despite its elaborate planning, the SCLC campaign experienced a less than auspicious start. The SCLC was forced to postpone the campaign in order to allow for the election of Albert Boutwell as mayor. When the protests eventually commenced on 3 May, King was taken aback by the strength of local black opposition. The black middle class in particular believed that the new administration should be given an opportunity to introduce reforms. The SCLC campaign could prove counter-productive, as it would arouse renewed racial hostilities. Although Connor continued to hold his position as Commissioner of Public Safety, he too confounded King. The SCLC anticipated that Connor would play into their hands by ordering a violent crackdown on civil rights protests. By exposing the brutal realities of white racism, the activists would create public pressure for federal government intervention. However, Connor exercised unusual self-control.

In an effort to improve the faltering momentum of the campaign, King was arrested during a march on Good Friday, 12 April. The timing of the arrest imbued King's actions with the symbolism of Christian martyrdom. In his prison cell, King read a letter published in the local newspaper from eight white clergymen, criticising him for creating renewed racial tensions at a time when real change had seemed imminent. King responded by penning his passionately worded 'Letter from Birmingham City Jail'. A scathing indictment of white liberals who urged greater caution, this document stands as the most thorough articulation of King's philosophy of non-violent direct action.

On his release from prison, King still faced the problem of how to crack the resolve of Connor. SCLC activist James Bevel offered the solution. On 2 May, thousands of black schoolchildren marched from the Sixteenth Street Baptist Church into the arms of arresting officers. Within a week, more than 2,000 children were in police custody. Confronted by the taunts of the children, Connor finally lost control. Under his command, the police turned dogs on the protesters. Those activists who failed to disperse were then assaulted with high-pressure water hoses.

There were some who criticised the SCLC for inciting the violence that erupted on the streets of Birmingham. The confrontational use of schoolchildren elicited particular criticism. However, as King asserted in the 'Letter from Birmingham Jail', the SCLC did not create the racial disorders that accompanied its campaigns, 'We merely bring to the surface the tension that is already alive.'[22] The SCLC also did its utmost to protect demonstrators from the threat of death or serious injury. It instilled in its supporters a strong sense of discipline, restricting the scale of violence by refusing to retaliate against white racists. The presence of the media also constrained the actions of the police. Although some of the demonstrators did suffer wounds, the repressive tactics used by Connor had a dramatic, rather than lethal, impact.

The scenes of racial brutality on the streets of Birmingham drew international condemnation. Soviet newspapers such as *Pravda* used the opportunity to ridicule the failure of the federal government to fulfil the ideals of American democracy. An embarrassed Kennedy administration sent Justice Department official Burke Marshall to negotiate a settlement between Birmingham merchants and the SCLC. The Birmingham campaign demonstrated the importance not only of television, but also of radio to the civil rights movement. As Brian Ward has shown, black radio stations helped to co-ordinate the mobilisation of demonstrators in the downtown area through the use of coded messages, such as the announcement of a 'big party' due to take place in Kelly Ingram Park. This form of communication enabled the SCLC to outmanoeuvre the police by restricting their information on where, and in what numbers, activists would march.[23]

Some activists, including Fred Shuttlesworth, believed that the SCLC should have used public outrage at the brutality of the police to push for more concessions. White racists also continued to resist enforcement of reform. On 15 September, Klansmen bombed the Sixteenth Street Baptist Church, killing four black girls and injuring twenty-two others. The Birmingham campaign was nonetheless a momentous achievement. Considering the strength of segregationist resistance before the SCLC arrived in the city, the settlement amounted to an important step forward in local race relations. The success of the SCLC in pressuring the Kennedy administration also represented a significant accomplishment for the movement. Birmingham was additionally important because it inspired other blacks to launch similar campaigns across the southern states. The scale of protest was unprecedented. Within ten weeks of the settlement, at least 758 demonstrations took place in seventy-five cities.[24] As Wyatt T. Walker anticipated, success in Birmingham encouraged southern blacks to believe that they could bring about the downfall of segregation throughout the region.

The dramatic demonstrations of black unrest and white resistance across the southern states compelled the Kennedy administration to reassess the civil rights issue. Faced with the threat of further racial disorder, President Kennedy accepted that he had underestimated the determination of white southerners to defend segregation. During his first two years in office, he had opposed presenting civil rights legislation to Congress on the grounds that it would split the Democratic Party along sectional lines. However, on 11 June 1963 – the day that Governor George Wallace performed his theatrical pretence of obstructing the entrance of two black students to the University of Alabama – Kennedy announced in a televised address to the nation his intention to secure passage of a comprehensive civil rights bill.

In an attempt to promote public support of the bill, civil rights leaders organised a March on Washington. On 28 August 1963, Martin Luther King addressed an audience of 250,000 people from the steps of the Lincoln Memorial. His stirring 'I Have a Dream' speech captured the popular imagination. King wrapped his language in the traditional symbols of American identity: patriotism, religious conviction, the Declaration of Independence and the Constitution. The speech resonated all the more powerfully because of the way the SCLC leader portrayed the black freedom struggle as part of the broader moral redemption of the entire American people: 'I still have a dream. It is a dream deeply rooted in the American dream that one day this nation will rise up and live out the true meaning of its creed – we hold these truths to be self-evident, that all men are created equal.'[25]

Despite the efforts of black leaders, the civil rights bill continued to face entrenched opposition from southern politicians. When President Kennedy was assassinated in Dallas on 22 November 1963, congressional resistance seemed insurmountable without serious concessions of a kind that would undermine the impact of the bill. The SCLC attempted to maintain the pressure on Congress through a direct action campaign in St Augustine, Florida. A series of violent assaults on black protesters during May and June 1964 maintained public focus on the civil rights issue. The outcome of the campaign was nonetheless inconclusive. Locally, the SCLC failed to secure significant concessions from the recalcitrant white political establishment. Nationally, the demonstrations did little to weaken the resolve of conservative opponents of the civil rights bill.

It took months of persistent pressure from civil rights and religious groups, coupled with the formidable political talents of new president Lyndon Johnson, to secure passage of the legislation. Johnson was not only more sympathetic than Kennedy had been to the civil rights cause, he also possessed more skill and experience as a political negotiator. As a senator, he had demonstrated considerable dexterity in establishing a middle position between northern liberals and southern conservatives, refusing to sign the Southern Manifesto in 1956 but helping to secure enactment of the Civil Rights Act the following year. Johnson now invested his enormous energy and ability to construct a bi-partisan coalition that defeated a southern filibuster to attain passage of the new civil rights bill.

Signed into law by Johnson on 2 July 1964, the Civil Rights Act was a more radical document than the bill his predecessor introduced to Congress. The act outlawed segregation in public accommodations and empowered the federal government to file suit to desegregate school districts and withhold funds from school boards that discriminated against blacks. It also established an Equal Employment Opportunities Commission and outlawed job discrimination on the grounds not only of race but also religion, national origin and sex. Despite some resistance in the Deep South, white southerners demonstrated relative calm in complying with the integration of public accommodations. However, opposition to school desegregation persisted in large parts of the region, as did the refusal to hire and promote black employees. The act also failed to address the pervasive problem of black disfranchisement. Although the new law represented a decisive victory for the movement, it needed to rally forces once more to win the crusade against white supremacy.

MISSISSIPPI GODDAM

Despite the success of the movement in securing federal legislation, the Civil Rights Act had little impact on the lives of African Americans in the state of Mississippi. SNCC had spearheaded civil rights protests in the state since the early 1960s, but the repressive political climate had impeded its progress. In 1964, the movement launched a massive campaign to publicise the plight of disfranchised blacks and pressure the federal government into taking interventionist action. However, the failure of the campaign would further sow the seeds of discontent among militant activists that would, in time, germinate into the Black Power movement.

Mississippi was the most notoriously racist state in the Union. According to journalist Nicholas Von Hoffman, the white power structure had succeeded in protecting against the civil rights reforms sweeping through other parts of the South. The state, he concluded, 'thinks of itself as a sovereign nation in loose affiliation with the rest of America'.[26] Although African Americans represented more than 40 per cent of the state population, they had no proportionate political power: only one in twenty adult blacks were registered to vote. The acceleration of mechanisation in agriculture after the Second World War had also brought economic ruin to many sharecropping families in the cotton-growing region of the Delta. By the early 1960s, the median family income of black families in Mississippi was a mere $1,444 per annum, one-third that of whites.[27]

What most distinguished Mississippi was the brute violence with which whites asserted their racial dominion over blacks. In the summer of 1955, Emmett Till, a black teenager from Chicago, went to visit his uncle in the small town of Money. Unaccustomed to southern racial mores, Till whistled at or flirted with the white female owner of a store at which he called in for refreshments. On 28 August, the husband of the woman, Roy Bryant, and his half-brother, J. W. Milam, kidnapped, tortured and murdered the black youth. Although police arrested the two men, a white jury acquitted them after little more than an hour of deliberation. One juror later remarked that the decision would have been reached even sooner if his colleagues had not stopped for a soda break. The political mobilisation of Mississippi blacks also led to a terrorist backlash by whites. On 12 June 1963, white supremacist Byron De

La Beckwith shot dead NAACP state leader Medgar Evers in the driveway of his home. The incident in part inspired one of the most confrontational protest songs of the era, Nina Simone's 'Mississippi Goddam':

> Oh, but this whole country is full of lies
> You're all gonna die and die like flies[28]

The frustration and bitterness of Simone towards both the federal government and the more cautious civil rights leaders would soon also be voiced by activists in Mississippi.

SNCC and CORE activists had first arrived in the state during the early 1960s, when they launched a series of voter registration drives. In February 1962, the two groups, in conjunction with the SCLC and NAACP, established the Council of Federated Organizations (COFO). State NAACP president Aaron Henry served as president, Robert Moses as programme director and David Dennis as his assistant. SNCC was the dominant force within the coalition. Between 1961 and 1963, its activists toiled in adverse conditions to mobilise Mississippi blacks as an electoral force. SNCC drew substantially on the community networks that local black women had long established through their families, churches and social groups. The commitment of SNCC to the cultivation of indigenous grassroots activism created important opportunities for local women such as sharecropper Fannie Lou Hamer, who defied eviction and assault in registering as a voter.

In July 1963, white activist Allard Lowenstein proposed that COFO organise a Freedom Vote, a mock ballot that would dramatise the determination of blacks to be included in the electoral process. Run parallel to the official gubernatorial election, the Freedom Vote resulted in 83,000 African Americans casting ballots in support of Aaron Henry as governor, and white chaplain Ed King as lieutenant governor. The success of the campaign encouraged activists to plan a larger demonstration the following summer. From the outset, the decision to recruit white northern volunteers drew fierce debate among black civil rights workers. Although white students had participated in the Freedom Vote, their patronising attitude towards SNCC staff members had created considerable friction. The efforts of Allard Lowenstein to commandeer the campaign had also antagonised SNCC activists because it threatened to undermine their efforts to build a sustainable local black leadership. Robert Moses nonetheless convinced the sceptics that the involvement of wealthy white northerners in the Freedom Summer would attract national publicity, creating pressure on the federal government to intervene.

The first group of volunteers had only recently arrived at a training school in Ohio, when word reached them of the disappearance of three civil rights workers. On 21 June 1964, Michael Schwerner, a white CORE staff member, set out with James Chaney, a black Mississippian who worked as a volunteer for CORE, and white student activist Andrew Goodman to investigate the burning of a black church in Neshoba County. They never returned. Arrested for an alleged traffic violation by Deputy Sheriff Cecil Price, the three men were released from prison but then stopped on a remote rural road by Klansmen who shot them dead. President Johnson ordered FBI director J. Edgar Hoover to launch an investigation. The search for the missing men eventually led to the discovery of their corpses, which had been buried in an earthen dam near the town of Philadelphia.

However, the prompt response of federal authorities simply served to antagonise SNCC and CORE activists, who believed that the Johnson administration had acted only because two of the murdered men were white. The failure of the federal government to provide protection for other Freedom Summer workers compounded their mistrust. During the course of the campaign, eighty civil rights activists suffered physical assault, a further four receiving serious injuries. Terrorists bombed sixty-five black homes and churches, and police made more than 1,000 arrests. The relentlessness of white violence contributed to voting rights workers registering a meagre 1,600 blacks.[29]

The apparent racial double standard amongst federal officials demolished what little faith many SNCC and CORE staff members still had in the conventional tactics of civil rights protest. Most black activists had embraced non-violence less as a moral principle than as a strategic means to an end. They were therefore willing to abandon it when it failed to secure results. Some black radicals had long since maintained the need for African Americans to practise armed self-defence against white racists. The most notable of these militants was Robert F. Williams, president of the NAACP chapter in Monroe, North Carolina. In the face of persistent violence from the Klan, Williams organised the Black Armed Guard to defend the local black community. The brutal repression of civil rights protest in Mississippi convinced many Freedom Summer activists that non-violence was no longer a viable strategy. Dave Dennis captured the spirit of disillusionment and anger shared by many when he delivered an emotional address at the funeral of James Chaney. As he later reflected, he 'was in a fantasy world' to have believed that racial progress could be accomplished through non-violence. On the contrary, 'you cannot make a man change by speaking a foreign language, he has to understand what you're talking about – this country operates, operated then and still operates, on violence'.[30] Other activists had drawn the same conclusion. Across the state line in Jonesboro, Louisiana, black militants, many of them war veterans, took up arms as members of the Deacons for Defense and Justice.

Relations between black and white Freedom Summer workers also caused the former to reassess the merits of inter-racial activism. Black activists bitterly resented the tendency of their white counterparts to push them aside and assume positions of leadership. The colour of white activists' skins also proved an impediment to their efforts to register local blacks as voters. Most Mississippi blacks had learned through experience not to trust whites, and it was difficult for them to overcome their suspicion of the white volunteers who offered promises of help. Finally, sexual relationships between white female volunteers and black male activists fuelled bitter resentment on the part of black women within the movement. Even a racially progressive organisation such as SNCC could be destabilised by the reactionary gender politics of male activists who, at times, pressured women into affairs. 'Sex is one thing;' concluded one black female activist shortly after the Freedom Summer; 'the Movement is another. And the two shouldn't mix.'[31]

The fate of the Mississippi Freedom Democratic Party (MFDP) confirmed to many activists the futility of mainstream civil rights tactics. COFO founded the MFDP in an attempt to unseat the all-white delegation sent by the regular Mississippi Democratic Party to the national party convention. When the convention met in Atlantic City in August 1964, many southern delegates supported the Mississippi regulars, and threatened to walk out if they were not seated. Lyndon Johnson, fearful that any public show of disunity would play into the hands of his Republican opponent Barry Goldwater, moved against the MFDP. When Fannie Lou Hamer made a moving plea to the credentials committee to recognise the legitimacy of the MFDP, Johnson interrupted television coverage by calling a sudden press conference. The administration also attempted to secure a compromise that would accommodate the regular Mississippi delegates but also allow the MFDP two at-large seats. It further promised that later conventions would not admit state delegations who tolerated disfranchisement. Despite pressure from white liberals and civil rights leaders, the MFDP refused to accept the compromise. As Charles Sherrod later reasoned: 'It would have said to blacks across the nation and the world that we share the power, and that is a lie! The "liberals" would have felt great relief for a job well done. The Democrats would have laughed again at the segregationist Republicans and smiled that their own "Negroes" were satisfied. That is a lie!'[32]

SELMA AND THE VOTING RIGHTS ACT

The increasing alienation of the more radical elements within the civil rights coalition would eventually cause irreparable damage to the cause of racial equality. Internal tensions within the movement were, however, concealed by the success of the SCLC voter registration campaign in Selma, Alabama. The political pressure created by the campaign led to the crowning triumph of the movement, the enactment of the Voting Rights Act of 1965.

The SCLC launched demonstrations in Selma in January 1965. Selma provided an ideal stage upon which to dramatise the problem of black disfranchisement. Although blacks comprised more than half the population of Dallas County, less than 2 per cent of them were registered to vote. The SCLC also anticipated that it could provoke local sheriff Jim Clark into a similar confrontation as it had had with Bull Connor in Birmingham. A series of marches to the county courthouse culminated in the arrest of King on 1 February. The SCLC used the occasion to publicise the black community's lack of political rights. In his 'Letter from a Selma Jail', King proclaimed: 'THIS IS SELMA, ALABAMA. THERE ARE MORE NEGROES IN JAIL WITH ME THAN THERE ARE ON THE VOTING ROLLS.'[33] However, despite the best efforts of black activists, the Selma movement struggled to gain national exposure.

On 18 February, Jimmie Lee Jackson was shot dead as he sought to protect his mother from state troopers during a protest in the nearby community of Marion. His death encouraged the SCLC to seek a direct confrontation with state authorities. On 5 March, King announced his intention to lead a fifty-four-mile march from Selma to Montgomery, to petition Governor George Wallace for the enforcement of black voting rights. Two days later, 600 demonstrators marched to the Edmund Pettus Bridge, where they were met by state troopers and members of Sheriff Clark's posse. The troopers charged the marchers with tear gas, billy clubs and bull whips. According to one newspaper report: 'The Negroes cried out as they crowded together for protection, and the whites on the sideline whooped and cheered.'[34] An estimated one hundred protesters were injured on what became known as 'Bloody Sunday'.

King was not actually among the marchers, having returned to Atlanta. His absence aroused intense criticisms from younger radicals, who accused him of cowardice. King responded by issuing a call to clergymen across the country to join him in a second march. However, the SCLC leader stirred further controversy when he ordered the marchers to turn around once they had crossed the Edmund Pettus Bridge. Confronted by a federal court injunction against the march, King feared that the protesters would be unprotected against a further outbreak of violence. However, his failure to inform SNCC activists of his intentions fuelled their resentment of his rather imperious leadership. King had come perilously close to losing completely the support of younger activists within the movement.

The campaign had nonetheless succeeded in arousing national indignation. Popular support for the SCLC was fuelled both by the violence of Bloody Sunday and the murder of James Reeb, a Unitarian minister from Boston who had answered King's call for religious leaders to support the campaign. On 15 March, Lyndon Johnson addressed a joint session of Congress. As he concluded his emotional appeal for passage of a civil rights law, the president invoked the anthem of the civil rights movement: 'And We Shall Overcome'. Never before had the federal government so completely embraced the cause of black civil rights. On 19 March, a federal court lifted the injunction against marching. Two days later, King set out for the state capitol. On the last day of the march, the movement gained another martyr when Klansmen shot dead northern white sympathiser Viola Liuzzo. The campaign was nevertheless a triumph. On 25 March, 25,000 demonstrators gathered outside the Alabama State Capitol Building. Reflecting on how far the movement had come, and how far it still had to go, King reassured his supporters that 'the arc of the moral universe is long, but it bends towards justice'.[35]

On 6 August 1965, President Johnson signed the Voting Rights Act into law. Only months earlier, Vice-President Hubert Humphrey had informed King that he doubted Congress would enact such a law so soon after the Civil Rights Act. The speed with which the Voting Rights Act passed into law is therefore a tribute to the remarkable ability of King and the SCLC to provoke public awareness of the race issue, creating the broad popular consensus that compelled federal government action. It is also important to stress the timing of the campaign. By the early months of 1965, the Johnson administration had become distracted from its domestic agenda by the military situation in Southeast Asia. On 13 February, Johnson authorised Operation Rolling Thunder, the sustained aerial bombardment of North Vietnam. Less than a month later, on 8 March, the first American combat troops set foot in South Vietnam. The Selma campaign succeeded in sustaining a sense of moral urgency about black civil rights that compelled federal government action at a time when the focus of the Johnson administration was shifting inexorably towards foreign affairs.

The Voting Rights Act had a transformative impact on southern politics. It prohibited literacy tests and provided for the appointment of federal registrars in areas where less than 50 per cent of potential voters had registered or cast a ballot in the 1964 presidential election. The act also mandated the need for federal approval of any changes to voting laws in districts whose populations were at least 5 per cent black. In 1964, the Twenty-fourth Amendment to the Constitution had abolished the poll tax, which had for so long impeded poor blacks from voting. The passage of the Voting Rights Act the following year further facilitated the enfranchisement of southern blacks. Between 1965 and 1969, the number of registered black voters in the South increased more than three-fold. The expansion of the black electorate was most dramatic in those states where disfranchisement had been particularly pervasive. By 1967, the number of blacks on the electoral rolls had increased from 19 to 52 per cent in Alabama, and from 7 to 60 per cent in Mississippi.[36]

The legal foundations that sustained white supremacist rule in the southern states had by 1965 been demolished. In attempting to explain the success of the civil rights revolution, it is important to stress from the outset that there was nothing inevitable about the collapse of Jim Crow. On the contrary, African Americans had to overcome incredible odds. Southern whites possessed the institutional power of law and government, and demonstrated their determination to resist racial reform at every turn, sometimes through the use of terrorist violence.

A number of forces nonetheless facilitated the success of black protest. Sociologist Aldon Morris has asserted that black churches acted as crucial movement centres since they provided a secure meeting space for protesters and a source of leadership and finance.[37] It is one of the richest ironies of southern history that many of the resources used by the black protest movement to defeat Jim Crow came from institutions and social networks that segregation had helped to create. However, the role of the churches should not be over-emphasised. In many instances black church leaders failed to provide support for civil rights campaigns. Religion was nonetheless an essential component in the success of the movement. The black population of the Bible Belt was a deeply devout people whose faith imbued them with a sense of moral righteousness that enabled them to withstand the brutal resistance of white racists.

The importance of religion also explains the presence of the disproportionately large number of women who swelled the ranks of the movement. The numerous local and state studies of the movement produced by scholars in recent years have cast considerable light on the integral role that women performed at a grassroots level. African American women drew in particular on the administrative skills and social contacts they had developed as members of civic clubs and churches during the Jim Crow era. Although most female activists did not rise above the position of foot soldiers, some did attain leadership positions. Daisy Bates served as president of the Arkansas

State Conference of NAACP branches, Septima Clark of the SCLC ran the citizenship schools in South Carolina that educated illiterate black adults and, in Maryland, Gloria Richardson led the Cambridge Nonviolent Action Committee.

Although there were personal and political conflicts between the competing factions within the civil rights movement, black activists demonstrated more unanimity than did southern whites, who were more decisively split between moderates and extremists. African Americans found common purpose through their religious convictions and their faith in the capacity of non-violent direct action to deliver them from racial oppression. From the outset, there were those within the movement who advocated their right to bear arms in self-defence. The persistence of white brutality and the failure of the federal government to protect civil rights workers further eroded support for non-violence among more militant blacks. However, it was when non-violence commanded the consensual support of southern blacks that the movement accomplished its most decisive victories.

With their emphasis on what Adam Fairclough describes as dramatic rather than deadly violence, the adroitly staged street protests of the 1960s successfully challenged segregation without incurring massive loss of lives. When compared with other liberation struggles around the world, the civil rights movement won an almost bloodless revolution. The number of African Americans murdered during the civil rights struggle was forty. By contrast, the sixty-seven victims of the Sharpeville massacre of 1960 demonstrates that more people died in a single day of protest against South African apartheid.[38]

Without the persistent pressure applied by black demonstrators, the federal government would not have made civil rights such a legislative priority. The enactment of the Civil Rights Act of 1964 and the Voting Rights Act of 1965 demolished the legal infrastructure of southern white supremacy. However, it was the grassroots insurgency of southern blacks that created the broad national consensus for reform needed to force federal government action. As Steven Lawson concludes: 'The federal government made racial reform possible, but Blacks in the South made it necessary.'[39] The role of Martin Luther King in communicating the aspirations and needs of southern blacks to a complacent white America should also not be underestimated. King instilled in the movement a sense of moral urgency, and succeeded in representing the black freedom struggle as an issue in which all Americans who believed in the democratic promise of their nation had a vested interest.

The years that followed the Selma campaign saw the focus of civil rights protest shift away from the South and towards the inner-cities of the North. However, many problems that affected southern blacks remained unresolved.

What follows in Chapter 12 is an assessment of southern race relations from the collapse of the national civil rights coalition in the late 1960s to the old and new controversies of the present day.

Notes

1. Jacquelyn Dowd Hall, 'The Long Civil Rights Movement and the Political Uses of the Past', *Journal of American History*, 91 (2005), pp. 1233–63. Some of the most important local and state studies of the civil rights movement include John Dittmer, *Local People: The Struggle for Civil Rights in Mississippi* (Urbana: University of Illinois Press, 1994); Charles M. Payne, *I've Got The Light of Freedom: The Organizing Tradition and the Mississippi Freedom Struggle* (Berkeley: University of California Press, 1995); Adam Fairclough, *Race and Democracy: The Civil Rights Struggle in Louisiana, 1915–1972* (Athens: University of Georgia Press, 1995); John A. Kirk, *Redefining the Color Line: Black Activism in Little Rock, Arkansas, 1940–1970* (Gainesville: University Press of Florida, 2002); and Stephen G. N. Tuck, *Beyond Atlanta: The Struggle for Racial Equality in Georgia, 1940–1980* (Athens: University of Georgia Press, 2001).
2. Stewart Burns (ed.), *Daybreak of Freedom: The Montgomery Bus Boycott* (Chapel Hill: University of North Carolina Press, 1997), p. 1.
3. Stephen B. Oates, *Let the Trumpet Sound: The Life of Martin Luther King, Jr.* (New York: Harper & Row, 1982), p. 75.
4. Burns, *Daybreak of Freedom*, p. 10.
5. 'Speech by Martin Luther King, Jr., at Holt Street Baptist Church', in Clayborne Carson, et al. (eds), *The Eyes on the Prize Civil Rights Reader: Documents, Speeches, and Firsthand Accounts from the Black Freedom Struggle* (New York: Penguin, 1991), pp. 50–1.
6. Taylor Branch, *Parting the Waters: Martin Luther King and the Civil Rights Movement, 1954–63* (New York: Simon and Schuster, 1988), p. 166.
7. Robert Weisbrot, *Freedom Bound: A History of America's Civil Rights Movement* (New York: W. W. Norton, 1990).
8. Henry Hampton and Steve Fayer (eds), *Voices of Freedom: An Oral History of the Civil Rights Movement from the 1950s through the 1980s* (London: Vintage, 1995), p. 58.
9. James Bevel, Bernard Lafayette, Joseph Carter and, Samuel Collier, 'You Better Leave Segregation Alone', *Sing For Freedom: The Story of the Civil Rights Movement Through Its Songs* (Smithsonian Folkways – SFW40032).
10. Numan V. Bartley, *The New South, 1945–1980: The Story of the South's Modernization* (Baton Rouge: Louisiana State University Press, 1995), pp. 301–2.
11. Ella J. Baker, 'Bigger than a Hamburger', in Carson, et al. (eds), *Eyes on the Prize Civil Rights Reader*, p. 121.

12. 'Student Nonviolent Coordinating Committee Statement of Purpose', in Carson, et al. (eds), *Eyes on the Prize Civil Rights Reader*, p. 119.
13. Irving Bernstein, *Promises Kept: John F. Kennedy's New Frontier* (New York and Oxford: Oxford University Press, 1991); James N. Giglio, *The Presidency of John F. Kennedy* (Lawrence: University Press of Kansas, 1991).
14. Robert Dallek, *John F. Kennedy: An Unfinished Life, 1917–1963* (London: Allen Lane, 2003), pp. 649–50.
15. Nick Bryant, *The Bystander: John F. Kennedy and the Struggle for Black Equality* (New York: Basic Books, 2006). Similar sentiments are expressed in David Niven, *The Politics of Injustice: The Kennedys, the Freedom Rides, and the Electoral Consequences of a Moral Compromise* (Knoxville: University of Tennessee Press, 2003).
16. Weisbrot, *Freedom Bound*, p. 54.
17. Diane Kunz, 'Camelot Continued: What if John F. Kennedy had lived?', in Niall Ferguson (ed.), *Virtual History: Alternatives and Counterfactuals* (London: Picador, 1997), p. 374.
18. Weisbrot, *Freedom Bound*, p. 95.
19. Branch, *Parting the Waters*, p. 618.
20. Adam Fairclough, *To Redeem the Soul of America: The Southern Christian Leadership Conference and Martin Luther King, Jr.* (Athens and London: University of Georgia Press, 1987), p. 89.
21. Andrew M. Manis, *A Fire You Can't Put Out: The Civil Rights Life of Birmingham's Fred Shuttlesworth* (Tuscaloosa: University of Alabama Press, 1999), p. 332.
22. Martin Luther King, Jr, 'Letter from Birmingham City Jail', in James M. Washington (ed.), *A Testament of Hope: The Essential Writings and Speeches of Martin Luther King, Jr.* (San Francisco: HarperSanFrancisco, 1991), p. 295.
23. Brian Ward, *Radio and the Struggle for Civil Rights in the South* (Gainesville: University Press of Florida, 2004), pp. 202–4.
24. Aldon D. Morris, 'Sustaining the Fight: The Importance of Local Movements', in Marjorie L. White and Andrew M. Manis (eds), *Birmingham Revolutionaries: The Reverend Fred Shuttlesworth and the Alabama Christian Movement for Human Rights* (Macon, GA: Mercer University Press, 2000), p. 28.
25. Martin Luther King,, Jr, 'I Have a Dream', in Washington (ed.), *A Testament of Hope*, p. 219.
26. Nicholas Von Hoffman, *Mississippi Notebook* (New York: David White Company, 1964), p. 4.
27. Harvard Sitkoff, *The Struggle for Black Equality, 1954–1992* (New York: Hill and Wang, 1993), pp. 156–7.
28. 'Missippi Goddam' first appeared on the 1964 album *Nina Simone in Concert* (Verve – B000DZ7V7C) and is available on numerous compilations of her work. An excellent analysis of Simone's political activism is provided by Ruth

Feldstein, '"I Don't Trust You Anymore": Nina Simone, Culture, and Black Activism in the 1960s', *Journal of American History*, 91 (March 2005), pp. 1349–79.

29. Len Holt, *The Summer That Didn't End: The Story of the Mississippi Civil Rights Project of 1964* (New York: Da Capo Press, 1992), p. 93; Sitkoff, *Struggle for Black Equality*, p. 167.
30. Hampton and Fayer (eds), *Voices of Freedom*, p. 195.
31. Lynne Olson, *Freedom's Daughters: The Unsung Heroines of the Civil Rights Movement from 1830 to 1970* (New York: Scribner, 2001), p. 309.
32. Charles M. Sherrod, 'Mississippi at Atlantic City', in Carson, et al. (eds), *Eyes on the Prize Civil Rights Reader*, p. 189.
33. James N. Colaiaco, *Martin Luther King Jr.: Apostle of Militant Nonviolence* (New York: St. Martin's Press, 1988), pp. 120–1.
34. *New York Times*, 8 March 1965.
35. Juan Williams, *Eyes on the Prize: America's Civil Rights Years, 1954–1965* (New York: Viking Penguin, 1987), p. 283.
36. David R. Goldfield, *Still Fighting the Civil War: The American South and Southern History* (Baton Rouge: Louisiana State University Press, 2002), p. 256.
37. Aldon D. Morris, *The Origins of the Civil Rights Movement: Black Communities Organizing for Change* (New York and London: Free Press/Collier MacMillan, 1984).
38. Fairclough, *To Redeem the Soul of America*, pp. 225–9; David L. Chappell, *A Stone of Hope: Prophetic Religion and the Death of Jim Crow* (Chapel Hill and London: University of North Carolina Press, 2004), p. 2.
39. Steven F. Lawson and Charles Payne, *Debating the Civil Rights Movement, 1945–1968* (Lanham, MD, and Oxford: Rowman & Littlefield, 1998), p. 42.

Chapter 12

A DREAM UNFULFILLED: RACE IN THE CONTEMPORARY SOUTH

During the late 1960s, the civil rights coalition collapsed under the strain of numerous political pressures. The rise of Black Power, the shift of political protest away from race relations towards the Vietnam War and the conservative white backlash to urban rioting in northern cities all contributed to the decline of the movement. Although at a national and regional level the civil rights movement ceased to exist, the struggle for racial reform continued in local communities across the South. Much was still needed to be done to improve the lives of millions of southern blacks. Schools continued to resist the enrolment of black schoolchildren, many adult blacks had not taken advantage of the political opportunities created by the Voting Rights Act and poverty afflicted thousands of families. Efforts to secure change have continued in the decades since the decline of the civil rights movement. While African Americans have overcome many obstacles, racial and class barriers continue to impede their progress towards equality.

THE DECLINE OF THE CIVIL RIGHTS MOVEMENT

'There is no more civil rights movement,' SCLC strategist James Bevel proudly proclaimed to news reporters after the Selma campaign. 'President Johnson signed it out of existence when he signed the Voting Rights Bill.'[1] The riot that erupted in the Watts ghetto of Los Angeles on 11 August 1965 brutally exposed the complacency of civil rights activists like Bevel. The riot was the worst outbreak of urban unrest since the Second World War. In its wake, thirty-four people lay dead, nearly 400 were injured and a further 4,000 were under arrest.[2]

The riot forced movement leaders to refocus the direction of their protest. While activists had invested enormous energy in the struggle to secure the constitutional rights of African Americans in the South, the plight of northern blacks had been largely overlooked. In contrast to the South, northern blacks did not endure legal discrimination. However, racism was as pervasive in the North as it was in the South. Social and institutional prejudice resulted in blacks suffering widespread unemployment, police brutality and political neglect. In 1964, 15 per cent of white families in the United States lived below the federal poverty line; the figure for African American families was 37 per cent.[3] By the summer of 1965, the SCLC had already made tentative plans to launch a northern campaign. The Watts riot hastened the decision of Martin Luther King to turn the direction of black protest from the South towards the deprived inner-cities of the North.

King launched his northern offensive in early 1966 with a campaign to eradicate slum conditions and promote open housing in Chicago. However, the SCLC failed to replicate the success of its crusade against southern racism. Its inability to secure meaningful concessions from city authorities owed to a number of factors including the wiliness of Mayor Richard Daley and the cynicism and apathy of ghetto blacks who did not respect the authority of the ministers who led the SCLC. Discrimination was also a less tangible issue than segregation, and therefore more difficult to dramatise.[4]

Following the failure of the Chicago campaign, King found himself criticised from all sides. Whites and moderate black leaders condemned his outspoken opposition to the Vietnam War. Black radicals conversely accused him of being too timid. By the time King launched his blistering assault on American foreign policy with a speech at the New York Riverside Church in April 1967, the civil rights coalition had already started to collapse.

On 6 June 1966, James Meredith – the first black student admitted to the University of Mississippi – set out on foot from Memphis to Jackson, in an attempt to encourage blacks to overcome their fear of white retaliation and register to vote. Thirty miles into the journey, a white racist shot and wounded Meredith. Although civil rights leaders resolved to continue the march in his name, they could not reach consensus on the purpose of their protest. Roy Wilkins of the NAACP and Whitney Young of the National Urban League walked out of a meeting in Memphis when they failed to secure agreement that the march take place in support of a new civil rights bill that would outlaw housing discrimination. Stokely Carmichael of SNCC and Floyd McKissick of CORE infuriated their moderate counterparts by denouncing President Johnson and asserting that they would not beg his administration for their rights and protection. King, caught uncomfortably between the two factions, chose to march alongside the militants.

The March Against Fear started in optimistic spirit but soon descended into chaos and disunity. On 16 June, police in Greenwood arrested Carmichael and two other activists. The SNCC leader used his arrest as a means of wrestling control of the march away from King. Following his release on bail, he and Willie Ricks worked a crowd of protesters into a commotion with the rallying cry 'Black Power!' 'It's time we stand up and take over,' exclaimed Carmichael. 'Every courthouse in Mississippi ought to be burned down tomorrow to get rid of the dirt and the mess.'[5] On 23 June, state troopers attacked protesters with tear gas in Canton. The failure to secure federal protection for the marchers fuelled militant anger. When the march concluded with a rally in Jackson three days later, King attempted to reassert his authority with a speech that articulated his utopian dream of a future multi-racial democracy. The dissent within movement ranks was nonetheless all too obvious.

Although Black Power attracted a constituency in northern cities, its impact on southern protest was minimal. The decision by SNCC and CORE to expel their white members undermined inter-racial activism in the region. Although Black Power advocates initially disavowed the use of violence as an instrument of revolutionary change, their increasingly inflammatory rhetoric also alienated blacks as well as whites. In August 1967, SNCC activist H. Rap Brown exclaimed to an audience in Cambridge, Maryland, that 'we're going to burn America down'. Hours later, a blaze tore through the black district of the city. The underlying cause of the riot may have been the persistent problems of unemployment, overcrowding and police brutality, but Brown had clearly acted as a catalyst. Police responded with a repressive crackdown on the black community and the arrest of the SNCC activist on charges of inciting a riot and committing arson.

Black Power did make a positive contribution to the struggle for racial equality. Its emphasis on community control and self-determination led to the mobilisation of urban blacks, who secured the election of more representative public officials, as was the case when Carl Stokes became mayor of Cleveland, Ohio, in 1968. Black Power also cultivated a new cultural aesthetic that emphasised the positive virtues of black history, customs and skin colour. However, the purging of white members from SNCC and CORE decimated the finances of both organisations, rendering them incapable of launching renewed direct-action campaigns. The reaction of white authorities further impeded black political protest. During the late 1960s, southern authorities also made discriminatory use of the draft as a means of sending black political dissidents overseas to fight in the Vietnam War. For instance, a draft board in Mississippi reclassified James Joliff, an epileptic, from 4-F to 1-A when he became president of his local NAACP chapter.[6]

There was one last drama to enact in the story of the southern movement. In his earlier career, Martin Luther King had individualised the problem of racism, perceiving it as an irrational hatred towards African Americans on the part of a minority of whites. It was therefore possible to accomplish racial equality within the existing economic and political structures of American society. The failure of the Chicago campaign, however, persuaded King that the capitalist system itself was the cause of black suffering. In October 1967, he announced plans for a Poor People's Campaign, which would involve thousands of impoverished citizens, black and white, marching on Washington to demand a 'Bill of Rights for the Disadvantaged'.

King never reached Washington. On 18 March 1968, he addressed a rally in Memphis, Tennessee, to express support for sanitation workers who were striking for union recognition. Ten days later, King led a sympathy march to City Hall, which collapsed into chaos when young militants known as The Invaders stirred unrest, smashing and looting store fronts. Police responded by firing tear gas and beating the blinded protesters. King was in part to blame for the disorder. The precipitate nature of his intervention in the strike meant that the SCLC was poorly prepared. King nonetheless agreed to return to Memphis for another rally on 3 April 1968. 'I just want to do God's will,' he proclaimed. 'And he's allowed me to go up to the mountaintop. And I've looked over. And I've seen the Promised Land. I may not get there with you. But I want you to know tonight that we as a people will get to the Promised Land.'[7] The speech proved tragically prophetic. The following night, as King stood on the balcony of the Lorraine Motel, an assassin named James Earl Ray shot and killed him. Although conspiracy theorists continue to propose alternative explanations for the murder of the civil rights leader, the official explanation remains that Ray, a white supremacist violently opposed to racial reform, acted alone.

Some commentators argue that the passage of the 1968 Civil Rights Act owed to the outpouring of public grief at the death of King, but this has not been conclusively proven. The act was, in any case, a less than fitting tribute to the slain civil rights leader. Although in principle it outlawed housing discrimination, without adequate enforcement mechanisms the new law accomplished little.

THE UNFINISHED REVOLUTION

Although the national civil rights movement had collapsed by the late 1960s, the struggle for racial equality continued, particularly at a local level. African Americans have made incremental advances over the near four decades since the demise of the movement; but measured by most social, political and economic indices, they still experience discrimination and marginalisation.

The eradication of de jure segregation resulted in black and white southerners sharing public spaces for the first time. However, personal social contact between both races remains minimal. For instance, in the 1967 case of *Loving* v. *Virginia*, the Supreme Court invalidated laws that prohibited inter-racial marriage. More than thirty years later, weddings between black and white partners represented only 0.6 per cent of all marriages. Marriages between whites and Hispanics or Asians have attained considerable social acceptance. By contrast, historical tensions between blacks and whites contribute to the continued stigma attached to mixed race marriages.[8]

The desegregation of southern schools has followed a difficult and what now appears increasingly circular course in the half-century since the *Brown* decision. By the late 1960s, most southern school boards still practised a policy of minimum compliance with the Supreme Court ruling. Freedom-of-choice plans allowed white parents to transfer their children out of integrated schools, but restricted the ability of black parents to enrol their children at predominantly white institutions. As a result, more than 80 per cent of black pupils still attended segregated schools. The Nixon administration provided tacit support to southern conservatives by pressuring the Department of Health, Education and Welfare not to withhold federal funds from school districts that had not desegregated.

While historians now recognise that Nixon was not an arch conservative on civil rights, the desegregation of southern schools owed less to his initiative than to the activism of the Supreme Court.[9] On 29 October 1969, the Supreme Court finally confronted the tokenism of southern school boards when it ruled in *Alexander* v. *Holmes County Board of Education* that the desegregation of thirty-three Mississippi school districts must begin 'at once'. The decision eliminated the ability of southern states to use the 'with all deliberate speed' standard to delay school desegregation. Within eighteen months, the number of black children enrolled at integrated schools rose sharply. Southern schools had achieved what would have seemed impossible a generation earlier, with a higher percentage of black children attending formerly white institutions than in the North: 38 per cent compared to 27 per cent.[10] Some school boards still attempted to postpone the complete desegregation of the public education system. On 20 April 1971, the Supreme Court in *Swann* v. *Charlotte-Mecklenburg Board of Education* upheld the use of busing to achieve a racial balance in schools. For more than a decade, the number of black children attending predominantly white schools in the southern states continued to increase, reaching a pinnacle of 44 per cent in 1983.[11]

However, during the last two decades the process has gone into reverse. In contrast to the prevalent historical pattern, it is now in northern cities that black schoolchildren are most segregated. In the academic year 2002–03, 79 per cent of pupils in the public school system of Philadelphia were black or Hispanic; in Chicago, the figure was 87 per cent; and in Detroit, a staggering 96 per cent.[12] The process of southern school re-segregation that started in the 1980s is nonetheless accelerating at a relentless pace. Southern schools are still more integrated than was the case before the *Brown* decision. Nonetheless, between 1988 and 1998, the percentage of black students in majority white schools fell from 43.5 per cent to 32.7 per cent.[13] There are numerous factors that account for school re-segregation. The relocation of whites to the suburbs has isolated blacks in urban areas and made it more difficult to maintain racial balance in public schools. A more conservative Supreme Court has also opposed efforts to enforce cross-district desegregation. White parents have also opted out of the public school system altogether and enrolled their children at private academies. From the late 1960s to the early 1980s, the desegregation of schools in the South raised the prospects of the United States fulfilling the promise of a multi-racial democracy. The re-segregation of schools demonstrates the failure of that dream.

Southern blacks still experience numerous forms of institutional racism. The criminal justice system, for instance, discriminates against African Americans in a number of ways. According to statistics published by Human Rights Watch in April 2003, African Americans represent on average 21.6 per cent of the southern population, but 55.8 per cent of all prison inmates across the region. It is worth noting that the disparity is even worse in northern states such as Vermont and South Dakota, where blacks are few in number but still form a disproportionate share of the prison population.[14] Racial bias is also evident in the administration of the death penalty. Southern states continue to execute more prisoners than the rest of the nation put together. Between 1976 and 2006, 832 of the 1,019 executions carried out in the United States occurred in the South. Southern states administer the death penalty most commonly in cases where the criminal is black and the victim is white. In Georgia, 60 per cent of murder victims are African American. However, since 1973 more than 80 per cent of executions have involved blacks who committed crimes against whites.[15] Conscious or unconscious, white prejudices about the supposedly inherent criminality of African Americans still persist. In 1994, a white woman in South Carolina named Susan Smith claimed to police that a black man had abducted her two sons. She later admitted to having invented the story as a means of deflecting the authorities from the fact that she herself had drowned the children by rolling her car into a lake. The unquestioning acceptance of her story by the police, press and public demonstrated the pervasiveness of racial stereotypes about black criminality.[16]

African Americans also suffer from fewer economic opportunities than whites. One of the most important battles that blacks still needed to fight after the collapse of the civil rights movement was the integration of the southern workforce. African Americans succeeded to some extent in securing access to sectors of the economy that had historically excluded them. For instance, by the late 1970s blacks occupied a quarter of all positions in the textile industry. While this brought better wages and benefits, black workers still suffered discrimination in terms of hiring and promotion. With the industry now in terminal decline, blacks have also found it difficult to secure employment in the expanding Sunbelt economy. The last several decades have seen the growth of a black suburban middle class, in part as a result of the re-migration of African American professionals and entrepreneurs from the northern to the southern states. In a reversal of the predominant demographic pattern of the twentieth century, blacks are now returning to the South in growing numbers. During the 1990s, the southern black population increased by almost 3.6 million.[17] Economic problems nonetheless persist. African Americans continue to work in disproportionate numbers in low-paying menial labour and service positions. In 1990, 28.4 per cent of southern black families lived below the federal poverty line, compared to 7.3 per cent of whites. The situation is worse than in the Northeast and West, but better than in the declining industrial heartlands of the Midwest.[18]

The economic prosperity of some southern blacks is a positive advance. However, the rise of the black middle class has arguably had a detrimental impact on the racial unity of African Americans. Class stratification within the black community had become a contentious issue as early as the late nineteenth century. A common experience of racial persecution during the Jim Crow era nonetheless promoted a collective identity that cut across economic lines. Yet many of those African Americans who now ascend the economic ladder leave the black underclass further and further behind, not only physically, as a result of their relocation to white suburban neighbourhoods, but also psychologically. The economic success of these middle-class blacks leads to their belief that race is no longer a barrier to equality. They therefore encourage poorer blacks not to rely on government aid but rather regain their personal initiative as a means of improving their condition. As David Goldfield argues, such reluctance to recognise the racial obstacles that still impede the upward mobility of poor blacks sounds uncomfortably close to the rhetoric of white conservatives who blame the underclass for their degraded status.[19]

Recent events have ruthlessly exposed the persistent reality of black poverty. On 29 August 2005, Hurricane Katrina hit the Gulf Coast of the

United States with storm windspeeds of 220 kilometres an hour. Katrina caused devastation to communities in Mississippi and Louisiana. The most extensive destruction occurred in New Orleans, where flood waters drowned 80 per cent of the city. Although New Orleans is situated below sea level, and therefore at constant risk of natural disaster, city authorities took no measures to plan for the evacuation of people who had no transport. Thousands of poor inhabitants, many of them black, therefore found themselves trapped after the hurricane hit. Incompetence rather than racism appears to have determined the slow response of federal authorities to the disaster. The reaction to Hurricane Katrina has nonetheless revealed the persistent and intertwined problems of class and race that afflict urban communities such as New Orleans. Three decades of deindustrialisation and white flight to the suburbs have created a large underclass of poor blacks ensnared in decaying inner-city neighbourhoods. Media reaction to the crisis also demonstrated the enduring racial stereotyping of African Americans. When desperate black people started to loot stores in search of supplies, the press depicted them as pathological criminals. The disaster also dramatised how poor blacks still suffer from a lack of political representation. African Americans had little voice in the recovery programme, and therefore found themselves confronted by recommendations from organisations such as the Bring New Orleans Back Commission that black neighbourhoods be bulldozed rather than rebuilt.[20]

The racial progress of the South appears more positive in political terms. The Voting Rights Act has by enabling blacks to become active participants in the electoral process permanently redefined the southern political landscape. Congress has protected and promoted black voter registration by renewing the provisions of the act three times: in 1970, 1975 and 1982. Its impact has been profound. At the start of the 1960s, only 29 per cent of potential southern black voters were registered. By the end of the decade, the figure had soared to 69 per cent.[21] The act also empowered black voters for the first time since Reconstruction to elect their own representatives to public office. The number of black elected officials in the South is higher in absolute numbers than in the North, and more proportionate to the size of the African American population. By 1995, the proportion of seats held by blacks in southern state legislatures – 16 per cent – precisely matched their share of the population.[22] The concentration of blacks in urban areas, a process facilitated by white flight to the suburbs, has created large electoral blocs that mobilise behind black candidates. One of the most symbolic demonstrations of black voting power occurred in 1979, when Richard Arrington became the first African American elected mayor of the former segregationist stronghold

Birmingham, Alabama. Black politicians have also succeeded in attracting the support of white voters needed to win election to high office. Such was the case in November 1989, when Douglas Wilder of Virginia became the first African American governor of a southern state since Reconstruction. The racial transformation of the electorate also forced white politicians, particularly Democrats, to abandon their prejudiced rhetoric and broaden their appeal to black voters. Dale Bumpers defeated Orval Faubus to become the governor of Arkansas in 1970 by constructing a populist coalition that cut across racial lines. That same year, racial moderate Jimmy Carter won election in the Georgia gubernatorial election over the demagogic incumbent Lester Maddox.

However, southern blacks still face problems in their efforts to secure full political representation. The election of African American officials has not necessarily translated into better provision of public services for their poor and unemployed black constituents. Douglas Wilder, for instance, was criticised for concentrating on policies that appealed more to white conservative voters, such as anti-crime programmes and support for the death penalty. The white political establishment also attempted to protect its power by redrawing the boundaries of electoral districts to reduce the number of eligible black voters. This racial gerrymandering occurred most commonly in those districts where blacks comprised a majority of voters and were more likely to elect public officials of their own race. During the 1980s, the Justice Department, under the auspices of the Voting Rights Act, pressured state authorities to increase the number of electoral districts in which minority groups comprised more than 50 per cent of voters. However, this effort to facilitate the election of minority candidates has come under increasing threat. In 1993, the Supreme Court ruled in favour of North Carolina whites who argued that they had been effectively disfranchised by the redrawing of electoral district lines. According to the decision reached in *Shaw* v. *Reno*, preferential treatment for African Americans reinforces the racial divisions that the civil rights struggle sought to eradicate. Officials elected in such districts would consider it their sole interest to represent the needs of their black constituents. In the opinion of the court, this could only impede the already slow and painful progress towards a colour-blind society. In reality, the decision is more likely to restore white political supremacy and marginalise minority representation.

The presidential election of November 2000 also demonstrated that southern blacks could still be the victims of political chicanery. Prior to the election, Florida Secretary of State Katherine Harris ordered the removal from the electoral rolls of more than 57,000 persons identified as convicted felons, and therefore prohibited under state law from voting. However, the company hired to compile the list made thousands of errors. A disproportionate number of the people illegally disfranchised – about 54 per cent – were African American and Hispanic. Black Floridians encountered numerous other obstacles on the day of the election, including police roadblocks that prevented their access to polling booths, the late arrival of some ballot papers and the discarding of others deemed spoiled. Republican candidate George W. Bush defeated his Democratic opponent Al Gore in Florida by a margin of only 537 votes. The electoral college votes gained from this narrow victory secured his election to the White House. Civil rights leaders accused the Republican state administration of deliberately targeting African Americans and Hispanics because they vote overwhelmingly Democrat. Although the Civil Rights Division of the Justice Department did not find evidence of racial discrimination, the NAACP filed a class action complaint against Secretary of State Harris that resulted in an agreement to re-process the list of persons removed from the electoral rolls.[23]

The battle over black voting rights reflects the rise of the Republican Party as the most powerful force in southern politics. This process of electoral realignment occurred after almost a century of Democratic dominance. White southerners first started to break ranks with the national Democratic Party as far back as the Dixiecrat revolt of 1948. Republican candidate Dwight Eisenhower also secured a number of peripheral southern states during the presidential elections of 1952 and 1956. The Republicans intensified their efforts to recruit disaffected white southern Democrats during the 1960s. In 1961, Arizona senator Barry Goldwater gave a speech that mapped out what later came to be known as the 'southern strategy'. Conceding that the Republicans were 'not going to get the Negro vote', Goldwater encouraged party activists 'to go hunting where the ducks are'.[24] The pursuit of white southern votes met with some success when Goldwater ran as the Republican candidate in the presidential election three years later. It was nonetheless not until 1968 that Richard Nixon used the southern strategy to help secure his election to the White House. While he eschewed demagogic appeals to white voters, there was a racial subtext to his rhetoric. Nixon exploited white anger and resentment at the advance of black civil rights by proclaiming his support for 'law and order' and opposition to 'forced busing'. This use of racially encoded language owed much to the influence of Alabama governor George Wallace, whose independent candidacy framed opposition to civil rights in terms of states' rights, crime and welfare.[25]

Recent scholarship has cast doubt on the significance of the southern strategy in the resurgence of southern support for the Republicans. Matthew

Lassiter, for instance, asserts that Republican efforts to manipulate white southern fears did not translate into electoral success. Instead, he attributes increased southern support for the Republicans to the growth of the suburban middle class, who were attracted to the party because of its policies of fiscal conservatism and restricted government.[26] This interpretation explains how the Republicans recruited racial moderates whose support was essential to their electoral success in the region. However, it is still the case that Republicans used racial code words in campaigning for the votes of more conservative whites. In 1980, Ronald Reagan launched his presidential campaign with a speech in Philadelphia, Mississippi, that emphasised his opposition to centralised government and respect for states' rights. Although Reagan made no mention of race, the timing and location of his address were loaded with symbolic meaning. It was almost sixteen years to the day since the bodies of the three civil rights workers killed during the Mississippi Freedom Summer were discovered near the small town. This was more than an unhappy coincidence. Republican manipulation of racial issues culminated in the election of former Klansman David Duke to the Louisiana state legislature in 1989. Duke campaigned on a platform that pandered to white resentment at the perceived preferential treatment that the government accorded to blacks, emphasising his opposition to welfare handouts and affirmative action. A similar manipulation of racial code words enabled Duke to win almost 60 per cent of white votes when he ran for the US Senate the following year, although he still lost the election.[27] The persistence of racism within the ranks of the Republican Party is illustrated by the South Carolina presidential primary of 2000. Campaign officials for George W. Bush helped to smear his opponent John McCain by claiming that his adopted Bangladeshi daughter actually came from an illicit relationship with a black prostitute.[28]

THE PAST HAUNTS THE PRESENT

In recent years, the South has confronted its racist history in an attempt to lay to rest the ghosts of the past. No attempt has been made to establish a Truth and Reconciliation Commission along the lines of post-apartheid South Africa. Southern whites have nonetheless implemented a number of substantive and symbolic measures to atone for the suffering inflicted on African Americans. Politicians, for instance, have made numerous acts of public contrition for the crimes of omission and commission committed by their predecessors in office. On 4 May 1994, Florida governor Lawton Chiles signed into law the Rosewood Compensation Act. The act recognised the failure of the state government to protect the black community of Rosewood, which white vigilantes burned to the ground in January 1923, and provided for the payment of $2.1 million to the families of the victims. In August 2005, the Georgia Board of Pardons and Paroles issued a posthumous pardon to Lena Baker, a black woman executed sixty years earlier for the murder of her white employer. Baker had been coerced into a sexual relationship with the man she had killed in self-defence when he attempted to assault her.[29] National institutions have also acknowledged their complicity in the oppression of southern blacks. On 16 May 1997, President Bill Clinton formally apologised to the eight remaining survivors of the Tuskegee syphilis experiment. In October 1932, the US Public Health service launched a clinical study to determine the natural course of untreated syphilis. It recruited 400 poor black men, who were not informed that they had the disease but only that they had 'bad blood' for which they could receive free treatment. Even when penicillin became widely available for the treatment of syphilis, the men still did not receive therapy. The failure to treat the men, and the fact that they had not given their informed consent, demonstrates the institutional racism of the white medical profession during the Jim Crow era. Another admission of institutional guilt came in June 2005, when the US Senate issued an apology for its historical failure to pass a federal anti-lynching law.[30]

Southern prosecutors have also re-opened a series of cases from the civil rights era in an attempt to convict white racists who have long eluded the law. According to the Southern Poverty Law Center, twenty-three cases of murder have been re-examined, resulting in twenty-seven arrests, twenty-two convictions, two acquittals and one mistrial.[31] The most publicised of these cases include the convictions of Byron De La Beckwith for the murder of Mississippi NAACP leader Medgar Evers; former Klan Imperial Wizard Sam Bowers for the murder of black activist Vernon Dahmer; and Thomas Blanton, Jr and Bobby Frank Cherry for the bombing of the Sixteenth Street Baptist Church in Birmingham that caused the deaths of four black girls. Most recently, a Mississippi jury found Edgar Ray Killen guilty of the manslaughter of civil rights workers James Chaney, Andrew Goodman and Michael Schwerner. In June 2005, authorities also exhumed the body of Emmett Till in a search for evidence connecting his murder to several white men still alive, although the FBI later announced that no charges would be filed.[32]

It took the authorities decades to prosecute the cases successfully. The time between the commitment of the crime and the conviction of the perpetrator was thirty-two years in the case of Bowers; thirty-seven and thirty-eight years respectively in the cases of Blanton and Cherry; and more than forty years in the cases of Beckwith and Killen. While the prosecution of white racists has brought comfort to the families of the victims, some whites in particular have criticised what they see as the reopening of old wounds. Time, they say, to forget the past and look towards the future. However, the most important criticism of the court cases is that they allow southern whites to demonise individuals rather than accept their collective responsibility for the historical mistreatment of African Americans. The imprisonment of a few white extremists cannot protect black people from the more impersonal institutional and cultural forms of racism that continue to oppress them.

The prosecution of white racists may convince some that the southern states can now close this chapter in their history, but acts of terrorist violence against African Americans are not entirely a thing of the past. In June 1998, three white men lynched an African American named James Byrd, Jr, in Jasper, Texas. The killers chained Byrd to the back of a pick-up truck and dragged his body two miles, severing his head and one of his arms. Although the incident was a morbid reminder of the not so distant past, there were important distinctions between what happened in Jasper and the lynchings that occurred so commonly during the Jim Crow era. During the late nineteenth and early twentieth centuries, white mobs acted with community sanction and the complicity of the authorities. By contrast, the townspeople of Jasper rallied around the family of James Byrd. A jury found the three men guilty of capital murder and sentenced two of them to death.[33] Although acts of racial violence may nowadays be the work of a small number of extremists, the victimisation of African Americans shows that the plague of white prejudice has been contained rather than cured. Between 1989 and 1996, arsonists attacked more than 200 black and multi-racial churches. Although the attacks took place across the country, the ten states with the highest number of incidents were all in the South.[34]

The bombing of black churches is not the only occasion when the spectre of the past has reappeared. It is an unfortunate irony that some of the whites who insist African Americans need to move on rather than pursue the prosecution of old Klansmen should themselves cling so tenaciously to one of the most potent symbols of southern history, the Confederate battle flag. Defenders of the flag insist that it is not an emblem of white supremacy but of the brave men who fought to defend their homeland from an autocratic federal government. This assertion rests on the tenuous notion that states' rights, rather than slavery, was the central issue that led to the Civil War. Critics of the flag contend that the Confederacy should be a cause of shame rather than pride, since its foundations were rooted in racial oppression. It is also the case that southern state governments explicitly intended the introduction of flags adorned with Confederate insignia as an emblem of white domination. The flags were first flown in the 1890s at the same time as new state constitutions mandated black disfranchisement and the separation of the races. While not all southern whites support the Confederate battle flag, the effort to remove it from public spaces shows how disputes over the meaning of the past continue to cause racial polarisation in the present. On 15 July 1999, the NAACP announced a tourist boycott of South Carolina in protest at the state flag. Faced with a loss of $20 million in revenue, the state legislature passed a compromise measure the following May that relocated the flag from the capitol building to a nearby Confederate monument. The racial divisiveness of the flag issue was further demonstrated in April 2001, when Mississippi voters opposed a proposal for a new state flag shorn of Confederate symbols. Most blacks supported the new flag, while most whites wanted to maintain the old one.[35]

These contemporary racial controversies reveal the complicated influence that race still has on the American South. The decades since the New Deal brought transformative change to the southern states. A region with an impoverished rural economy reliant on a single staple crop has become an expanding urban and industrial centre. Racial violence has lost its legitimacy as an instrument of social control. African Americans have, through the intervention of the federal government, attained their full civil rights. The political system once monopolised by a white elite now provides southern blacks with the opportunity to vote, hold office and direct local, state and national government policy. Yet the burden of race still weighs heavily on the southern states. Old problems, such as black poverty and social and institutional prejudice, persist. New challenges also face the region, not least the rising influx of large numbers of Latin American immigrants. Race will continue to be a central influence in the shaping of southern society. Only once the region has become completely reconciled to its racist history will there be any prospect of African Americans attaining full equality. How long that may be is unclear. Time, it is said, heals all wounds. The deeper the wounds, the more time that is needed. In the American South, those wounds run very deep.

Notes

1. August Meier and Elliott Rudwick, *CORE: A Study in the Civil Rights Movement, 1942–1968* (New York: Oxford University Press, 1973), p. 329.
2. Gerald Horne, *Fire This Time: The Watts Uprising and the 1960s* (New York: Da Capo, 1997), p. 56.
3. Robert Weisbrot, *Freedom Bound: A History of America's Civil Rights Movement* (New York: W. W. Norton, 1990), p. 161.

4. The most extensive analysis of the Chicago campaign is James R. Ralph, Jr, *Northern Protest: Martin Luther King, Jr., Chicago, and the Civil Rights Movement* (Cambridge, MA, and London: Harvard University Press, 1993).
5. Taylor Branch, *At Canaan's Edge: America in the King Years, 1965–68* (New York: Simon and Schuster, 2006), p. 486.
6. Weisbrot, *Freedom Bound,* p. 247.
7. Martin Luther King, Jr, 'I See The Promised Land', in James M. Washington (ed.), *A Testament of Hope: The Essential Writings and Speeches of Martin Luther King, Jr.* (San Francisco: HarperSanFrancisco, 1991), p. 286.
8. *New York Times,* 4 June 2006.
9. The most thorough revisionist analysis of the Nixon administration's civil rights record is Dean J. Kotlowski, *Nixon's Civil Rights: Politics, Principle, and Policy* (Cambridge, MA, and London: Harvard University Press, 2001).
10. David R. Goldfield, *Promised Land: The South Since 1945* (Arlington Heights, IL: Harlan Davidson, 1987), p. 179.
11. Gary Orfield, et al., 'Deepening Segregation in American Public Schools', *Southern Changes,* 19 (Summer 1997), p. 14.
12. Jonathan Kozol, 'Still Separate, Still Unequal', *Harper's Magazine* (September 2005), p. 41.
13. Gary Orfield, 'Schools More Separate: Consequences of a Decade of Resegregation', Civil Rights Project of Harvard University, July 2001, p. 29, http://www.civilrightsproject.harvard.edu/research/deseg/Schools_More_Separate.pdf (accessed 9 May 2006).
14. 'Incarcerated America: Human Rights Backgrounder, April 2003', http://www.hrw.org/backgrounder/usa/incarceration/us042903.pdf (accessed 12 May 2006).
15. Death Penalty Information Center, 'Facts About the Death Penalty, April 27, 2006', http://www.deathpenaltyinfo.org/FactSheet.pdf (accessed 10 May 2006); Pew Forum on Religion & Public Life, 'Religious Reflections on the Death Penalty', http://pewforum.org/publications/reports/DeathPenalty.pdf (accessed 12 May 2006).
16. *New York Times,* 6 November 1994.
17. James C. Cobb, *The* Brown *Decision, Jim Crow, & Southern Identity* (Athens and London: University of Georgia Press, 2005), p. 60.
18. Andrew Hacker, *Two Nations: Black and White, Separate, Hostile, Unequal* (New York: Charles Scribner's Sons, 1992), p. 233.
19. David R.Goldfield, *Black, White, and Southern: Race Relations and Southern Culture 1940 to the Present* (Baton Rouge and London: Louisiana State University Press, 1990), pp. 219–22, 250–4.
20. Mike Davis, 'Who Is Killing New Orleans?', *The Nation,* 10 April 2006, pp. 11–20.
21. Numan V. Bartley and Hugh Davis Graham, *Southern Politics and the Second Reconstruction* (Baltimore, MD: Johns Hopkins University Press, 1975).

22. David R. Goldfield, *Still Fighting the Civil War: The American South and Southern History* (Baton Rouge: Louisiana State University Press, 2002), p. 257.
23. John Lantigua, 'How the GOP Gamed the System in Florida', *The Nation*, 30 April 2001; Gregory Palast, 'Vanishing Votes', *The Nation*, 17 May 2004.
24. Numan V. Bartley, *The New South, 1940–1980: The Story of the South's Modernization* (Baton Rouge: Louisiana State University Press, 1995), p. 385.
25. Dan T. Carter, *From George Wallace to Newt Gingrich: Race in the Conservative Counterrevolution, 1963–1994* (Baton Rouge: Louisiana State University Press, 1996).
26. Matthew D. Lassiter, *The Silent Majority: Suburban Politics in the Sunbelt South* (Princeton, NJ, and Oxford: Princeton University Press, 2006).
27. John C. Kuzenski, Charles S. Bullock and Ronald Keith Gaddie (eds), *David Duke and the Politics of Race in the South* (Nashville, TN: Vanderbilt University Press, 1995).
28. *The Guardian*, 2 January 2003.
29. *New York Times*, 14 March 1994 and 19 December 1995; *The Independent*, 17 August 2005.
30. Susan M. Reverby, 'History of an Apology: From Tuskegee to the White House', *Research Nurse*, 3 (July/August 1997), pp. 1–9; *The Observer*, 12 June 2005.
31. 'Remembering Reality', *Intelligence Report* (Summer 2000), http://www.splcenter/intel/intelreport/article.jsp?aid=256 (accessed 10 May 2006). We have added Edgar Ray Killen to the list of those defendants convicted.
32. *New York Times*, 8 February 1994; *The Observer*, 23 August 1998; Associated Press, 19 November 2004; *The Guardian*, 22 June 2005 and 6 June 2005.
33. Jonathan Markovitz, *Legacies of Lynching: Racial Violence and Memory* (Minneapolis and London: University of Minnesota Press, 2004), p. 201, n.25.
34. Sarah A. Soule and Nella Van Dyke, 'Black church arson in the United States, 1989–1996', *Ethnic and Racial Studies*, 22 (July 1999), pp. 724–42.
35. James C. Cobb, *Away Down South: A History of Southern Identity* (New York: and Oxford: Oxford University Press, 2005), pp. 298–301.

CONCLUSION

The history of race is inextricably intertwined with the historical development of the American South. The rich cultural mix of this region reflected three integral elements: Native Americans, Europeans and Africans. Negotiating differences between these groups and deciding on their wider meaning and significance is a complicated process. This book has stressed the importance of race, class and gender but also ethnicity, religion and local circumstances. The balance of these forces has varied at different times and in different places. Race was hesitant and uncertain in the colonial period. Slavery became the bedrock foundation of southern society, inculcating the association of blackness with servility, but not necessarily the further assumption of African *racial* inferiority, at least not on a wide scale. The eventual expulsion of the Indians advanced and legitimated ideas of natural white supremacy, but the high point of southern racism came only after slavery's abolition. The full ideological and institutional weight of the South, eventually supported by the federal government, enforced the racial order and created apartheid in the southern states. Race was the single most important determinant of identity under Jim Crow, but the horrific oppression endured by African Americans under this regime fostered their collective resistance. Blacks and Indians were never passive victims and always contested and resisted white supremacy as best they could. The seeds of Jim Crow's demise were planted from within. The civil rights movement, built on the enduring courage and fortitude of the black community, exposed the ugliness of southern racism and brought about the dismantling of legal segregation.

From colonial origins, European settlers interacted with the diverse indigenous populations they encountered, relying on them for their very survival in many ways. Even before arriving in the New World, colonists had conceptions of exotic and sometimes frightening peoples passed on in tales and stories of adventurers who circumnavigated the globe in the early modern period. Similar impressionistic stories circulated within Native

American tribes who had had sporadic contact with European visitors. The English colonies were extremely vulnerable in their early years. It took many decades to establish stability and subdue the threat posed by Native American tribes, enabling the emergence of a region known as 'the South'.

Some historians argue that race was a significant factor at this early point, that Europeans and Indians felt themselves to be innately separate from one another and that this fundamentally determined relations between the two. Unquestionably, there was an immense religious and cultural divide, but we suggest that this did not constitute a racial identity at this point, on either side, because difference was not rooted in the body. As Michael Omi and Howard Winant remind us, 'A racial project can be defined as *racist* if and only if it *creates or reproduces structures of domination based in essentialist categories of race.*'[1] No single overarching response characterised first contact in the Chesapeake; on the contrary, a multitude of encounters ensued, both individual and collective, and a bewildering array of fleeting and more substantive impressions took root in the minds of settlers and Indians.

As the southern colonies secured their position, increasing in size and numbers, the relationship with Native Americans changed significantly. If the first stage of settler-native relations was characterised by exchange of goods, knowledge, values and ideas, the second stage was a power struggle. The overwhelming desire of Europeans was to acquire land for planting crops. All other considerations were secondary to this imperative and relations between Indians and the colonists deteriorated as a result. In this context, positive impressions became more negative; mutual exchange, friendship in some cases, was generally undermined by the perception of the bloodthirsty savage. This was a powerful stimulant to white group identity, widening the gap that already existed between heathens and Christians. Deep fissures of gender and class within the white community in the early South, however, considerably reduced the social, economic and psychological potency of whiteness. Indentured servants working in the field, for example, found that their white skin brought little tangible reward or upward mobility. In the seventeenth century, the most important divide in practical terms was between the free and the unfree and between men and women. The small number of Africans coming to the Chesapeake fitted very easily into that dynamic.

The growth of slavery in the Upper and Lower South in the eighteenth century nurtured the development of an overarching racial ideology positing a natural and irrevocable divide between whites, blacks and Native Americans. To what extent this process was inevitable, refracting cultural, political and religious differences through the prism of race, is fiercely debated. South Carolina's founding as an extended Caribbean slave colony was crucial. It is possible to envisage alternative roads that might have been taken in Virginia and Maryland in the eighteenth century, roads in which emancipation was a possibility. Racial attitudes might have taken a different form as a result. However, the very early black majority in South Carolina galvanised and focussed the white population. Unlike the situation several hundred miles to the north, the class divide between indentured servants and planters in the Lowcountry was not such a significant factor in a colony where land was freely available.

Even so, the great rice planters in their Charleston mansions were just as wealthy and aristocratic as their counterparts in the Chesapeake by the mid-eighteenth century. Power was unquestionably held by a small elite in societies built on class privilege. Somewhat bridging the gap between colonial males was the consolidation of a white identity offering status and opportunity to ordinary white men. Modelling itself on the English sugar colonies of the Caribbean, South Carolina quickly embedded the notion of a permanent divide between Africans and Europeans in its social, political and legal system. Maryland and Virginia eventually did the same, but over a much longer period of time. Certain types of work became considered suitable only for blacks, while white men alone were granted some form of political input. Gender was also crucial. Developing hand in hand with the idea of white supremacy was the ever more firmly-held assumption of natural male dominance over women and children. The workload of black women in the Chesapeake – labouring in the tobacco fields with little or no gendered consideration for female status – became significantly different to that of white women, many of whom withdrew from the fields to the domestic sphere. The southern colonies were hierarchical societies in which identity and power were negotiated via a complex intersection of race, class, gender and other status differences.

Questions of inclusion and exclusion became more urgent in the revolutionary era, just as a measure of stability and order had been established. Whiteness was codified in the eighteenth century, Native Americans were pushed back and European settlers became southerners with their own identity autonomous from Great Britain, but the status quo was threatened by the American Revolution. The political rhetoric of universal equality, as well as Enlightenment and evangelical notions of the essential similarities of human beings, combined to challenge the institution of slavery. For the first time in world history, the idea of owning other sentient beings became morally and religiously unacceptable to significant numbers of people, and also considered a serious economic encumbrance, stimulating the growth of various anti-slavery organisations. From tentative beginnings, the transatlantic movement against slavery forced southerners to justify the peculiar institution in an increasingly bitter war of words in the antebellum era.

Scientific racism, conceptualised and disseminated outside of the American South as much as within it, was utilised by pro-slavery ideologues not only to defend slavery but claim it as a positive good, because, the argument went, blacks were racially inferior. Racial dogma was also used to justify Indian removal in the 1830s. How far the antebellum masses accepted the radical theory of polygenesis and absorbed the finer points of racial doctrine is debateable. White men believed in their superiority over African Americans and Native Americans, but this was based on longstanding political, cultural and economic differences as much as it was on the internalisation of racial ideology. Religion exerted a much greater influence than science and continued to preach the message of universal equality before God.

The concept of Caucasians maintaining their position at the top of a hierarchy of races because of superior racial stock was strongest by far in the minds of slaveholders and was projected most vocally by pro-slavery spokesmen and politicians defending the South from outside attack. It was an ideological position that grew organically from the master-slave relationship and validated and justified the power wielded by slaveholders. Outside the slaveholding ranks, however, most antebellum southerners did not need to look beyond slavery to understand the nature of southern society or their place within it. Whites were free and the overwhelming majority of blacks were slaves. This powerful dynamic explained and structured race relations in the South and arguably did so until the Civil War for the majority of non-slaveholding whites.

The Civil War was a crucial turning point in the history of race in the South. Slavery's demise resulted in not only the emancipation of African Americans but the granting of citizenship, drastically disrupting and overturning the social hierarchy. Aspects of the old racial order certainly endured amid the social, political, economic and psychological flux of war and Reconstruction but, in many ways, conceptualising race relations had to be started again at this point. Slavery was the South's sheet anchor. Once gone, a period of uncertainty and turmoil ensued as whites and blacks had to learn how to relate to one another again.

For a very brief moment, class threatened to supersede race in parts of the South. Southern lower-class whites and blacks had often interacted with one another for mutual advantage and the fledgling Republican Party in the South attempted to build on that alliance. Planter interests were also challenged in the immediate post-war period by the federal government, illustrating how important political institutions were to the construction and maintenance of the racial order. However, evolving configurations of race and gender combined to head off the internal class revolt and return power to the white elite. Horrific images of the black man as beast and as a threat to white women were used to whip up racial tension. Politicians such as Tom Watson demanded the unity of white southern males, no matter how dire their economic circumstances. The commitment of national politicians and the northern public to black civil rights also waned not least because the North basically shared a belief in white supremacy and was persuaded by southern assertions of the danger posed by African Americans. In an ideological sense, the South lost the war but won the peace, as most whites across the United States accepted the scientific doctrine of black inferiority and white superiority.

The Jim Crow system that emerged in the New South, legitimised by Supreme Court rulings such as the 1896 *Plessy* v. *Ferguson* decision, constituted the apex of white supremacy. Racism commanded unprecedented intellectual and institutional support. The rise of what Joel Williamson calls 'radical racism' displaced paternalistic attitudes towards African Americans and precipitated a relentless wave of violence.[2] The late nineteenth and early twentieth centuries witnessed the highest recorded levels of lynching in American history. With little or no recourse to local, state or federal authorities, African Americans were relatively powerless to withstand the brutal enforcement of white supremacist rule. As Rayford Logan ruefully observes, this era represented 'the nadir' of American race relations.[3]

A series of structural and intellectual changes that occurred during the 1930s and 1940s provided the preconditions for the collapse of the southern caste system. First, the decline of the traditional plantation economy and the rise of a new urban and industrial order undermined white control of the black labour force. The migration of African Americans from the countryside to the cities led to an increased concentration of numbers and institutional resources that facilitated their political mobilisation. Second, the increasing intervention of the federal government in southern affairs, sometimes, if often tentatively in support of black rights and aspirations, weakened resistance to racial reform as an increasing number of white business and civic leaders realised the financial cost of maintaining segregation. Third, the emergence of new political alliances between African Americans and a number of groups including organised labour and the national Democratic Party strengthened opposition to Jim Crow. Fourth, the Second World War had a powerful ideological impact. The American experience of waging war against racist regimes such as Nazi Germany undermined the intellectual legitimacy of segregation back home. The Second World War and then the

Cold War raised awareness of the disparity between the principles of democracy and the practice of racial discrimination, pricking the consciences of some whites and instilling in African Americans a more militant political consciousness. Fifth, the rise of northern, and indeed global, liberalism focused renewed political attention on the racial problems of the South, increasingly seen as one of the most serious impediments to the advancement of American democracy. While the victories of the civil rights movement were often hard won, the forces of white resistance were fatally undermined by the changes that occurred during the preceding decades.

To what extent, though, did the civil rights movement represent a decisive break from the past; or was it rather the culmination of a continuous process of resistance by African Americans? The creation and maintenance of a racist social system relies in part on its ability to inculcate the notion that socially constructed differences between two sets of people are natural and inherent. In the context of the American South, blacks as well as whites needed to believe that the social hierarchy represented an innate order determined by the hereditary characteristics of both groups. White superiority and black inferiority were a force of nature, not the fictional creations of man.

Some southern blacks did internalise the ideology of white supremacy. The numerous advertisements for bleaching creams and hair straighteners in African American newspapers suggest an idealisation of white aesthetic standards. So too does the construction of social hierarchies based on skin colour within the black community; lighter complexioned African Americans intermarrying as a means to protect their privileged status. Historian Leon Litwack has also illustrated how the southern caste system instilled an immobilising racial self-hatred among some blacks. Martin Luther King described this as a 'degenerating sense of "nobodiness"'.[4] This condition was not unique to southern blacks. A lack of self-esteem similarly led some black northerners to aspire to white ideas of physical attractiveness. Malcolm X, who as a young man lived in Boston, endured excruciating pain when he conked his hair in imitation of whites. He later interpreted this, along with his sexual interest in white women, as a mark of his 'self-degradation'.[5]

Despite this internalisation, many African Americans resisted their subordinate status within the social order, as they had done for centuries. Through their collective and private acts of protest, and through the cultivation of distinctive cultural practices, African Americans prevented the material oppression of Jim Crow from crushing their sense of pride, self-respect and worth. Initially drawing their inspiration from the black political protest of the civil rights era, historians have during the last several decades placed a strong emphasis on black resistance to white supremacy.

Over the course of four centuries, African Americans established a tradition of resistance that included the slave rebellions of the colonial and antebellum eras, the labour strikes that accompanied emancipation and the legal challenge to Jim Crow laws during the twentieth century. The efforts of African Americans to build and sustain their own social and cultural institutions and networks represented a less confrontational form of opposition to white supremacy. As Evelyn Brooks Higginbotham observes, even when African Americans accepted that there were inherent differences between the races, they did so in a manner that empowered them by celebrating the distinctiveness of their historical and cultural practices and accomplishments.[6]

There is a need to caution against placing too much emphasis on black agency. If all that was needed to create the civil rights movement was African Americans' recognition of their oppression and a desire to end it, then the freedom struggle would have emerged much sooner than it did. Nonetheless, while the changes that occurred both within and outside the South during the 1930s and 1940s were important in expanding the range of possibilities for African American protest, without the sustaining power of black culture, there would not have been the sense of pride and self-respect that was necessary to take advantage of those new opportunities.

This tradition of protest has led some scholars to caution against a simplistic periodisation of African American history and to place more emphasis on the continuity of the black experience. In particular, historians dispute what they regard as the false dichotomy drawn between the accommodationist tactics of black leaders during the late nineteenth and early twentieth centuries, and the later confrontational protests of the civil rights movement. According to Robert Norrell, the representation of accommodation and confrontation as mutually exclusive tactics 'has functioned as virtually a Manichean divide in writing about African American leadership'.[7]

The revisionist approach, however, is in danger of constructing a seamless narrative of black protest. The accommodationist philosophy did not represent a complete capitulation to racism, but rather represented an attempt to secure incremental improvements in the condition of African Americans at a time of otherwise unremitting racial hostility from whites. While recognising the limitations of an immediate assault on white supremacy, accommodationist leaders worked towards the longer-term advantage of their people. Far from being passive in their acceptance of southern apartheid, they helped to establish the foundations for the direct action protests of the civil rights era.

Those demonstrations did nonetheless represent a new and more radical phase of black protest. Where earlier activists had attempted to secure reform within the structure of a segregated society, the civil rights movement made a revolutionary assault on the system itself. Historian Glenn Eskew may be too emphatic in stating that that the civil rights movement represented a complete departure from the accommodationist tactics that preceded it. However, he has a point in accusing scholars who chart a continual process of black resistance of acting 'within a cloud of relativism that borders on ahistoricism'.[8]

The direct action phase of black protest also resulted in profound changes to southern society constituting a decisive break from the past. The Jim Crow South was what George M. Fredrickson describes as an 'overtly racist regime'.[9] Its social, political and economic systems reinforced an ideology of white supremacy and black inferiority. Whites used not only the power of law, but also extra-legal force to maintain their hegemony. The civil rights movement performed a crucial role in eroding both segregationist laws and the racist ideology that underpinned them. Violence lost its legitimacy as an instrument of white political control as a result of the actions of movement activists. By directly confronting their oppressors, blacks gained a sense of empowerment and overcame the social conditioning of Jim Crow which demanded deferential public behaviour towards whites.

While the contemporary political culture of the South is no longer based on an ideology of racial oppression, inequalities remain. The state does not pursue an overt policy of discrimination and exclusion but the historical legacy of institutional arrangements perpetuates structural barriers which, combined with enduring prejudice, continues to deny many African Americans equality of opportunity. The American South today is not so much a racist society, but a society in which racism continues to exist. The idea of race – of whites, blacks and reds – lives on, despite overwhelming evidence of its historical specificity and ultimate obsolescence in the twenty-first century. As the controversy surrounding the public display of the Confederate flag demonstrates, race continues to inform the collective memories and traditions of southerners. It will probably continue to do so as long as the myth of race helps to sustain what scholar George Lipsitz terms 'the possessive investment in whiteness': better housing, health care, education and job opportunities for whites not just within the South, but across the United States, and the concomitant disadvantaging of other groups.[10]

Notes

1. Michael Omi and Howard Winant, *Racial Formation in the United States: From the 1960s to the 1990s* (New York: Routledge, 1994), p. 71.

2. Joel Williamson, *The Crucible of Race: Black-White Relations in the American South Since Emancipation* (New York: Oxford University Press, 1984), pp. 11–223.
3. Rayford W. Logan, *The Betrayal of the Negro from Rutherford B. Hayes to Woodrow Wilson* (New York: Da Capo Press, 1997).
4. Leon F. Litwack, *Trouble In Mind: Black Southerners in the Age of Jim Crow* (New York: Alfred A. Knopf, 1998), p. 33; Martin Luther King, Jr., 'Letter from Birmingham City Jail', in James M. Washington (ed.), *A Testament of Hope: The Essential Writings and Speeches of Martin Luther King, Jr.* (San Francisco: HarperCollins, 1986), p. 293.
5. Malcolm X with Alex Haley, *The Autobiography of Malcolm X* (London: Hutchinson and Co., 1966), especially Chapter Three.
6. Evelyn Brooks Higginbotham, 'African-American Women's History and the Metalanguage of Race', *Signs*, 17 (Winter 1992), p. 268.
7. Robert J. Norrell, 'Understanding the Wizard: Another Look at the Age of Booker T. Washington', in W. Fitzhugh Brundage (ed.), *Booker T. Washington and Black Progress: 'Up From Slavery' 100 Years Later* (Gainesville: University Press of Florida, 2003), pp. 74–5.
8. Glenn Eskew, *But for Birmingham: The Local and National Movements in the Civil Rights Struggle* (Chapel Hill: University of North Carolina Press, 1997), p. 14.
9. George M. Fredrickson, *Racism: A Short History* (Princeton, NJ: Princeton University Press, 2002).
10. George Lipsitz, *The Possessive Investment in Whiteness: How White People Profit From Identity Politics*, revised and expanded edition (Philadelphia: Temple University Press, 2006).

CHRONOLOGY

1492	Christopher Columbus sails to the Caribbean on the first of four voyages
28 August 1565	Spanish admiral Pedro Menéndez de Avilés establishes a settlement at St Augustine, Florida
1584–87	English colonists fail to establish a permanent settlement at Roanoke Island, off the coast of North Carolina
14 May 1607	The Virginia Company establishes the first English colony in North America at Jamestown
Winter 1609–10	The so-called 'starving time' in Virginia, when the colony teeters on the brink of disaster due to a lack of food supplies
1614	One of the earliest English settlers in North America, John Rolfe, marries Pocahontas
	Tobacco exports leave Virginia for Great Britain in large quantities
1619	First documented arrival of Africans in the South at Point Comfort in Virginia
	First meeting of the Virginia House of Burgesses
22 March 1622	Opechancanough, chief of the Powhatan confederacy, attacks colonists in Virginia, in an attempt to force them to abandon the region

1624	King James I dissolves the Virginia Company and thereby creates a royal colony
25 March 1634	Lord Baltimore sends the first settlers in to establish the royal colony of Maryland
1644	Opechancanough attacks colonists in Virginia for a second time
1660s	Slave laws placing Africans in a debased position are passed in Virginia and Maryland
1672	The Royal African Company is founded, with a monopoly to supply slaves to the British colonies
June 1676	Bacon's Rebellion in Virginia, led by colonist and planter Nathaniel Bacon, culminates in the burning of Jamestown
1680	Charles Town is established at the confluence of the Ashley and Cooper Rivers
1701	Delaware is founded by splitting from Pennsylvania
1 May 1707	The Acts of Union between England and Scotland come into effect, dissolving both parliaments and creating the Kingdom of Great Britain
1711–13	The Tuscarora War is fought in North Carolina, with colonial authorities enlisting the aid of other Native Americans to defeat the Tuscarora tribe
1712	Formal division of the Carolinas into North and South
1715–16	The Yamasee War is fought by the Yamasee (and other tribes) against the British in South Carolina, ending in defeat for the Native Americans at Saltketchers on the Combahee River
1719	South Carolina becomes a royal colony

1729	North Carolina becomes a royal colony
12 February 1733	Georgia is founded, as 113 settlers land at a location that was to become the city of Savannah
9 September 1739	The Stono Rebellion is sparked when a group of South Carolina slaves gather at the Stono River to begin an armed march for freedom
1751	Georgia ends its ban on slavery
1754	Georgia becomes a royal colony
1754–63	French and Indian War (Seven Years War 1756–63)
10 February 1763	The Treaty of Paris is signed, dividing French possessions in North America between Britain and Spain
1775	First shots are fired in the American War of Independence
4 July 1776	The United States Declaration of Independence is ratified by the First Congress
19 October 1781	Following a siege, Lord Cornwallis surrenders to the Americans at Yorktown
3 September 1783	The Peace of Paris is signed, as the British formally recognise American independence
May–September 1787	Constitutional Convention is held at Philadelphia
4 March 1789	US Constitution comes into effect
30 April 1789	George Washington becomes the first American president
1793	Invention of the cotton gin
30 August 1800	A literate and charismatic blacksmith known as Gabriel has his planned uprising thwarted by the authorities in Richmond, Virginia

1803	The Louisiana Purchase sees the United States double in size, as it acquires vast tracts of territory from France, at the cost of about three cents per acre
1 January 1808	Formal termination of the international slave trade to the United States
1812–15	War of 1812 between the United States and Great Britain
9 August 1814	Andrew Jackson defeats the Red Stick (Creek) Indians, who subsequently sign the Treaty of Fort Jackson
1820	The Missouri Compromise prohibits slavery north of Missouri
28 May 1830	Congress narrowly votes to accept the Indian Removal Act, facilitating the forced relocation of remaining Native American tribes east of the Mississippi River
21 August 1831	Nat Turner's slave rebellion in Southampton County, Virginia
1832	The Virginia state legislature conducts a vigorous debate over slavery's future, in which emancipation is a serious possibility
1835–38	The 'Trail of Tears', as the Cherokee are forced to relocate to the Indian Territory, resulting in an estimated 4,000 deaths
1836	Texas declares independence from Mexico
1846–48	Mexican–American War
1850	A series of measures collectively known as the Compromise of 1850 attempts to resolve the territorial and slavery issues arising from the Mexican–American War
30 May 1854	The Kansas-Nebraska Act comes into force, stipulating that western territories can decide

	for themselves whether to permit slavery within their borders
7 March 1857	The US Supreme Court's *Dred Scott* decision rules that slaves are property, and cannot be taken from their owners without following due process of law
16 October 1859	Abolitionist John Brown leads eighteen men in a raid on the Federal arsenal at Harpers Ferry, Virginia
6 November 1860	Abraham Lincoln becomes president-elect
4 February 1861	Representatives from seven southern states draw up the Confederate Constitution at Montgomery, Alabama
12 April 1861	Confederates forces fire on Fort Sumter, Charleston, signalling the beginning of the American Civil War
16 April 1862	The first Confederate Conscription Act comes into force, applying to all white men between the ages of eighteen and thirty-five (later extended to those aged forty, and then fifty)
22 September 1863	Abraham Lincoln announces the Preliminary Emancipation Proclamation
1 January 1863	Abraham Lincoln issues the Emancipation Proclamation
9 April 1865	General Robert E. Lee surrenders to Ulysses S. Grant at Appomattox Court House in Virginia
14 April 1865	Abraham Lincoln is shot by John Wilkes Booth at Ford's Theatre, Washington DC, and dies the next day
6 December 1865	The Thirteenth Amendment abolishing slavery is ratified
1865–66	Southern states pass Black Codes: laws designed to restrict the civil rights of freed slaves

3 March 1867	The Reconstruction Act divides the South into five military districts and sets out terms of readmission to the Union
9 July 1868	The Fourteenth Amendment protecting civil rights is ratified
3 February 1870	The Fifteenth Amendment is ratified, prohibiting the denial of voting rights on the grounds of race or previous condition of servitude
November 1876	Disputed presidential election, with Republican Rutherford B. Hayes eventually declared victorious
1877	Reconstruction ends, as remaining Federal troops withdraw from the South
Spring 1879	Twenty thousand African Americans ('the Exodusters') abandon the South in search of new opportunities in Kansas
1 November 1890	Mississippi becomes the first southern state to adopt a new constitution disfranchising African Americans
1892	The highest number of lynchings in one year is recorded at 230
18 September 1895	Booker T. Washington delivers the 'Atlanta Compromise' address
18 May 1896	The US Supreme Court upholds the principle of 'separate but equal' in *Plessy* v. *Ferguson*
10 November 1898	Riot in Wilmington, North Carolina
24 July 1900	Riot in New Orleans
1903	W. E. B. Du Bois publishes *The Souls of Black Folk*, which establishes him as the leading critic of Booker T. Washington
22–5 September 1906	Riot in Atlanta, Georgia
12 February 1909	Foundation of the National Association for the Advancement of Colored People (NAACP)

November 1915	The Ku Klux Klan is reborn at cross-burning ceremony in Stone Mountain, Georgia
6 April 1917	The United States declares war with Germany and enters European conflict
28 June 1919	The First World War I is formally concluded by the Treaty of Versailles
1 October 1919	Race riot in Elaine, Arkansas
1 January 1923	Whites destroy black township of Rosewood, Florida
March 1931	International outcry at sentencing to death of nine black youth convicted of raping two white women near Scottsboro, Alabama
8 November 1932	Franklin D. Roosevelt is elected president and soon introduces his New Deal programmes to combat the depression
8 December 1941	The United States declares war with Japan following the bombing of Pearl Harbor
	Germany declares war with the United States three days later
3 April 1944	The US Supreme Court outlaws the white primary in *Smith* v. *Allwright*
25–6 February 1946	Race riot in Columbia, Tennessee
5 December 1946	President Harry S. Truman establishes a Committee on Civil Rights, which issues a critical report on American race relations the following year
July 1948	Southern Democrats organise a States' Rights convention and nominate Strom Thurmond as their presidential candidate
	Truman is re-elected president in November
5 November 1952	Dwight Eisenhower elected president

17 May 1954	The US Supreme Court rules, in *Brown* v. *Board of Education of Topeka, Kansas* that segregation in public schools is unconstitutional
31 May 1955	The US Supreme Court issues implementation ruling, in *Brown II*, that school desegregation must proceed 'with all deliberate speed'
1 December 1955	Arrest of Rosa Parks precipitates 381-day boycott of buses in Montgomery, Alabama
14 February 1957	Southern Christian Leadership Conference (SCLC) founded under leadership of Martin Luther King, Jr
24 September 1957	President Eisenhower sends troops to enforce school desegregation in Little Rock, Arkansas
29 August 1957	Civil Rights Act attempts to increase black electorate by making it a criminal offence to obstruct voter registration
1 February 1960	African American students in Greensboro, North Carolina, hold the first in a wave of sit-in protests that sweeps across the South
15–17 February 1960	Student Non-Violent Coordinating Committee (SNCC) founded in Raleigh, North Carolina
9 November 1960	John F. Kennedy is elected president
4 May 1961	Congress of Racial Equality (CORE) launches the Freedom Rides in support of the desegregation of interstate transportation
30 September 1962	A riot breaks out at the University of Mississippi in opposition to the admission of black student James Meredith, who successfully enrolls the following day
22 November 1963	President John F. Kennedy is assassinated in Dallas, Texas
3 April 1963	SCLC launches a campaign against segregation in Birmingham, Alabama

21 June 1964	Three civil rights workers are murdered during the Mississippi Freedom Summer campaign
29 June 1964	Civil Rights Act signed into law
25 March 1965	White civil rights supporter Viola Liuzzo is shot dead by the Ku Klux Klan following Selma-to-Montgomery march
6 August 1965	Voting Rights Act signed into law
12 June 1967	The US Supreme Court outlaws anti-miscegenation laws in *Loving* v. *Commonwealth of Virginia*
4 April 1968	Martin Luther King, Jr is assassinated during sanitation workers' strike in Memphis, Tennessee
6 November 1968	Richard Nixon is elected president
29 October 1969	The US Supreme Court rules, in *Alexander* v. *Holmes County Board of Education*, that 'all deliberate speed' is no longer acceptable and orders immediate desegregation of 33 Mississippi school districts
20 April 1971	The US Supreme Court, in *Swann* v. *Charlotte-Mecklenburg Board of Education*, upholds court-ordered busing plan to ensure racial balance in public schools
4 August 1980	Ronald Reagan launches his presidential campaign at location of murder of three Mississippi civil rights workers
7 November 2000	George W. Bush is elected president amidst accusations of black voters in Florida being disfranchised
21 June 2005	Edgar Ray Killen is convicted of the manslaughter of civil rights activists killed during Mississippi Freedom Summer
29 August 2005	Hurricane Katrina causes devastation to the Gulf Coast

GUIDE TO FURTHER READING

GENERAL WORKS

The literature on the American South is enormous and potentially overwhelming for any student approaching it for the first time. However, there are a number of books that provide an accessible survey of southern history and culture. The most recommended of these titles are William J. Cooper, Jr, and Thomas E. Terrill, *The American South: A History* (New York: McGraw-Hill, 1996) and John B. Boles, *The South Through Time: A History of an American Region* (Englewood Cliffs, NJ: Prentice Hall, 1995). J. William Harris, *The Making of the American South: A Short History, 1500–1877* (Oxford: Blackwell, 2006) is an excellent survey of southern history up to Reconstruction, and is particularly good on southern politics. Peter Kolchin raises many important issues in defining and understanding what actually constitutes 'the South' in *A Sphinx on the Land: The Nineteenth-Century South in Comparative Perspective* (Baton Rouge: Louisiana State University Press, 2003). A more thematic approach, with helpful analysis of the historiography of the region, is provided by John B. Boles (ed.), *A Companion to the American South* (Malden, MA: Blackwell, 2002). A valuable reference guide to the region is Charles Reagan Wilson and William Ferris (eds), *Encyclopedia of Southern Culture* (Chapel Hill: University of North Carolina Press, 1989).

AMERICAN SLAVERY

Even though slavery was not confined to the southern states until the nineteenth century, the history of American slavery is firmly entwined with the historical and cultural development of the South. Few subjects in American history have been so extensively and productively explored as slavery. Two excellent overviews of the origins, growth and maturation of North American plantation society are Ira Berlin, *Generations of Captivity: A History of African-American Slaves* (Cambridge, MA: Harvard University Press, 2003) and Peter Kolchin, *American Slavery, 1619–1877* (London: Penguin Books, 1993). Berlin's book condenses material from his earlier work *Many Thousands Gone: The First Two Centuries of Slavery in North America* (Cambridge, MA: Harvard University Press, 1998), which provides a detailed interpretation of slavery before 1800. See also John B. Boles, *Black Southerners, 1619–1869* (Lexington: The University Press of Kentucky, 1984). James Walvin, *Questioning Slavery* (London: Routledge, 1996) is highly recommended for its comparative view of slavery's impact on the Atlantic world, while Robin Blackburn, *The Making of New World Slavery: From the Baroque to the Modern, 1492–1800* (London: Verso, 1997) also places North American slavery within the context of the wider New World colonies.

The rich and complex historiography of American slavery is surveyed in Peter J. Parish, *Slavery: History and Historians* (New York: Harper & Row, 1989). There are many good collections of primary source documents, but Willie Lee Rose (ed.), *A Documentary History of Slavery in North America* (New York: Oxford University Press, 1976) remains the most comprehensive.

RACE

A growing number of scholars focus on the development of racial ideology in North America. Students wanting to familiarise themselves with key issues in the context of the American South should begin with two extremely influential articles: Barbara Jeanne Fields, 'Ideology and Race in American History', in J. Morgan Kousser and James M. McPherson (eds), *Region, Race and Reconstruction: Essays in Honor of C. Vann Woodward* (New York: Oxford University Press, 1982), pp. 143–77; and Evelyn Brooks Higginbotham, 'African-American Women's History and the Metalanguage of Race', *Signs* 17 (Winter 1992), pp. 251–74. George M. Fredrickson's work is highly recommended, especially *The Black Image in the White Mind: The Debate on Afro-American Character and Destiny, 1817–1914* (New York: Harper and Row, 1971) and *Racism: A Short History* (Princeton, NJ: Princeton University Press, 2002). Ronald T. Takaki, *Iron Cages: Race and Culture in Nineteenth-Century America* (New York: Alfred A. Knopf, 1979) remains extremely useful in thinking about race, class and gender in the nineteenth century, and Joel Williamson, *The Crucible of Race: Black–White Relations in the American South Since Emancipation* (New York: Oxford University Press, 1984) continues the analysis of these themes into the twentieth century. See also Thomas F. Gossett, *Race: The History of an Idea in America* (Dallas, TX: Southern Methodist University Press, 1963); Audrey Smedley, *Race in North America:*

Origin and Evolution of a Worldview (Boulder, CO: Westview Press, 1993); William Stanton, *The Leopard's Spots: Scientific Attitudes Towards Race in America, 1815–1859* (Chicago: University of Chicago Press, 1960); Reginald Horsman, *Race and Manifest Destiny: The Origins of Racial Anglo-Saxonism* (Cambridge, MA: Harvard University Press, 1981); Mia Bay, *The White Image in the Black Mind: African-American Ideas About White People, 1830–1925* (New York: Oxford University Press, 2000); Bruce Dain, *A Hideous Monster of the Mind: American Race Theory in the Early Republic* (Cambridge, MA: Harvard University Press, 2002); and Elazar Barkan, *The Retreat of Scientific Racism: Changing Concepts of Race in Britain and the United States Between the World Wars* (Cambridge: Cambridge University Press, 1992). John Solomos and Les Back, *Racism and Society* (London: Macmillan, 1996) provide a succinct and very readable sociological analysis of race as a concept, as does Robert Miles, *Racism* (London: Routledge, 1989).

NATIVE AMERICANS

There is a growing literature about Native Americans and their responses to colonial settlement, although it is not as plentiful as that written about black–white relations. The only general survey of southern Indians is J. Leitch Wright, Jr, *The Only Land They Knew: The Tragic Story of the American Indians in the Old South* (New York: The New Press, 1981), but this is a bit dated now. Students are advised to consult Alan Gallay, *The Indian Slave Trade: The Rise of the English Empire in the American South, 1670–1717* (New Haven: Yale University Press, 2003) for a broad overview, albeit within a limited time period. See also Timothy Silver, *A New Face on the Countryside: Indians, Colonists, and Slaves in South Atlantic Forests, 1500–1800* (Cambridge: Cambridge University Press, 1990) and Nancy Shoemaker, *A Strange Likeness: Becoming Red and White in Eighteenth-Century North America* (New York: Oxford University Press, 2004).

Tribal histories are extremely valuable and tend to take a long chronological view outlining change over time. For southern tribes, see James H. Merrell, *The Indians' New World: Catawbas and Their Neighbors from European Contact through the Era of Removal* (Chapel Hill: University of North Carolina Press, 1989); Robbie Ethridge, *Creek Country: The Creek Indians and Their World* (Chapel Hill: University of North Carolina Press, 2003); Theda Perdue, *Slavery and the Evolution of Cherokee Society, 1540–1866* (Knoxville: University of Tennessee Press, 1979); Claudio Saunt, *A New Order of Things: Property, Power and the Transformation of the Creek Indians 1733–1816* (New York: Cambridge University Press, 1999); J. Leitch Wright, Jr, *Creeks and Seminoles:*

Destruction and Regeneration of the Muscogulge People (Lincoln: University of Nebraska Press, 1986); and William G. McGoughlin, *Cherokee Renascence in the New Republic* (Princeton, NJ: Princeton University Press, 1987).

Theda Perdue, *'Mixed Blood Indians': Racial Construction in the Early South* (Athens: University of Georgia Press, 2003) is a fine examination of Indian racial attitudes. Daniel H. Usner, Jr, paints a vivid picture of interaction between different groups in the Deep South in *Indians, Settlers, and Slaves in a Frontier Exchange Economy: The Lower Mississippi Valley Before 1783* (Chapel Hill: University of North Carolina Press, 1992). Daniel F. Littlefield considers interactions between blacks and Indians in *Africans and Creeks: From the Colonial Period to the Civil War* (Westport, CT: Greenwood Press, 1979). Indian removal is succinctly analysed by Philip Weeks in *Farewell, My Nation: The American Indian and the United States, 1820–1790* (Arlington Heights, IL: Harlan Davidson, 1990); for more detail, see Michael Paul Rogin, *Fathers and Children: Andrew Jackson and the Subjugation of the American Indian* (New York: Alfred A. Knopf, 1975).

SLAVERY AND RACE IN THE COLONIAL SOUTH

For many years colonial slavery was the poor relation to a rich series of books on antebellum slavery, but that has changed in the past two decades. The origins and contested status of the first Africans in North America are discussed in Betty Wood, *The Origins of American Slavery: Freedom and Bondage in the English Colonies* (New York: Hill and Wang, 1997). A valuable compilation of major competing historiographical views is collated by Edward Countryman in *How did American Slavery Begin?* (Boston, MA: Bedford/St. Martin's, 1999). Edmund S. Morgan, *American Slavery, American Freedom: The Ordeal of Colonial Virginia* (New York: W. W. Norton, 1975) and Winthrop D. Jordan, *White Over Black: American Attitudes Toward the Negro, 1550–1812* (Chapel Hill: University of North Carolina Press, 1968) remain key texts on the development of slavery and the evolution of racial views. The position of free blacks in early Virginia is examined in Timothy H. Breen and Stephen Innes, *'Myne Owne Ground': Race and Freedom on Virginia's Eastern Shore, 1640–1676* (New York: Oxford University Press, 1980). David J. Weber discuses Spanish influence in the South, among other things, in *The Spanish Frontier in North America* (New Haven: Yale University Press, 1992).

Philip D. Morgan, *Slave Counterpoint: Black Culture in the Eighteenth-Century Chesapeake and Lowcountry* (Chapel Hill: University of North Carolina Press, 1998) masterfully compares and contrasts slave society in the Upper and Lower South in the eighteenth century. On the development of slave society in the southern colonies, see Peter H. Wood, *Black Majority: Negroes in Colonial South Carolina from 1670 through the Stono Rebellion* (New York: W. W. Norton, 1974); Daniel C. Littlefield, *Rice and Slaves: Ethnicity and the Slave Trade in Colonial South Carolina* (Baton Rouge: Louisiana State University Press, 1981); Betty Wood, *Slavery in Colonial Georgia, 1730–1775* (Athens: University of Georgia Press, 1984); Anthony S. Parent, Jr, *Foul Means: The Formation of a Slave Society in Virginia, 1660–1740* (Chapel Hill: University of North Carolina Press, 2003); Judith A. Carney, *Black Rice: The African Origins of Rice Cultivation in the Americas* (Cambridge, MA: Harvard University Press, 2001); Allan Kulikoff, *Tobacco and Slaves: The Development of Southern Cultures in the Chesapeake, 1680–1800* (Chapel Hill: University of North Carolina Press, 1986); Gwendolyn Midlo Hall, *Africans in Colonial Louisiana: The Development of Afro-Creole Culture in the Eighteenth Century* (Baton Rouge: Louisiana State University Press, 1992); Mechal Sobel, *The World They Made Together: Black and White Values in Eighteenth-Century Virginia* (Princeton, NJ: Princeton University Press, 1987); Marvin L. Michael Kay and Lorin Lee Cary, *Slavery in North Carolina, 1748–1775* (Chapel Hill: University of North Carolina Press, 1995); and Thomas N. Ingersoll, *Mammon and Manon in Early New Orleans: The First Slave Society in the Deep South, 1718–1819* (Knoxville: University of Tennessee Press, 1999). An excellent synthesis of the colonial black experience is Donald R. Wright, *African Americans in the Colonial Era: From African Origins through the American Revolution* 2nd edition (Wheeling: Harlan Davidson, 2000).

WHITE SOCIETY IN THE COLONIAL SOUTH

Most of the books listed above have much to say about the development of white society, so students looking for information about planters and indentured servants should not overlook them. For studies concentrating more intensively on the colonial planter elite and the society which they led, however, see Robert Olwell, *Masters, Slaves, and Subjects: The Culture of Power in the South Carolina Low Country, 1740–1790* (Ithaca, NY: Cornell University Press, 1998); T. H. Breen, *Tobacco Culture: The Mentality of the Great Tidewater Planters on the Eve of Revolution* (Princeton, NJ: Princeton University Press, 1985); Rachel N. Klein, *Unification of a Slave State: The Rise of the Planter Class in the South Carolina Backcountry, 1760–1808* (Chapel Hill: University of North Carolina Press, 1990); and Rhys Isaac, *The Transformation of Virginia, 1740–1790* (Chapel Hill: University of North Carolina Press, 1982). On indentured servants, see Kenneth Morgan's *Slavery and Servitude in North America, 1607–1800* (Edinburgh: Edinburgh

University Press, 2000), which does a good job of summarising current historical writing on this subject.

Several recent studies have placed gender at the heart of the colonial experience. Kathleen M. Brown, *Good Wives, Nasty Wenches and Anxious Patriarchs: Gender, Race and Power in Colonial Virginia* (Chapel Hill: University of North Carolina Press, 1996) is the key text, but see also Kirsten Fischer, *Suspect Relations: Sex, Race, and Resistance in Colonial North Carolina* (Ithaca, NY: Cornell University Press, 2002) and Jennifer L. Morgan, *Laboring Women: Reproduction and Gender in New World Slavery* (Philadelphia: University of Pennsylvania Press, 2004). Catherine Clinton and Michele Gillespie (eds), *The Devil's Lane: Sex and Race in the Early South* (New York: Oxford University Press, 1997) present a valuable collection of essays about race, gender and sexuality.

THE SOUTH AND THE AMERICAN REVOLUTION

The literature on the South during the American Revolution is comparatively less substantial than for other periods. David Brion Davis, *The Problem of Slavery in the Age of Revolution, 1770–1823* (Ithaca, NY: Cornell University Press, 1975) provides a general overview of the international situation and the origins of anti-slavery. Numerous themes are covered in Ira Berlin and Ronald Hoffman (eds), *Slavery and Freedom in the Age of the American Revolution* (Charlottesville: University of Virginia Press, 1983) and Jeffrey J. Crow and Larry E. Tise (eds), *The Southern Experience in the American Revolution* (Chapel Hill: University of North Carolina Press, 1978). Sylvia R. Frey, *Water From the Rock: Black Resistance in a Revolutionary Age* (Princeton, NJ: Princeton University Press, 1991) and Benjamin Quarles, *The Negro in the American Revolution* (Chapel Hill: University of North Carolina Press, 1961) give the most detailed examination of African Americans in the revolutionary era. Gary B. Nash, *Race and Revolution* (Madison, WI: Madison House Publishers, Inc., 1990) and Duncan J. MacLeod, *Slavery, Race and the American Revolution* (Cambridge: Cambridge University Press, 1974) explore the paradox of revolutionary equality. The Native American response is covered in Colin G. Calloway, *The American Revolution in Indian Country: Crisis and Diversity in Native American Communities* (Cambridge: Cambridge University Press, 1995).

THE EXPANSION OF SLAVERY IN THE NINETEENTH CENTURY

Two important books establish the extent of the inter-regional slave trade: Michael Tadman, *Speculators and Slaves: Masters, Traders, and Slaves in the Old South* (Madison: University of Wisconsin Press, 1989) and Steven Deyle,

Carry Me Back: The Domestic Slave Trade in American Life (New York: Oxford University Press, 2005). On the growth of slavery in the Deep South, see John Hebron Moore, *The Emergence of the Cotton Kingdom of the Old South-West* (Baton Rouge: Louisiana State University Press, 1988); Daniel S. Dupre, *Transforming the Cotton Frontier: Madison County, Alabama, 1800–1840* (Baton Rouge: Louisiana State University Press, 1997); Christopher Morris, *Becoming Southern: The Evolution of a Way of Life, Warren County and Vicksburg, Mississippi, 1770–1860* (New York: Oxford University Press, 1995); Edward E. Baptist, *Creating an Old South: Middle Florida's Plantation Frontier Before the Civil War* (Chapel Hill: University of North Carolina Press, 2002); and Adam Rothman, *Slave Country: American Expansion and the Origins of the Deep South* (Cambridge, MA: Harvard University Press, 2005). Planter migration is explored in James David Miller, *South by Southwest: Planter Emigration and Identity in the Slave South* (Charlottesville: University of Virginia Press, 2001) and Joan E. Cashin, *A Family Venture: Men and Women on the Southern Frontier* (New York: Oxford University Press, 1991).

ANTEBELLUM SLAVE LIFE AND CULTURE

There is a vast and fascinating literature on this topic. The influential work of Kenneth M. Stampp, *The Peculiar Institution: Slavery in the Ante-Bellum South* (New York: Alfred A. Knopf, 1956) and Stanley M. Elkins, *Slavery: A Problem in American Intellectual and Institutional Life* (Chicago: University of Chicago Press, 1959) should not be overlooked. The best revisionist scholarship of the 1970s includes: Eugene D. Genovese, *Roll, Jordan, Roll: The World the Slaves Made* (New York: Pantheon, 1974); Herbert G. Gutman, *The Black Family in Slavery and Freedom, 1750–1925* (New York: Pantheon, 1976); Lawrence W. Levine, *Black Culture and Black Consciousness: Afro-American Folk Thought From Slavery to Freedom* (New York: Oxford University Press, 1977); John W. Blassingame, *The Slave Community: Plantation Life in the Antebellum South*, revised and enlarged edition (New York: Oxford University Press, 1979). An econometric approach is taken in Robert William Fogel, *Without Consent or Contract: The Rise and Fall of American Slavery* (New York: W. W. Norton, 1989), which develops many of the themes in Robert William Fogel and Stanley L. Engerman, *Time on the Cross: The Economics of American Negro Slavery* (Boston, MA: Little, Brown and Company, 1974). A post-revisionist view is presented by William Dusinberre, *Them Dark Days: Slavery in the American Rice Swamps* (New York: Oxford University Press, 1996); Walter Johnson, *Soul by Soul: Life Inside the Antebellum Slave Market* (Cambridge, MA: Harvard University Press, 1999); and Brenda E. Stevenson, *Life in Black and White:*

Family and Community in the Slave South (New York: Oxford University Press, 1996). Charles Joyner's *Down by the Riverside: A South Carolina Slave Community* (Urbana: University of Illinois Press, 1984) is an outstanding local study. Studies of antebellum slavery continue to appear at an astonishing rate; students should consult Chapter 5 for details of the latest scholarship.

Slavery came in many forms and was not confined to the plantation. John C. Inscoe, *Mountain Masters, Slavery, and the Sectional Crisis in Western North Carolina* (Knoxville: University Press of Kentucky, 1989) is an excellent study of slavery and white society away from the plantation district. Recent works on industrial slavery include Charles B. Dew, *Bond of Iron: Master and Slave at Buffalo Forge* (New York: W. W. Norton, 1994) and T. Stephen Whitman, *The Price of Freedom: Slavery and Manumission in Baltimore and Early National Maryland* (Lexington: The University Press of Kentucky, 1997). John Hope Franklin and Loren Schweninger, *Runaway Slaves: Rebels on the Plantation* (New York: Oxford University Press, 1999) is the most thorough analysis of slave resistance.

PLANTERS

Writing about the southern elite has been extensive, because planters were influential beyond their small numbers, and because they tended to leave abundant records. Eugene D. Genovese's seminal, but controversial, interpretation of the South's ruling class as in, but not of, the capitalist world, is presented in its most succinct and sophisticated form in *The Slaveholders' Dilemma: Freedom and Progress in Southern Conservative Thought, 1820–1860* (Columbia: South Carolina University Press, 1992). For a wide-ranging and incisive analysis of intellectual culture see Michael O'Brien, *Conjectures of Order: Intellectual Life in the Old South, 1810–1860* 2 vols (Chapel Hill: University of North Carolina Press, 2004). Drew Gilpin Faust's study, *James Henry Hammond and the Old South: A Design for Mastery* (Baton Rouge: Louisiana State University Press, 1982), is an outstanding biography of one planter. William Kauffman Scarborough focuses on the wealthiest planters in *Masters of the Big House: Elite Slaveholders of the Mid-Nineteenth-Century South* (Baton Rouge: Louisiana State University Press, 2003). Elite families and their social, familial and political values are evaluated by Bertram Wyatt-Brown in *Southern Honor: Ethics and Behavior in the Old South* (New York: Oxford University Press, 1982) and *The Shaping of Southern Culture: Honor, Grace and War, 1760s–1880s* (Chapel Hill: University of North Carolina Press, 2002); Jane Turner Censer, *North Carolina Planters and Their Children, 1800–1860* (Baton Rouge: Louisiana State University Press, 1984); and Kenneth S. Greenberg,

Masters and Statesmen: The Political Culture of American Slavery (Baltimore, MD: Johns Hopkins University Press, 1985). James Oakes, *The Ruling Race: A History of American Slaveholders* (New York: Alfred A. Knopf, 1982) contends that the southern elite did not have it all their own way, but he revises his position somewhat in *Slavery and Freedom: An Interpretation of the Old South* (New York: Alfred A. Knopf, 1990).

WOMEN IN THE OLD SOUTH

Female southerners, both black and white, were essentially overlooked by historians for many decades. Anne Firor Scott's pioneering analysis *The Southern Lady: From Pedestal to Politics, 1830–1930* (Chicago: University of Chicago Press, 1970) was eventually followed by Catherine Clinton, *The Plantation Mistress* (New York: Pantheon Books, 1982); Suzanne Lebsock, *The Free Women of Petersburg: Status and Culture in a Southern Town, 1784–1860* (New York: W. W. Norton, 1984); and Deborah Gray White, *Ar'n't I a Woman? Female Slaves in the Plantation South* (New York: W. W. Norton, 1985). Elizabeth Fox-Genovese, *Within the Plantation Household: Black and White Women of the Old South* (Chapel Hill: University of North Carolina Press, 1988) argues that class was more powerful than gender, and so elite women generally supported the slave regime. Sally G. McMillen, *Motherhood in the Old South: Pregnancy, Childbirth, and Infant Rearing* (Baton Rouge: Louisiana State University Press, 1990) considers both black and white mothers, while Marie Jenkins Schwartz, *Born in Bondage: Growing Up Enslaved in the Antebellum South* (Cambridge, MA: Harvard University Press, 2000) is the best study of slave childhood. More recent works, discussing various aspects of the female experience, include Marli Weiner, *Mistresses and Slaves: Plantation Women in South Carolina, 1830–1880* (Urbana: University of Illinois Press, 1998); Emily West, *Chains of Love: Slave Couples in Antebellum South Carolina* (Urbana: University of Illinois Press, 2004); Kirsten Wood, *Masterful Women: Slaveholding Widows from the American Revolution Through the Civil War* (Chapel Hill: University of North Carolina Press, 2004); Elizabeth R. Varon, *We Mean to be Counted: White Women and Politics in Antebellum Virginia* (Chapel Hill: University of North Carolina Press, 1998). Sally G. McMillen's *Southern Women: Black and White in the Old South* (Arlington Heights, IL: Harlan Davidson, 1992) is a useful synthesis.

NON-SLAVEHOLDERS

Planters and slaves have dominated the focus of southern historians, and so ordinary whites have not received the attention they deserve. There are signs that this is changing, however. Many excellent community studies consider non-elite whites and class relations: J. William Harris, *Plain Folk and Gentry in a Slave Society: White Liberty and Black Slavery in Augusta's Hinterlands* (Middletown, CT: Wesleyan University Press, 1985); Orville Vernon Burton, *In My Father's House are Many Mansions: Family and Community in Edgefield, South Carolina* (Chapel Hill: University of North Carolina Press, 1985); Steven Hahn, *The Roots of Southern Populism: Yeoman Farmers and the Transformation of the Georgia Upcountry, 1850–1880* (New York: Oxford University Press, 1983); Lacy K. Ford, *The Origins of Southern Radicalism: The South Carolina Upcountry, 1800–1860* (New York: Oxford University Press, 1988); Stephanie McCurry, *Masters of Small Worlds: Yeoman Households, Gender Relations, and the Political Culture of the Antebellum South Carolina Low Country* (New York: Oxford University Press, 1995); Timothy James Lockley, *Lines in the Sand: Race and Class in Lowcountry Georgia, 1750–1860* (Athens: University of Georgia Press, 2001). Two outstanding works consider lower-class whites in detail: Bill Cecil-Fronsman, *Common Whites: Class and Culture in Antebellum North Carolina* (Lexington: University Press of Kentucky, 1992) and Charles C. Bolton, *Poor Whites of the Antebellum South: Tenants and Laborers in Central North Carolina and Northeast Mississippi* (Durham, NC: Duke University Press, 1994). A vivid insight into the lifestyle of one individual is found in Scott P. Culclasure and Charles C. Bolton (eds), *The Confessions of Edward Isham: A Poor White Life of the Old South* (Athens: University of Georgia Press, 1998). Hinton Rowan Helper's claim to be a non-slaveholding spokesman is assessed in David Brown, *Southern Outcast: Hinton Rowan Helper and The Impending Crisis of the South* (Baton Rouge: Louisiana State University Press, 2006).

Little has been written specifically about lower-class women, with the exception of Victoria E. Bynum, *Unruly Women: The Politics of Social and Sexual Control in the Old South* (Chapel Hill: University of North Carolina Press, 1992). Michele Gillespie, *Free Labor in an Unfree World: White Artisans in Slaveholding Georgia, 1789–1860* (Athens: University of Georgia Press, 2000) is the best study of southern artisans. Ethnicity in the Old South is not a prolific area of study, but David T. Gleeson's *The Irish in the South, 1815–1877* (Chapel Hill: University of North Carolina Press, 2001) shows that it merits much greater study.

SECESSION, CIVIL WAR AND RECONSTRUCTION

The political history of the antebellum South is dominated by the growing momentum of the secession movement. William W. Freehling, *The Road to*

Disunion: Volume I, Secessionists at Bay, 1776–1854 (New York: Oxford University Press, 1990), comprehensively examines the far from uniform southern response to the growth of sectionalism and *The Road to Disunion: Volume II, Secessionists Triumphant* (New York: Oxford University Press, 2007) takes events up to the beginning of the Civil War. Valuable studies of secession in specific locations include: William L. Barney, *The Secessionist Impulse: Alabama and Mississippi in 1860* (Princeton, NJ: Princeton University Press, 1974); William A. Link, *Roots of Secession: Slavery and Politics in Antebellum Virginia* (Chapel Hill: University of North Carolina Press, 2003); Daniel W. Crofts, *Reluctant Confederates: Upper South Unionists in the Secession Crisis* (Chapel Hill: University of North Carolina Press, 1989); Michael P. Johnson, *Toward a Patriarchal Republic: The Secession of Georgia* (Baton Rouge: Louisiana State University Press, 1977); J. Mills Thornton, III, *Politics and Power in a Slave Society: Alabama, 1800–1860* (Baton Rouge: Louisiana State University Press, 1978); and Manisha Sinha, *The Counterrevolution of Slavery: Politics and Ideology in Antebellum South Carolina* (Chapel Hill: University of North Carolina Press, 2000). John McCardell's *The Idea of a Southern Nation: Southern Nationalists and Southern Nationalism, 1830–1860* (New York: W. W. Norton, 1979) is the fullest consideration of the development of sectionalism from a southern perspective.

The split from the Union and creation of the Confederacy is a critical period in southern history, and the Confederate home front has been a topic of great interest. Emory M. Thomas, *The Confederate Nation, 1861–1865* (New York: Harper and Row, 1979) remains the best general text. Two important books provide a different interpretation of the southern response: Gary W. Gallagher, *The Confederate War* (Cambridge, MA: Harvard University Press, 1997) emphasises the loyalty and resilience of ordinary southerners, but William W. Freehling, *The South* vs. *the South: How Anti-Confederate Southerners Shaped the Course of the Civil War* (New York: Oxford University Press, 2001) stresses conflict over consensus. These two competing views dominate the historiography. On Confederate nationalism, see Drew Gilpin Faust, *The Creation of Confederate Nationalism: Ideology and Identity in the Civil War South* (Baton Rouge: Louisiana State University Press, 1988) and Anne Sarah Rubin, *A Shattered Nation: The Rise and Fall of the Confederacy, 1861–1868* (Chapel Hill: University of North Carolina Press, 2005). The essays in Gabor S. Boritt (ed.), *Why the Confederacy Lost* (New York: Oxford University Press, 1992) summarise the various factors cited to explain southern defeat.

Local studies of the war's impact on soldiers and civilians are a good way in which students can gain an understanding of important issues. Especially recommended are Martin Crawford, *Ashe County's Civil War: Community and Society in the Appalachian South* (Charlottesville: University of Virginia Press, 2001); Stephen V. Ash, *When the Yankees Came: Conflict and Chaos in the Occupied South, 1861–1865* (Chapel Hill: University of North Carolina Press, 1995); William A. Blair, *Virginia's Private War: Feeding Body and Soul in the Confederacy, 1861–1865* (New York: Oxford University Press, 1998); David Williams, *Rich Man's War: Caste, Class and Confederate Defeat in the Lower Chattahoochee Valley* (Athens: University of Georgia Press, 1998); and John C. Inscoe and Gordon B. McKinney, *The Heart of Confederate Appalachia: Western North Carolina in the Civil War* (Chapel Hill: University of North Carolina Press, 2000). The position of southern Unionists has been examined in detail recently. See, in particular, Richard Nelson Current, *Lincoln's Loyalists: Union Soldiers from the Confederacy* (Boston, MA: Northeastern University Press, 1992) and Margaret M. Storey, *Loyalty and Loss: Alabama's Unionists in the Civil War and Reconstruction* (Baton Rouge: Louisiana State University Press, 2004).

There are several excellent texts about the difficult experiences of southern women during the war: Drew Gilpin Faust, *Mothers of Invention: Women of the Slaveholding South in the American Civil War* (Chapel Hill: University of North Carolina Press, 1996); Catherine Clinton, *Tara Revisited: Women, War, and the Plantation Legend* (New York: Abbeville Press, 1995); Laura F. Edwards, *Scarlett Doesn't Live Here Anymore: Southern Women in the Civil War Era* (Urbana: University of Illinois Press, 2000); and LeeAnn Whites, *The Civil War as a Crisis in Gender: Augusta, Georgia, 1860–1890* (Athens: University of Georgia Press, 1995). The best works on the end of slavery and the coming of emancipation include Clarence L. Mohr, *On the Threshold of Freedom: Masters and Slaves in Civil War Georgia* (Athens: University of Georgia Press, 1986); Steven Hahn, *A Nation Under Our Feet: Black Political Struggles in the Rural South From Slavery to the Great Migration* (Cambridge, MA: Harvard University Press, 2003); and Armstead L. Robinson, *Bitter Fruits of Bondage: The Demise of Slavery and the Collapse of the Confederacy* (Charlottesville: University of Virginia Press, 2005).

The best survey of the complex history of Reconstruction is Eric Foner's monumental *Reconstruction: America's Unfinished Revolution* (New York: Harper and Row, 1988), but also useful is Michael Perman's shorter *Emancipation and Reconstruction, 1862–1879* (Arlington Heights, IL: Harlan Davidson, 1987). Dan T. Carter, *When the War Was Over: The Failure of Self-Reconstruction in the South, 1865–1867* (Baton Rouge: Louisiana State University Press, 1985) focuses on the South in the immediate post-war period, while James L. Roark, *Masters Without Slaves: Southern Planters in the*

Civil War and Reconstruction (New York: W. W. Norton, 1977) considers the southern elite. Roger L. Ransom and Richard Sutch, *One Kind of Freedom: The Economic Consequences of Emancipation* (Cambridge: Cambridge University Press, 1977) remains the starting point for evaluating changes in the southern economy. Leon F. Litwack, *Been in the Storm so Long: The Aftermath of Slavery* (New York: Alfred A. Knopf, 1979) is a superb study of the black response to emancipation; see also Julie Saville, *The Work of Reconstruction: From Slave to Wage Laborer in South Carolina, 1860–1870* (Cambridge: Cambridge University Press, 1994). Gender issues are explored in Jane Turner Censer, *The Reconstruction of White Womanhood, 1865–1895* (Baton Rouge: Louisiana State University Press, 2003) and Laura F. Edwards, *Gendered Strife and Confusion: The Political Culture of Reconstruction* (Urbana: University of Illinois Press, 1997).

THE JIM CROW SOUTH

The appropriate starting point for any investigation of the Jim Crow era is with the debate on the origins of the southern caste system. Students can find summaries and critical evaluations of the most important contributions to this debate in John David Smith (ed.), *When Did Southern Segregation Begin?* (New York: Palgrave, 2002). The most comprehensive analysis of southern race relations during these years is Leon F. Litwack, *Trouble in Mind: Black Southerners in the Age of Jim Crow* (New York: Alfred A. Knopf, 1998). A superb case study of segregation in one state is Neil R. McMillen, *Dark Journey: Black Mississippians in the Age of Jim Crow* (Urbana: University of Illinois Press, 1989).

There are a number of important works that assess the construction of white racist ideology during this era. The way in which white supremacists manipulated gender issues to promote their political agenda is the subject of Glenda Elizabeth Gilmore, *Gender and Jim Crow: Women and the Politics of White Supremacy in North Carolina, 1896–1920* (Chapel Hill: University of North Carolina Press, 1996) and Stephen Kantrowitz, *Ben Tillman and the Reconstruction of White Supremacy* (Chapel Hill: University of North Carolina Press, 2000). Another important text is Grace Elizabeth Hale, *Making Whiteness: The Culture of Segregation in the South, 1890–1940* (New York: Pantheon Books, 1998).

The most substantial analysis of how white supremacists stripped southern blacks of their right to vote is Michael Perman, *Struggle for Mastery: Disfranchisement in the South, 1888–1908* (Chapel Hill and London: University of North Carolina, 2001). An important revisionist work that assesses how poor whites succumbed to racist appeals in supporting disfranchisement, only to lose the vote under the same constitutional reforms, is Glenn Feldman, *The Disfranchisement Myth: Poor Whites and Suffrage Restriction in Alabama* (Athens: University of Georgia Press, 2004).

The efforts of the populists to form a bi-racial alliance that challenged the political and economic power of the Bourbon elite has been assessed by a number of scholars. The classic work on southern populism is C. Vann Woodward, *Tom Watson, Agrarian Rebel* (New York: Macmillan, 1938). Other recommended titles include Robert C. McMath, Jr, *The Populist Vanguard: A History of the Southern Farmers' Alliance* (Chapel Hill: University of North Carolina Press, 1975); Lawrence Goodwyn, *Democratic Promise: The Populist Moment in America* (New York: Oxford University Press, 1976); and Barton C. Shaw, *The Wool-Hat Boys: Georgia's Populist Party* (Baton Rouge: Louisiana State University Press, 1984).

The exploitative economic system that operated on the farms and plantations of the rural South is the focus of Pete Daniel, *The Shadow of Slavery: Peonage in the South, 1901–1969* (Urbana: University of Illinois Press, 1990). Historians have in recent years paid increasing attention to the working lives of black labourers in the southern urban and industrial economy. Many of these works stress the agency of African Americans despite the repressive environment in which they lived and laboured. See, for example, Tera W. Hunter *To 'Joy My freedom: Southern Black Women's Lives and Labors after the Civil War* (Cambridge, MA: Harvard University Press, 1997); Brian Kelly, *Race, Class, and Power in the Alabama Coalfields, 1908–21* (Urbana: University of Illinois Press, 2001); and William P. Jones, *Black Ulysses: African American Lumber Workers in the Jim Crow South* (Urbana: University of Illinois Press, 2005). A seminal essay that stresses the agency of working-class blacks is Robin D. G. Kelley, '"We Are Not What We Seem": Rethinking Black Working-Class Opposition in the Jim Crow South', *Journal of American History*, 80 (June 1993), pp. 75–112.

Leon Litwack discusses in considerable detail the pervasive racial violence against southern blacks, but students interested in this aspect of Jim Crow should also consult in particular W. Fitzhugh Brundage, *Lynching in the New South: Georgia and Virginia, 1880–1930* (Urbana: University of Illinois Press, 1993). Two other important studies of lynching are Christopher Waldrep, *The Many Faces of Judge Lynch: Extralegal Violence and Punishment in America* (New York and Basingstoke: Palgrave Macmillan, 2002); and William D. Carrigan, *The Making of a Lynching Culture: Violence and Vigilantism in Central Texas, 1836–1916* (Urbana: University of Illinois Press, 2004). The race riots of the late nineteenth and early twentieth centuries are assessed in David S. Cecelski and Timothy B. Tyson (eds), *Democracy Betrayed: The Wilmington Race*

Riot and Its Legacy (Chapel Hill: University of North Carolina Press, 1998); *Carnival of Fury: Robert Charles and the New Orleans Race Riot of 1900* (Baton Rouge: Louisiana State University Press, 1976); David Fort Godshalk, *Veiled Visions: The 1906 Atlanta Race Riot and the Reshaping of American Race Relations* (Chapel Hill: University of North Carolina Press, 2005); and Gregory Mixon, *The Atlanta Riot: Race, Class, and Violence in a New South City* (Gainesville: University Press of Florida, 2005).

The institutional racism of the southern criminal justice system is assessed in Alex Lichtenstein, *Twice the Work of Free Labor: The Political Economy of Convict Labor in the New South* (London and New York: Verso, 1996); Mary Ellen Curtin, *Black Prisoners and their World, Alabama, 1865–1900* (Charlottesville: University Press of Virginia, 2000); and Vivien M. L. Miller, *Crime, Sexual Violence, and Clemency: Florida's Pardon Board and Penal System in the Progressive Era* (Gainesville: University Press of Florida, 2000).

The lives of the two most prominent black leaders of the era are assessed in Louis R. Harlan, *Booker T. Washington: The Making of a Black Leader, 1856–1901* (New York: Oxford University Press, 1972) and *Booker T. Washington: The Wizard of Tuskegee, 1901–1915* (New York: Oxford University Press, 1983), and David Levering Lewis, *W. E. B. Du Bois: Biography of a Race, 1868–1919* (New York: Henry Holt, 1993). The most prominent black female activist of the era is the subject of Patricia Ann Schechter, *Ida B. Wells-Barnett and American Reform, 1880–1930* (Chapel Hill and London: University of North Carolina Press, 2001).

THE BLACK MIGRATION

The causes and consequences of the black exodus from the South that started during the inter-war era are assessed in James R. Grossman, *Land of Hope: Chicago, Black Southerners, and the Great Migration* (Chicago: University of Chicago Press, 1989); Carole Marks, *Farewell – We're Good and Gone The Great Black Migration* (Bloomington: Indiana University Press, 1989); Nicholas Lemann, *The Promised Land: The Great Black Migration and How It Changed America* (New York: Alfred A. Knopf, 1991); and James N. Gregory, *The Southern Diaspora: How the Great Migrations of Black and White Southerners Transformed America* (Chapel Hill: University of North Carolina Press, 2006).

THE NEW DEAL AND THE SECOND WORLD WAR

The inter-war era established some of the preconditions for the later civil rights movement. On the changes that the Great Depression and the New

Deal had on southern race relations, see Harvard Sitkoff, *A New Deal for Blacks: The Emergence of Civil Rights as a National Issue* (New York: Oxford University Press, 1978); John B. Kirby, *Black Americans in the Roosevelt Era: Liberalism and Race* (Knoxville: University of Tennessee Press, 1980); Nancy J. Weiss, *Farewell to the Party of Lincoln: Black Politics in the Age of FDR* (Princeton, NJ: Princeton University Press, 1983); James C. Cobb and Michael V. Namorato, (eds), *The New Deal and the South* (Jackson: University Press of Mississippi, 1984); and Patricia Sullivan, *Days of Hope: Race and Democracy in the New Deal Era* (Chapel Hill: University of North Carolina Press, 1996).

The Second World War had a particularly transformative impact on race in the South. The influence of the war and its immediate aftermath is the focus of Pete Daniel, 'Going Among Strangers: Southern Reactions to World War II', *Journal of American History,* 77 (December 1990), pp. 886–911; Neil A. Wynn, *The Afro-American and the Second World War,* revised edition (New York and London: Holmes and Meier, 1993); and Neil R. McMillen (ed.), *Remaking Dixie: The Impact of World War II on the American South* (Jackson: University Press of Mississippi, 1997). The changing racial climate of the South in the aftermath of the war is assessed in Gail Williams O'Brien, *The Color of the Law: Race, Violence, and Justice in the Post-World War II South* (Chapel Hill: University of North Carolina Press, 1999) and Jennifer E. Brooks, *Defining the Peace: World War II Veterans, Race, and the Remaking of Southern Political Tradition* (Chapel Hill: University of North Carolina Press, 2004).

Some scholars have seen the years during and immediately after the war as a time when black and white workers could have forged an alliance rooted in their common class interests, were it not for the manipulation of employers. See Robert Korstad and Nelson Lichtenstein, 'Opportunities Found and Lost: Labor, Radicals, and the Early Civil Rights Movement', *Journal of American History,* 75 (December 1988), pp. 786–811; Robert Korstad, *Civil Rights Unionism: Tobacco Workers and the Struggle for Democracy in the Mid-Twentieth Century South* (Chapel Hill and London: University of North Carolina Press, 2003); and Bruce Nelson, 'Organized Labor and the Struggle for Black Equality in Mobile during World War II', *Journal of American History,* 80 (December 1993), pp. 952–88.

THE FEDERAL GOVERNMENT AND RACE

There are a number of books that assess the civil rights record of individual administrations. These include Donald R. McCoy and Richard T. Ruetten,

Quest and Response: Minority Rights and the Truman Administration (Lawrence: University Press of Kansas, 1973); Michael R. Gardner, *Harry Truman and Civil Rights: Moral Courage and Political Risks* (Carbondale: Southern Illinois University Press, 2002); Robert Frederick Burk, *The Eisenhower Administration and Black Civil Rights* (Knoxville: University of Tennessee Press, 1984); Carl M. Brauer, *John F. Kennedy and the Second Reconstruction* (New York: Columbia University Press, 1977); Robert Mann, *The Walls of Jericho: Lyndon Johnson, Hubert Humphrey, Richard Russell, and the Struggle for Civil Rights* (New York: Harcourt Brace, 1996); Nick Kotz, *Judgment Days: Lyndon Baines Johnson, Martin Luther King, Jr., and the Laws that Changed America* (Boston, MA: Houghton Mifflin, 2005); and Dean J. Kotlowski, *Nixon's Civil Rights: Politics, Principle, and Policy* (Cambridge, MA: Harvard University Press, 2001).

Students interested in a broader interpretative overview of how the federal government did or did not promote black civil rights are recommended to consult the following titles: William Leuchtenburg, *The White House Looks South: Franklin D. Roosevelt, Harry S. Truman, Lyndon B. Johnson* (Baton Rouge: Louisiana State University Press, 2005); Harry Ashmore, *Hearts and Minds: The Anatomy of Racism from Roosevelt to Reagan* (New York: McGraw-Hill, 1982); and Garth E. Pauley, *The Modern Presidency & Civil Rights: Rhetoric on Race from Roosevelt to Nixon* (College Station: Texas A&M University Press, 2001).

THE CIVIL RIGHTS MOVEMENT

Much of the literature on the civil rights movement inevitably focuses on the leadership of Martin Luther King. The most substantial accounts of the civil rights leader's life are David J. Garrow, *Bearing the Cross: Martin Luther King, Jr., and the Southern Christian Leadership Conference* (New York: William Morrow, 1986) and the monumental trilogy by Taylor Branch, *Parting the Waters: America in the King Years, 1954–63* (New York: Simon and Schuster, 1988); *Pillar of Fire: America in the King Years, 1963–65* (New York: Simon and Schuster, 1998); and *At Canaan's Edge: America in the King Years, 1965–68* (New York: Simon and Shuster, 2006). The sheer amount of detail in these books can be intimidating. For those seeking shorter and more accessible assessments of King, the following titles are suggested: Adam Fairclough, *Martin Luther King, Jr.* (Athens: University of Georgia Press, 1995); Peter J. Ling, *Martin Luther King, Jr.* (London and New York: Routledge, 2002); and John A. Kirk, *Martin Luther King* (Harlow: Longman, 2005).

Too narrow a focus on King can obscure the important contributions made by other individuals and organisations at national, regional and local levels.

The more militant elements within the civil rights coalition are the focus of August Meier and Elliott M. Rudwick, *CORE: A Study in the Civil Rights Movement, 1942–1968* (New York: Oxford University Press, 1973) and Clayborne Carson, *In Struggle: SNCC and the Black Awakening of the 1960s* (Cambridge, MA: Harvard University Press, 1981).

A number of scholars have produced studies of black protest in individual states. The best of these include John Dittmer, *Local People: The Struggle for Civil Rights in Mississippi* (Urbana: University of Illinois Press, 1994); Adam Fairclough, *Race and Democracy: The Civil Rights Struggle in Louisiana, 1915–1972* (Athens: University of Georgia Press, 1995); John A. Kirk, *Redefining the Color Line: Black Activism in Little Rock, Arkansas, 1940–1970* (Gainesville: University Press of Florida, 2002); Charles M. Payne, *I've Got the Light of Freedom: The Organizing Tradition and the Mississippi Freedom Struggle* (Berkeley: University of California Press, 1995); and Stephen G. N. Tuck, *Beyond Atlanta: The Struggle for Racial Equality in Georgia, 1940–1980* (Athens: University of Georgia Press, 2001).

The influential role of women both in positions of leadership and at the grassroots is assessed in Vicki L. Crawford, Jacqueline Anne Rouse and Barbara Woods (eds), *Women in the Civil Rights Movement: Trailblazers and Torchbearers, 1941–1965* (Brooklyn, NY: Carlson, 1990) and Peter J. Ling and Sharon Monteith (eds), *Gender and the Civil Rights Movement* (New Brunswick, NJ: Rutgers University Press, 2004). Two of the best biographies of individual black female activists are Chana Kai Lee, *For Freedom's Sake: The Life of Fannie Lou Hamer* (Urbana: University of Illinois Press, 1999) and Barbara Ransby, *Ella Baker and the Black Freedom Movement: A Radical Democratic Vision* (Chapel Hill: University of North Carolina Press, 2003)

One of the most interesting recent developments in the scholarship on the civil rights movement is the attempt to place the domestic race struggle in the larger context of global politics. A number of historians have assessed how the Cold War influenced federal policy on civil rights, as Washington attempted to reconcile the disparity between its promotion of democracy abroad and the persistence of racism at home. See Brenda Gayle Plummer, *Rising Wind: Black Americans and U.S. Foreign Affairs, 1935–1960* (Chapel Hill: University of North Carolina Press, 1996); Mary L. Dudziak, *Cold War Civil Rights: Race and the Image of American Democracy* (Princeton, NJ: Princeton University Press, 2000); Azza Salama Layton, *International Politics and Civil Rights Policies in the United States, 1941–1960* (New York: Cambridge University Press, 2000); Thomas Borstelmann, *The Cold War and the Color Line: American Race Relations in the Global Arena* (Cambridge, MA: Harvard University Press, 2001); Carol Anderson, *Eyes off the Prize: The United Nations and the African American Struggle for Human Rights, 1944–1955* (New Cambridge University Press, York: 2003); and Jonathan Rosenberg, *How Far the Promised Land? World Affairs and the American Civil Rights Movement from the First World War to Vietnam* (Princeton, NJ: Princeton University Press, 2006).

WHITE MODERATES AND MASSIVE RESISTANCE

For many years historians of the civil rights struggle focused their attention almost exclusively on the black and white activists who campaigned for the abolition of Jim Crow practices. This stripped the accomplishments of the movement from its proper context, since it ignored the strength and character of the southern white opposition that needed to be overcome. Some of the most important new scholarship by civil rights historians focuses on the ideology and tactics of segregationists. Recommended works include Dan T. Carter, *The Politics of Rage: George Wallace, the Origins of the New Conservatism, and the Transformation of American Politics* (New York: Simon and Schuster, 1995); Pete Daniel, *Lost Revolutions: The South in the 1950s* (Chapel Hill: University of North Carolina Press, 2000); Jeff Woods, *Black Struggle, Red Scare: Segregation and Anti-Communism in the South, 1948–1968* (Baton Rouge: Louisiana State University Press, 2004); George Lewis *The White South and the Red Menace: Segregationists, Anticommunism, and Massive Resistance, 1945–1965* (Gainesville: University Press of Florida, 2004); and Clive Webb (ed.), *Massive Resistance: Southern Opposition to the Second Reconstruction* (New York: Oxford University Press, 2005). Two classic works on segregationists that have stood the test of time are Numan V. Bartley, *The Rise of Massive Resistance* (Baton Rouge: Louisiana State University Press, 1969) and Neil R. McMillen, *The Citizens' Council: Organized Resistance to the Second Reconstruction, 1954–64* (Urbana: University of Illinois Press, 1971).

Historians for a long paid more attention to white moderates, no doubt because they were more sympathetic to their politics. Recommended works on this subject include Morton Sosna, *In Search of the Silent South: Southern Liberals and the Race Issue* (New York: Columbia University Press, 1977); Irwin Klibaner, *Conscience of a Troubled South: The Southern Conference Educational Fund, 1946–1966* (Brooklyn, NY: Carlson, 1989); Frank T. Adams, *James A. Dombrowski: An American Heretic, 1897–1983* (Knoxville: University of Tennessee Press, 1992); David L. Chappell, *Inside Agitators: White Southerners in the Civil Rights Movement* (Baltimore, MD: Johns Hopkins University Press, 1994); and Catherine Fosl, *Subversive Southerner: Anne Braden and the Struggle for Racial Justice in the Cold War South* (New York: Palgrave, 2002).

SOUTHERN POLITICS SINCE 1945

The southern strategy used by Republicans to break Democratic control of the region is discussed in Earl Black and Merle Black, *The Rise of Southern Republicans* (Cambridge, MA: Harvard University Press, 2002) and Dan T. Carter's books *The Politics of Rage: George Wallace, The Origins of the New Conservatism, and the Transformation of American Politics* (New York: Simon and Schuster, 1995) and *From George Wallace to Newt Gingrich: Race in the Conservative Counterrevolution, 1963–1994* (Baton Rouge: Louisiana State University Press, 1996). A number of important recent works have provided a more complicated understanding of the rise of contemporary white conservatism in the South. The most impressive of these books are Kevin M. Kruse, *White Flight: Atlanta and the Making of Modern Conservatism* (Princeton, NJ: Princeton University Press, 2005) and Matthew D. Lassiter, *The Silent Majority: Suburban Politics in the Sunbelt South* (Princeton, NJ: Princeton University Press, 2006).

THE PERSISTENT PAST AND THE UNCERTAIN FUTURE

Controversies over such issues as the Confederate battle flag and the prosecution of old Klansmen demonstrate how the past continues to impact upon the contemporary South. The contested meaning of southern history is assessed in a number of important recent works, including David R. Goldfield, *Still Fighting the Civil War: The American South and Southern History* (Baton Rouge: Louisiana State University Press, 2002); John Shelton Reed, *Minding the South* (Columbia: University of Missouri Press, 2003); W. Fitzhugh Brundage, *The Southern Past: A Clash of Race and Memory* (Cambridge, MA: Harvard University Press, 2005); James C. Cobb, *Away Down South: A History of Southern Identity* (New York: Oxford University Press, 2005); and Renee C. Romano and Leigh Raiford (eds), *The Civil Rights Movement in American Memory* (Athens: University of Georgia Press, 2006).

The increasing participation of African Americans in the southern electoral process made possible by the Voting Rights Act of 1965 is discussed in a number of books by Steven F. Lawson, including *Black Ballots: Voting Rights in the South, 1944–1969* (New York: Columbia University Press, 1976) and *In Pursuit of Power: Southern Blacks and Electoral Politics, 1965–1982* (New York: Columbia University Press, 1985). The threat that the clock is currently being turned back to the era before the civil rights revolution is assessed in Raymond Wolters, *The Burden of* Brown: *Thirty Years of School Desegregation* (Knoxville: University of Tennessee Press, 1984) and John

Charles Boger and Gary Orfield (eds), *School Resegregation: Must the South Turn Back?* (Chapel Hill and London: University of North Carolina Press, 2005). A more optimistic assessment is offered by John Shelton Reed, *Surveying the South: Studies in Regional Sociology* (Columbia: University of Missouri Press, 1993).

INDEX

Page numbers in **bold** indicate maps

1545